THE QUESTION IS "WHY?"

STANFORD M. ADELSTEIN: A JEWISH LIFE IN SOUTH DAKOTA

BY ERIC STEVEN ZIMMER
PREFACE BY STANFORD M. ADELSTEIN

CONTENTS

Note to the Reader		6
Preface		7
Introduction		11
Chapter 1:	From Russia with *Libe*	26
Chapter 2:	Heading West	40
Chapter 3:	A Son of Skyline Drive	50
Chapter 4:	Life in Colorado	67
Chapter 5:	Becoming a Builder	79
Chapter 6:	From the Holocaust to Israel	88
Chapter 7:	Finding Purpose	97
Chapter 8:	Making the Adelstein Empire	110
Chapter 9:	Politics *Is* Business	118
Chapter 10:	Family and Community	132
Chapter 11:	Taking Over	142
Chapter 12:	The Continual Struggle	180
Chapter 13:	Remaking the Gate City	189
Chapter 14:	True Republican	204
Chapter 15:	Lakotas and Israelis	225
Chapter 16:	Family Business	246
Chapter 17:	Politics and Service	262
Chapter 18:	New Love	275
Chapter 19:	State Senator Adelstein	285
Epilogue		300
Acknowledgments		310
Sources		312
Index		345

© 2019 by Stanford M. Adelstein and Vantage Point Historical Services, Inc.

Published by Vantage Point Historical Services, Inc., 1422 Clark Street, Rapid City, SD 57701. www.vantagepointhistory.com

Book design by Matt McInerney at Motel.

Printing by Lulu.

ISBN 978-0-9903972-5-0

Except for the following, all photos were provided by Stanford M. Adelstein: Cars overturned, Rapid City flood (169), *Rapid City Journal*; Rapid City Public Library (170), Rapid City Public Library; Adelstein with horn (177), Chris Benson Photography; Adelstein and Cleveland (179), Dick Brown; "Dignity" statue (309), Katie LeClair. Cover photo courtesy of *Rapid City Journal*. All rights reserved.

DEDICATION

Stanford M. Adelstein dedicates this book to the memory of his father, Morris, who came home with honor from the "War to End All Wars," and to his only uncle, Lt. (j.g.) Jack Greenberg, a naval aviator who perished in World War II.

NOTE TO THE READER

Allowing Stan Adelstein's voice to show through—both as a historical actor *and* as a man reflecting back on his life's journey—is a primary goal of this book. In addition to extensive archival and secondary research, I conducted several taped interviews, exchanged many emails, and engaged in follow-up working sessions with Stan and other interviewees over the course of nearly three years.

Throughout this process, Stan had an opportunity to clarify his meaning and solidify the details of personal anecdotes. I did my best to ensure that all language that appears *"in italics and in quotes"* throughout this work reflects Stan's words, as he told them to me. I lightly edited his words when it was necessary to finesse the spoken word to match the written word, adjust tense or syntax, or include implied meanings or contextual details that might not be clear to the reader. I took care, however, not to modify the intent of his words, so all *"italicized quotes"* reflect Stan's meaning, if not his exact phrasing. Occasionally, I paraphrase Stan's stories without using quotes to stitch elements of a specific anecdote together or to emphasize a story's significance.

I did not cite these *"italicized stories"* with endnotes, nor did I fact-check them. While my contributions to this work—the majority of the main, unitalicized narrative—reflect a historian's research, synthesis, and analysis, Stan's words are just that—his own memories told the way he remembered them, with slight touch-ups for clarity. All of his contributions are drawn from our interviews or follow-up conversations, working sessions, and correspondence. To set them apart from stories Stan told me directly, I did not italicize his words when they came from archival materials or secondary sources. Instead, Stan's letters, notes, and written reflections appear in quotation marks but with unitalicized text and are cited in the endnotes, as are quotes by others drawn from archival and secondary sources.

PREFACE
BY STANFORD M. ADELSTEIN

Over half a century ago, former Prime Minister of Israel David Ben-Gurion asked me a question that profoundly affected the rest of my life: "The question is not 'where?' It is 'why?'"

In the spring of 1965 I was in Israel along with my wife, Ita, and twenty-one other young couples from across the United States. For most of us, this leadership mission was our first trip there. Our journey—the first of many that would follow—had been sponsored by the American Jewish Committee (AJC). Although today that organization has a special relationship with Israel, this trip was perhaps the first that the AJC organized to what was, at the time, the barely seventeen-year-old nation of Israel.

We were introduced to many people during our trip, and after hearing where I was from, a quizzical look would come over their faces. People often asked me a two-word question wrapped in an exclamation: "South Dakota?!" This brief phrase hinted at their confusion and was often followed by additional questions ranging from "Where is South Dakota?" to "How did you end up there?" to "There are Jews in South Dakota?!"

This happened so many times during our travels that I eventually drew a little map of the United States on a small piece of paper, showing our location in the center of America.

One night, our group was honored with a reception with Israel's first prime minister, David Ben-Gurion, which began with him sharing his thinking about the future of Israel. Afterward, he went around the room, sharing a few words with each person as he sought to better understand what was clearly a change among us emerging leaders of the AJC. Our questions and comments revealed an attitude far different from those that the AJC had expressed in the Blaustein–Ben-Gurion declaration that had been signed on August 23, 1950, and made it clear that the Israeli government could only speak for its own citizens, not for all Jews.

When Ben-Gurion came toward me, he voiced the familiar question, "South Dakota?" As I reached into my pocket for that map, he held up his hand to cut me off—seemingly knowing what was about to be said.

Then he said "South Dakota? I know where, but the question is not where, it is 'why?'"

How had he known what I was reaching for? What did he expect to hear? After being surprised with that one word—"why?"—my instinctive reply was to say that "this is my mission as a Jew." I surprised even myself with this response.

You have to remember that this was a time when Zionists would often ask Jews like me "Why aren't you in Israel?," largely because they were certain that no Jew could be safe anywhere else in the world. Just twenty years after the end of World War II, our group was often asked what made us believe that what happened to the Jews in Europe wouldn't happen in the United States.

Ben-Gurion pressed me on my meaning for a few more minutes, and I tried to clarify by quoting Isaiah, who said that as Jews, we were meant to be "as a light unto the Nations."

In other words, I believed that my Jewish mission was to share our traditions and viewpoints wherever we lived, whether it was in Eretz, Israel, or anywhere else. For the moment, Ben-Gurion seemed to accept my response.

Now in my eighty-eighth year, I am reflecting on all that has transpired since that fateful meeting in Israel all those years ago. My lifelong attempts to live out the answer to the question Ben-Gurion asked my thirty-four-year-old self are the subject of this book. It tells my story—the story of one Jew in the land of America's heart. (I deliberately put this spin on the phrase "heartland," because I believe South Dakota really is *where America's heart resides.) Some Jews think that life's happenings or events—things that seem to me to be coincidental—are actually* beshert, *a Yiddish word that implies a sense of divine fate: the idea that all things happen for a reason. Mine is an opposite conviction. There is no plan. How could there be, when I grew up in happiness and comfort, attending public schools and playing in Wilson Park, while half the Jewish children in the world were murdered on the other side of the planet?*

In recent years, friends, family, and colleagues encouraged me to document my story. To contextualize my life and offer an outside perspective and analysis, the historian Eric Zimmer was chosen to write this book.

I have spent many hours with Eric over the last few years trying to articulate my views about my role in the world. I've lived a life full of opportunity and coincidence, and it has allowed me to travel widely and become involved in some incredible stories. But I know deep down that I am a product of the world around me. After all, a seed dropped into the ground may blossom into something special, but not purely of its own will. A seed is shaped by the genetic makeup of all the species that came before it, the timing of its planting, the quality of the soil into which it fell, and the climate and atmosphere that allowed it to mature. My Jewish heritage, combined with the rich and nurturing soil of South Dakota's core values of acceptance and support—not just "tolerance"—allowed me to become who I am today.

My father and family prospered, and South Dakota offered us remarkable opportunities. Indeed, being "that Jew from South Dakota" amplified my voice and influence onto much larger platforms. Yes, sometimes there was a struggle with the isolation that accompanied the anomaly of our Jewish presence. We faced occasional acts of discrimination, but mostly our challenge lay in figuring out how to survive as ethnic outsiders, alone in a predominantly Christian region. Not too many years ago, while serving in the South Dakota legislature, peering out the window of my home high on the hillside at 1999 West Boulevard on a cold winter's day, proudly looking out over the homes of the thousands of people I represented, I realized that only two other Jews lived in my entire district.

There is no such thing as the "self-made man." As you read this book, you will encounter dozens of individuals who shaped me as a person, a professional, a public servant, and a citizen. They are representative of the hundreds—or maybe thousands—of people who I bumped into on the streets of Pierre or Denver, New York or Jerusalem. Many you will meet, as I did, through organizations like the AJC, the Young Presidents' Organization, the Republican Party, or many others.

Born to special circumstances, inspired by my father, Morris, and an army chaplain-turned-mentor named Rabbi Joseph Messing; supported all along by friends, family, and my Jewish values, I developed an absolute conviction that there was no choice but to give my time, talent, and treasure to worthy causes. All of this is for a simple reason: because I can. More than that, I have come to learn, with total certainty, that I cannot not *help but assist others when they are in need.*

This is not to say that I never made any mistakes. I did! Throughout my life I have fought against personality traits that, at times, led me to act with rashness or to allow my passions to consume me. With time, I learned to listen to others. Lecturing to my students at the South Dakota School of Mines & Technology, I tried to teach them that listening and empathetically understanding others is the key to accomplishing successful negotiation. If you can achieve what is your objective, don't think how much the other side gets or achieves. Ignore what's "left on the table!"

A memory helps me illustrate this feeling. I decided to run for the state legislature in the year 2000. At the time, I was seventy years old and well established in the Rapid City and regional business communities. Yet polling showed that the public perceived me as rich, unapproachable, and out-of-touch with regular people. My response was to knock on doors and host Saturday morning coffees at McDonald's to meet people and hear what they had to say. Over time, the public perception seemed to change, and people met my more relatable side—and then, after earning their trust, allowed me to represent them in Pierre for more than a decade.

Every day reminds me of the incredible privilege, security, and opportunities set before me. Once, while serving in the state legislature, there was an abortion debate that went long into the evening. For hours I held firm to my pro-choice stance. When the heated discussion ended for the evening, my side lost every one of our proposed amendments, and the bill passed. That night and for years after, many people thanked me for my "courage" in the chamber—a comment that seemed wrong to me. Didn't I have to face real danger, I thought, in order to express "courage?"

Nearing the door on my way out of the state capitol, a uniformed state trooper told me "good evening Representative" and wished me well, just as he did every other lawmaker—no matter his or her position on the night's hot-button issue. Strolling to my car, I was consciously aware that there was no need to check it for bombs. I remembered that when it came time to speak again in the morning, all I would need to do is rise and say "Mister Speaker," and I would assuredly have the chamber's absolute recognition. Deep down, I knew that the ultimate truth was that South Dakota and the United States had granted me freedoms—freedoms that had not often been available to many Jews around the world during my life. Unlike many of our people, I knew then—as I know now—that I am free to stand up for my beliefs without fear of violence or retribution.

That is exactly what I've been trying to do all these years: make my voice heard, and, with it, amplify the needs of the people and issues I care about. The story that follows charts the unusual possibilities of a Jewish life that began in 1931, on the eve of the Holocaust—the time of my planting—and when the State of Israel was only a dream.

Israel was "The Hope," which is the meaning of that nation's national anthem, "Hatikvah." My hope is that, faced with a lifetime of opportunities, I made the most of them, giving purpose to my life—and, through my actions, some semblance of an answer to the question posed by David Ben-Gurion all those years ago.

Stanford M. Adelstein
Rapid City, South Dakota
2019

INTRODUCTION

Stanford M. Adelstein remembered that *"it was snowing hard on a Saturday morning, and I was looking forward to a quiet weekend. That's when I received a very unexpected call."* It was January 1964, and blustery winter winds whipped across the Dakota plains. When he reached for his receiver, Adelstein had no way of knowing that this call would send him on a grueling tour across South Dakota. The exhaustion, however, would be worth the effort. If the thirty-two-year-old played his cards right, he could help alter the course of American history.

Sporting horn-rimmed glasses and a high-and-tight haircut left over from his Reserve Officer Training Corps (ROTC) days, Adelstein seemed like an unlikely political operative. An engineer and executive at the Northwestern Engineering Company (NWE), a heavy construction firm that his father had founded four decades earlier in Kadoka, a small town in southwestern South Dakota, he had grown up in the state, but graduated from high school and college in Colorado. After two years in the U.S. Army Corps of Engineers, he moved back to South Dakota, settling in Rapid City with his new wife and young son in 1957. By 1964, he had begun to immerse himself in Republican politics and international Jewish activism.

A familiar drawl boomed through the receiver, which vibrated Stan's hand whenever his caller spoke. The voice belonged to Morris Abram, president of the American Jewish Committee (AJC). Perhaps the most powerful Jewish advocacy organization in the United States, the AJC had been building support for minority rights for decades.

Stan tried to contain his surprise. As he was fond of saying, *"South Dakota has fewer rabbis than U.S. senators,"* so even though Adelstein and his wife, Ita, had been members of the AJC for a little over four years, at that moment he could scarcely imagine what interest the AJC had in them.

Not coincidentally, Morris Abram had called to talk politics. *"He told me that the final ratification of the Twenty-Fourth Amendment to the United States Constitution was dependent"* on pushing one more state to approve the document.

Stan hadn't been following that particular issue, so he asked Abram to elaborate. Along with other unjust Jim Crow restrictions, state legislatures had for decades been passing "poll taxes," or fees that a citizen had to pay before voting. Generations of white politicians had sworn, with their fingers crossed behind their backs, that poll taxes were necessary to raise revenue for cash-strapped states. But this thin facade hid an insidious function: poll taxes kept blacks and poor whites away from the voting booth and out of power. The Twenty-Fourth Amendment would outlaw poll taxes (or any similar restrictions) in federal elections and prevent five southern states from continuing to use this repressive tool.[1]

On January 16, Maine had become the thirty-seventh state to approve ratification of the amendment. With the approval of one more state, the amendment would become part of the founding document of the United States of America.[2]

"At that time," Stan remembered, *"there were only three legislatures, two in the South, and South Dakota"* that had ratification bills in the works. One of these pivotal three could become the magic number thirty-eight. But *"Morris said that it was going to be impossible to get either of the southern states to ratify. It was his understanding that ratification had been stalled in the South Dakota legislature."* Abram called to ask Stan *"if I would take some action to solve the problem."* It was an enticing invitation for someone who had a deep sense of the problems of social injustice and who aspired to help rectify them.

Public criticism of the poll tax extended back decades. Every president from Franklin Roosevelt to John F. Kennedy spoke out against restrictions on African American suffrage, with varying degrees of assertiveness. Congress, too, raised the issue every year from the late 1940s forward, but burying assaults on the poll tax became an annual ritual for the Dixie Democrats who defended Jim Crow.[3]

Finally, in 1962, the Kennedy administration cautiously pressed Congress to draft legislation for a constitutional amendment. Kennedy's Justice Department, which was led by his younger brother Robert Kennedy, believed this was the only legal strategy that could break the Dixiecrats' grip. The amendment had been approved by Congress that September, and over the next year and a half, states inched the ratification along.[4]

On the phone, *"Abram told me this issue was 'vital in order to secure voting rights for tens of thousands of black people in the South in the 1964 general election.'"*

Despite his sympathy for the cause, Stan was reticent at first. As a Jewish person, he had long been aware of the sting of bigotry, even though he had limited personal experience with it. He had spent years competing alongside his high school debate partner, who happened to be African American. As a youth, friendships like that one made it difficult for Adelstein to conceive of the racism that blistered his nation's skin. Nevertheless, he hesitated to take on the task because he needed a moment to weigh the politics—to ask himself if he had the leverage to succeed. *"I told him I would give this matter some thought, decide what I could do, and see what I could find out."* He thanked Abram for the call and said he would be in touch soon. *"After talking to him,"* Stan recalled, *"I visited with my wife, Ita."*

A Holocaust escapee who understood better than most the travesty of racial oppression, Ita had been born in Poland and later trained as a teacher. She spoke with a precision befitting her trade. *"She asked me, 'Stan, why have you spent so much time developing a political position, if not for the purpose of taking on this sort of responsibility?'"*

"Ita was right," Stan remembered. *"I called Morris back and told him I would do what I could."* After dropping the receiver just long enough to reset the dial, Stan *"called our company pilot, Bob Higgins,"* a retired air force colonel, *"in Hill City, and told him that we would be flying to Pierre the next day."* Higgins agreed that the weather should be good enough to fly, *"though it certainly was going to be unpleasant and cold."*

Then Stan called the governor of South Dakota, Archie Gubbrud. Four years earlier, Stan had helped Gubbrud win the governor's office. To do so, Adelstein had talked some business associates into funding a phone bank in the basement of one of the buildings his family owned in downtown Rapid City, from which the campaign team blanketed voters with calls for Gubbrud. *"This was the first get-out-the-vote effort in South Dakota, and even though it's now a pretty well-accepted practice, in those days, people were skeptical that it would work at all."* Against the odds, Gubbrud had unseated popular Democratic Governor Ralph Herseth in 1960.[5] Afterward, Adelstein and the governor *"had a very warm and special relationship. I had been deeply involved in his campaign, and after he won the gubernatorial election, he asked me to serve as the youngest member—by over ten years—on his transition team."*

On the phone, the governor agreed to meet with Stan the following day on one condition, *"if I would be willing to go for a ride with him. I said, 'What's that all about?' He said that the Ford Motor Company had just given all of the nation's governors the use of a very beautiful Lincoln automobile, that he had never seen such a fancy car, and that he enjoyed driving it, but since it was a long weekend and most legislators and lobbyists had gone home, he could not find anyone to go riding."* Adelstein agreed, and when the pair took a Sunday tour through downtown Pierre and across the countryside, Stan brought up the Twenty-Fourth Amendment.

The governor searched his mind for a moment before remembering that a ratification bill had been proposed earlier in the session. He had decided to sit on it *"and had no intention of bringing the bill forward during that session."*

Adelstein told Gubbrud that the Twenty-Fourth Amendment was good public policy. Failure to ratify might also pose a risk for their state. *"South Dakota's refusal to ratify would give the impression that we had some sort of a major political or racial bias."* And this would not be the first time the state faced these charges under Gubbrud's watch. A little over a year earlier, the *New York Times* had run a story about racism in South Dakota. The newspaper took the state to task after a report by a local civil rights organization claimed that "90 per cent of the bars and barber shops and 30 per cent of the restaurants and motels" in Rapid City refused service to African Americans, most of whom were airmen at nearby Rapid City Air Base.[6] With the *Times* story on his mind, Gubbrud agreed with Adelstein, but only tacitly—*"he said he would go along with the ratification and sign the bill without any hesitance, but that he was unwilling to invest any political capital in the process."* Moving the legislation forward would be Stan's burden, and his alone.

As the governor's glossy black Lincoln rolled up to the curb along East Capitol Avenue, Adelstein thanked his friend for the conversation and the ride. Stepping onto the curb, Stan inhaled brisk air. His collar rubbed the nape of his neck as he looked up at the yellow bricks of the St. Charles Hotel. In South

Dakota, the legislature met between January and March each year, depending on the agenda, and for years the St. Charles hosted the state's political class. Entering the hotel, Adelstein hoped to find E.C. "Ping" Murray, a Rapid City businessman and state senator from Stan's own district.[7]

Fortunately, Murray and several other legislators had elected to stay in the capital city for the weekend rather than risk the icy drive home. After a warm reception in his suite, Murray, like Archie Gubbrud, agreed to support the ratification bill *"but made it clear that he had no influence in the matter because he was not even a member of the State Affairs Committee,"* which held the bill. Murray explained that it was Representative Joe R. Dunmire, the chairman of his chamber's State Affairs Committee, who had decided to freeze the legislation. His support would make all the difference.

By the time Stan's visit with Murray had ended, winter darkness blanketed the town and the icy surface of the Missouri River to the west. With directions to Dunmire's motel suite just two blocks away, Adelstein bundled up and then slogged through the ice and snow. When he arrived, the sixty-two-year-old Dunmire welcomed him. After commiserating about the weather, Adelstein got to the purpose of his visit.

Dunmire told Stan that *"he had no intention of releasing the ratification bill. He said, 'We need to teach that son-of-a-bitch a lesson in constitutional law.'"*

Like Stan, Dunmire was a Republican, and *"the son-of-a-bitch he was referring to was President Lyndon B. Johnson."*

Johnson had only been in the Oval Office for about two months, following the assassination of John F. Kennedy the previous November. Kennedy's murder had placed incredible political capital in the new chief executive's hands, and he did not want to be a placeholder president. With the 1964 election eleven months out, Johnson realized that passing the Twenty-Fourth Amendment would secure a significant victory for civil rights. It would also bolster his own candidacy by enfranchising legions of African American voters who had increasingly cast their ballots for Democrats since the days of FDR's New Deal.[8]

Doing what Johnson did best, *"he called each member of the State Affairs Committee in South Dakota, told them how important it was, and demanded that they ratify the amendment."* Johnson's lobbying irked Dunmire, who believed that the president had no business pressuring members of state government.

As a Republican and as a Jewish man, Stan's loyalties were divided, but he had committed himself to Abram and the AJC, and at a higher level he believed in the inherent justice of the cause. *"The historical denial of the franchise and political opportunity for Jews in Europe was never far from my heart, and I realized that I had a chance to do what Jews in other places could not. Our knowledge of the boundless privileges South Dakota offered us had been precious to my family since the day my grandmother first stepped foot on her desolate homestead near the Badlands."*

Driven by these motivations, Stan spent a lengthy conversation *"trying to convince Dunmire that he had sufficiently made his point to the president,"* and that the issue *"had moved out of the political environment into the social environment, and that our failure to act would place the state in a very, very difficult light and would be against everything that those in our state believed in."*

That is when Dunmire revealed that he possessed the two fundamental traits of any successful politician: a firm belief in his ideals and a willingness to bend them for just the right price. Adelstein had no doubt that Dunmire was sincere in his belief that Johnson lacked the constitutional authority to pressure states and their legislators into affirming a constitutional amendment. Then again, Dunmire had let on that the owners of the Homestake Mine—the largest gold mine in the world and the largest employer in his home district of Lead, South Dakota—had been pushing an amended state tax bill that would be favorable to them. As their representative, and as an individual whose political future was beholden to Homestake, Dunmire wanted that bill passed.

Adelstein asked him what was impeding the tax legislation. In an odd coincidence—and that weekend in 1964, not to mention his entire life, was full of them—it turned out that none other than Ping Murray, whose foyer Stan had just left, was the chairman of the Taxation Committee, and the very individual stalling Dunmire's bill. Adelstein knew what he had to do. *"By now it was about eight o'clock at night, and I trudged back to Ping's apartment"* at the St. Charles to change Murray's mind.

Inside his toasty room, Murray explained his problem with Dunmire and Homestake. He intimated his belief that even though the mine employed thousands of South Dakotans and was a major part of the state's economy, it was only one company in one district of an expansive state. It was inappropriate, Murray believed, for the company to be tailoring tax law. So he had decided to humble Dunmire and his gilded lobby by delaying their bill. When Adelstein asked Murray to consider the weight of the Twenty-Fourth Amendment, the legislator agreed that enough was enough, and that *"he had taught Dunmire the lesson he needed to have taught—that Homestake did not own West River,"* the common moniker for the portion of South Dakota west of the Missouri River. *"Murray said that if I wanted it, Dunmire could have his tax bill."*

That hurdle crossed, for the fifth time that day—it was now about nine o'clock—Stan donned his overcoat and headed out into the cold. Back at Dunmire's place, he told the chairman that Murray would let his tax bill move to a floor vote, then asked him to release the ratification bill. Dunmire agreed. Victory.

Or so Stan thought. There was another catch: Dunmire said he could get the bill through the House, but it had been tied up for too long and *"the date for the introduction of committee bills in the state Senate had passed, and to get the ratification bill to the floor would require a suspension of the rules."* That was something that the legislature rarely did, and *"only in the most severe cases."* Furthermore, the action *"would have to be agreed to by Lieutenant Governor Nils A. Boe,"* who was, per the South Dakota Constitution, president of the Senate.[9]

Time was running short, and as Stan traipsed through the snow toward his own motel, he wondered whether Boe would take a meeting. Unlike his colleagues in the House and the Senate, Boe had returned home for the weekend to Sioux Falls, where he was a successful and very busy attorney with a Monday schedule that almost certainly had no room to spare.

Stan called Boe late Sunday night. Boe said he had a brief, ten o'clock window in the next morning's schedule. If Stan could be in Sioux Falls, Boe would happily meet with him. So, a furious thirty-six hours after getting that fateful call from Morris Abram, Adelstein dialed his final numbers for the day. Bob Higgins answered, and Stan *"told him that we needed to be up and about, wheels up, no later than 8:00 A.M., which was fine with Bob."*

The next morning in Sioux Falls, Adelstein explained the situation. He made it clear that he believed South Dakota had a moral and political imperative to support the Twenty-Fourth Amendment. Boe agreed. *"He was very sympathetic, understood the seriousness of the problem, and had no particular axe to grind by withholding the ratification."* But he also had a couple of things on his mind. First, Boe was concerned about suspending the Senate's rules, as doing so was a rarity. He took his powers seriously and did not want to use them without good cause. Stan respected that. *"I also knew that Boe was engaged in a difficult primary election with former Governor Sigurd Anderson, and being no stranger to politics, I knew exactly what he wanted."*[10]

Adelstein was not surprised when Boe casually asked, *"Where will the Young Republicans be in the June primary?"* Stan understood the gambit. *"At that time, I was state chairman of the Young Republicans, a very powerful group with say in the convention, and certainly a lot of say in terms of the communities we represented."*

Stan silently counted the members of the executive committee of the Young Republicans that would support him if he hinted that the Young Republicans were leaning toward Boe. His math complete, Adelstein suggested that *"we would be in favor of the youngest candidate,"* since that person would be best suited to relate with the Young Republicans and their concerns. Boe knew he was that man, but Adelstein did not have to say it. Stan added that some Young Republicans were concerned that the efforts of Sigurd Anderson—who had already served two terms as governor in the 1950s and was running again—*"suggested that he was overly concerned with public power."*[11]

Boe seemed satisfied with Stan's response and reached for his calendar. After a few moments, he told Adelstein that he would suspend the legislature's rules at the end of Thursday's session, January 23, clearing the way for a vote to ratify the Twenty-Fourth Amendment to the Constitution. When the day came, the House passed the measure, and the Senate—allowed by Nils Boe's suspension of the regular rules—followed at 2:26 P.M. with minimal debate. With this roll call vote, South Dakota played a pivotal role in the history of the long battle for civil rights.[12]

WHY STAN?

Adelstein's long winter weekend in South Dakota in 1964 played an important—if unexpected—part in the process that changed the U.S. Constitution and removed one trenchant barrier between thousands of American citizens and their right to vote. Over the years, Stan has been asked to recount this story many times, in part because it reveals much about the character of politics in the United States in middle of the twentieth century. Yet it is the subtext of his story—the coincidence and nuance of the entire scenario, and indeed, his part in it—that tells us even more about him and his place in the annals of state and national history.

At first blush, Adelstein seems like an unlikely candidate for the role he played. He was a young Jewish man in a very Christian state. His people had been repeatedly oppressed and marginalized throughout their history, and in 1964 they were barely two decades from the genocide that attempted to burn them from the face of the earth.

Was it a question of place? Perhaps South Dakota was simply an exceptionally welcoming space for Jewish people and minorities. The state's long, ugly record of violence and malfeasance toward its Native American population—not to mention the pockets of anti-Catholic and harshly nativist activity that had popped up occasionally in its history—suggests otherwise. But even if it were, South Dakota was, despite its expansive landscape, a demographically small and rural state. With no major cities and only four electoral votes in 1964, it hardly seemed consequential in the broader scheme of national politics.

In other ways, Adelstein might have seemed the perfect character. He was an ambitious, intelligent, and wealthy man whose family connections and life experience had placed him well beyond his years, both professionally and politically. In 1964, he was only two years away from assuming the corporate presidency of NWE, the multimillion-dollar Adelstein family construction business that employed thousands of people across the West. Stan was also vigorously active in an array of civic, political, and Jewish causes and slowly spinning himself into a network of influence through Republican politics and organizations like the AJC, the Young Republicans, and, later, the Young Presidents' Organization. Finally, he was exceptionally dedicated—largely because of his wife's Holocaust experience and the teachings of a single mentor he met in the army—to a lifetime of service. That was, as he understood it, the Jewish way.

Stan's lobbying on the Twenty-Fourth Amendment marked a pivotal moment in his life, roughly midway between the time of his birth in Iowa in the 1930s as the first son of immigrant and second-generation parents and his gradual retirement from a lifetime of entrepreneurship, civic and political activism, and religious advocacy in the second decade of the twenty-first century. Indeed, over the course of more than eight decades, Adelstein's life story offers a window into the history of Jewish people in South Dakota and the Midwest as well as the physical creation of many communities in those places. It is a story of national and global Jewish activism and of local, state, and national Republican politics. It is also one of success and failure in business and politics, of personal achievement, and of familial strain. Stan's story tells of the power of philanthropy, the risks and rewards of business, and the sprawling web of luck and perseverance, coincidence and calculation, that brought a young Jewish man from Rapid City's Skyline Drive to the streets of Israel, the White House, and back.

Stan Adelstein commissioned this work. It is only fair, however, that readers understand that the book in their hands is far different from what he envisioned. Stan pictured a series of anecdotes from his long and full life, the sum total of which would operate as an antibiography. Rather than focusing on him, it would emphasize small vignettes about events, interactions, and processes that—as he considers them—he was simply lucky enough to stumble into. Coincidence, he believed, not effort or exception, drove his story, and that was how he believed it should be told.

As my research and writing continued, however, I came to see that only by centering the work on Stan as an individual and a life could one weave together the many strains of the narrative. Tales of loyalty, immigration, power, faith, politics, industry, philanthropy, federalism, community, disaster, activism, marriage, reflection, and much more sprawl and cross in the tangle of his life. With this in mind, I—along with my colleague, friend, and editor, Eric John Abrahamson—made the case for a broadly contextualized biography that would be punctuated by Stan's personal stories.

He agreed, and as we went along, Stan opened the doors to his past, allowing access to the memories and issues that shaped his life. He submitted to hours of oral history interviews, as did members of his family and his closest associates. Stan also shared thousands of pages of primary source material held by the Northwestern Engineering Company. I supplemented these records with secondary literature and additional holdings at several archives, as well as informal conversations with people across the Black Hills. In fact, one of the singular challenges of this book has been to capture the many stories and insights for which there are no documentary records. Some of these were personal examples of Stan's incredible generosity—moments in which he paid the law school tuition for an intern of his in the South Dakota State Senate or that of a young nurse's assistant who cared for him in the hospital and dreamed of attaining further vocational training. Some of the things unearthed in this process, of course, were less flattering and uncomfortable for Stan to confront, let alone share publicly. His decision to continue the process reflects both his courage and his candor.

INTRODUCTION

Through more than two years of interviews, conversations, exchanges, and research, I learned many things about Stan Adelstein—some of which he found copasetic, others he challenged, and still others he had long forgotten. Perhaps the most compelling thing I absorbed, however, involves his insistence that—despite ample evidence to the contrary—his remarkable and expansive life was simply a product of coincidence. He firmly believes that he just happened to be "that Jew from South Dakota" that people somehow heard about and decided to look up. More often than not, he answered, and the following pages offer a glimpse into the wide-ranging repercussions of the relationships "that Jew from South Dakota" brought to life. I think, or perhaps hope, that over the last few years, Adelstein has come to see that even if the many episodes described here—and the many more that did not make the final cut—were actually mere coincidences, they were seasoned and spurred along by his strong devotion to helping people when and how he could.

Since the moment Stan's mother brought him across the Missouri River, his Jewish heritage has set him apart from most of his peers. He sought to carve a space on the prairie he called home, while steamrolling his way through business, politics, and all manner of civic and Jewish affairs across the nation and the world. Much of this he did because he felt a strong compulsion to assist those around him; parts of this were innate, others were learned through experiences and acquaintances. He enjoyed trying to solve problems, many too large for any single person to reconcile, but Stan threw himself at them anyway. Sometimes, it was a phone call to a powerful person; a $100,000 donation; or the use of company resources. He happily deployed his considerable oratorical talents when they were requested, and sometimes when not. Frequently, however, Adelstein simply sat and listened, giving the well-intentioned or the ambitious five minutes of his time before connecting people and ideas. He cross-pollinated the messy systems through which power and business flowed and helped populate the corridors where decisions were made. Sometimes Stan hampered progress or engendered enemies. But even when he erred, he tried to learn, to soak up experiences and information around him, and to make sense of life.

In South Dakota, it seems that everyone has an opinion of Stan Adelstein. News articles, individual stories and letters to the editor (from Stan's personal and political friends and foes), and the documentary record provide a mélange of memories, rumors, and opinions. To some, he is a visionary, courageous leader, a fiery reminder of the "true" Republican Party and original spirit of South Dakota Republicanism. To others, he is a liberal in conservative clothing, a wealthy heir soiled by "politics-as-usual." Some view his perceptions of anti-Semitism in contemporary South Dakota as overly sensitive or deployed toward political ends. Others understand that his views on race, religion, and belonging have roots two generations back. Some see a committed philanthropist, others a coldhearted businessman. Some see a father, brother, and husband—for better and worse. Some perceive a lifelong leader too egocentric to quit. And others think of Adelstein as a man who is, as the years stretch on, too committed to give up.

Each description carries some degree of accuracy. He, like all humans, is inherently complex. More important than any single take on Stan and his identity, perhaps, is the wide berth of influence he has wielded for his city, his state, his nation, and his people. In this sense, Stan's story is about the relationship between the individual and his community, the insider and the outsider, and the ways in which these tensions play against one another to fulfill the promise of American democracy.

ADELSTEIN FAMILY TREE

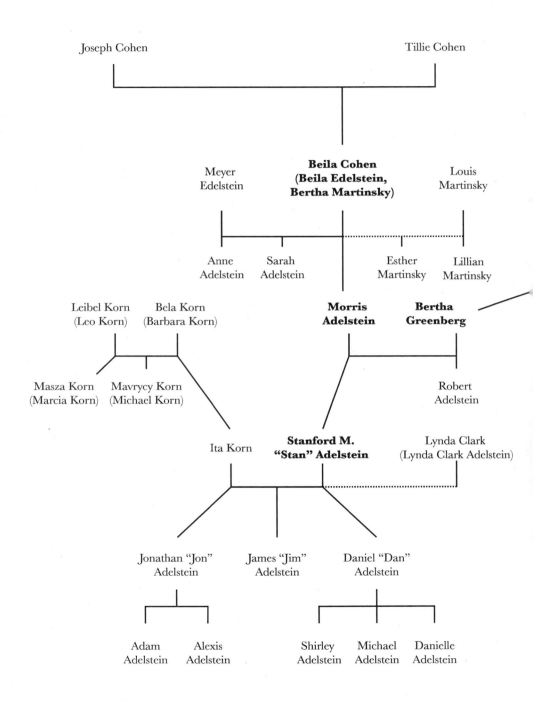

ADELSTEIN FAMILY TREE

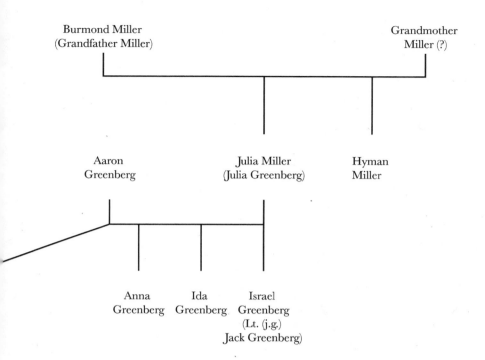

This chart represents several generations of Stan Adelstein's family. Children are not listed in birth order, and this chart is not a comprehensive genealogy of the Miller, Cohen, Edelstein, Adelstein, Korn, Martinsky, or Greenberg families. Instead, it shows the connections between the families discussed in this book. Marital and other name changes are noted in parentheses.

CHAPTER 1
FROM RUSSIA WITH *LIBE*

In the autumn of 1891, the golden dome of Iowa's state capitol blended into the hazy sky around Des Moines. For a hurried few months every year, thousands of farmers harvested corn and other produce from the world's best soil. By late fall, their army of hoes and reapers would leave only the brittle, ten-inch skeletons of once verdant stalks and air thick with particulates. Wiping sweat from their brows, laborers spread manure over the earth. Such was the cycle of Iowa agriculture: many farmers grew corn to feed pigs and cows, whose flesh they sold at market and whose waste they recycled as fertilizer for the next year's yield. As each day passed, temperatures waned and the sun arched a little lower in the sky, its rays piercing the dust at an angle just sharp enough to cast the atmosphere in a golden hue.

As their New York City–based steam engine lumbered into Des Moines in 1891 or 1892, Beila and Meyer Edelstein may have witnessed this Iowa ritual. They might have also admired the genius of Mifflin E. Bell and W.F. Hackney, the architects who so masterfully intertwined the shining capitol dome and surrounding sky.[1] To those who crafted the heroic story of the American frontier, Beila and Meyer were clearly outsiders.

For decades, writers, politicians, and the American public adhered to a vision of the settlement of the American West that included teams of self-assured, divinely inspired Christians, who packed their goods into covered wagons and headed with their families for greener pastures. Rare were tales of Native peoples who were anything but violent and obstructive, African Americans who came to and through Iowa as they escaped slavery's grip,

Asian immigrants who built the railroads, the few Latino families that trickled into the Middle West, or white settlers who did not fit the Euro-Christian mold.[2] And yet all of these people shaped the region.

The Edelsteins were Jewish, two of about 5,000 other Jewish people who were living in Iowa in 1900.[3] Over the next ten years, they were joined by nearly 13,000 others who shared their faith, including Aaron and Julia Greenberg, who also came from Russia. The two families did not know each other. The Edelsteins lived in Des Moines, while the Greenbergs chose to settle in a Jewish neighborhood along the Missouri River on Iowa's western edge.[4] But their shared experience in Russia would provide the basis for the confluence of their family lines in America.

CHAOS IN THE CATHERINE CANAL

In the middle of the afternoon on March 1, 1881, two bombs heaved Russia into chaos. The sixty-three-year-old emperor, Alexander II, had spent part of the day with his cousin at Mikhailovsky Palace in St. Petersburg. It was a mere twenty-minute walk from the mansion to the tsar's residence at the Winter Palace, which had housed successive Russian monarchs for more than a century. Alexander, of course, was no pedestrian. Quite the opposite, a heavy guard surrounded his carriage. Such precautions were necessary since several assassins had tried to kill the tsar over the course of his long reign.[5]

As the emperor's entourage—six guards on horseback and two additional security sleighs—turned onto the Catherine Canal on its return to the Winter Palace, a young man threw a small package beneath Alexander's car. The explosion decimated the carriage, sending the tsar, who was otherwise unhurt, to the ground. As Alexander gained his bearings—reports claim he began casually pacing the scene, likely in shock—a second bomber tossed another parcel at his feet. This explosion shattered the emperor's legs and disfigured his face. When the surviving guards gained control of the situation, they rushed Alexander to his residence, where doctors struggled to halt the torrent of blood that gushed from his femoral arteries. Within the hour, however, Alexander II lay dead.[6] His family and admirers would mourn the fallen monarch, but they were not the only Russians who suffered in the fallout from his death. Jewish people were next.

Life in Russia had been difficult for Jewish people long before Alexander's demise. They had been blamed, as elsewhere in the world, for a variety of national problems.⁷ Since 1791, anti-Semitic administrators within the imperial Russian government had relegated the Jewish families to the "Pale of Jewish Settlement," a swath of land situated along the southwestern corner of the Russian Empire. It encompassed the modern states of Poland, Ukraine, and Belarus, among others. Acquired by Russia at the end of the eighteenth century, the Pale was, with few exceptions, the only place where Jewish people—who comprised just 4.2 percent of the empire's population—were allowed to live. Even there, Jewish people were the minority; they made up only about 12.5 percent of the nearly three million people inside the Pale.⁸ The government also capped the number of Jewish people who could be educated in a given community, limited Jewish suffrage, and otherwise oppressed this tiny ethnic and religious minority.⁹

Four out of five Jewish people in the Pale lived in small shtetls, or villages, and most eked out meager livings as craftspeople and artisans. The remainder were spread over rural areas. In Jewish spaces, the tradition of *tzedakah* (righteousness and charity) compelled community members to develop systems of collective care. But by the end of the nineteenth century, industrialization created economic strife across the Pale. Railroads snaked their way over the empire, and after the comparatively progressive Alexander II emancipated the Russian serfs in 1861—thereby increasing competition in the labor market—conditions grew steadily worse. Unemployment in the shtetls skyrocketed by the 1880s, and many Jewish people faced starvation.¹⁰

As though the economic slide and the weight of political repression did not pose sufficient problems, Alexander II's assassination ushered in a new wave of terror for Jewish Russians. The tsar's murder had been orchestrated by a group of revolutionaries known as Narodnaya Volya, which translated to "will of the people." Active since 1878, this organization favored terrorist bombings and sought to bring about a socialist revolution in Russia—one it believed would replace the monarchy with a government led by the peasantry.¹¹ At least one Jewish woman—Hessia Helfman—spent the rest of her life in prison for a minor role in the assassination plot.¹²

When the slain emperor's son, Alexander III, assumed the throne, his government crushed Narodnaya Volya, and he and elements within the Russian population aimed vengeance at their Jewish neighbors. For four years beginning in 1881, a swarm of violent pogroms swept across what is now Ukraine, and later, into portions of present-day Poland.¹³

The pogroms were followed in 1882 by the "May Laws." Issued by the government, these mandates pushed Jewish people from villages and relegated them to shtetls inside the Pale. The government also expelled Jewish residents from Moscow and temporarily shuttered the Choral Synagogue, the construction of which had begun in 1880.[14] Anti-Semitism then carried into the tumultuous, two-decade reign of Russia's last tsar, Nicholas II, who abdicated the throne under pressure from Bolshevik revolutionaries in 1917 and was executed alongside his family in a basement in Yekaterinburg the following year.[15]

The continuing threats of violence, starvation, and the forced conscription of young men into the Russian military spurred a variety of reactions within the Russian Jewish community.[16] Scores of Jewish people had been forced into service since 1827, when Tsar Nicholas I made them eligible for the draft. While the minimum age was eighteen for non-Jewish men, Jewish boys could be conscripted as young as twelve years old. Although the Russian army maintained some provisions allowing Jewish soldiers to keep Torahs, build synagogues, and sometimes even cook in separate, kosher pots, they were required to attend Christian prayers, and perhaps as many as 15,000 converted, or pretended to convert, over the course of the century. At different times, Jewish soldiers earned respect for valor on the battlefield, but they were barred from attending military academies, and regulations capped their promotions below the rank of corporal. Indeed, the Russian military had only a single Jewish officer in the four decades prior to World War I, and even then, he had been promoted after retirement.[17] And, given the constant tribulations that accompanied the waning years of Russia's tsarist rule, conscription was a hard life at best and a death sentence at worst.

The Russian pogroms, the threat of conscription, and other oppressions made life in Russia a daily struggle for survival for Jewish people. Accordingly, waves of them left for central and western Europe, and others migrated to the United States. Among this latter group were the Edelsteins and the Greenbergs, for whom abandoning their homeland must have seemed like the only option.

FROM THE PALE TO THE HEARTLAND

Escaping the strife of eastern Europe, the Edelsteins and the Greenbergs joined a long wave of Jewish migration to the United States. For about fifty years beginning in 1820, some 250,000 Jewish people emigrated to America.[18]

Another two million—a full third of eastern Europe's Jewish population—flooded in between 1880 and 1920.¹⁹ Most Jewish families settled along the eastern seaboard, in port cities like New York and Charleston, South Carolina.²⁰ Others, however, searched inland for a place to make a living, and the ever-expanding networks of riverboats and railroads slowly brought them to the Midwest.

In Iowa, Jewish immigrants built enclaves along the western banks of the Mississippi River.²¹ They settled in river towns like Keokuk and Davenport, whose names betrayed the process of American Indian removal that was still clearing Iowa of its Native inhabitants when the first settlers entered the territory. Iowa's first known Jewish settler entered the state in 1833.²² Within twenty years, Jewish families were becoming a fixture on the Iowa landscape. Cities along the Mississippi and its sprawling tributaries were home to small Jewish communities. Their members joined one another for Sabbath and holiday services, organized synagogues, held reading and discussion groups, and had small, Jewish fraternities. When they could, families pooled money to buy property for the establishment of Jewish cemeteries.²³

As time and settlement crept along, the Jewish settlers pushed farther into the heart of Iowa. By the 1870s, the small Jewish congregation in Des Moines was growing steadily. Other Jewish people slowly made their way toward western Iowa. At the end of the decade, Sioux City and Council Bluffs each had at least two Jewish residents. In 1877, brick and mortar signaled the end of early Jewish settlement in Iowa. That year, the Jewish community in Keokuk built the state's first synagogue. Their Hebraic community was there to stay.²⁴

Small Jewish congregations sometimes struggled with traditions and logistics. Custom dictated, for example, that a minyan—or a minimum of ten Jewish men older than thirteen—had to be present for public prayer. Scattered, rural communities of Jewish migrants also tended to lack the training and materials necessary for keeping kosher kitchens and holding worship. One had to assume that *Sefer Torahs*, the meticulously hand-scribed scrolls used during services, for example, were few and far between. Yet these communities made due. Some could afford *hazanim*, non-rabbis who led synagogue services, while others, out of sheer necessity, combined families of Orthodox and Reform Jews—who in many places had sharp disagreements about the other's beliefs—into a single congregation. By carrying forth their traditions, Jewish people not only brought their faith to the Midwest, they revised it in the process, contributing to the development of the distinctly American brand of Judaism that was taking shape at the end of the nineteenth century.[25]

EXODUS AND SETTLEMENT: THE EDELSTEINS

Beila Cohen was born in the Pale of Settlement in the early 1870s. She died nearly seventy years later, almost 5,000 miles away, in a new country, and under a different name. She and her family shared many similarities with other immigrants of various religions. Tight finances meant that the family came to America in stages. Beila's father, Joseph, arrived first and earned what he could to cover the cost of his family's trip from Russia.[26] Like many migrants, basic details about the Cohens' lives were lost in their transcontinental shuffle. Was Beila born in Poland or Lithuania, and in what year? Was "Cohen" the family's original surname, or was it "Gabalski" or "Gabowski," as some of Beila's descendants believe? If that is the case, when and why did their name change?[27]

Despite this uncertainty, it is clear that Beila was about nineteen years old when she left Russia in 1891. By that time, she had married a man named Meyer Edelstein and had assumed his last name. They traveled with Beila's mother and several siblings. After leaving their home, this small group of Jewish refugees temporarily separated in order to sneak across the Russian border. It is unclear how they did so and exactly where they reconvened. But it is likely that Brody, Austria—which was a known haven for Jewish émigrés—was the family's last stop in central Europe before they emigrated from a port on the Black Sea. The family sailed to New York, possibly stopping in Liverpool on the way west. Their immigration papers were processed, and that may have been the moment at which the family's surname became "Cohen." In any event, the family boarded a locomotive that carried them to the confluence of the Des Moines and Raccoon Rivers, where the golden dome of Iowa's state capital towered over the river bluffs.[28]

The Cohens, along with Beila and Meyer, found a supportive network of Jewish families waiting for them in Des Moines. In fact, the family had chosen the city specifically because friends from Europe had settled there. The geographical organization of the Des Moines Jewish community mirrored that of the old country: Jewish families from Germany congregated in the west, while Ukrainian, Lithuanian, Polish, and other eastern European families assembled on the east side of town.²⁹

The Edelsteins shared a small apartment with Beila's parents, Joseph and Tillie Cohen, before moving into a nearby flat in 1893.³⁰ They were surrounded by other Jewish families who comprised the B'nai Israel, an Orthodox congregation that had been active in East Des Moines since 1869.³¹ By 1912, three other Orthodox congregations and one group of Reform Jews had been established in the city, so Beila likely found a peer group among the Hebraic community in eastern Des Moines.³² According to one account from the period, "the real spirit of the Jewish community were the ladies; they have not only been the helpers of the poor, the deliverers of the distressed, but have been foremost in perpetuating Judaism in their newly adopted country."³³

Meyer and Beila's life in Iowa differed markedly from their experience in Russia. For one thing, Jewish people could vote, move, work, and live in relative peace. Yet the family struggled to make ends meet on Meyer's scant earnings. Like three out of four young Jewish men in Iowa, Meyer was a traveling peddler who spent most of his life on the road. He carried a heavy backpack or pushed a cart laden with pots and pans, dishes, eyeglasses, and a menagerie of other wares. He sold them to families in the city and the countryside.³⁴

Young men like Meyer had to develop people skills, acquire goods (often on credit), and account for their wares and revenues. Trudging across the Iowa and Illinois countrysides in the sweltering, mosquito-laden summer and the bitter, windy winter tested every peddler's endurance. Because they carried goods and cash, traders were frequent victims of assault and robbery. Their work also imposed a hefty psychological burden: condemned to a life of isolation, with rare opportunities to visit their families, peddlers like Meyer had little more than the hope of saving enough money to open a shop or buy their way into another industry to encourage them along.³⁵

Vestiges of Old World prejudice also existed: in the late nineteenth century, virulent nativism drew sharp lines in the American public's conception of who did and did not belong. Strains of anti-immigrant thought appeared throughout the early phases of European migration. When the United States erected the russet Statue of Liberty—it would not fully acquire its iconic aqua shade until about 1920—the sculpture bore the immortal inscription by the Jewish American poet Emma Lazarus, who begged the world to "Give me your tired, your poor, / Your huddled masses . . . The wretched refuse of your teeming shore."[36]

Yet not all who sought passage through New York's golden door were welcomed with open arms. Catholics came under fire in the 1840s and again beginning around the 1870s. Nativists also turned their furor against Italians, Chinese, Irish, and other immigrant groups with some regularity. The degrees of their hatefulness ranged from social persecution and localized violence to institutional repression embodied in laws like the Chinese Exclusion Act of 1882, which banned the immigration of Chinese workers.[37]

In the United States, Jewish writers first noted anti-Semitic activity just before the Civil War. It started quietly, with a subtle but clear sense of social ostracism. By the 1880s, outspoken anti-Semites cropped up in the merchant-filled port towns of the Gulf Coast. Shortly thereafter, they appeared, more virulent than ever, in urban centers like New York. Anti-Semitism spread widely in the twentieth century, usually arising during times of economic unease, and was particularly prevalent in the eras of the First and Second World Wars.[38] For much of the history of the United States, even Americans who were not outspokenly anti-Semitic often considered Jewish people to be a distinct and "nonwhite" race.[39]

It does not appear that either the Edelsteins or the Cohens experienced any persecution in Des Moines. Central Iowa does not seem to have hosted a significant amount of anti-Semitism around the time of their arrival. But the Midwest was not free of this brand of bigotry. In 1893, a group of Christian activists requested that Chicago close its elaborate World's Fair on Sundays out of respect for the Christian Sabbath. Historians have connected such "Sunday laws" to Protestant complaints that Jewish and Catholic immigrants were upsetting the American social order.[40] Academics have also identified strains of anti-Semitism among the agrarian Democrats and Populists on the Northern Plains, although some writers claim that these connections are overblown. Nevertheless, in their 1896 platforms, both parties included language about the negative impact "European moneychangers"—an indirect term for "Shylocks," which was in turn a euphemism for "Jews"—were having on the American economy.[41] And some politicians openly complained that the Republican Party had "sold out to the Jews."[42]

Given the tense circumstances of Gilded Age ethnic relations and the complicated, churning waters of race and belonging, a heavy consciousness of their minority status must have weighed on Beila and Meyer Edelstein and the rest of the Jewish community in Iowa and the Midwest. They lived their lives with a careful awareness—informed by personal experience in Russia and millennia of history from around the world—of the perils that all Jewish people faced as racial and ethnic outsiders.

GROWING IN SIZE AND GROWING APART

Despite the challenges inherent to their arrival in this new country, the young Edelstein family underwent several significant changes in the last decade of the nineteenth century. Two daughters, Anne and Sarah, were born in 1893 and 1896, respectively. Meyer and Beila's middle child, a son named Moisha, or "Moses" in Yiddish, arrived on June 2, 1894. Shortly thereafter, a mistake by one of young Anne's schoolteachers forever altered the Edelstein name, mishearing it as "Adelstein" instead of "Edelstein." Over time, this enunciation brought about an orthographic shift to which the children and all their descendants would forever adhere.[43]

Almost immediately after Sarah's birth, Meyer and Beila Edelstein separated. According to one account, Tillie Cohen disliked Meyer, believed him beneath Beila and the family, and encouraged the split. Other iterations point to Meyer's frequent absences and the accrual of large debts from his peddling business, which he either could not afford or simply did not want to pay. Still other stories suggest that Meyer may have left for Chicago and, without a word, never returned. Beila rarely spoke of her husband, although they may have kept in touch. By the latter half of the 1890s, the couple had permanently separated. Meyer lived in Chicago, and his three children grew up believing him dead. In fact, it would not be until Chicago authorities reached out to Anne in the 1930s that she even knew of his fate.[44]

Moisha would eventually Americanize his name, changing it to Morris *"at the suggestion of his elementary school teacher who,"* according to Stan Adelstein, *"told him he would need an English name if he was going to get anywhere"* in life. And Morris only learned of his father's death years later, when a telegram arrived announcing Meyer's demise. It left Morris furious that he and his siblings had never been told the truth. To add insult to injury, *"The first time my father ever saw the family name spelled 'Edelstein,'"* his son Stan recalled, *"was when he first visited his own father's grave in Chicago."*

If Beila ever preferred "Adelstein," the change was only temporary. In 1899—and likely out of necessity as much as romance—she married an old family friend named Louis Martinsky. He was several years Beila's senior, and their marriage was not affectionate. The two were simply "not compatible," as Morris would recall years later. "Mother was always ambitious," he said, constantly in search of somewhere to go and something to do. Louis, on the other hand, was distant and lacked drive. A warehouse laborer, he often struggled to keep jobs. Although the pair had another two daughters—Lillian and Esther—their marriage quickly deteriorated. As their relationship wound to a close, the couple bought a grocery store and moved into the adjoining apartment. Beila hoped the family could make a living running the shop. When Louis turned out to be a passive partner, she procured a small property just outside Des Moines. She filled it with a handful of chickens and dairy cows. From 1903 forward, and although she and Louis remained legally married, Beila lived as a single mother of five.[45]

It is unclear exactly when Beila Edelstein changed her first name to "Bertha." Perhaps the nickname developed in Des Moines in the 1890s and simply stuck. Maybe it came about during her second marriage. Or it may have been part of the personal transformation that accompanied her metamorphosis into a lone parent and proprietor. But one thing is clear: by the first decade of the twentieth century, she was "Bertha Martinsky," a moniker she would use for the rest of her life.

Bertha continued running her dairy farm for a few years. But by 1910, the dispossession of Native peoples on the Northern Plains had once again created an opportunity for the settlement of non-Native people. Among them was a Yiddish-speaking woman whose life had been characterized by migration and rebuilding. South Dakota, Bertha Martinsky knew, was teeming with free and open land, so she set her sights on the western prairie.[46]

EXODUS AND SODA POP: THE GREENBERGS

Just as the image of hearty farmers heading out in covered wagons has dominated the tale of westward expansion, so has the popular imagination painted the story of Jewish settlement. Indeed, the visage of exhausted but determined Jewish immigrants arriving at Ellis Island and elsewhere is a fixture in the American consciousness.[47] The Cohens, Edelsteins, and Greenbergs fit this basic narrative—their experience was, without doubt, one of exodus and resettlement. Yet the divergences in these families' experiences give texture to the broader history of the Jewish experience on the Northern Plains.

Julia Greenberg's father, Burmond Miller, was a successful businessman who lived in Minsk, the present capital of Belarus in what was then the Pale of Jewish Settlement. His name derived from his trade, and Burmond made a good living milling grain. He was a relatively wealthy man whose position afforded the family a comfortable life, insofar as that was possible for Jewish people in that time and place. And yet this comfort could not insulate the family from the threats that their Jewish peers faced in eastern Europe. In 1904, only months before Julia's first daughter, Bertha, was born, Julia's older brother, Hyman, received the dreaded notice to report for service in the Russian military.[48]

Burmond Miller's status could not protect the family from Russian laws. But it could help them skirt their oppressors. And Grandfather Miller, as he was known, wanted to save his son. A stern and authoritarian patriarch—Miller was known for forcing his married children to live with him in order to receive the compulsory, parental blessing—Miller was used to getting his way. When the news of his son's conscription arrived, Miller ordered Julia's husband, Aaron Greenberg, to secure a passport and passage to the United States, using the guise of his own emigration to sneak the twenty-eight-year-old Hyman to America. Miller believed that with Julia pregnant, Aaron had the best argument for relocation—he would need an American job to send money back to care for his wife and child. Miller also had faith in Aaron's ability to dupe the authorities and customs agents. Miller's optimism, it seems, was not ill-founded: Aaron and Hyman made it to New York, where the pair lived briefly before heading to Sioux City, Iowa, to join Aaron's relatives.[49]

Aaron Greenberg started a small bakery in Sioux City and quickly made plans to bring Julia and baby Bertha to the United States. He saved money and planned their departure but struggled to convince Julia to leave. Her father did not want to lose his daughter and grandchild and had never intended that Aaron not return to his family in Minsk. After pleading with her father for four years, Julia finally received his permission and left for the United States. Just as Joseph and Tillie Cohen and Meyer and Beila Edelstein had done more than a decade earlier, she and young Bertha sailed across the Atlantic, boarded a steam engine in New York, and left for Iowa.[50]

Situated in the state's northwestern corner, Sioux City was flanked by the Loess Hills on the east and the Missouri River—which also served as the border with South Dakota and Nebraska—to the west. Two years after the Greenbergs reunited in Sioux City, the town was home to some 47,000 people.[51] It had a small but active Jewish community that traced its origins to the Jewish Cemetery Association founded in the city in 1869. Sixteen years later, a group of Orthodox women established the Jewish Ladies' Aid Society, which hosted a reading group as well as a Sabbath school and worked with Jewish men to hold services on the High Holidays of Rosh Hashanah and Yom Kippur.[52]

According to historian Michael J. Bell, by the middle of the 1890s, a group of Orthodox Jews had founded the Congregation Adath Jeshrun in Sioux City. Over the next few decades, three other congregations existed in the city: Anshe Kapull, Tifereth Israel, and Beth Abraham. Together, these four congregations had around 450 members and served about a thousand Jewish people.[53]

The Anshe Kapull congregation was comprised almost entirely of Jewish immigrants from the same region in Russia. As an Orthodox family from the Pale who lived in an east-central Sioux City neighborhood, the Greenbergs likely made this their spiritual home. Sioux City also had a significant number of German Reform Jews, whose thirty-one members structured their services around the teachings of Chicago-based firebrand Emil G. Hirsch and formed the Mt. Sinai congregation in 1899.[54]

The Greenbergs' experience in Iowa differed significantly from that of most other Jewish families. Firmly upper-middle class before and after his arrival, Aaron was among the fraction of lucky Jewish men who did not have to rely on the high-risk, low-reward life of a peddler. Running his bakery was challenging work, but it proved successful and, unlike the peddler's life, kept the family together. Young Bertha, who had never met her father before her arrival in the United States, would see him regularly while growing up—a luxury the Adelstein and Martinsky children did not have.[55]

Within a few years of Julia and Bertha's arrival, Aaron began to feel that the family bakery, which provided them a comfortable life, offered little room for expansion. After searching for new opportunities, Aaron found a seltzer bottling plant that was for sale. The company, Sioux City Bottling Works, delivered seltzer to neighborhoods around town. Work at the plant would be difficult. If he took over, Aaron would spend early mornings driving the city, dropping off wooden cases, each filled with a dozen bottles, at his customers' homes and collecting empties. His afternoons and evenings would be filled by endless hours of cleaning and refilling the bottles for the next day's delivery.[56]

The question was not, however, whether Aaron could handle the challenge—he had grown accustomed to early mornings at the bakery—but how he would raise the $6,000 (some $177,000 in 2019) he would need to buy the business. Where another immigrant or working-class American might have scrimped for years or taken out a bank loan, Aaron could turn to his father-in-law. After Grandfather Miller sent the money, Aaron went to work. Within a year, he added a second route and brought on Julia's brother, Hyman, to handle the deliveries.[57]

Aaron and Hyman remained partners for several decades, expanding their business beyond seltzer water and slowly developing their own line of soda drinks. *"Sioux City Bottling Works had a secret formula for the best strawberry soda I ever had in my life,"* Stan Adelstein remembered, *"and other people felt the same way."*[58] Coca-Cola even offered Greenberg a franchise, which he turned down, signing instead with a company called Dr. Pepper in 1937. Years later, Hyman's son Morris would manage the family business.[59]

As a result of their father's success, Bertha Greenberg and her siblings had comfortable childhoods. Her sisters, Anna and Ida, and a brother named Israel—who later went by "Jack" Greenberg—were all born between 1910 and 1915. Aaron and Julia purchased a large home in 1911, furnishing it with plush sofas and chairs. They quickly became leaders in Sioux City's Jewish community. Their children played almost exclusively with other Jewish children, even though they attended public school. Strict Orthodox Jews who spoke Yiddish at home, cooked kosher meals, and observed all religious holidays, Aaron and Julia also brought yeshiva students—young scholars who specialized in Hebrew texts—to teach Bertha and her siblings about Jewish traditions.[60]

Bertha Greenberg, a sharp, olive-skinned young woman with dark eyes and a soft smile, grew up in this world. Her family life was not perfect, but their home was generally a joyous and comfortable place. It was free from the paternal absence, tension, remarriage, and displacement that shaped the lives of the Adelstein children only a few hundred miles away. Where Morris Adelstein and his sisters often lived with relatives and sometimes suspended their own goals and aspirations to help their mother run her business, Bertha and the other Greenberg children set their sights on dreams of their own.[61]

Like thousands of high schoolers across the country, Bertha wanted to attend university. She mapped out a loose fantasy of her college experience, fixating on the adventure and intellectual journey that would accompany attendance at a prestigious coastal school. Bertha wanted to attend the University of California at Berkeley and become a librarian. She mailed her application in the spring of 1923, but life took her in a different direction.[62]

CHAPTER 2
HEADING WEST

Around 1908, Bertha Martinsky started looking for another fresh start. She had been toiling away on the outskirts of Des Moines for years, squeezing a meager living from her small dairy farm. The thirty-eight-year-old had not received any support from her estranged husband in several years, making advertisements promising that she could become "independent and rich, at [a] very low cost" quite attractive. All Martinsky had to do to reap these benefits, the newsprint read, was secure a homestead patent on 160 acres in South Dakota.[1] A single Jewish mother, Martinsky was intrigued.

Settlers had been moving west to claim 160-acre tracts under the Homestead Act since the presidency of Abraham Lincoln. Encouraged by the prospect of free, open, and purportedly uninhabited land, droves of Euro-Americans steadily pushed westward over the latter half of the nineteenth century. After using violence and coercion to force the *Oceti Sakowin* ("Seven Council Fires," often called the "Great Sioux Nation") and other Native Americans onto remote and semiarid reservations, the United States further dispossessed them through a program known as "allotment." After giving each Native American family a parcel of reservation land comparable in size to that available under the Homestead Act, the federal government sold the remaining "surplus" lands to non-Natives. The government's action devastated tribal land bases across the nation. Eager to snag a piece of the surplus, scores of these settlers arrived in western South Dakota in the decades surrounding the turn of the twentieth century. Many stayed and continued to interact with American Indians and Dakota transplants for decades.[2]

When Bertha Martinsky came to claim a piece of South Dakota prairie, she became part of a decades-long process that dispossessed area Lakotas of their federally protected treaty lands. Established by the Fort Laramie Treaty of 1868, the Great Sioux Reservation encompassed all of West River South Dakota, spare the sliver containing the Black Hills, which the government removed from the treaty lands in 1877. In 1889, a piece of legislation known as the "Sioux Agreement" divided what remained of the Great Sioux Reservation into smaller reservations and primed the region for allotment. Settlement exploded, and in 1908, some 115,000 hopefuls sought after 4,000 available homesteads. Martinsky traveled to Washington, D.C., two years later, speaking with government officials about procuring a homestead. Shortly thereafter, she visited her future home in rural South Dakota.[3]

Settlers had founded the tiny town of Interior on a "surplus" plot in 1907. The ground had been baked hard for several years prior to Martinsky's arrival. She nevertheless attempted to make a living there, filing a homestead patent on a parcel just outside the hamlet in late 1911. Although there were more than 600,000 people in South Dakota, Interior was so sparsely populated that, in 1910, it listed a non-Native population of zero.[4] By that time, frustrated settlers were fleeing the region in droves, but that did not deter Martinsky from loading her daughters onto a wagon and hauling them to the Badlands in the spring of 1912. There, the Yiddish-speaking mother and her girls would make a run at homesteading.[5]

The Martinskys were not the only Jewish people in South Dakota. As was the case in Iowa, small Jewish communities began to crop up across the state as Jewish settlers pressed west and, once there, sought a sense of religious and ethnic comradery. Unlike the wind-swept expanses of West River where Bertha Martinsky lived, the eastern half of South Dakota was home to "a good many Jewish families," predominantly "merchants, businessmen, and even some farmers."[6] As a result, several small Jewish enclaves had cropped up on the eastern side of South Dakota in the latter years of the nineteenth century. Two groups of Jewish emigres launched short-lived attempts to build agricultural communes near Mitchell in the 1880s.[7] By the 1890s, Jewish families from farm towns across northeastern South Dakota were celebrating the High Holidays together in the railroad town of Aberdeen and established the Congregation B'nai Isaac there in 1917.[8] Similarly, Sioux Falls was home to groups of Orthodox and Reform Jews who worshipped together for several years under the banner "Sons of Israel" around 1916. Disagreements over matters of tradition and orthodoxy, however, pushed the Reform Jews to split off and form the Mount Zion Synagogue in 1924.[9]

As for West River, the famous Black Hills mining town known as Deadwood had the closest Jewish community to Bertha Martinsky and her daughters. By the late 1870s, the town's colorful and occasionally violent character had earned it national notoriety. Jewish citizens were an important part of Deadwood's earliest years. Sol Bloom established a clothing and shoe store on Main Street, while Jacob Goldberg ran a grocery. Another prominent Jewish man, Nathan "Beaver" Colman, served as a postmaster and later as an electoral judge in Deadwood. He was not a rabbi, but led holiday services and religious rites, including weddings that were conducted in the Jewish-owned Franklin Hotel.[10]

The Deadwood Jewish community used a Torah that had been shipped over from Germany to bless the marriage of a young Jewish couple. Many years later, this same Torah would inspire a synagogue that Bertha Martinsky's grandson, Stanford Adelstein, would help to establish in South Dakota.[11]

MARTINSKY'S OF KADOKA

Alone on their desolate homestead for several harsh years, Bertha Martinsky and her daughters learned that a strictly agricultural life was untenable. *"Growing up,"* Stan said, *"I always heard that the girls rode a blind horse five miles to school in Interior every day."* At home, they helped their mother, but the bone-dry land, chilling winters, and personal inexperience produced little to eat or sell.

Despite these hardships, Bertha expanded her property, gaining an additional quarter section under the Enlarged Homestead Act in 1916. When she did, Bertha *"signed her full name in Hebrew cursive, probably because she couldn't in English,"* just above the line that read "sign here, with full Christian name."[12]

The additional land also bore little fruit, so Martinsky tried again, applying for a ranch homestead in 1920. None of these endeavors paid off—she was only able to grow about ten acres of alfalfa and grains, all of which came up crispy as periodic droughts plagued the region. Rather than relying solely on her farm during these hard years, Martinsky opened a small bakery in a little wooden shack in Interior. She sold loaves of bread, a kind of bagel/

doughnut hybrid, and small wares from her shop and a wagon she would park at powwows and other community events.[13] In a sense, she found herself living the peddler's life that her husband, Meyer, had tried so many years earlier.

When her homestead failed, Martinsky moved her small shop 25 miles north to the town of Kadoka, where she dusted off her grocer's skills. Area Lakotas had been regular customers in Interior—Bertha even learned to speak conversational Lakota—and they continued to patronize the new store she opened in 1917. Bertha called the place "Martinsky's of Kadoka," and from it she sold dry goods, clothes, and groceries.[14]

The seat of Jackson County, Kadoka was a center of activity. Like many small towns across western South Dakota, the community was filled with people who came to prove up free land, sell out, and move on. Others seemed to move from boomtown to boomtown, capitalizing on the frenetic early energy of municipal growth. Still others came to stay, establishing businesses of all kinds and investing their lives in the town. Banks, lumberyards, doctors' and dentists' offices, and shops of all kinds lined the city's handful of streets, while civic and church groups drove the town's social and political lives. Native Americans came up from the reservation, and cattle ranchers and passers-by stopped to stock up and do business.[15]

Martinsky stayed in West River South Dakota for decades. There, she adhered to halacha, or the biblical mandates prescribed for all Jewish followers. This included recognition of Shabbat, the Jewish Sabbath, and keeping kosher. She would not work on Saturdays or the High Holidays, for example, and some accounts suggest that she hired non-Jewish women to run the store in her stead.[16] Stan Adelstein, however, *"always heard that she didn't need to hire anyone. The women simply volunteered to run my grandmother's shop and the rooms she rented above it. They probably didn't really understand why she refused to work, other than that it had something to do with her faith."*

Bertha also practiced *tzedakah* in small ways when she could, and relentlessly observed Jewish holidays. Despite the challenges inherent to lacking a ritual slaughterer, hers was known as one of the few kosher kitchens in many miles—possibly because her sister, who still lived in Iowa, would send canned kosher meat by rail. For that reason, Jewish travelers sometimes called on Martinsky for a hot meal and a warm bed. For decades, she would maintain her reputation as a savvy businesswoman whose softer side hid beneath the grit and gristle of a hard life and a soft Yiddish accent. In her final years, she moved to her adult daughter's home in Mitchell, South Dakota.[17]

THE CONSTRUCTION BUG

When his mother started her dairy farm outside Des Moines, Morris Adelstein lived with his two sisters and his aunt and uncle, Sarah and Sam Aliber, in the city. He was a serious student who earned a B average at Des Moines's East High School. He would have graduated around 1912, but Morris dropped out of school because, when times were tough—and they often were—Bertha needed him to milk cows, collect eggs, and deliver the fruits of their farm to customers.[18] When his mother went west to the dry, Dakota grasslands, however, she left Morris in Iowa where he could complete his studies.[19]

At seventeen years old, Morris was clean-cut, with a shock of dark, neatly parted hair and bangs that waved over his high forehead. The Alibers encouraged Morris to continue his education. He had accumulated enough credits to graduate, but it is unclear whether he ever took a diploma. In any case, Highland Park College in Des Moines accepted him into its engineering program in 1914, and he began school that fall. In college, Morris was an avid debater and partnered with the future matinee actor Conrad Nagel. He was also active in the school's literary society and editor of its newspaper, *The Highlander*. Highland Park operated on an accelerated schedule, which Morris exploited, earning his engineering degree in only two years. He quickly enrolled in a summer program to add an endorsement in Liberal Arts, which he received that August. Shortly thereafter, Morris taught at a grammar school in LeMars, Iowa. Over the next year, he continued teaching and taking summer classes at the University of Iowa, but never received any further degrees.[20]

Instead, just as it had for both sets of his Russian Jewish grandparents, the assassination of a European monarch in Sarajevo in 1914 changed Morris Adelstein's life.[21] By early 1917, World War I had been raging across Europe for nearly three years. The death toll and physical destruction left much of the continent in ruins. On the other side of the Atlantic, Americans argued ferociously about whether the country should get involved in the Great War. In 1917, the isolationists lost out, and the United States joined Great Britain, France, Italy, and Russia in their fight against the German, Austro-Hungarian, and Ottoman Empires.[22]

Twenty-three-year-old Morris Adelstein enlisted in the U.S. Army looking for adventure. As he later said, "The draft was just being instituted. We all thought that if we enlisted we could pick the branch of service that we wanted to be in."[23] He spent six weeks training at Camp Dikes, Iowa, before shipping out to France. He left "untrained [and] ill-equipped," joining the 528th Engineers, a company comprised mostly of African American soldiers from the Deep South. Identified early on as a well-educated soldier, Morris was promoted to corporal and named the company clerk—his superiors tasked him with administrative duties like managing the soldiers' government-subsidized life insurance policies—and he learned the leadership skills that would serve him throughout his career. If he had imagined army life would entail a strict observance of the chain of command, he discovered instead a kind of controlled chaos. Fights were common in camp, and an individual had to earn his fellow soldiers' respect—regardless of his rank or theirs—in order to get by.[24]

Morris spent the long sail to France seasick. Dispatched to the northeastern corner of France, he got his first taste of the work that would define his life. The 528th had been sent to build battlefield hospitals and ammunition transport railroads. Overcome with sadness when the first casualties arrived, Morris was also surprised to see that entire units returned from the front without officers. Those with formal military training were hard to come by and even harder to replace. Yet among this devastation, he found that he deeply enjoyed field-based construction.[25]

Morris had to survive the carnage. According to one story, every officer in the 528th perished at St. Mihiel in the fall of 1918. This left Adelstein the highest-ranking member of the unit, converting him instantly into a battlefield commander. He directed forward operations while coordinating the construction of a critical bridge, all under an onslaught of German fire. *"My father once told me that a general had seen the 528th working under attack, then turned to a subordinate and barked an order to 'make that sergeant a lieutenant!' This gave my father an officer's field commission, a rarity for a Jewish officer in the U.S. Army at that time."*[26]

"My father always told me that he was only 'brave' in that moment because he could see the string of ambulances that needed to get wounded soldiers behind the front lines," Stan Adelstein recalled, *"and the screams of the wounded were more frightening than the sound of German bullets, so he did what he could do to make them stop."*

Following the episode on the bridge, Morris left for officer's training in Langres. Later on, he recounted how, in the rush to get his unit deployment-ready, his commanders in Iowa skipped over some of the army's more ceremonial commands. During an early training session in Langres, a drill sergeant told the trainees to "present arms." At that, Morris launched his hands toward the sky as though he had fallen victim to an Old West stickup.[27]

Morris learned the ropes over the laughter of his fellow trainees. But his time in Europe was waning. The Allied and Central Powers signed an armistice in November 1918, just two months after the victorious campaign at St. Mihiel. The U.S. government, however, wanted to slow the reintroduction of soldiers into the U.S. economy, thereby dampening the recession that tends to follow military scale-downs. Thousands of soldiers idled for months. Some took classes from vocational teachers sent over by the American government. Morris spent most of early 1919 interacting with locals and working as a translator, using the Yiddish and Russian he had learned as a child. He returned to the United States as a commissioned lieutenant in August 1919, but he was done with army life. Having tasted the life of a builder, though, he had a new ambition.[28]

TWO BERTHAS ON THE OPEN PRAIRIE

Bertha Greenberg received her acceptance to Berkeley in the summer of 1923, but never matriculated. Intent on getting a degree and working as a librarian somewhere far from Sioux City, she had focused on school and social events while waiting for news from California. The Sioux City Jewish community was close, and bar and bat mitzvahs, weddings, and funerals drew large crowds. Given her parents' prominence in local Jewish affairs, invitations to dance or mourn with neighbors came frequently to the Greenberg home.[29]

In fact, there was nothing to suggest that the invitation to a family friend's wedding would bend the trajectory of young Bertha's life. Philip Mizel was the son of a Russian Jewish couple named Isaac and Rose, who had settled in Mitchell, South Dakota. He met a young woman named Esther Martinsky, who had come to Mitchell in the early 1920s in search of wholesale goods that she could sell at her mother's store in Kadoka. After a brief bout of family drama—some of Philip's aunts feared that he would be unable to care for his mother once he had a wife of his own—the pair married.[30]

Although Philip and Esther lived in South Dakota, their wedding took place in Sioux City, the closest town with a rabbi, J. Kopstein, who could consecrate their union. The Greenberg family attended the ceremony in January 1922. There, Bertha Greenberg met the bride's brother, a charming army veteran named Morris Adelstein.[31]

After the war, Morris had returned to Des Moines and was working as a design engineer for the Iowa State Highway Commission. He was also recovering from hernia surgery. Unaware of the operation, Morris's mother and sisters in South Dakota took umbrage when he did not visit them immediately after returning from France. He finally spent a week in Kadoka in late 1919. His mother encouraged him to move west to help the family. The idea slowly grew on Morris, and he returned for a second visit the next spring.[32]

While there, Morris met a cattleman and lawyer with a reputation as a cunning dealmaker. One contemporary even called Chet Leedom "South Dakota's greatest politician."[33] Rather than the state legislature or Congress, however, Leedom's purview was local politics and law. He was a longtime South Dakota highway commissioner, and he would later be named a U.S. marshall by President Calvin Coolidge. But it was in his former capacity that Leedom made his mark on the South Dakota landscape. "It was largely through Mr. Leedom's efforts," a county history reads, "that the west river country was so generously endowed with the state road building program."[34] Leedom, a Republican, encouraged Adelstein to run for county engineer. Under Leedom's wing and on his billowing coattails, the unknown transplant from Des Moines won the position around 1920.[35]

Morris spent the early 1920s traveling across Jackson, Jones, Stanley, and Haaken Counties surveying sites for the sprawling new roads that had begun to connect West River towns. The job paid well—Morris served five counties, taking about $170 in wages each month. It also offered him the opportunity to conduct the survey work that so enthralled him in France. He helped his mother at the store and spent long days away, traveling the gravel reservation roads, meeting new people, but also passing dozens of miles of prairie scrub without seeing another soul. His work frequently left him far from home, and he regularly stayed with white settlers or area Lakotas, all of whom seem to have welcomed him. These travels connected Morris to a wide array of people, and the proclivity for debate that he had mastered in college made him a popular speaker at community events. Morris fixed his mind on Republican politics and the events hosted by the many civic clubs of which he was a part. But his heart was elsewhere.[36]

Morris and Bertha Greenberg kept in touch after their fateful meeting in Sioux City in early 1922. Morris, in fact, returned to western Iowa several times to court her. She was initially cold to his advances, still nursing the dream of attending college in California. Eventually, however, she agreed to visit Kadoka. The visit almost ended in disaster. According to Chet's son Boyd Leedom, who worked for Morris, "the emotional side of the boss was becoming more and more visible" in the summer of 1923. Morris, it seems, had taken to waxing on about his young love, and once invited her to join him and the boys in the field. Hoping to impress Bertha, Morris took a larger, faster vehicle than usual, and when the group fell behind schedule, he raced to pick her up. Leedom and another coworker, caught between the terror of an impending crash and of incurring their superior's wrath, silently tried to decide which of them should tell Morris to slow down. Just as one tried, Morris swerved to avoid a small wagon pulled by aged horses—whom he no doubt blamed for the accident—but smashed squarely into the carriage.[37]

Bertha's relationship with Morris posed a serious dilemma, given her goals. Like many young women of her time, she was being asked to trade her own ambitions for a man's hand and a hard life in a desolate place. She weighed both propositions carefully, ultimately accepting Morris's proposal—and abandoning her dreams of a California education—before heading off to Kadoka to spend time getting to know his mother immediately after graduating from high school in June 1923.[38]

The two Berthas in Morris's life collided with one another just as he had with that wagon outside Kadoka. Bertha Martinsky studied the younger woman, offering the kind of scrutiny only a mother-in-law could. A deep, personal schism between the two Berthas was already apparent in late 1923, but despite significant tension between the women, both Martinsky and the Greenbergs understood that their children were in love and gave Morris and Bertha their blessings—an unquestioned prerequisite in Orthodox families like theirs.[39]

These blessings cleared the way for the young couple's marriage, and the ceremony took place on January 27, 1924, in Sioux City. It was overseen by Rabbi Kopstein, the same man who had conducted the wedding at which

Bertha and Morris first danced. After a short honeymoon in Iowa, they returned to Kadoka and lived with Morris's mother.[40]

In the coming years, the tension between the two Berthas toggled between a terse, mutual forbearance and icy castigations. The pious and protective Martinsky distrusted young Bertha, once accusing her of robbing the store's cash drawer. The younger Bertha, too, drove the divide. In the early years of their marriage, Morris and Bertha lived with Martinsky. Morris gave a portion of his income to help cover the home's expenses, but allowed his wife no personal cash. Eventually, with the scornfulness between her and her mother-in-law already at a fever pitch, Bertha protested this arrangement, and the young couple moved out of Martinsky's home.[41] Yet they remained in Kadoka, where they would set about building a future and a firm.

CHAPTER 3
A SON OF SKYLINE DRIVE

As he rushed across South Dakota, Morris Adelstein worried whether his wife and child would survive. It was mid-August 1931, and he had just learned that Bertha and their firstborn son had suffered through a long and dangerous delivery. The young engineer's anxieties were well-founded. In 1930, nearly 57 of every 1,000 infants born in South Dakota, and 1 in 100 women, did not survive childbirth.[1]

Despite these odds, Morris had stayed behind when Bertha traveled from the couple's new home in Rapid City to her parents' house at the feet of the Loess Hills. The bump and chug of Dakota rail lines spelled misery for any woman in her third trimester, but a sense of foreboding had enveloped Bertha in the final weeks of her pregnancy. Back home in Sioux City, where she could be near her parents and the trusted Greenberg family physician, she believed, all would be better. Morris had assured her that everything would be fine. He would be along to visit her and the baby, he swore, as soon as he wrapped up some work.[2]

August 19, 1931, did not go according to plan. The details of Bertha's labor are vague, but it was "extremely difficult," and Bertha and her baby were "very ill" for several weeks. When he heard the news, Morris dropped everything and raced to Sioux City, where he found mother and child weak, but stable.[3]

Over the course of the next few days, as Bertha and the baby rebounded, the couple turned to the question of a name. *"In Jewish tradition, a child is usually named for a close family member who is deceased, and since the baby's grandfather was named 'Schmuele,'"* the new parents liked that name, which translated to "Samuel" in English. Realizing that the baby's nickname would inevitably be "Sammy," which Morris detested, they moved on to Stamford—the name of a tiny town near Kadoka where Morris was working around the time of the baby's birth. A close friend named Louis "L.A." Pier, however, was critical of that decision. So, after much deliberation, they settled on a name: "Stanford Mark Adelstein."[4]

That Stan's birth certificate bears the seal of the state of Iowa is a detail that would irk the lifelong South Dakotan for decades. *"When I meet people, I often tell them that I'm 'foreign' born. Then they ask where I'm really from. When I tell them I mean Iowa, they usually chuckle, then I ask them not to hold it against me,"* Stan said.

THE SONS OF SKYLINE DRIVE

By the time Stan Adelstein was born, his parents were living in Rapid City. Morris and Bertha first met their friend L.A. Pier shortly after their wedding in 1924. Morris had been dreaming of starting his own enterprise—an outfit he would call the Northwestern Engineering Company (NWE)—since he studied at Highland Park. In those days, he did not have the education, the experience, or the means to make it happen. By the mid-1920s, however, he was a married man with a steady salary, and, since the tension between his mother and wife had continued after the couple moved out of Martinsky's home, he had a reason to make some changes.[5]

Pier was a banker from the tiny hamlet of Belvidere just east of Kadoka. With his capital and Morris's experiences, the pair founded NWE over little more than a handshake and a half-page of ruled paper in 1924. They started work in 1925, and the business grew slowly, with Bertha and Morris living in field camps on the arid open prairies of southwestern South Dakota and Pier running the numbers from his offices in Belvidere, checking on projects when he could.[6] By the late 1920s, as the trio hitched their fortunes to the explosion of state and government spending on West River roads, bridges, and parks, the company was well on its way to becoming the largest construction company in the state. This success demanded that Northwestern establish a permanent office.[7]

Situated halfway between northern hills attractions like Devil's Tower and Spearfish Canyon and the many monuments and parks of the southern hills,

Rapid City's centrality to the region made it a prime location for NWE's new headquarters. After living in a rented room for several months in 1928, Morris and Bertha purchased a small home at 1307 St. Joseph Street, just off the city's picturesque West Boulevard neighborhood.[8]

Like many other communities in the West, Rapid City's history was rooted in the restless pursuit of gold and land, the expansion of railroads, and conflicts between Native and non-Native peoples. White settlers had founded the town—which they initially called Hay Camp—along the base of a small sandstone bluff on the edge of Rapid Creek in February 1876, during the height of the Black Hills gold rush. They were by no means the first to recognize the utility of the site. An accessible and centrally located water source where the Black Hills met the plains, the stream was a logical meeting place that—according to oral traditions and archaeological evidence—Cheyennes, Lakotas, and other Native communities had used for generations. Always a contested space, this gap in the ridgeline was at once a creator and emblem of the frictions that developed as different groups overlapped and interacted.

The earliest attempts to make Hay Camp nearly failed. During the violent summer of 1876, gold miners swarmed the many creeks in the Black Hills in violation of U.S. treaties with the Lakotas and other tribes. Fighting between Native and non-Native peoples led to the Battle of the Little Bighorn in Montana and continued skirmishes as Native peoples sought to protect their treaty lands and survive in a new context characterized by warfare and starvation. The threat of Indian raid was overblown in the public discourse, but two attacks left four whites dead just south of Rapid City in 1876. In a frenzy—no doubt exacerbated by news of Custer's demise at the Little Bighorn the month before—all but 20 of the city's 200 citizens fled to Fort Pierre, some 170 miles to the east. They returned the following year after hearing that most tribes had been confined to reservations and that the Black Hills had officially opened to white settlement. Rapid City grew steadily thereafter, containing 2,500 people by 1885.[9]

By the time Stan Adelstein arrived as a baby in his mother's arms in 1931, Rapid City was a bustling hub of activity. The vertex of four major rail lines, it had surpassed the Lead/Deadwood area as the population center of the Black Hills. With over 10,000 people, it was the largest South Dakota city west of the Missouri River.[10] As a toddler, when Stan went downtown with his parents, the

Hotel Alex Johnson towered above the other buildings with its iconic orange sign affixed at its apex. Legions of nearly identical Model T's lined the wide streets—a couple of which had been paved. Saturday afternoon shoppers streamed along the sidewalks in front of local cafés, shops, and chain stores like Woolworth's and J.C. Penney.[11]

Rapid City lacked the stark class distinctions of Chicago, New York, or even Denver. Small-town culture permeated the city, and the children of wealthy families attended public school with those from all walks of life. At the same time, however, some families—like the Adelsteins—could afford luxuries like new cars and domestic help. Morris, for example, traded in his shiny black Buick for a new model every two years.[12]

Stan's younger brother, Robert "Bob" Adelstein, was born in December 1934. The two boys spent a great deal of time with nannies and maids who came to assist Bertha around the house. None were live-in au pairs, but Stan and Bob became close with a young Lakota woman who sometimes stayed and watched them when Morris and Bertha traveled out of town. As Stan recalled, his father *"often entertained guests like the chief of police or traveling entertainers,"* so Stan and Bob lived much of their childhood surrounded by community leaders and well-known visitors.[13] In fact, many of Stan's closest boyhood friends were the progeny of Rapid City's most successful and influential citizens. He played regularly with the sons and daughters of university deans and presidents, judges, and doctors. His best friend, Ted Lamb, was the scion of the Warren Lamb Lumber Company, the region's leading timber producer.[14]

The Adelsteins lived among these small-town luminaries. After spending their first few years in the small house on St. Joseph Street, Morris and Bertha looked for a bigger home, and moved shortly before Robert's birth in 1934. James Doyle, a local physician, had begun construction on a stylish new house at 1702 West Boulevard. Drastically underestimating the expense, however, Doyle soon ran into financial trouble. A friend and prominent local banker named Art Dahl knew Morris had his eye on the housing market and suggested that he wait until Doyle's home approached foreclosure before snatching it up at a rock-bottom price.[15]

A businessman who "enjoyed a bargain . . . as much, or more, than most," Morris knew that he could follow this path.[16] As Stan remembered, *"My father told 'Banker Dahl,'"* as he was known, *"about a Jewish expression to 'never drink your* tea with someone else's tears in it.' Since Dad knew he had to raise his children there, he didn't want to acquire the house through someone else's distress, so he paid full market price."

Years later, the family learned from Doyle's son that the interaction had changed Doyle's opinion of Jewish people. According to his son, Jim, prior to selling his house to Morris, Doyle "had been an avowed anti-Semite" who carried entrenched misgivings about Jewish people and their character.[17] If Morris knew of Doyle's anti-Jewish reputation, he buried this knowledge in both the transaction and his recollections of it. *"After he heard what my father had done, Doyle realized that he never really had a good reason for disliking Jewish people, and once said, 'In fact, I never even knew one. If this is really how they think, I must have been wrong.'"*

Only eleven blocks separated the Adelsteins' old and new homes, but in another sense the residences were galaxies apart. To be on West Boulevard was to fit squarely within Rapid City's well-to-do. "It was," as one of Stan's childhood friends remembered, "one of the most desirable places to live."[18] The new Adelstein house was flanked by that of another major contractor, Henry Hackett of Henry H. Hackett & Sons. Across St. Charles Street, the massive limestone mansion inhabited by the local Catholic bishop, John Jeremiah Lawler, presented a regal facade to passersby.[19]

The Adelsteins' deep lot at 1702 crescendoed into a large house that wrote its grace in its twin-peaked, brick construction. Two limestone arches broke from the crimson exterior, surrounding the front entrance and window, while a light cream facade accentuated the exposed, molded beams that framed the exterior of the upper floors.[20]

The house bore a Bavarian elegance, like an oversize cottage that might have fit more naturally among Black Forest firs than the two large deciduous trees that soared over the Adelsteins' lawn. Although Bertha disliked this new home, to have a corner lot in the heart of the leafy West Boulevard neighborhood—even if the streets were still gravel—spelled success.[21] *"When the new road was eventually paved,"* Stan recalled, *"I got to ride in the motor grader, since Northwestern had been awarded the job."*

No matter what his mother thought of their house, through its front windows young Stan began to frame his conception of the world. As a boy, he ventured up to play among the stately ponderosa pines around Rapid City's Skyline Drive. At night, he listened to the rumble and horns of the Chicago &

North Western and the Milwaukee Railroad engines as they moved through the heart of the city.²²

When he was old enough to attend grade school, Stan walked to Wilson Elementary, a brown brick schoolhouse situated a block from West Boulevard and adjacent to a lush city park. He and his peers came from enterprising families. Parents involved themselves deeply in school activities and the PTA. A number of his classmates would go on to illustrious careers. *"At least a full third of my classmates went on to earn advanced degrees of one sort or another,"* Stan remembered. At least one of his playmates, David Burrington, would gain national repute. The son of a prominent dentist, Burrington lived only seven blocks from the Adelsteins on the north end of West Boulevard.²³ He became a famous broadcast journalist, covering the 1968 Tet Offensive in Vietnam and, five years later, Israel's Yom Kippur War, among many other events during his quarter-century with NBC studios.²⁴

In some ways, Stan's childhood resembled a staged snapshot of twentieth-century Americana. As a boy, he read the *Wizard of Oz* and followed the adventures of Tom Swift. He consumed every one of the Bobbsey Twins books. His parents had a phonograph player and a radio. Through crackly speakers he and his friends listened to the *Lone Ranger*. He was a Cub Scout and spent afternoons with his friends crunching pine cones beneath Skyline Drive. They played among the tall green triceratops, brontosaurus, tyrannosaurus rex, and other concrete figures that the Works Progress Administration (WPA) had installed at Dinosaur Park on the crest of Skyline Drive in 1936 to evoke the Black Hills' ancient past.²⁵

At the base of Skyline Drive, the twelve-block radius around Stan's house made for an excellent stomping ground. Stan, Ted, David, and their friend Sam Crabb—who lived a few blocks down on Ninth Street—could head west and upward from the Boulevard.²⁶ In less than a quarter mile they disappeared among chunky boulders and tall pines to get lost in their own imaginations. In the winter, Wilson Park, another WPA project, offered an outdoor ice pond next to the elementary school.²⁷ Sledding runs covered the slopes off Skyline Drive.²⁸ On hot summer days, children could abandon the wilderness and ride their bicycles a few blocks into the heart of town. Dodging automobiles that bounced and sputtered along Rapid City's streets, the squad could make its way to the ornate brick buildings at city center. There, they wandered through the aisles at the Duhamel Company's 45,000-square-foot mercantile store or grabbed a cool treat at Doherty's Drug, with its soda fountain mounted behind a mosaic-tiled counter.[29]

As an adolescent, Stan attended Camp Kawaga, a 160-acre haven in the thick northern woods outside Minocqua, Wisconsin. Founded by a rabbi in 1915, Camp Kawaga offered a monthlong adventure that included camping, swimming, canoeing, and other outdoor activities. Like many summer camps of its time, Kawaga played on a romanticized sense of Native American history and culture, organizing campers into two "honorary tribes of Mawanda and Sachem," and giving the children a feather and headband or a special "Indian name" when they achieved certain goals.[30]

Stan preferred Kawaga's theater troupe to physical activities like swimming. He had a few friends there, but felt out of place when surrounded by children from extremely wealthy families. Although all of the other campers were Jewish—indeed, his attendance was one way Morris and Bertha sought to connect him to his heritage—most lived a life far different from Stan's. Arriving one summer, he remembered, *"I saw a family drive up in a chauffeur-driven limousine."*

Back home in Rapid City, Stan could *"remember when we lived in our first home on St. Joseph Street, before the brick house on the Boulevard, that my mother would often give me money and send me off on my little pedal car to buy a loaf of bread or a few eggs from a grocery store half a block away."* Up to and through high school, he would occasionally find a $20 bill stuffed into his jacket pocket—a small gift from his mother. *"We would spend the weekends at a little cottage that L.A. Pier had built next to his own near Canyon Lake. He built it because he wanted my family to have a place to stay when we visited."* The Adelsteins also picnicked at the foot of Mount Rushmore and played Monopoly and other board games. Bertha and Morris traveled together regularly, visiting Hawaii, Florida, and other places that most members of the Rapid City community could not afford to see. Sometimes they brought Stan and his younger brother, Bob, on trips to California, Louisiana, and Colorado. But Stan and Bob usually stayed home, tracking their parents' travels with toy cars on a huge map in their bedroom. The family even had a cocker spaniel named Spot.[31]

Frequent trips ensured that Stan knew his grandparents. He took the train to Sioux City several times as a child, where he spent time with Aaron and Julia Greenberg. *"Many of the small-town merchants along the railroad had general stores just like Grandma Martinsky's,"* Stan remembered. People in that trade were *"sort of like an extended family, and many of them had been married in Sioux City, so they got to know us when we came through. I would stand in the small open space between the train cars when we would stop, and people would give me cookies and tell me how much I had grown. That was a real treasure as well as experience."* In 1938, when Julia Greenberg became gravely ill, Bertha took the boys to Sioux City for six months, where they lived while she cared for her dying mother.[32]

Stan's grandfather was a devout man whose American brand of Jewish Orthodoxy differed from that practiced in Europe.[33] Aaron rigidly observed the Sabbath, prayed in Hebrew three times a day, and kept three sets of dishes: one each for kosher foods that were not allowed to touch, and a third used only during Passover. Bertha even kept a second kosher cooking area stocked for Aaron's visits to Rapid City. Stan remembered Grandfather Greenberg's affection above all else. Aaron regularly took Stan to synagogue in Sioux City, *"and he would proudly introduce me as 'mein grandson'"* in his thick Yiddish accent. *"I didn't have to be smart, skinny, fat, handsome, or anything else,"* Stan fondly recalled, *"because I was 'mein grandson,' and that was good enough."*

Traveling to Kadoka was an altogether different adventure. Getting there by automobile in the 1930s and 1940s *"was a day's journey from Rapid City, with at least two flat tires on gravel roads."* Behind the counter at Martinsky's, Stan recalled his grandmother as *"small and severe,"* but her shop was an adventure for two young boys. In addition to its food, clothes, and dry goods, the shop housed a small, second-floor apartment with a kitchen. Additional living quarters, which Morris had built, were hidden at the back of the store, *"and Grandmother had two or three other rooms that she would rent out to travelers coming through Kadoka."* Martinsky, like Aaron Greenberg, had a soft spot for her grandchildren. Her shop was full of small, fruit-flavored yellow-and-red mints. Other youngsters inevitably found their way to the candy barrel and reached in, only to earn the sharp crack of Martinsky's hand. But not Stan—*"I could have as many as I wanted."*

FAMILY STRAIN

Although Stan's memories project an idyllic childhood, several realities highlight the latent tensions at home and in the community. A three-year difference separated Stan and Bob. Despite—or perhaps because of—their close age, the pair were not especially close when they were boys. They rarely played together, even though they shared a bedroom. In fact, Stan would occasionally loan Bob's bicycle to other friends. While Stan and friends rode through town, Bob was often off on his own, building models and tinkering with toys and small machines.[34]

Personality differences established themselves early on, and *"we fought about everything, from toys to friends."* The preferential treatment that Stan received from their father exacerbated the problem. Whether it was because he was the first born, was more attuned to Morris's personality, or for some other reason, Stan always seemed to receive a little more attention.

Stan remembered his father fondly and has vivid memories of time he spent with his father as a boy. He was *"somewhat overweight and not very tall, but a man who laughed easily and was a great public speaker."* On Memorial Day holidays in the late 1930s, *"our father was in high demand because he was a war hero and a well-known public speaker,"* so he was invited to speak about World War I. One year Stan traveled with his father as Morris made a series of speeches. Morris started somewhat awkwardly in the morning in a Rapid City auditorium and then drove to Kadoka, where he gave a talk in the high school auditorium while Stan played with other children outside. Later in the afternoon, father and son drove to a little church on the prairie, where Morris drew inspiration from the dozens of farmers and ranchers who had carved precious time from their spring planting to pack a small church and celebrate the holiday. With the chapel bursting at its seams, Stan had to wait outside with other kids while his father addressed the community. *"I remember hearing loud applause and the stamping of feet"* coming from inside the church, Stan said, *"and watched people excitedly slapping each other's backs as they came out,"* clearly fired up from Morris's talk.[35]

Stan and Morris also bonded over other activities. *"I loved collecting stamps, and Dad would always bring a few back from business trips."* Morris also took Stan on the road for NWE business. *"Once, we were in Wyoming and pulled up to an intersection. One sign read 'Yellowstone Park' and the other pointed towards Rapid City. I asked my father, 'Would it ruin our lives if we took the time to go to Yellowstone?' He turned the car right around,"* and the pair shared a memorable, spur-of-the-moment trip to peer at the stunning canyons and sulfurous geysers of the nation's first official national park.[36] This good fortune, however, had consequences: for the rest of his life, whenever he and Stan disagreed, *"Dad would always say 'Would it ruin our lives if . . .' as he tried to change my mind."*

Bob had very different recollections of his father, and he was especially close to his mother. But, as he recalled, "no matter what I did, I couldn't quite get it done right" in Morris's eyes. His father "had a way of making me feel almost good," Bob continued, but would "find fault and express it in a way that made me feel rather bad."[37] Stan remembered that although Morris was often very busy with NWE, he was still a *"loving . . . father who enjoyed the company of his young sons."* Bob perceived Morris as "distant and unreachable" and less apt to reveal his warm side.[38] Indeed, Morris *"didn't seem to consider Bob as capable as I was,"* Stan said, *"at least not in the ways he thought we should be."* Even in the areas in which he excelled, Bob's achievements *"never had the recognition that mine did."*

Morris and Bertha's marriage was far from perfect. They rarely expressed their affection in front of their children, and when they did, they were reserved and cool. Arguments sometimes spilled out before the boys. Morris was the family's provider, and when he was home, he was in charge. He was often away for work, however, and his absences left a void, as he was "gone a great deal of the time." Bertha and the boys also went days at a time without hearing from him, a casualty of the breadwinner mindset of that time.[39]

Bertha, on the other hand, walked a fine line between firmness and indulgence. She could be stern and domineering, but in many ways spoiled the boys. *"I remember during World War II, with ration stamps, there was a little bit of a black market where people found ways to buy whatever they wanted despite the restrictions. Being an army man, my father absolutely forbade that. You don't cheat the ration system. But my mother would somehow get meat or other rare items. She always found little ways to indulge us kids, especially me, but also found a way to do it that satisfied our father as well."* A Chicago shopping trip, for example, always prefaced a summer at Camp Kawaga and resulted in Stan having an expensive new wardrobe.

Bertha also betrayed a quiet dissatisfaction—with herself, or perhaps just as a matter of temperament. She was an attractive, socially active woman. Her husband was a Mason, and Bertha was involved with the Order of the Eastern Star, the society's coed affiliate. *"My mother was very socially conscious,"* Stan said, *"and she had a group of friends, women in town. But she was also much more of an introvert than my father, and was very, very bothered by what other people thought."* Bertha also helped organize and chair the local chapter of the United Service Organization during World War II, and assisted Sarah Crabb, the founder of Rapid City's Young Women's Christian Association, which helped young women in need—many of whom were pregnant, partnerless, and often desperate after an influx of military men following the construction of Ellsworth Air Force Base. Sarah was the mother of one of Stan's closest friends, Sam Crabb, and *"even as a young boy I understood that the Crabbs were a very religious Methodist family and quite strict, in terms of their observance. But that was secondary to their care for human beings, especially pregnant girls in this case."* Sarah Crabb *"took a lot of flak for it. People said it wasn't the Christian thing to do. But caring was an inherent part of her character, and she was a real model for behavior."*

In addition to this kind of work, Stan's own mother read voluminously, teaching herself about many subjects, yet she never really shook a sense of self-consciousness about her lack of a university degree.[40]

The occasional strains in the Adelstein family's dynamic were not the only trying aspects of Stan's childhood. He also wrestled with the subtle and sometimes explicit anti-Semitism that infused Rapid City and much of the United States in the first half of the twentieth century. This prejudice extended far beyond the misgivings of a single individual like James Doyle, and it was not easily reversed by simple demonstrations of good nature and moral fortitude. Even though it was rarely apparent to him, this anti-Semitism quietly shaped Stan's life and began to push him to slowly and carefully consider his own Jewish identity.

BIGOTRY IN THE BLACK HILLS

Late in life Morris Adelstein would say that there was "no anti-Semitism [in Rapid City] until a certain time," which he pegged to the beginning of World War II. He was being polite. Strains of bigotry had long infected western South Dakota. Settlers, for example, had long subscribed to entrenched stereotypes about "savage" and "uncivilized" Native Americans.[41] And if ethnocentrism ever lacked a foothold in western South Dakota, it found one in the 1920s.

Masked by their terrible ivory hoods, the Ku Klux Klan (KKK) had unleashed violence and terror against African Americans, their white supporters, and other groups in the American South in the nineteenth century. The organization, however, lay dormant after being pushed underground during Reconstruction, only to be revived in the second decade of the 1900s. Films like *Birth of a Nation* and rallies at Stone Mountain, Georgia rekindled the Klan's prominence. In the 1920s, the KKK consolidated its support among white Protestants in many corners of the United States, including the Midwest. The group promoted a stark, nativist vision of white supremacy and "100 Percent Americanism." African Americans, Asian Americans, Jewish people, Catholics, and immigrants all came under the Klan's scrutiny. The organization relied upon vigilantism and terror, policing prostitution, adultery, bootlegging, and a wide array of activities its members deemed un-American.[42] Even Gutzon Borglum, who would later carve the "Shrine to Democracy" at Mount Rushmore, was involved with the Klan.[43]

In the middle of the 1920s, the KKK had as many as five million members across the United States. It arrived in the Black Hills in 1922. Most Klan activity came in the form of public meetings, socials, and parades; at least two-dozen Klansmen marched on Sixth Street in downtown Rapid City in the middle of the 1920s. In the Midwest, the Klan often presented itself in the tradition of service clubs or social orders like the Masons, but for people in the community who did not fit the Klan's view of the ideal citizen, the group was a foreboding presence. Local Klansmen tarred and feathered at least one woman suspected of adultery or prostitution in Rapid City. They burned crosses near the Catholic church in Sturgis and in the yard of a minister who preached against the Klan in Spearfish. They also campaigned to rid the public school system in Rapid City of Catholic influences.[44]

As with its rise, the waning of the Black Hills KKK mirrored that of the national Klan. While internal politics tore the organization apart, the 1925 conviction of the Indiana-based Grand Dragon David G. Stephenson for the kidnap, rape, and murder of a young woman threw the Klan into scandal. By late 1927, the Klan—which had become a powerful, ugly force in American politics and society in a stunningly short period—was once again relegated to the shadows.[45]

Although public Klan activity dissipated around 1927, the Adelsteins—like members of other minority communities in the area—were right to fear that the absence of hoods on city streets did not confirm the total abandonment of racial hatred. Given that they were among the few Jewish families in western South Dakota during this time—and despite Morris's later comments—the Adelsteins felt the sting of discrimination in their earliest years in West River. When Morris first sought L.A. Pier's partnership in the early 1920s, for example, some local businessmen chastised Pier. Stan remembered hearing his father talk about how the tax assessor balked at Pier, saying, *"'You're going to give $6,000 to that Jew?,'* to which L.A. sternly replied, *'You mean Morris Adelstein?'* then turned around and walked away."* Later, when Morris and Bertha moved to Rapid City, they believed that county tax assessors—ascribing stereotypes about greedy, conniving Jewish people onto the Adelsteins—always seemed to subject the family's annual property tax reports to extra scrutiny, looking for evidence that they were cooking the books.[46]

Once, Stan remembered, *"a Pennington County auditor called the purchase price and invoice for the first hot-mixed asphalt plant in South Dakota a 'Jew Deal'"* after L.A. Pier secured the equipment at a 5 percent discount. NWE was uncommonly successful in the context of the Depression, and, as such, Pier was able to offer a Minneapolis heavy machine dealer cash on the spot in exchange for the reduced price. After hearing the assessor's comment, an angry Morris had all of NWE's equipment relicensed in Jackson County, including his own car. *"It took me years,"* Stan mused, *"to figure out why our license plates started with '62' instead of '2' like all the other cars in Pennington County,"* per the state transportation department's codification system.[47]

Another story encapsulates the socially encoded, and often contradictory, forms of bigotry that permeated parts of the Black Hills. When Stan was a young boy, he and his father headed out on another of Morris's work trips. Their travels took them to Belle Fourche, the seat of Butte County at the northeastern edge of the Black Hills, which had hosted a massive "Klonklave" years earlier.[48] Stan waited in the Buick while his father worked. As the clock ticked toward five o'clock, Morris told Stan it was time to go, but Stan *"told him I had a good book and that we could stay longer if he had more work to do. That's when my father told me something I'll never forget: 'Butte County doesn't like black people or Jews after dark, and I don't need the trouble.'"*

For the Adelstein family, existing as Jewish people—even prosperous, socially and civically active ones—in the very Christian Black Hills was a challenge. As a result, Morris downplayed his own Jewish identity. *"He was never a very public Jew,"* Stan remembered. Morris even attended the occasional Episcopalian service because he had befriended the minister and several members, many of whom he knew through the Masons and the American Legion.[49]

Morris had never been especially devout, due in equal parts to personal belief and necessity. Living with his mother in Kadoka, he assented to her *frum* (or pious) lifestyle. But it was difficult to keep kosher in the field. With no network of fellow Jewish residents of Jackson or the other counties he represented, he rarely had opportunities to practice his faith publicly.[50] On the other hand, he remained close friends with his sister and her husband, Philip Mizel, and in that sense was linked to Jewish communities in eastern South Dakota and in Sioux City.[51]

The product of her parents' intense orthodoxy, Bertha Adelstein respected Jewish dictum and raised Stan and Bob in the faith. She observed the Sabbath, took painstaking care to ready her home for Passover, and insisted that the family visit the Greenbergs during the High Holidays when they could. In Sioux City, Grandfather Aaron instilled in his grandchildren an early sense of their heritage.[52] According to Bob, Greenberg "never demanded that we do as he did," but "made us aware that [Judaism was] a part of the world in which we lived."[53]

The Adelsteins were not the only Jewish family in Rapid City—in fact, some of their relatives had moved to town and lived only a few blocks away. Bob was especially close to their cousins Patricia and Carolyn Seff, whose parents emigrated from Russia like Stan's grandparents. The Adelsteins and the Seffs, Bob recalled, socialized regularly.[54] But there was no synagogue or even a regular worship group. The only time Rapid City's Jewish community came together was during Rosh Hashanah and Yom Kippur, when they met at the Masonic Lodge in downtown Rapid City. Other than that, there were few opportunities to study their faith.[55] The Adelstein children never learned much of what Stan called *"the Prophets, the Abraham kind of thing,"* until well into their teens, after the family had left South Dakota.

This spiritual isolation influenced the ways in which Stan and Bob conceived of their Judaism. Try as they did, the family lacked the kind of social and theological connection to Jewish history or current events that they could have gleaned in a place with a larger Jewish population. This lack of awareness of the place of Jewish people in history and the world became most important to Stan in the years leading up to and through World War II.

ANOTHER COMING EXODUS

In early 1933, with Klan-style hatred buried again, the Adelsteins might have felt that a new dawn had broken. There were signs that things were faring better for Jewish people at the national level. The historian Arthur Herzberg points out that many Jewish Americans saw the election of Franklin Delano Roosevelt as a turning point. They considered FDR a guardian who respected Jewish culture, and some 70 percent of Jewish voters supported Roosevelt in 1932. Many were pleased when the new president appointed an unusually high number of powerful Jewish figures to positions in his administration. Felix Frankfurter, a Harvard law professor and later Supreme Court justice, regularly visited the White House. Benjamin Cohen and Samuel Rosenman advised FDR, and Henry Morgenthau Jr. ran the Treasury Department—more Jewish people, Hertzberg writes, than in any previous president's administration.[56]

This apparent progress proved short-lived. In the mid-1930s, anti-Semitism once again gained momentum. The Depression reinvigorated claims that Jewish people had somehow connived their way into Americans' pocketbooks, securing for themselves and a closed network of their Yiddish-speaking kin an advantageous economic position. Using similar logic, Adolf Hitler brought his Third Reich to power. Jewish Americans held huge rallies—one at New York City's Madison Square Garden in March 1933—and tried to pressure Roosevelt to denounce Germany's new Nazi chancellor. They failed. To the disappointment of many Jewish Americans, the Roosevelt administration reasoned that it was still trying to normalize relations with Germany in the wake of World War I. As the decade wore on, anti-Semitism swelled in the United States. In 1937, one study found that some 40 percent of Americans perceived an increase in anti-Semitism. The next year, 41 percent of poll respondents agreed that Jewish Americans had garnered undue influence. The acclaimed novelist Sinclair Lewis took note of this rising tide of anti-Semitism, publishing a satirical novel in 1935 called *It Can't Happen Here*. His message, of course, was that it could.[57]

Jewish people responded to this phenomenon in several ways. Zionism gained traction among Jewish leaders and intellectuals across the world. Zionists had searched for a unifying strategy for several decades. By the middle of the twentieth century, however, the atrocities of the Holocaust and continued geopolitical tensions with Arab nations consolidated the movement's leaders around a firm belief in Jewish statehood.[58] In the United States, Jewish individuals and organizations also focused on the immediate concerns of Germany's Jewish community, raising millions of dollars to aid their emigration.[59] These efforts took many forms. One prominent Jewish businessman and philanthropist, Louis Bamberger, founded the Institute for Advanced Study in Princeton, New Jersey, which quickly became a sanctuary for Jewish scientists who fled Nazi Germany in the early 1930s. Among them was Albert Einstein.[60]

The Adelsteins sensed these shifts in Rapid City. Anti-Semitic sentiments first expressed themselves in the family's business affairs. By 1935, NWE had become a juggernaut in western South Dakota. That year, Adelstein and Pier purchased a quarry, which they called the Hills Materials Company, and used it to supply their own projects with crushed stone and other building products while also selling these materials to other businesses. This vertical integration kept production costs low and created additional revenue sources.[61] While the success of Hills Materials represented one sign of NWE's clout, the company's finances reflected another. During an earlier "bank holiday" mandated by the federal government in 1932, Northwestern began issuing IOUs in Rapid City. *"These were printed certificates in the amount of the weekly payroll,"* Stan recalled, *"which the company made up so that employees would be able to pay for food and other needs,"* and local businesses treated them like cash.[62]

Unfortunately, success in the tight Depression-era economy bred resentment, and Morris Adelstein's heritage became an easy target. On several occasions Adelstein overheard his own employees disparaging "the old Jew" at job sites. A long grudge between Morris and Pete Lien—the president of the Summit Construction Company and later Pete Lien & Sons, a quarry—for example, was peppered with racism. Lien was a hard man, famous for once suing his own father over unpaid construction debts. He was also known to toss racial epithets at the minorities around him, insensitive to any harm his words might inflict.[63]

The conflict in Europe drew dividing lines in Rapid City. In late 1939, the Nazis invaded Poland, launching World War II. Continuing an earlier pattern of violence and persecution, the German troops rounded up Jewish families, forced them into ghettos, and sent them to concentration and death camps. News of these developments slowly made its way to the United States. *"In those days,"* Stan said, *"people socialized in their homes. They didn't go out to eat or things like they do today."* At one party in the late 1930s or early 1940s, *"there were heated discussions, with some people saying that the Jews 'must have done something to deserve'"* their tragic treatment in Europe. Morris and Bertha were not at the party, but a friend later told them that the debate quickly devolved into *"essentially two* camps: positive and negative towards the Jews. After the party, people couldn't remember who was on which side, so when they would invite people to other events, they figured the best way to avoid the issue was not to invite my parents."* Thereafter, *"the number of invitations they got evaporated."*[64]

As a youth, Stan was largely unaware of the plight of Jewish people around the world. *"I first learned about the Shoah"*—a Hebrew term that many Jewish people used to describe the Holocaust—*"right after the war."* The acclaimed Ukrainian Jewish cellist Gregor Piatigorsky—who had played across Europe and the United States—came to perform for the Rapid City Concert Association. The Adelsteins frequently hosted traveling Jewish performers, and they were eager to give Piatigorsky a tour of the Black Hills. Bouncing along in the backseat next to Piatigorsky's accompanist one day, Stan *"heard this thing that I couldn't conceive of, what the Nazis had done to Piatigorsky's pianist. They'd broken every finger in each hand, and he'd had to learn to play the piano all over again."*

By 1945, Bertha and Morris were increasingly *"bothered by my brother and myself not having adequate Jewish education and socialization, and maybe even a slight fear of mixed marriage"*—that is, the idea that Bob or Stan would marry a non-Jewish woman. With this on their mind, the Adelsteins decided to relocate somewhere with an established synagogue. Bertha Martinsky had passed away in 1940, and without her as a tie to West River South Dakota, they packed up their two children, sold their West Boulevard home, and cut across the arid landscape around Wyoming's Medicine Bow Mountains toward Colorado.[65] All but Stan would settle in Denver, where NWE already had an office, for good.

CHAPTER 4
LIFE IN COLORADO

Denver was a cosmopolitan center of about 400,000 people when the Adelsteins arrived in 1945.[1] The Northwestern Engineering Company office in Commerce City, a suburb on Denver's northeast side, oversaw operations in Colorado.[2] When the family moved to Colorado, Morris made the Commerce City office the corporate headquarters and extended the company's reach to Utah, New Mexico, Texas, western Nebraska, and Wyoming. The Rapid City office remained open, managing work in the Dakotas, Montana, and parts of Nebraska. Morris bounced back and forth between the two offices, overseeing his company's sprawling operations.[3]

At fourteen years old, Stan had no desire to leave Rapid City and the group of friends he had known all his life. Over the next several years, he was perennially uneasy. *"I wasn't comfortable with the move to Denver,"* Stan remembered, *"I just wasn't a happy person. I had a couple of car accidents. I drank a little. No drugs; they didn't have any drugs in those days."* But his parents quickly noticed the pall that hung over their eldest son and scheduled appointments with a counselor. Time and therapy helped, and Stan eventually adjusted to life on the Front Range. But *"my heart was never really there."*

Starting his freshman year at Denver's East High School in 1945, shortly after the atomic bomb attacks on Hiroshima and Nagasaki, Stan was relieved along with the rest of the country by the end of the war. But like most teenagers, he was quickly absorbed by life in his new school. Opened in 1925 and recognizable throughout the neighborhood for its soaring brick clock tower, East High was regarded as one of the top high schools in the nation.[4] When it was built, the student population at East High "serv[ed] primarily well-to-do Anglo students," but as the city grew diverse, so went the student body. By Stan's time, it was still fairly homogenous, but that was changing. Although residential segregation divided much of the Denver area by race, often forcing African American families to the Five Points neighborhood, Stan had several black classmates at East High.[5]

As he adjusted to his new community, Stan immersed himself in activities. He was an artistic soul and had become enamored with the French horn while in Rapid City, and he carried this interest to the high school orchestra. He would continue to play for the rest of his life. *"I was the principal chair in the University of Colorado Symphony and was occasionally a pickup player at the Denver Symphony when they needed a sixth horn or a regular musician was sick. I loved every minute of it, and the only thing I disliked about the whole experience was that, even just to play the occasional job, I had to join the musicians' union."*

Like his father, Stan also relished debate. Early in high school, he partnered with Mark Gibson, an African American student with soft features, a bright smile, and *"an incredible tenor voice. Mark was an outstanding orator."* The only black member of the school ROTC's drill squad or debate team, Gibson was also the best high school speaker at East. In 1949, he even won the national championship in the original oratory division.[6] Stan was the debate team's manager and was a talented extemporaneous speaker, a category in which judges gave competitors a theme, then scored their ability to articulate an original, cogent analysis with little preparation and few notes. Stan and Mark were a formidable team. As seniors, they won the regional championship based on a careful strategy that they duplicated in victory after victory: Mark would give the first, prepared oration while Stan assembled an extemporaneous contribution. Capitalizing on his momentum, Stan would give the first rebuttal, another oratory, to their opponents while Gibson wrote their closing statement, which he hammered home.[7] Over the course of his high school career, Stan earned 216 competition points, according to the records of the National Speech and Debate Association. This earned him a slot in the organization's "excellence" category.[8]

Denver had a significant Jewish community of nearly 20,000 people, spread across a series of well-established synagogues.[9] It was separated geographically: Orthodox Jews lived in the west, while Reform Jews lived in the east. Never a fan of his mother's orthodoxy, Morris and his family attended Temple Emanuel, a turreted castle on the corner of Sixteenth and Pearl Streets that was the spiritual home of more than 1,000 followers of Reform Judaism. Morris loved the congregation. He became its vice president and, after a few years, represented Emanuel on the board of the Union of American Hebrew Congregations.[10]

Despite the presence of organized Jewish congregations, Denver was not free from the prejudice that the Adelsteins had hoped to leave in South Dakota. One of Stan's high school friends belonged to what Stan called *"kind of the Denver aristocracy, and his mother wasn't very happy with his friendship with me, a Jewish kid."* So their friendship fizzled. Morris, moreover, had been a longtime member of the Rapid City Rotary Club. *"My father really, really liked Rotary, and he tried to meet 100 percent attendance. If you were out of town, you could make up for it by attending a different chapter's meeting, and he would do that often"* when he was in Denver on business. *"So when he moved to the Denver, he wanted to change his membership, but they wouldn't let him—somehow the leadership there made it clear that he couldn't join because he was a Jew. So he started a separate Rotary chapter in Commerce City."*

Even among his Jewish friends, Stan often felt like an outsider. Most of the Jewish kids his age, he remembered, *"were far more sophisticated than I was used to."* They lived in large fancy homes, carried themselves with erudition, and spoke with a formality to which he was unaccustomed. He socialized with Jewish kids and attended many of the parties that they hosted after Saturday religious school at in-home recreation rooms. He enjoyed these events, but never felt entirely comfortable, mostly because *"in Denver, you dressed better, went to nicer places. That whole thing felt strange because many upper-class kids sort of poo-pooed religious school. I was interested in what I was learning, but many just did it because their parents said so."*

He was, however, plenty relaxed around girls. Stan's position on the East High debate team regularly brought him to other schools for competitions. Slight of stature, Stan sported thick-rimmed glasses and neatly slicked hair. Neither athletic nor bookish, he had a kind face and oversized ears, and struck an easy conversation.[11] That is all it took. He dated girls from St. Regis Catholic School; *"for them, a Jewish debater from off campus was forbidden fruit."* He also met young women from different parts of town, including a talented musician from the Five Points neighborhood. But her family was fairly poor, and economic tensions quickly pushed the two apart.

Stan and his dates spent flirtatious Saturdays over lunch and a movie or at the occasional social event. They were never serious, even though social events *"were almost ritualized, in the sense that it seemed like the Jewish parents were trying to set their children up to marry the other Jewish kids some day."* His first love was Patricia Fitzsimmons, whom he saw off-and-on throughout high school and into his freshman year at the University of Colorado. But he never went steady, even with Pat—in part because her father disliked him. But dating was different then, because, as he put it, *"'serious' today means you sleep with them. But you didn't sleep with anybody in those days. They'd get pregnant."*

Fraught though they were, these first years in Denver started to frame Stan's personal faith and moral framework. The values and choices inherent in the celebration of Jewish holidays began to register with him. He was especially taken with the concept of *tzedakah,* the commitment to charity. In the years immediately following World War II, and especially after the creation of Israel in 1948, *tzedakah* took on an additional meaning for Jewish Americans. It had long been a mitzvah, a biblical precept, that Jewish people should support the needy. But by the 1940s, a clear tension had presented itself between Jewish Americans' concerns with their individual lot—a product, writes one scholar, of their increasingly "liberal American values"—and those of collective, Jewish survival. As Jewish Americans struggled to assuage this friction, many used philanthropy as a tool for making their voices heard and supporting the nascent State of Israel.[12]

Affluent families filled the East Denver suburbs. *"The Jewish community was really stratified, and that wasn't the way it was in Rapid City. Back home, we were fairly well-to-do, but we had friends and neighbors of lesser means, and it really wasn't an issue. In Denver, the elite were wealthier and clearly made an effort to demonstrate their social position. And while we were pretty rich by Rapid City's standards, our family wasn't nearly as wealthy compared to many people in Denver. In fact, we didn't really appear wealthy in Colorado, because my father couldn't buy the home he first wanted—we had a nice home, but it was in a neighborhood off Lower Monaco Street, where the larger homes were more upscale. As a result, I didn't feel accepted until much later on, when my parents finally got a home on Monaco and people knew Dad ran a big business."*

Giving was an expectation at Temple Emanuel and elsewhere. *"It was different than I knew. In Rapid City, people would borrow money to have a fancy car. In Denver, conspicuous consumption was the amount of money you gave to the community, and all the gifts were listed every year in what was called 'the blue book.' People even took out loans to give more money,"* Stan said. This social pressure even affected high schoolers: when a boy dated a Jewish girl, her parents would look up the boy's family name in the blue book to ensure that his family was in good standing.

Stan also struggled to reconcile the relationship between Israel and the United States during his time in Colorado. Through the family's involvement at Temple Emanuel and in Jewish organizations, Morris Adelstein had become close with Herbert Friedman, the fiery rabbi who had served Emanuel since 1943.[13] Friedman was a devout and outspoken Zionist, committed to Israel and the democratization of his faith. He left Colorado during World War II to be an army chaplain. He then served as an American contact for the Israeli paramilitary force known as Haganah under the visionary leader David Ben-Gurion. In that capacity, he assisted with the campaign called Aliya Bet, which illegally shuffled Jewish refugees from Europe into Palestine prior to the establishment of Israel in 1948.[14] At Temple Emanuel, Friedman injected Hebrew into weekly services, bolstered the temple's educational programming, and worked to inspire congregants to become more involved in the Temple community and its operations.[15]

As Morris got to know Friedman, he began to view the creation of Israel as a vital factor in the lives of Jewish people everywhere. A man who had spent much of his life feeling forced to downplay, if not conceal, his religion and ethnicity, Morris came to believe that the existence of Israel made non-Jewish people more familiar with Judaism and encouraged Jewish people across the world to be more confident and involved in their communities. Morris became so committed that in 1947 or 1948, he participated in an effort to stockpile and then smuggle weapons to help defend Israel.[16] Morris also contributed heavily to the United Jewish Appeal, the predominant organization that raised foreign money to support Israel, which Rabbi Friedman took over in 1954 after leaving Temple Emanuel two years earlier.[17] Over the next twenty years, Friedman would raise more than $3 billion in support of the Jewish homeland.[18] Some of those dollars came from Morris, Bertha, and, later, Bob Adelstein.[19]

Stan, like many of Denver's Jewish residents, was slower to identify with Israel. In addition to class hierarchies in the local Jewish community, there was a *"profound difference"* between the Zionists and those who did not support Israel.

"Elite Jews in Denver at that time had a very strong membership in the American Council for Judaism," a group that, Stan said, "was openly anti-Israel."[20] And although "my dad was a Zionist, he also had friends and owned a big business," and could transcend these differences. As many of Stan's friends were the children of elite, non-Zionists, he was less convinced, in part because he struggled to rectify his support for both the United States and a foreign country. Although he attended a small Sunday study group led by Friedman, he drew an "us and them" division between his country and the Jewish state—a position that would, in time, evolve into his ardent support for Israel.

UNIVERSITY OF COLORADO BOULDER

In his senior year in high school, Stan considered several colleges, including Northwestern University outside Chicago—perhaps because that's where his old friend Mark Gibson matriculated on a debate scholarship. Stan chose the University of Colorado Boulder (UC Boulder). Although he flirted with a few majors and was attracted to the law, *"my father made it clear that, to his thinking, anybody could graduate from university, but it took skill to become an engineer. It was his expectation that I would do that—but it was one I resisted for several years."*

Stan's lack of passion was compounded by the fact that he had never been an especially dedicated student. In his first couple of years at Boulder, he cut classes so frequently that his grade point average floundered well below the "C" requisite for graduation. This poor performance resulted from a combination of disinterest and rebellion. Morris had long oscillated between fatherly encouragement for Stan's independent choice of a career and his personal desire to have his firstborn follow in his footsteps. For years, Stan resisted these pressures and wondered if engineering was right for him. He hated the curriculum and found many distractions during his freshman and sophomore years. Stan *"went to the classes I liked and didn't go to the ones I didn't. I had a car and an apartment, and I knew the difference between good-looking women and not good-looking women."* Chasing them, he observed, *"was kind of a hobby,"* so much so that it derailed his work.

The French horn was the only other activity Stan truly enjoyed during his early years in Boulder. He played with swing bands from time to time, and was the principal horn in the University Symphony. *"I'm not sure I was the best player our director, Horace Jones, had,"* Stan said. *"But he was a great man and a great teacher, and he was kind of an iconoclast. I eventually figured out that he put me at first chair because he knew it irritated the dickens out of his colleagues to have an engineer as principal chair!"*

During that period, his musical interests led him to another, more ancient instrument that would tighten his bond with his Jewish heritage. In 1952, a well-known musician from Hebrew Union College named Abraham Binder had composed a closing service for Yom Kippur, *"combining the organ, French horn, and shofar."* The shofar is a corkscrew-shaped ram's horn that emits a powerful, crying note when one blows through its narrow end. Jewish celebrants sound the shofar during the High Holidays and on special occasions. *"The rabbi at Temple Emanuel, Rabbi Joel Zion, was a devotee of modernizing ritual music. Knowing that I played French horn, he asked me to give Binder's song a try"* during a service in Denver. *"That was the first time I blew the shofar and I got kind of interested in it,"* he remembered. *"It's a very intriguing thing for me. This is a dangerous thing for me to say, because there's a myth that if you become prideful of your ability to blow the shofar, the sound will come out badly. I just close my eyes and I go with the shofar. And I'm not really exactly sure where it's going to go."*

Unfortunately, however, Stan continued to spend more time playing music and chasing women than hitting the books. People noticed. One day the dean of the engineering school, Clarence L. Eckel, summoned Stan into his office. Eckel had been at UC Boulder for nearly thirty years and had seen his share of unmotivated students. A native Coloradan and an uncommonly skilled engineer, Eckel had graduated from Boulder's program in 1914 before serving as an instructor on the department's faculty. Like Morris Adelstein, he had been an army engineer during World War I and dedicated much of his professional life to assisting in local engineering associations.[21]

Eckel had a deep personal reverence for the engineering profession, and once told an interviewer that his trade was his only hobby.[22] Seeing Stan Adelstein—or any student—so disengaged bothered him. Eckel knew Stan's father through the Associated General Contractors of America, a national organization led by construction executives. Morris had served as the Colorado chapter president. Their mutual, very similar service in World War I made for an easy acquaintance. Although Eckel's instinct was to expel Stan outright, he first consulted with Morris out of professional courtesy. Eckel then sat Stan down in his office and described the conditions of his continued enrollment. Eckel had convinced Morris to take away Stan's car and put him in a university dorm. Finally, Stan had to meet with Eckel weekly and report his progress.[23] Whether Stan would heed this opportunity remained to be seen.

SMITTEN

Equal parts independent, attractive, and introspective, Ita Korn had enrolled at UC Boulder in the fall of 1948. A few short years later, she changed Stan Adelstein's life. Korn fit in well at the picturesque college town on the eastern slope of the Rocky Mountains, but when she spoke, it was obvious that she was not from Colorado. *"She had no particular accent, but a very distinctive way of speaking, sort of how Audrey Hepburn spoke,"* Stan said, *"except Ita never made grammatical errors."* She wore little makeup, sewed her own clothes, and almost never drank alcohol. For most people, her past was a mystery.

Despite her diffidence, Ita was friendly and an avid student. In college, she hoped to study philosophy, but her father demanded that she pursue something with more practical applications. Since she could not bear the sight of blood, she chose an education degree over nursing and was determined to work after college.[24]

Ita may have been more closely studied than any book on the UC Boulder campus. She was tall, thin, and fashionable, with a wide, thin smile and angular features. Her trendy, strawberry-blonde hair bounced when she strolled between university buildings. According to Stan, two Jewish fraternities existed on Boulder's campus, and both asked her to run for homecoming queen, hoping to seat the first Jewish person to hold that position. They were confident that she could win because she was one of the two best-looking women on campus, and the other woman had been queen the year before. Ita, however, *"didn't want to be honored only for her appearance,"* because she believed it derogatory to women. *"She was a feminist before the term was really even used,"* Stan claimed.

Meanwhile, young men across campus knew the building in which Ita lived.[25] *"I mean, she was so noticeable that when she had to walk from her dorm to Liberal Arts, she passed the engineering classrooms and laboratories, and fellows would come out to watch her walk by, including a young surveying professor, Roland Rautenstraus, who would later serve as president of the university and was on my company's board of directors. Years later, we all joked about it."*

Ita had a sister, Marcia, who bore a stunning resemblance to a future first lady of the United States, Jacqueline Bouvier Kennedy. Like Morris Adelstein,

Marcia's parents had changed her name. Originally bearing the Polish moniker "Masza," the girl became "Marcia" when her family came to America. At a fraternity gathering at the beginning of the fall semester in 1951, Marcia introduced Ita to Stan. The two had met once before, at a Temple Emanuel meeting in 1949, and Stan had been entranced from the beginning. But it took him years and an acquaintance with Marcia to build up his courage and set the stage for another introduction. When the moment arrived, he invited her to the new Bing Crosby movie, *Here Comes the Groom*, even though he had already seen the film the night before. *"She thought I was really, really bright,"* he recalled, *"because I seemed to sense what was going to happen next in the movie."* The pair spent a lovely autumn night as Crosby warbled through the film.

Ita and Stan dated regularly over the course of the next fourteen months. Although he was in love, Ita continued to survey her options. She dated a young journalist from New York, a holdover from her precollege life who even came to visit her in Denver on several occasions. When Ita's other beau came for a visit, she took him out to the sharp, angled mountains outside Boulder known as the Flatirons. *"I knew about when they were going, and there was a place where you did your surveying along the Boulder Toll Road."* Stan had a surveying project in the area to complete, so he headed up the toll road and waited for the pair to drive by. *"I never said anything, and she knew I was in the area and caught me following them in the rearview mirror."* The move did not go as Stan had hoped: *"Ita was furious with me."*

With that, Stan had had enough of the careful dance that had thus far characterized their courtship. For the first time in his life he asked a woman for a real commitment. He offered Ita his Zeta Beta Tau (ZBT) fraternity pin—the signal of exclusivity in their day—and she accepted. Stan then donned his white tuxedo jacket and black bow tie, escorting Ita—clad in a light, strapless gown—to the ZBT spring formal. They attended with Stan's childhood friend from Rapid City, Sam Crabb, who went to the University of Denver, and his date.

In the weeks that followed, Stan picked Ita up every day from her student teaching assignment, and the pair spent most evenings together. But, like many people their age, they had little time to relish their budding relationship. Ita was set to graduate in the spring of 1952, and they had to decide whether to pursue their careers together or go their separate ways.[26]

Ita had decided against trying for teaching jobs right away and wanted to explore other opportunities. She spent the summer after her graduation in Southern California, studying at the Brandeis Collegiate Institute, a 2,200-acre Jewish-owned compound for cultural study at the feet of the Santa Susana Mountains outside the Simi Valley.[27] Meanwhile, Stan headed off to an ROTC camp in Fort Lewis, which was located just outside Tacoma, Washington. After a long summer of drills and training, he drove down the rocky Pacific coast to see Ita.

Stan had assumed that it would be easy to get a job to fill out the remainder of the summer after his ROTC training was over, but the only position he landed was as a clerk in a brewery, and even that came on the recommendation of a great uncle who knew the owner. Nevertheless, Stan was happy: he and Ita spent what was left of the summer attending concerts and plays and having wonderful dinners at the Victor Hugo Restaurant in Laguna Beach.

As the trip came to a close, Ita delivered some devastating news. Although Stan had another year of school at UC Boulder and a military commitment to finish by the end of that year, she had no intention of returning to Colorado. *"She said she was happy in Los Angeles,"* Stan remembered.

Stan was devastated by Ita's decision. As he contemplated the future, he couldn't imagine it without her.

LOVE LEAVES LOS ANGELES

With their relationship at a critical impasse in the summer of 1952, Stan and Ita contemplated a long-distance relationship. The thousand miles between Boulder and Los Angeles could be traversed by letters, phone calls, and regular visits, but the question of diverging fates proved far more pressing. For a moment, it looked as though their time together had ended.[28]

But Stan was not ready to let go. Somehow, he convinced Ita to come home. Although he did not propose on the spot, both of them understood that a wedding was fast approaching, even if Stan would have preferred to wait until after college.[29] Shortly after that fateful conversation in Los Angeles, Stan proposed, and Ita accepted. The couple were married less than six months later.[30]

The ceremony took place back in Colorado, in the basement of Temple Emanuel, on December 19, 1952. *"We were married downstairs,"* Stan recalled,

CHAPTER 4

"because her parents both had to be there, and they were in the process of getting divorced." Instead of a grandiose showing, *"our wedding was not a big deal."* Stan and Ita erected a flowery arch—which replaced the traditional chuppah, a fabric canopy that usually hung above a Jewish bride and groom—before the bookcases inside the temple's library. Stan stood in a dark suit and spotted tie, while Ita wore a conservative pink jacket, cap, and dark birdcage veil. Marcia and Bob attended as their respective siblings, *"and then we had a little reception at the house."*

Then "the Adelsteins," Stan and Ita went back to work. Ita had taken a job as a second grade teacher at an elementary school in southeast Denver, making her the primary breadwinner in an era nostalgically portrayed as one of stay-at-home housewives and career men.[31] She also became involved in community affairs and ensnared more than one photographer. A *Denver Post* spread advertising crystal tableware featured her in 1953.[32] A year later she looked like royalty in a white gown, elbow-length satin gloves, and diamond earrings as she strode the catwalk in a charity fashion show that raised funds to fight polio.[33]

Marriage finally spurred Stan to clean up his act at school. Realizing that he now had Ita's well-being to consider, Stan began attending classes and grinding toward graduation. In order to do so, he actually registered at the University of Colorado's Denver campus. In the days before computerized course administration, he recalled, a person could pull off a dual-enrollment without the registrars at either campus realizing it. He got his car back once his grades improved, and during his final year of college, Stan overloaded on concurrent courses at both campuses. He drove twenty-six miles from Boulder to Denver each evening and pushed himself hard to bring up his GPA and meet all of his requirements. College would not be the only time Stan took this approach, sitting back before kicking in when the stakes were high. Risky though this was, it succeeded in the near term. Just as his father had done some thirty-seven years earlier, Stan graduated with a degree in civil engineering in 1953. He then dual-enrolled with UC Boulder's Business School and began working toward another bachelor's degree, this time in business administration, which he completed in 1955. In the early spring of 1954, however, Stan had another good reason to focus on his career and his family: Ita was pregnant.[34]

Initially, Ita and Stan worried more than usual for first-time expectant parents. *"Because Ita didn't know she was pregnant, she'd been taking horseback riding lessons in Boulder and fell off once or twice."* She was concerned that these accidents somehow had injured the fetus. Like expectant mothers everywhere, she also had doubts about what kind of a mother she would be, even as Stan tried to reassure her.

For Stan, a new father who had for years been involved with ROTC and the Colorado National Guard, a poignant coincidence surrounded the birth of their son. Sitting in the waiting room in the maternity wing at Denver's General Rose Memorial Hospital with Ita's father, Leo, *"we heard the baby's first cry at the stroke of midnight. We knew what time it was because the TV set in the room had just started playing 'The Star-Spangled Banner,'"* just as it did each midnight, when broadcast channels signed off for the day.[35]

When the song ended, a silence nearly as penetrating swept through the waiting area. The delivery room physician (who happened to be a close friend of Morris and Bertha's) Dr. Eugene Auer, walked in. *"He said, 'What day do you want on the birth certificate?' since our son had been born at exactly midnight. I could choose the 22nd or the 23rd of November. And I took the 23rd because that was his grandfather Leo's birthday."* The boy's birth certificate thus declares his arrival at three minutes past midnight on November 23, 1954.[36]

Ita and Stan were overjoyed following their son's birth. Their excitement was evident in the birth announcement, which came in the form of a memo from the "Adelstein Engineering Company," noting that "Chief Engineer and Designer Ita" and her "Assistant Engineer, Stanford" had completed a project entitled Daniel Jeffrey Adelstein, whose materials were "superior throughout, as specified by the AIBB (American Institute of Baby Builders)."[37]

Daniel's birth precipitated a significant shift in Stan's life—one that extended beyond the expected transition from carefree college student to husband and father. He still owed the U.S. Army a stint of service and planned accordingly. With a wife and son to look out for, he also began to round out his personal journey from disinterested, rebellious student to trained engineer and professional. With Dan's birth, Stan abandoned his antipathy toward the career that his father had long ordained. It became clearer and clearer that Stan would join the NWE ranks as soon as his military obligation was up. *"All of a sudden,"* as he put it, *"I was going to have a family, so I got immersed in the family business. Being a father was kind of a big deal to me."*

CHAPTER 5
BECOMING A BUILDER

Right after graduation in 1955, Stan began what he would later call the hardest months of his entire life. Set to report for service in the U.S. Army Corps of Engineers that fall, he sought some practical field experience and extra money in construction. He was no stranger to the field. As a high school student in the late 1940s, he cut his teeth doing the same hard, manual work that his father had performed in France and Kadoka years earlier, digging up a steam pipe for a joint-venture project in downtown Denver. *"The ditch could only be dug to a fairly shallow level, and the rest had to be mucked out by hand. I was common labor, tossing dirt and using a jackhammer."* The next summer, he was a field clerk when the Northwestern Engineering Company built a road near the Silverton Railroad in southwestern Colorado. In 1950 and 1951, he worked several other projects, but rode low in the corporate hierarchy and barely stood out. As a result of these experiences, Stan got to know the world of construction, but he had few meaningful interactions with higher-ups at NWE. After graduating from college, however, Stan became an engineer and project estimator, joining a team that had already begun work on a section of Interstate 25 that stretched from Denver to the town of Castle Rock.[1]

On the Interstate 25 project, Stan encountered Edwin Vandervort, a manager for NWE's Denver office.[2] He had been with the company for almost a decade, and was the company enforcer. When fifty NWE supervisors convened their annual meeting—held each winter after 1948 in either the luxurious Cosmopolitan Hotel in Denver or the Hotel Alex Johnson in Rapid City—the task of pressing company estimators and foremen to keep better track of their jobs and expenses usually fell to Vandervort.³

Perhaps it was a clash of personalities. Or maybe Vandervort was just hard on those who worked beneath him, or that Stan rejected authority. But it was clear that Vandervort did not like Stan. As the boss's son, Stan was in an uncomfortable position: Vandervort, the head of the Denver office, answered to Morris, but understood that the bond between father and son outweighed that between the executive and even his most trusted employees. Vandervort was also outnumbered: Stan's brother, Bob, had joined the Denver office as a full-time staff member in 1955, even though he had not finished college.⁴ Perturbed that two twenty-somethings with family connections and little practical experience seemed to be leaping over seasoned and loyal employees like him, Vandervort *"wanted to prove that I couldn't do a good job."*

Vandervort piled on tasks and watched the young engineer fall behind. The strain nearly broke Stan, who spent a summer suffering one laborious fourteen-hour day after another, noting that he never lagged when other foremen assigned him work.⁵ Furthermore, when Stan left for the season, Vandervort split his assignments between two men, rather than passing them all to one. Ever wary of earning the ire of his coworkers, however, Stan had refused to bring his issues with Vandervort to his father. When he left for active duty, Stan found himself at once relieved (military service, he thought, could not be as crushing as Vandervort's vendetta) and wondering if his entire career would follow that grueling pattern when he returned to Northwestern.⁶

LIEUTENANT ADELSTEIN

Whether in the classroom or on a survey project, young civil engineers faced neatly defined foes. One could surmount a tricky equation with extra hours of study. In the field, terrain sometimes called for complex grading, and unreliable workers and equipment occasionally stalled progress. Or, as Stan had learned, a vindictive boss could render days miserable. In the military, however, antagonisms stemmed from something larger, more complex, and more consequential than any challenge Stan had faced on a construction job: the Cold War.

Even before World War II had come to a close in the summer of 1945, the bond between two uncomfortable allies—the United States and the Soviet Union—began to fray. For the next half-century, the world would watch nervously as the two powers jostled for superiority. Their chess match brought about the massive buildup of catastrophic weapons, a race to the reaches of outer space, decades of espionage and skullduggery, and famous moments like the Cuban Missile Crisis, during which the fate of humankind seemed to hinge on the temperaments of John F. Kennedy and Nikita Khrushchev. Both nations, moreover, meddled in the affairs of African, Asian, and Latin American nations as they sought to prove the dominance of their respective states and economic systems.[7]

Mistrust at home mirrored tensions abroad. The autumn of 1954 brought the much-observed conclusion to the "Army-McCarthy Hearings," a long and dramatic series of congressional investigations centered on accusations by a Republican senator, Joseph McCarthy of Wisconsin, who claimed to have information about communist subversives operating inside the U.S. government. The hearings turned up little evidence of subversive activity, and, indeed, ended up spawning new probes into whether McCarthy had abused his position, inciting a national panic for purely political reasons. South Dakota's own senator, Karl Mundt, oversaw the hearings that investigated and ultimately exonerated McCarthy. Although he was found not guilty of criminal wrongdoing, McCarthy's Senate colleagues censured him in December 1954.[8]

With the world wrapped in turmoil and suspicion still running deep in early 1955, the newly activated Lieutenant Stan Adelstein reported for training at Fort Belvoir, Virginia. Twenty miles southwest of Washington, D.C., the complex jutted out on a Potomac River peninsula. Even though most of the young lieutenants lived in more affordable housing in nearby Arlington, the Adelsteins rented an apartment in Alexandria. *"We used all of our housing allowance, which was already higher because I was an officer. We also had some financial support from my family,"* so he and Ita got a nicer place in a nicer neighborhood. Chuck Johnson, one of Stan's friends from officer's training a few years earlier, whose father was a contractor in Wisconsin, lived nearby. The two men carpooled to Fort Belvoir each morning, leaving a car for Ita and Jen Johnson, Chuck's wife, to use during the day. Stan and Ita's time in Virginia was short-lived, however, as Stan was reassigned to Fort Lewis, Washington, after just a few months of active duty.[9]

Unlike his father, Stan never deployed to the trenches. On active duty from 1955 to 1957, Stan served during a short Cold War respite.[10] The United States and North Korea had reached an armistice in July 1953, and the former was still in the early stages of what would, by the mid-1960s, morph into a long and bloody intervention in Vietnam.[11] Otherwise, the military waited out the mid-1950s in relative calm.

Stan served in the U.S. Army Corps of Engineers, which had been founded in 1802 and conducted a wide berth of government-sponsored construction, research, and development in the United States and abroad. By the middle of the twentieth century, it oversaw flood control projects across the United States. During World War II, the Corps trained army engineers, built bases for the army and air force, and made military maps, among other duties. After the war, the Corps continued building bases, dug silos for the nation's nuclear missile programs—many of which were scattered across western South Dakota—and laid infrastructure of all kinds in the United States and across the world.[12]

For Stan, military life was a bittersweet affair. In one sense, he loved it. *"I liked the army. I liked uniforms."* The drills and the sense of responsibility and purpose—all of these trappings suited him perfectly. Photographs from Fort Lewis depict Lieutenant Adelstein proudly clad in his sidecap and uniform, an olive necktie tucked between the second and third buttons of his tan shirt. He wore thick glasses, and a leather patch bearing a six-pointed star adorned his left shoulder. This was the insignia of the Sixth Army that Stan served, and mere coincidence connected this Star of David—which had a crimson "A" (for army) in the center—to this young Jewish officer.

A member of "C" Company of the Sixth Army's Ninth Engineer Battalion, Stan served in a variety of capacities. Writing to his parents just before ten o'clock at night on the second day of January 1956, he could not help but reflect on the similarities between his career and Morris's: "I spent this week," he wrote with noticeable sarcasm, "doing what Dad did so many years ago—that is the high level job of pouring sidewalks." Army fieldwork was different from pencil work in the classroom or estimator's office. Stan quickly learned his strengths and weaknesses. "I probably would go broke in the sidewalk contracting business," he noted, "as I always seem to lose a quarter of a bag [of] cement" in a half-yard of mix.[13]

Stan also taught water purification techniques to local groups of reservists, and his first major job was supervising the construction of "Little Remagen," a tank transport bridge over the Nisqually River that drains from the Cascade Mountains outside Tacoma. His platoon camped at the site, which meant leaving Ita alone five days a week for nearly a month. The Little Remagen project proved to be a strange experience, since Stan was the only officer on site. He had a separate tent and latrine from the rest of the troops. Always an extrovert, the clear lines between him and his men created a level of isolation that made Stan uncomfortable. The company christened the platform—which it had named after a fierce and famous 1945 bridge battle near the village of Remagen on Germany's Rhine River—in late June 1956.[14] "C" Company had received a presidential unit recognition for its efforts during the war, and Stan's unit always toasted this history at formal events.[15]

Throughout his military service, Adelstein had a personal policy of volunteering for any opportunity that arose. This resulted in one of the weightiest aspects of his army career: that of defense counsel. *"I'm not sure it was the most gratifying work,"* Stan recalled, *"but it certainly was challenging and I enjoyed it."* Today, military trials are usually counseled by the Judge Advocate General's Corps. In Stan's time, it was not uncommon for units to follow a provision of the Uniform Code of Military Justice that allowed any commissioned officer to represent a defendant.[16]

With two college degrees, a knack for public speaking, and an interest in law, Stan was well suited for the task. Plus, he served while *The Caine Mutiny*, a 1954 Humphrey Bogart film based on a Pulitzer Prize–winning novel, was still very popular among servicemen. In the film, two naval officers, angry with their new commanding officer's efforts to instill discipline on their ship, relieve their superior of his duties. In their subsequent court martial, a Jewish defense attorney gets one of the mutineers acquitted.[17] Stan believed that he was chosen for defense cases because everyone on base had seen the movie, and, he added with a smirk, *"everybody knew that if you had a Jewish guy as your attorney, he'd get you off."*

Stan quickly mastered military evidence procedures. "Generally no one except graduate attorneys," he boasted to his parents, was allowed to "plead cases in General Courts," and officer counsel like him normally only represented servicemen being tried in the lower, summary courts. "But I did so well in my last case that I was requested by the defendant" for a general court martial. That man's case exposed the heavy emotional toll that accompanied criminal defense. The soldier faced a thirty-year prison sentence. Although Stan could not reveal any details, he did tell his parents that the case was "a really rough one and believe me I spend many nights worrying." "As an engineer you are responsible for a structure," he said, since a job gone wrong meant losing money, and in an extreme worst-case scenario could lead to a fatal accident. In the courtroom, however, "I have a man's life, his wife, and three children's future to think about."[18]

In addition to the strain these cases put on his psyche, Stan reviled the physical training associated with his military service. He spent the summer of 1952 at Fort Lewis, squeezing his officer's training program between semesters. When he passed out on the running track during his cohort's first jog, an angry drill sergeant pressed Adelstein to explain why he failed to keep running. *"I don't know why not,"* he sputtered between gasps and heaves, *"but I don't think I can."*

Running was not his only challenge. To nobody's surprise, hours of solving equations and conducting field surveys had not translated to upper body strength, and when it came time for the recruits to do pull-ups, Chuck Johnson had to hold Stan's legs for support. *"He'd been a football player, and he looked like it because his arms were long and he was stronger than anything. Chuck would hold my legs, but he would actually lift me"* above the chin-up bar.

Other aspects of military life also rubbed Adelstein the wrong way. Sent to Utah as a technical adviser to the state's National Guard, he was frustrated by the way the unit seemed to disregard the chain of command. *"It was a disaster and I raised hell about it."* Stan identified two serious problems: *"Because one of the sergeants had a higher position in the Mormon Church,"* Stan observed, *"the company commander deferred to his judgment on nearly everything."* Second—as a result of this confused chain of command—*"the engineering group had organized the headquarters so it was cut off from all of its units, and heavy rains washed out access to the command center."*

"You can imagine that I wasn't exactly willing to 'go along' with what they were doing, and I told the Utah folks what I thought. I then issued a pretty negative report about their operation. Well, the adjutant general sent another negative report on my disrespect to the headquarters of the Sixth Army at the Presidio" in San Francisco. A letter like that could ruin a young officer's career. But it did not: instead, the envelope landed on the desk of a lieutenant colonel in the engineering division, who happened to have been one of Stan's ROTC instructors in Colorado. Knowing Adelstein, the man pocketed the letter, and on his next trip to Fort Lewis, personally showed it to Lieutenant Colonel Joseph Gurfein, a senior officer at Fort Lewis, rather than sending the complaint up the chain of command in San Francisco.

CHAPTER 5

Already a West Point graduate and veteran of both World War II and the Korean War when Stan came under his command, Gurfein would later earn a Silver Star for gallantry in Vietnam.[19] He was by no means fun to disappoint. Letter in hand, Gurfein called Stan to his office. Two stern, decorated superiors stared Adelstein down during his salute. *"He looked at me and said, 'Lieutenant, what does T-A-C-T spell?'"*

"Tact, sir," Stan responded.

"'Then why the hell don't you have any?!'" Gurfein barked from behind his imposing wooden desk. His opprobrium clear, Gurfein tore up the Utah general's letter and allowed the pieces to flutter ominously toward the ground. Coincidence, or perhaps his personal connections, had saved the brash young lieutenant from anything more than a slap on the wrist.

Lieutenant Adelstein's days were filled with travels, projects, and new experiences. His wife's lacked excitement. Ita hated military life. In Virginia, she could at least spend time with Jen Johnson, but when she and Stan moved to Washington in 1955, Ita was just another young, lonely army wife. She had a toddler, no job beyond her home, and few people with whom to relate. There were, of course, legions of Fort Lewis wives who, like her, were caught up in the changing tide of the military's culture. For years, an old axiom held true: *"They'd say 'if the army wanted you to have a wife and child, they'd have issued you one.'"* Yet throughout the 1950s, soldiers' dependents began to outweigh military personnel on bases. By 1960, a full 84 percent of officers were married. The military responded by increasing soldier pay and expanding on-base housing for servicemen and women, but in 1955 army wives did not have an easy time.[20]

Opportunities for social interaction cropped up occasionally, but Ita could barely stomach the rigid hierarchies to which most of the officers' wives ascribed. At one function, an older woman approached Ita. She cordially introduced herself—carefully noting that her husband was a general—and, without any further niceties, asked Ita to walk her dog. Stan remembered how Ita grew incensed, *"looked the woman square in the eye and told her, 'No, I'm Lieutenant Adelstein's wife, and I don't do that kind of thing.'"*

Stan, too, became swept up in the unspoken rules of military society. Once, Ita met a young woman named Susan Willens, who was married to an enlisted man named Howard who had been drafted just after completing law school. She and Ita became friends at a Jewish chapel meeting on base and made plans for a double date. Stan initially balked at the idea, telling Ita that he believed it would be inappropriate to socialize with an enlisted man. Ita rebuked this logic, reminding Stan that the Willenses were friendly fellow Jewish people, and well accomplished at that. Indeed, Howard Willens had graduated from Yale Law School. He would later become a deputy assistant attorney general in Robert F. Kennedy's Justice Department and serve on the Warren Commission, which investigated the assassination of President John F. Kennedy.[21] Once Ita broke Stan of his social parochialism, the two couples became friends.

Army life exacerbated tensions in the early years of their marriage, largely because Stan devoted himself almost entirely to his work.[22] Stan pushed himself hard, as he sought the approval of his superiors and to satisfy his own self-imposed expectations. Busy with drills, projects, and court defenses, he regularly left Ita and Dan from five o'clock in the morning until seven o'clock at night.[23] *"Forty-two second lieutenants were assigned to the Ninth Engineer Battalion at Fort Lewis. Almost all went to the post at 7:00 A.M. and came back at 5:00 P.M. I went to the post at 5:00 A.M. and came back at 7:00 P.M. because I enjoyed the level of responsibility that no one else my age would have outside the army."* This devotion compounded Ita's isolation. When she miscarried what they hoped would be their second child, she suffered through the tragedy alone. Ita felt isolated and unhappy, and she and Stan experienced their first serious bout of marital strain.

In 1957, Stan had only a year left of his initial military commitment. Would he re-up, go back to NWE, or take an altogether different path? On one hand, Stan was warming up to the idea of his eventual return to the family business, yet he never shook the military's allure. Court defenses stoked Stan's interest in the law; Ita also thought he would make a good lawyer. *"I even went and took the LSAT at the University of Washington in Seattle. Before the test, I decided that if I didn't end up in the top 3 percent, I would abandon the idea of becoming an attorney because I thought I needed that score to get into a top school. Because I lacked any liberal arts training, I couldn't answer many questions, and came in just above 5 percent, so that was the end of that."*

And Lieutenant Adelstein still pondered a longer military career. Shortly before his active duty expired, Gurfein had ordered Stan to apply for a commission in the regular army—a high honor for members of the Army Corps of Engineers. *"I received a letter in Rapid City, while Ita and I were on a*

CHAPTER 5

thirty-day leave, telling me I was one of only 100 soldiers selected for that distinction." Despite this honor, the army was in the middle of reducing its force, meaning soldiers like Stan could elect to cut their term of service. Although he had signed up for three years of active duty in the Corps—which would have kept him in the service through 1958—and otherwise would have stayed, Ita's depression changed his mind, and he took the early discharge. Stan left active duty in 1957 but remained on reserve status. He did so because *"the military just wasn't Ita's kind of life."* As Stan reflected on his wife's experience, he understood why.

CHAPTER 6
FROM THE HOLOCAUST TO ISRAEL

When Ita and Stan first met, he was attracted to her personality and striking good looks. But a certain darkness loomed in her past. Stan would only come to fully appreciate it during their early years in Colorado, Virginia, and Washington. The wrenching details of her story, perhaps more than anything else in his life, nudged Stan down a path that would land him in Israel in 1965 and engaged in a conversation that would change his life.

Ita's story began in Lodz, Poland, in the autumn of 1939. At ten years old, she was the eldest child of Leibel and Bela Korn, a wealthy, secular Jewish couple who owned a textile manufacturing company.[1] Ita remembered the first weeks of school that fall, when her teacher had the class sing and celebrate the strength of the Polish army.[2] In a matter of days, however, German Panzers rolled through the countryside, devastating the Polish defense, which still relied, in part, on horse-mounted cavalry. Nazi soldiers burst into Ita's home, their jackboots trampling the family's rugs. They confiscated the radio and returned to plunder. Knowing that the Nazis targeted wealthy Jewish families, Bela and Leibel hid some Persian rugs under a bed, as Bela said, because they were "trying to make the place look not so rich." But the Gestapo found them, and a soldier with a whip forced Leibel "to schlep these things down" two flights of stairs and load them into a German truck. The Korns lost almost everything.[3]

Aware of the anti-Semitism that had historically coursed through Poland, Leibel had stashed "a fortune, a real fortune" in diamonds and gold in banks in England and the Free City of Danzig, a small, semi-independent city-state on the Baltic Sea that had been founded in 1920 and lasted until the Nazi invasion.[4] As tensions rose over the summer and fall of 1939, Bela moved around—she took the children to the countryside to avoid air-raid bombings of industrial cities like Lodz and Warsaw. Leibel stayed behind, unaware that the Germans were making plans to round up Jewish people across the region.

Some German soldiers seemed unaware as well; Bela recalled one German soldier, Hans, who spoke with her about his own wife and children, and later brought chocolate and coffee for the children. The man acquiesced when Bela begged him to prevent the army from confiscating a cow that was the only source of milk for the family with whom she and her children stayed. Other soldiers were brutal—one saw Bela sitting near an apple tree and asked if it bore any apples. When she glanced and told him it had no fruit, the man stormed over, threatening to execute her on the spot if she had lied to him. Holding her breath as he inspected the tree, she only exhaled after the soldier confirmed that Bela's report had been true.[5]

The Korns stayed in Lodz for a while, but then the Gestapo began rounding up Jewish people—starting with the wealthy and intelligentsia. The Germans took one group of thirty from a local coffeehouse known to host salons, forcing them to a farmhouse in the country, where they were executed. Only one survived—a painter friend of Bela's who had been warned at the last minute by the landowner, who had overheard the soldiers discussing their plans.[6]

The Korns fled to Warsaw, where they stayed in an apartment building Leibel owned with a partner. They hoped conditions there would be better. They were not—there was a 5:00 P.M. curfew for Jewish people, who were also not allowed to cross the city's main street in order to keep them segregated from the rest of the community.[7] Jewish people had to wear a yellow armband marked with the Star of David. It may as well have been a bull's-eye. Standing in the bread line one day, the adolescent Ita witnessed a group of young men beat an elderly Jewish man within an inch of his life. Scrambling for survival, he leapt for a streetcar. When the passengers saw his armband, they recoiled, burying any empathy for their countryman. They pushed him, broken and bloodied, back to the thugs.[8]

The Korns waited anxiously as they searched for opportunities to bribe their way out of the country. Meanwhile, the ghetto became a holding area while Nazis built concentration camps like Auschwitz and Triblenka, where the SS planned to deport the Jewish residents of Warsaw for extermination.[9]

To escape Warsaw, the Korns purchased fake identification papers, a dangerous move because it meant crossing the main street to leave the ghetto. They took the risk because Bela spoke German so well and their very German last name offered no hints at their ethnicity.[10] On their new documents, Leibel and Bela became "Leopold 'Leo'" and "Barbara Korn"—names they would bear for the remainder of their lives. Then in the spring of 1940, Barbara and Leo (they began using their new names straightaway) heard about a Jewish official in the Bulgarian consulate who had access to a visa stamp, but needed money to flee Europe. The Korns had bought currency on the black market, stockpiled jewelry and other valuables, and remained wealthy enough—even after the lootings—to purchase the falsified documents.[11]

Visas in hand, Barbara charmed the young Jewish family past a group of soldiers whose job was to keep people like them off the train. Leo knew a hotelier who allowed the family to stay the night in Vienna. He and Barbara searched for food while Ita watched her eight-year-old sister, Masza, and four-year-old brother, Mavrycy. After their next move, the family found some relief in the coastal village of Trieste, Italy. But this lasted only a few months. Trieste was no longer safe after Italy's fascist dictator, Benito Mussolini, joined Hitler in the summer of 1940.[12]

The Korns fled again and over the course of a harrowing year bounced through almost a dozen countries. They drove across Syria, floated down the Tigris River on a sheepskin raft, and made it to Turkey and then Bombay, India. There, they boarded a ship called the *President Harrison* on January 14, 1941, where the ship's manifest listed their "Race or people" as "Polish," not "Hebrew," like the other Jewish passengers. According to Barbara, they passed as Catholics in order to end their difficult escape, then steamed to New York City's Ellis Island, where they arrived on February 22 with hopes that somehow they might be allowed to land.[13]

Unfortunately, the Korns could not be certain that they would be allowed refuge in the United States, as the country rejected many Jewish refugees before and during the war. Perhaps most infamously, the Coast Guard stopped the steamer *St. Louis*, which carried more than 900 German Jewish refugees, and prevented it from docking in 1939. The Canadian and Cuban governments also rejected the ship. It returned to Europe, where over 200 of its passengers were ultimately killed by the Nazis.¹⁴

Decades later, Stan Adelstein would escort Senator Larry Pressler to Israel, where he showed the senator letters and documents telling the story of the *St. Louis*. *"I knew the story and knew that the Roosevelt administration had faced strong criticism for its inaction with regard to the* St. Louis. *When I told Pressler, he just looked right at me and said, 'Why haven't I ever heard of this before?!'"*

In February 1941, while the Korns were still waiting to see if they would be allowed into the United States, a group of journalists boarded the *President Harrison*. Barbara had heard rumors that the U.S. government was preparing to stop ships from bringing any more European immigrants to New York because German mines and U-boats dotted the North Atlantic. Searching for a way to negotiate her family's stay, Barbara caught the eye of a reporter.¹⁵ The woman asked Barbara what language she spoke. Barbara could barely understand the question, but replied that she spoke Polish, Yiddish, German, and French. The pair cobbled together a conversation in German and Yiddish. Barbara explained how badly she and her family wanted to stay in the United States. As a backup plan, they had purchased tickets for Brazil, one of the few places still amenable to Jewish immigration. They were running out of time if they wanted to stay in the United States, Barbara told the journalist, because they had only been granted a two-week transit visa, which allowed them to remain in New York until their ship set sail for Brazil.¹⁶

Moved by Barbara's story, the reporter—who, Barbara surmised, was also Jewish based on her knowledge of Yiddish—"started pulling strings" to get the Korns a meeting with representatives of the Hebrew Immigrant Aid Society (HIAS) in New York City, an organization that had been helping Jewish refugees settle in the United States since 1881.¹⁷

This meeting helped the Korns get set up in an HIAS-sponsored room in the city. "Every day," Barbara said, "Leo went to the Jewish bigwigs, you know, from the Jewish organizations, to help us stay in America." Meanwhile, the clock ticked toward the end of their two-week transit visa. But "every night he came back. Nothing." Then, as their visas neared expiration, a woman approached the family on the street. She said she had read about them in the news story about the *President Harrison,* then sought the family out and was able to spot them based on the reporter's description of Barbara. The woman asked if the Korns had met with a "Congressman Dickstein." They had not.[18]

Samuel Dickstein, a Jewish immigrant from Lithuania, had represented New York in Congress for over twenty years. He would go on to serve as a justice on the New York State Supreme Court until his death in 1954, and decades later, documents from the former Soviet Union would also reveal that he was a spy for a Soviet intelligence agency.[19] In 1941, when the Korns went to meet with him, Dickstein was not around.

The Korns met instead with one of Dickstein's staffers, a Jewish lawyer, who explained that there was a legal way for the Korns to become citizens of the United States, but it was complicated and would take several years. According to Barbara, he told them to have their transit visa converted to a visitor's visa. "Then, after five months you change it for immigration," the man said. After that, the family would need to go to Canada for five years while they waited for the American quota for their home country to open up. When that happened, they could finally return, reapply, "and you become a citizen." The lawyer later helped the Korns' applications along, and Leo paid him a nominal fee.[20] Ita would later tell an interviewer that her family survived their traumatic voyage only via "a real miracle."[21]

Leo and Barbara became American citizens in July 1948, following the requisite stint in Canada, and the family settled in New York. The Korns had used all of what was left of their wealth to escape to the United States.[22] According to Stan, *"Leo got back into the business of buying and selling fabrics, something he was already good at because he had the experience running such a big manufacturing company in Poland."*

But the Korns were not comfortable in Gotham. *"They had come to feel that the climate and air quality—what we now call 'pollution'—was too bad in New York. So the family toured a few cities and determined Denver was the best place to be,"* Stan recalled. After Ita graduated from George Washington High School in New York, the family moved west.[23]

TESTS OF FAITH

Ita carried her Holocaust experience with her for the rest of her life. It crushed her faith in God while simultaneously cementing her commitment to the ethnic and cultural bonds that connected Jewish people everywhere. As a result of her childhood trauma, Ita said, she "was an atheist for a long time." As she put it, "I had been taught about a righteous, kind God. How could he let this happen?" Instead of delving into the "ritualistic aspect of religion," she focused on the "peoplehood bound together by common experiences." Jewish people, she said, "have a profound, ancient, historic tradition."[24]

Her husband, who had always struggled to conceptualize the Holocaust and reconcile it with his own, relatively plush childhood, internalized these ideas. *"The further I went in life, the more I realized that the world had done nothing, and the United States had done nothing. Then as time went on, I began to understand how the United States had actually reacted very negatively toward the Jews."*

As with Ita, Stan had always found the existence of a higher power illusive, even as he dutifully attended temple and prayed during Shabbat. These rituals, he came to believe, were as important for preserving his people's cultural and historical traditions as they were for connecting with a deity. If Jewish people stopped practicing and believing, who would?

While at Fort Lewis, Stan met a man who, in addition to Ita, *"was really probably the biggest influence"* on his nascent devotion to Jewish activism. By 1956, Rabbi Major Joseph "Joel" B. Messing had been ordained for just over a decade.[25] He was one of four Jewish chaplains to serve in the Korean War and, although he was only thirty-six years old, his meaty jowls made him appear distinguished beyond his years. As a regular officer, Messing was entitled to one year of graduate study following his assignment to Fort Lewis, which he elected to take at the University of Washington.[26]

Messing sat on the first board of the Reform Temple Beth Am on Seattle's north side. While the synagogue was under construction, he led prayers at the University of Washington's Hillel House and would later move to a Unitarian church in the city.[27] Stan and Ita drove from Fort Lewis to Seattle to attend one of Messing's services one Friday night. Upon entering, they found the church packed almost to capacity; Rabbi Messing's services, they found, were enormously popular. Messing was so well liked, in fact, that the new synagogue at Temple Beth Am offered to install him as its permanent rabbi, starting at twice his army salary. He declined, however, *"because he decided that his real place in life was 'only with the soldiers.'"*

Later in his career Messing would be stationed in Germany, where, along with Protestant and Catholic chaplains, he helped lead a memorial service attended by some 1,500 soldiers and their families, all of whom had packed a tiny church in Heidelberg to mourn the death of JFK.[28] Several years after that 1963 service, as Stan recalled, *"Messing was even considered to become the first Jewish chief chaplain of the United States Army, but was ultimately passed over because some higher-ups did not believe the military was ready for such a high-ranking Jew."* Stan also recalled a time when *"Rabbi Joel came to visit us in Rapid City and told us of his terrible disappointment"* when he learned he had been passed over for the prestigious post. *"He had heard that two non-Jewish generals had flown to Washington to plead his case. One had been the commander at Fort Hood, Texas, while Joel was chief chaplain there. The other had deep concerns about having a Jewish chaplain as chief, but decided that Messing was the best chaplain he'd ever dealt with."*

During services at Fort Lewis and in the Seattle Unitarian church, Stan came to know "Chaplain Joel." Messing was such a talented speaker that within a matter of months, the Unitarians stopped distinguishing between their services and the Shabbat meetings, blurring denominational lines in order to deliver a good message to the widest possible audience. Between 300 and 400 people attended Messing's sermons. *"He always kept them to 'fifteen minutes, and not a minute longer,' as he always said, because he believed that was the only way to keep a bunch of soldiers' attention."*

Messing's talks were always powerful, and Stan Adelstein was not the only individual he influenced. During the Korean War, for instance, Messing had served as the chaplain for a battalion that included a young Lutheran soldier named Herb Cleveland. As time went on, according to Stan, Cleveland and Messing *"began to discuss the idea of what Christians call 'ministry.'"* As a result of these conversations, Cleveland decided to become an ordained minister at war's end.

In 1959, Cleveland and his wife, Connie, came to the Black Hills, where he worked closely with the Fort Meade Veterans Hospital in Sturgis. There, he ushered in a sensitivity toward what is now called post-traumatic stress disorder (PTSD), which had long been diagnosed as "shell shock" or "battle fatigue." Over the years, Cleveland saw that Veterans Administration chaplains with battlefield experience could relate closely with soldiers returning from the horrors of war, and designed programming to that end. He also built bridges with American Indian communities by hiring Lakota chaplains and hosting powwows and sweats for those returning from battle. Cleveland's passion and innovative approaches would later bring him national repute, and in 1988 President Ronald Reagan asked him to become the first Lutheran (and South Dakotan) to serve as the chief chaplain of the Department of Veterans Affairs.[29]

Each year, Cleveland organized a special commemorative reenactment of the sinking of the SS *Dorchester*, a troop transport destroyed by a Nazi U-boat in the North Atlantic in February 1943. *"As the* Dorchester *was going down,"* Stan recalled, *"four military chaplains, each of a different faith, gave up their life jackets and their spaces on the lifeboats to desperate soldiers."* As the soldiers looked back from the freezing, salty water, *"they saw the four chaplains with arms around each other, singing as they went down with the ship."*[30] To honor the sacrifice of the "Four Chaplains," Cleveland would invite local ministers to Fort Meade to reenact the event. Because the Black Hills had no rabbi, Cleveland invited Stan to play the role of Rabbi Alexander D. Goode, the army chaplain who died on the *Dorchester*. Stan's participation in the event *"started a friendship that would last the rest of our lives."*

One day, as Adelstein and Cleveland were driving somewhere in the Black Hills, Cleveland asked Stan how he had become so active in Jewish affairs and worship. *"When I told him it was because of my own army chaplain, Herb asked me his name. When I told him, he said, 'You mean Chaplain Joel?!'"* It turned out that Cleveland also knew Messing and was flabbergasted by the connections they shared.

Of all the stories and lectures he heard from Joel Messing over the years, one shook Adelstein to the core. In an impassioned speech, the rabbi underscored the "obligation to leadership" with which every Jewish person had been born.[31] He pushed the members of his congregation to embrace their collective past as well as the responsibilities that many—especially the most privileged among them—had. He encouraged the congregation to seek out positions of leadership and to give fully and frequently to their communities and those in need, telling the group, *"If you have any kind of leadership position, exercise your leadership as a Jew, according to Jewish values."*

For Messing, this imperative stemmed from the very qualms with which Stan had been wrestling for years. One did not have to understand and embrace every aspect of Jewish ritual. It was nobody's fault, moreover, that they had not been ensnared in the Holocaust; fortune and circumstance indiscriminately spared some from the atrocities. For reasons nobody could explain, Messing said, some Jewish people had been blessed with opportunity and wealth. It was their responsibility not to squander these gifts, but to leverage them toward a more equitable world for the Jewish and non-Jewish people around them.[32] As Chaplain Joel's words washed over him that Friday night—and in a hundred smaller, private conversations before and after—Stan Adelstein cemented his belief in himself and his heritage. As he prepared to leave the military and return to the Black Hills, this new sense of duty and destiny would infuse much of his work and civic life.

CHAPTER 7
FINDING PURPOSE

The Rapid City to which Stan, Ita, and three-year-old Daniel moved in 1957 was far different than that which Stan had left more than a decade earlier. For one thing, it was bigger. A full two months before Japanese Zeroes dive-bombed Pearl Harbor, members of a military board paced the prairie twelve miles east of Rapid City, mapping out a new installment. Earlier in 1941, Congress had authorized a massive defense spending bill aimed at bolstering the U.S. military as the nation faced the growing belligerency in Europe and Asia. Prescient South Dakota politicians like Senator Karl Mundt and Congressman Francis Case pushed for the creation of an air base near Rapid City. By mid-1942, the project was under way, with Rapid City attorney Boyd Leedom—Morris's best friend and former employee from their Jackson County days—deeply involved in planning the $8.5 million base, which would hold around 4,000 army air corps personnel.[1]

Throughout World War II, the Rapid City Air Base was a training field for B-17 bomber crews. Briefly deactivated at war's end, the facility reopened in March 1947, and another multimillion-dollar investment expanded the base and converted it into a home for B-36 long-range bombers.[2] Aptly named the "Peacemaker," the B-36 was a cornerstone of the United States' Cold War arsenal: it was the first air force bomber that could deliver an intercontinental nuclear payload from a base in the United States. Wielded by both American and Soviet forces, weapons like the B-36 deterred both nations from launching a presumptive attack. The Rapid City Air Base was, accordingly, a key part of the U.S. military's Strategic Air Command. In June 1953, President

Dwight D. Eisenhower traveled to the Black Hills to rename the facility "Ellsworth Air Force Base" only months after General Richard E. Ellsworth, who had served as wing commander in Rapid City since 1950, died in a B-36 training accident in Canada.[3]

Ellsworth Air Force Base was, from its very founding, a boon to Rapid City businesses. Over the next decade—encouraged, in large part, by the $8 million added to the regional economy by air force salaries alone—Rapid City boomed to over 25,000 people, an 82 percent increase in ten years. As residents of the surrounding rural areas flocked to Rapid City, nearly everyone got a boost, from shopkeepers to utilities operators like the Black Hills Power and Light Company, whose customer base expanded from under 10,000 in 1941 to nearly 30,000 twenty years later.[4] Even long-marginalized Native American communities benefited—if only fleetingly—from the wartime boom: some 2,000 Lakotas from the Pine Ridge Indian Reservation, which sits about 60 miles south of Rapid City, had moved to town looking for jobs.[5] And the Northwestern Engineering Company got its piece of the pie after becoming "a prime contractor in the construction of the base."[6]

By the early 1960s, NWE was flying high. With forty-seven projects spread over seven states in 1961 alone, work had not slowed, and the company set several consecutive earnings records.[7] Projects ranged from building huge shopping centers, to "pouring . . . enough concrete" on two interstate jobs "to make a sidewalk four feet wide that would stretch 3,300 miles—enough to cover the United States from coast to coast." The company also contracted with Boeing and the federal government to develop grading, streets, and utilities for over 300 miles of access roads to Minuteman Missile sites and weapons systems. Like the B-36 before them (which would soon be phased out at Ellsworth by even larger and more lethal B-52 bombers), these intercontinental missiles could rain a torrent of nuclear destruction on targets all over the world at the push of a button. As Morris boasted in that year's annual report, "once again, Northwestern was called upon and performed the work in record time, breaking all construction schedules for such work and beating" delivery dates.[8]

In addition to Northwestern, which was by far the most lucrative of their ventures, the Adelstein family had also invested in several other businesses. The quarry Morris and L.A. Pier had acquired in 1935, Hills Materials Company, operated as an NWE subsidiary and quickly became a powerful producer of construction materials like "Reddy Con-Crete," a fast-forming, portable cement. NWE also had derivative companies in several states, which bid projects and complied with local regulations.[9]

Other ventures had little to do with construction. Adel Jewelers sold watches and diamond jewelry from a small, checker-floored shop in downtown Rapid City.[10] The Harney Lumber Company, which started out in 1943 as a timber sales operation during the wood shortages of World War II, leased vehicles and construction equipment to contractors from its office in Rapid City. Hills Tire and Supply was a wholesale agency for the B.F. Goodrich Company, which the Adelsteins opened in 1959 in order to make it easier for NWE to buy and use rubber and to sell its surplus at a profit.[11] As it turned out, Stan remembered, *"getting into the tire business was a mistake since Goodrich gave a better wholesale discount to contractors than they did to tire dealers."* Also in Rapid City was a loan firm called Automobile Bankers of South Dakota, which Morris and Bertha founded in 1948.[12] Finally, Stan and Bob shared a mutual interest in real estate. They started a joint development and holdings venture called the Robford Company in 1959, which Bob suspected that Stan brought him in on because he needed extra leverage for loans. This was fine with him since Stan always earned a handsome return managing properties in South Dakota and outside Casper, Wyoming, from an office on Rapid City's Kansas City Street.[13] Stan saw the arrangement differently. *"I didn't need the leverage, but thought I had an obligation to cut Bob in since I was using company time and our reputation to secure capital for these investments."*

As Northwestern's newest estimator and a partner in many of these enterprises, Stan was doing well as the 1950s wound to a close. The median annual earnings of a South Dakota family whose major breadwinner worked in the construction industry was $5,164 in 1959.[14] Around that same time—and working his first full-time job since college and the military—Stan pulled in about $7,425 from his NWE salary alone.[15]

With more disposable income than most Rapid Citians, Ita and Stan lived in relative comfort. They built a large, modern house in 1958. It perched near the southern terminus of West Boulevard, just three blocks from Stan's childhood home. When first constructed, the house was beyond the Adelsteins' means to furnish, and for a time furniture only existed in the bedrooms, living room, and kitchen. In fact, *"the size of the house was more than we could afford. I arranged to have much of the work done with day labor, with me serving as foreman, and I occasionally borrowed company equipment to get the job done."* After a series of remodels over more than twenty years, the home grew to some 5,800 square feet, racking up six bedrooms, five-and-a-half bathrooms, and an indoor swimming pool situated inside a vast, cedar-lined chamber.[16] It was, to say the least, far beyond the ranch-style starter homes that cropped up in Robbinsdale and other new Rapid City neighborhoods during the postwar housing boom. The family of three had space to spare, but they would fill it in coming years: Ita and Stan had two more boys, James and Jonathan, in 1960 and 1962, respectively.[17]

Stan worked beneath a chief estimator named Al Marvin, but was more closely mentored by his father's longtime deputy, John Materi. At fifty-two years old, Materi had broad shoulders that he wrapped in a sharp tweed jacket and patterned tie.[18] A picture of the 1950s American businessman, Materi had little time for nonsense. His work correspondence revealed a straightforward business sense, deep pragmatism, and intense devotion to Northwestern.[19] Like his employer, Materi was the son of eastern European parents who had fled Russian chaos. Born in Aberdeen, a railroad town in northeastern South Dakota, in 1905, Materi attended the South Dakota School of Mines (the university would add "& Technology" to its name in February 1943) and business colleges in Aberdeen and in Denver.[20] Somewhere along the way, he impressed L.A. Pier, who encouraged Morris Adelstein to hire the young Materi to fill in for Bertha Adelstein while she was pregnant with Stan. He remained with the company for the rest of his life.[21]

Called the "dean of contractors" by his peers, Materi was known for giving advice to colleagues both inside and outside of NWE.[22] It would have been difficult for Stan to find a better mentor, and both he and Morris knew it. Morris wanted Stan to "create in John Materi the feeling that you are his right-hand-man, and that he can depend on you and that you are always available."[23] Stan, likewise, told his father that he was "well satisfied" with the guidance Materi provided, which he called "a product of [Materi's] maturity and insight."[24] Eventually, Stan and Materi became close, even as Materi drew sharp lines between himself and those he oversaw. The pair did not socialize outside work, something the old-school Materi considered an unacceptable breech in the chain of command. *"In those early days, John even told me not to socialize with my own coworkers because even though they were my peers at the time, one day I'd have to supervise them."*

On the whole, things went well for Stan during his first few years at Northwestern—indeed, he became the assistant to the executive vice president in 1960. But he frequently tested his superiors' patience. They thought he often got ahead of himself, a habit perhaps best illustrated in a series of stern letters that an exasperated Morris wrote in the summer of 1959. First, Morris wrote, Stan had a tendency toward distraction. During a recent visit to Rapid City, Morris continued, he had gleaned from Materi the sense that Stan "was spending more time doing everything except taking care of Northwestern work." Morris further complained that he had come to the office several times during his trip but was disappointed when he "failed to find [Stan] in the office."[25]

Committing himself to various charitable and community-centered organizations was Stan's way of living out the kind of devotion Rabbi Messing preached. To Morris and Materi, however, Stan's sprawling involvement in these activities eroded his focus. Dripping with frustration, Morris decried Stan's penchant for constantly "flitting around with Boy Scouts, political ventures," and the like, instead of devoting all of his attention to business. Materi once stayed up several nights performing work that should have been Stan's. In his defense, Stan told his father that he had offered to take care of it, but that Materi declined. What Stan perceived as Materi letting him off early, Morris saw as an effort to ensure quality, focused work. Materi probably sent Stan home, Morris told his son, because he was "not consistent with [his] help and [did] not follow through on assignments." This had to change.[26]

Full of youthful confidence, Stan sometimes overestimated his position. "Whether you realize it or not," Morris wrote, "you tend to give the impression that you are now the Top Boss. I heard someone who met you [on a recent project] refer to the fact that you said you were running the Rapid City outfit." "One day this may be more than true," he continued with a salty rebuke, but "let's don't distort values."[27]

Morris found his son slow to heed his instructions. "I must not have made myself clear," Morris remarked in reference to another, earlier reprimand for meddling in the operations at Auto Bankers. That business already had an employee named Ely, Morris reminded his son, "who is supposed to be the manager of this operation, good or bad." Given his army experience, Morris had assumed that Stan understood the importance of hierarchy. "We can't destroy a man's dignity—go over his head, etc.—because many of our people have spent many long years in our services and have earned the right to our respect for their jobs."[28]

"I have asked you," Morris stated, "to devote all your energies to NWE. Everything this family has stems from NWE" and "regardless of the fact that we might have other ventures, basically NWE is our bread and butter."[29] He hoped Stan could slow down and focus.

Materi, with no small encouragement from his own boss, stuck by the young Adelstein.[30] Together, Materi and Morris hoped they could push Stan to think more carefully about his priorities. Stan, meanwhile, worked on calibrating his ambitions and his drive to be involved with community affairs.

THE SYNAGOGUE OF THE HILLS

While Stan worked out his place in NWE, his financial success and growing network in Rapid City helped make him and Ita, like Morris and Bertha before them, an influential part of their local community. Creating a space for Jewish Rapid Citians was of fundamental import. When he left active duty in 1957, Stan immediately signed up for the South Dakota National Guard. As an officer, training, meetings, and other events frequently brought him to Ellsworth Air Force Base.[31]

When the Adelsteins arrived in the Black Hills in 1957, they encountered a small Jewish community in Rapid City, anchored largely around the servicemen and women who were stationed at Ellsworth. Myron and Sarah Rivkin, a young couple with five children, had moved to Rapid City from North Dakota in 1947, joining the small group of Jewish residents already living there. According to one history, a reverend at the local Congregational church recognized that Rapid City's Jewish community lacked a house of worship and cleared an upstairs room in his Fifth Street church of any "crucifixes or other symbols of Christianity."[32]

There, a congregation of about four-dozen Jewish worshippers attended High Holidays services under the direction of Neal Shandler, Sarah Rivkin's brother, who, having studied Hebrew and the liturgy, was probably the most qualified Jewish leader around. Myron sang during services, and into the 1950s arranged for rabbis from cities like Denver to visit Rapid City and conduct services in a small cabin on the edge of Canyon Lake.³³ It was a small but comfortable arrangement. When other Jewish people complained about feeling isolated in the Black Hills, Ita was quick to remind them how much worse it could be. *"Once,"* Stan remembered, *"Ita heard someone refer to our local Jewish community as 'the Shtetl of Rapid City,' and she was furious. 'Never, never call this place a shtetl,' she said, 'You've never seen one like I did in Poland. It was a miserable place for Jews!'"*

Later in the decade, the group moved to the chapel at Ellsworth, and for a time even had a Jewish chaplain named Robert Hammer, but he was reassigned shortly thereafter, and the congregation "became self-functioning."³⁴ When the Adelsteins got to town, Myron was the de facto head of the annual Passover celebration, *"and for Passover you want to have really, really hot horseradish. So Myron gave me, as a new young member, the job of crushing the real, wild horseradish that they brought. And it was just impossible, so what I did was I put on my National Guard gas mask, and I crushed the stuff up in the driveway of our office on South Street."*

Given that he was an Adelstein, a reservist, and—by the late 1950s—more empowered and confident in his role as a Jewish activist than ever before, Stan was a natural catalyst between local Jewish residents and Ellsworth. At some point—likely when Morris and Bertha still lived there—a man named Bert Jacobs brought the Deadwood Torah to Stan's childhood home on West Boulevard, where the Adelsteins, it seems, were entrusted with caring for the sacred object. The Adelsteins, after all, were likely the most prominent Jewish family in Rapid City at the time, and Jacobs may have believed that they could best care for the Torah. It is unclear where it went when the Adelsteins went to Denver, but when Stan returned to Rapid City, he located the scroll and arranged to have it moved to the Ellsworth chapel.³⁵

Working with Ellsworth's leadership—two of the base's highest commanders were Jewish—Stan helped found the "Synagogue of the Hills" around 1960. In these early years, the Synagogue of the Hills was an incorporated, nonprofit entity that served the local Jewish community rather than an actual, physical place. The synagogue met every other Friday night for Shabbat services, often at Ellsworth Air Force Base. Educational programs, marriages, funerals, bar and bat mitzvahs, and High Holidays services continued to be held in this way on a semiregular basis for the next four decades. Stan was deeply involved in the organization, serving in a variety of capacities, as "president, lay leader, community liaison, and benefactor" throughout that time.³⁶

The Adelstein family's growing influence in prominent Jewish organizations helped secure some much-needed long-term support for the fledgling Synagogue of the Hills. Following the long pattern of midwestern Jewish communities who had to make do with what they had, the congregation was, out of necessity, a mixture of Conservative, Reform, and Secular Jews. It got along fine in this manner for a few years, but by the middle of the 1960s the need for firmer institutional support became clear. So the synagogue applied for an affiliation with the Union of American Hebrew Congregations (UAHC)—the same organization with which Morris Adelstein had, through Herb Friedman, become deeply involved. The UAHC offered resources to its member congregations—it even generated informational "kits" to help fledgling groups organize. Membership opened small assemblies like the Synagogue of the Hills to a network of rabbis and Hebrew educators who could visit them. But in order to reap these benefits, Jewish enclaves had to gain the approval of the UAHC Board of Trustees.[37]

That's where the Adelsteins came in. Over his years of service, Morris had become close with Rabbi Maurice Eisendrath, the UAHC's executive director, and other members of the leadership, who asked him to serve on the organization's executive committee. At the annual meeting in 1965, Morris was on his way from one session to the next. Stan said: *"What happened was my father had gotten very involved in Denver and was very close to Rabbi Eisendrath and Nelson Glueck, of the UAHC leadership. So during this meeting, he just happened to stick his head in the membership committee when he heard them discussing the application of the Synagogue of the Hills, and obviously he paused. A man moved that the committee deny us membership, because the group was too remote, had few people, and would be expensive to maintain. And as some discussion was under way, somebody saw Dad in the back of the room and said, 'Oh, there's Morris Adelstein, a member of the executive committee. Morris, do you have something to say?' And my dad said, 'Yes. Most of you think of me as coming from Denver, but I'm originally from South Dakota, where my mother lived in the little town of Kadoka. Let me tell you about this Synagogue of the Hills'—I don't think he had ever heard us called that before, even though he knew about the group—'it's mostly military. They're serving the United States with honor. But there are a number of civilians, and these civilians bring their children out for religious school on ice and snow, and they drive eight or ten miles to get there. And this is a vibrant congregation, and they should be supported. And besides, my son is the president.' After that, the group quickly withdrew its motion, and with that, the Synagogue of the Hills became a member of the UAHC that year, 1965."*

CHAPTER 7

His life filled with small interactions like this, where he and his family's success and influence had a notable effect on those around them, Stan Adelstein had changed considerably by the mid-1960s. Stan, who had in his early life scarcely heard of the Holocaust, who only vaguely comprehended the scent of anti-Semitism that wafted through his hometown, and who never really fit in at temple and summer camp, now found himself the lay leader of western South Dakota's only synagogue—an organization that, with his family's help, gained a firm footing.

GETTING TO KNOW ISRAEL

In high school and college, and unlike his parents and brother, Stan was uncertain about his support for Israel. After he joined the ROTC in college, he had a hard time devoting himself to another nation. Stan's unit, the 557th Aircraft Control and Warning Squadron, was activated about a year into the Korean War. *"We came back from summer training camp in the summer of '51, and we were called to active duty."* While the bloody conflict raged across the Pacific, Stan's sense of nationalism surged.

The tension between his patriotism and his support for Israel was put to the test during one winter while Stan was in high school. The Israel Philharmonic Orchestra made its first-ever tour of the United States, which included a February performance in Denver. When the deep orchestral chant of "Hatikvah," the Israeli national anthem, began, much of the mostly Jewish audience stood up. Stan and his friends, however, were steadfast products of the diametric patriotism that characterized the early Cold War. They believed it un-American to stand for a foreign country's national anthem and rose only when the band churned out a rendition of "The Star-Spangled Banner."[38]

After marrying Ita and understanding her story, Stan's perspective on Israel began to change. His efforts to launch the Synagogue of the Hills and his increasing involvement with national Jewish organizations deepened his understanding. Soon, Stan found himself involved in changing the relationship between the American Jewish Committee (AJC) and Israel, an experience as personally significant for him as it was for any broader agenda.

In the early 1960s, while visiting New York City, Stan and Ita had walked into the office of the AJC at 165 East 56th Street in Manhattan. They told the woman at the front desk that they were from South Dakota, and said they wanted to know more about what the committee did. She picked up the phone, Stan recalled, and told whomever was on the other end of the line, with no small hint of surprise, *"'There are two people down here who say that they are from South Dakota—and are Jewish.'"* A few moments later Isaiah Terman came down to the front desk and took the Adelsteins on a tour of the building. He was a senior administrator at the AJC and was surprised to hear that Elliot Cohen, one of Morris Adelstein's closest cousins in Iowa, had founded *Commentary* magazine, which the AJC published. *"My father had been recruited to the AJC years before, when the committee sought representation from different industries and parts of the country,"* Stan recalled, *"but had not been very active."* Nonetheless, these connections proved enough to inspire a warm welcome, and by the end of the tour the young Adelsteins were AJC members.

By 1965, Stan had come a long way, both geographically and spiritually. He and his bride had boarded a plane in South Dakota and leapfrogged their way to Paris before finally landing at the Lod Airport just outside Tel Aviv. Traveling with twenty-one other young Jewish couples from across the United States, the Adelsteins were part of the AJC's first "leadership mission" to Israel.[39] It was a historic journey for that organization and for the relationship between Jewish Americans and their Israeli peers. Over the course of the next two weeks, the group would travel to the far reaches of the Jewish state, visiting politicians, dignitaries, and intellectuals. They had three goals: to "get a more dynamic understanding of 'church-state' relationships in Israel," which was a matter of great concern to Americans like Stan who worried about claims of religious intolerance toward non-Jewish people. The AJC also hoped to confirm for the Israelis "the strength of American Jewish feeling" about their role in the Jewish diaspora and their desire to help Jewish people everywhere. Finally, the Americans wanted to "get a 'feel'" for Israel, its achievements, and its strategies.[40]

The trip was a key moment in the history of the AJC, an organization that had been founded in 1906 in response to continued anti-Jewish pogroms in Russia. *"I knew the story well,"* Stan said: *"a small group of American Jews had visited President Theodore Roosevelt to express their concern about violence in Kishinev, and it was he who suggested they found a committee on American Jewish affairs."* That November, several dozen Jewish activists organized around their core objective: "to protect the civil and religious rights of Jews in the United States and abroad" and to "alleviate the consequences of persecution and to afford relief from calamities affecting Jews wherever they may occur."[41]

For many years, the AJC struggled to develop its relationship with Israel. Major philosophical and political questions, like Zionism, inspired debate and disagreement among Jewish Americans and Israelis. The purpose of the excursion was to strengthen those relationships, but it had a much deeper impact. Of the twenty-two couples on that initial trip, Stan would later write, almost all of them became officers or lifelong AJC members.[42] *"Two of the people on that trip became national presidents of the organization, and three of us became national vice presidents,"* he said. Together, Stan said, *"this group had a really big impact over the years. The trip connected us twenty-two couples together, but it also connected the AJC to Israel in ways that it previously had not been. We helped create a new generation of leadership, strengthened political and financial support for Israel, and made the AJC more robust overall. The whole organization really changed and took on a new life during the 1960s, 1970s, and 1980s as a result of that trip."*

The journey was also a pivotal moment in Stan's life. For decades, his sense of belonging had been fraught with uncertainty. More recently, however, he had found his place in the Jewish community, settling in with prominent activists and professionals and contributing to Jewish causes in the United States. Chief among them was his membership in the AJC—though he would contribute to many Jewish causes over a long career.

And the trip deepened Stan's connection to the shofar. The first one he had blown at Temple Emanuel had been small enough to hold in one hand. In Israel, however, Stan wandered into a shop in Tel Aviv, *"and the woman who owned it had a number on her arm—she was a survivor"* of the Holocaust. *"And I tried a shofar she had for sale, and it had a wonderful sound,"* so he bought it. Although he would amass a small collection of ram's horns over the years, he would blow this one at special events for decades to come. It was a long, dark, curving Sephardic shofar made from the horn of an African kudu ram that required both arms to support and was too thick at its middle to enclose with one hand. Before he left the shop, *"the woman said, 'I sell these, but I don't know how most of them sound because so few people can do it. Would you come back tomorrow and blow some so I know which are high and which are low, or which will even blow at all?'"* Stan agreed. *"When I came back the next day as promised,"* he said, chuckling, *"she had seventy-five shofars waiting for me to test!"*

Yet the most memorable moment of the entire journey came during a Sunday at Sde Boker, a kibbutz, or agricultural community, in the Negev Desert of southern Israel. There, Stan met David Ben-Gurion—who was, as Stan wrote to his family back in the States, "one of the greatest Jewish leaders of the twentieth century."[43] Called by one biographer the "Father of Modern Israel," the Polish-born Ben-Gurion was approaching his eightieth year when the AJC couples arrived in the Negev.[44] The son of a devoted Zionist, Ben-Gurion was a driving force behind the creation of Israel, which had achieved statehood—to the great displeasure of local Palestinians and regional Arabs—in 1948.[45] His head flanked by an almost comical puff of wiry white hair that shot outward above each ear, Ben-Gurion served as the nation's first prime minister and bounced into and out of politics until his death in 1973.[46]

Ben-Gurion had been scheduled to meet with the AJC group for just forty minutes, but was so engaged by the Americans that they "ended up spending four hours in conversation."[47] After breaking the ice with a few jokes, Ben-Gurion expressed his optimism for the future of Jewish people everywhere, a sentiment rooted in the long pattern of cultural fortitude that undergirded most of Jewish history. He found it curious that the world's two largest powers, the United States and the Soviet Union, were not only locked in a dangerous Cold War but also happened to be the two places in the post-Holocaust world with the largest Jewish populations. He could not help but wonder, he told the small crowd, whether "the future of either of these powers [was] linked to the future of" Israel. Indeed, he added, "if Judaism was ever made un-tenable in the United States for American Jews, then certainly there was little hope for the State of Israel."[48]

Ben-Gurion then spoke of his fear for the survival of Jewish Americans. He worried that they "would either experience annihilation," just as they had "on a rather consistent basis in every country in which they have lived over the last 3,000 years," or that the community as a whole would fray under the pressure to assimilate.[49] *"Ben-Gurion had always expressed this sentiment,"* Stan said. *"Like every committed Zionist, he sincerely believed that every Jew in the world should move to Israel."* He had several critiques of the ways in which Jewish people had organized themselves in the United States. He worried that they were overly concentrated in urban areas, which made them too dependent on non-Jewish people for food. (Israel, the group had been told, had gone from importing

90 percent of its food in 1948 to only about 5 percent by 1965.[50]) Too few Jewish people spoke Hebrew or Yiddish, Ben-Gurion complained, but Jewish Americans had a chance if they could preserve their language, gain an understanding of Hebrew history, and maintain a strong connection to Israel, even if they lived abroad.[51] Then, Stan had his fateful conversation with Ben-Gurion, where the historic Israelite told him: "the question is not *where*, but *why?*"

On its face, this offered nothing profound. Ben-Gurion had not set forth the kinds of distinct instructions that other Jewish mentors had provided Stan in recent years. But with that single, contemplative word—"why?"—he had pushed Adelstein to rethink his role in that room and in the world. That question was an end and a beginning—the start of a new phase in Stan's life of activism and the terminus of a slow process that had been more than a decade in the making. Stan had transformed from a rebellious, uncertain student who respected his Jewish heritage but felt unsure of his place in the broader Jewish community—and who had refused to stand for the "Hatikvah" and was skeptical of Israel—to a devoted activist locked in a face-to-face meeting with David Ben-Gurion himself. In the study of Stan's life, the central question surrounding this metamorphosis was, as Ben-Gurion posited, *why?* Stan's efforts to fulfill his answer were wrapped tightly around his heritage as the progeny of Jewish immigrants, a child of the Northern Plains, and the son of a successful entrepreneur.

CHAPTER 8
MAKING THE ADELSTEIN EMPIRE

Long before Stan and Ita made their way to Israel, Morris and Bertha Adelstein had spent restless nights on a small cot. Unforgiving winds pummeled the walls of their canvas tent somewhere in southwestern South Dakota. Each year, dusty summers turned into frigid winters. In the spring, the earth soaked up even sparse rains, transforming the taupe dirt into clay that could swallow the tires of trucks at a moment's notice.[1]

The year was 1924. The Adelsteins had just gone into business with L.A. Pier, a resolute, even stubborn, man with an optimistic outlook on life. He had been banking in Belvidere since 1908, and in his professional life toggled between two competing extremes. He was a kind and dedicated man whose deep Christian spirituality inspired his faith in the people around him, and Stan Adelstein would recall hearing stories about the Depression, when *"bankers in South Dakota were foreclosing on farmers and ranchers that could not pay their mortgages, but L.A. found ways to extend loans and saved literally dozens of family farms and ranches."* Yet Pier was also a frugal businessman, and his daughter Virginia remembered him as "the most conservative banker imaginable" who often held clients to high standards before loaning them a dime.[2]

Morris Adelstein, on the other hand, was no longer the unknown Iowan that Chet Leedom had made county engineer. He was a well-respected member of the broader West River community. More important, he was a friend: Morris and L.A. had grown fond of one another in several fraternal orders, and it was Pier who pushed Morris to start his own business. After weeks of planning and preparation, Morris presented his idea and offered Pier a partnership. Whether he simply believed in Morris, recognized a good investment, or both, Pier financed the creation of the Northwestern Engineering Company in 1924.[3]

Their yearly contracts were short and straightforward. A half-page, typewritten contract from 1928, for example, named Pier as Northwestern's president and Morris as treasurer. Adelstein, the agreement read, was to "give his full time and attention" and be paid $100 a week—a significant decrease from his county salary. Morris and Pier agreed to split any profits up to $6,000 evenly, with three-quarters of additional margins going to Adelstein and the remainder to Pier. They would split any losses the same way.[4] *"The amazing thing about it,"* Stan recalled, *"was how much they trusted one another. That $6,000 was worth more than $160,000 in purchasing power today, and neither worried about defining the details of how the company would operate, what my dad did for his salary, or how profits would be determined. Today, that kind of agreement would be thirty pages long, written by a team of lawyers, and full of specific details and safeguards."*

Signing on was the easy part. Even with Pier's financial support and business acumen, NWE started with little more than "a suitcase and a bunch of papers."[5] The company lacked machines, and the partners had to subcontract much of the labor. Profits were excruciatingly thin. When they finally landed some equipment and their first job, Bertha accompanied her husband in the field and slept alongside him on her own cot at night. The months that followed were some of the most exciting of her life.[6]

Camp days oscillated between degrees of adventurousness, fulfillment, danger, and crippling loneliness. The crew was constantly exposed to venomous snakes and the elements. Heavy machinery invited accidents, but most projects sat far from emergency services. Tragedy could, and did, strike: a sudden lightning storm—among the hallmarks of prairie life—killed one and wounded several other crew members on one of NWE's first projects in 1925. Morris and a local priest drove victims to the hospital. Bertha waited alone, wondering all night if the crew would survive the stormy trek back to camp.[7]

Morris and Bertha lived with their team, and Bertha filled roles that at once adhered to and diverged from the standard expectations of prairie wives of her time. She was the camp cook, responsible for most of the domestic labor that kept the NWE team fed and clothed. Yet she also kept Northwestern's books and managed corporate records while Morris ran fieldwork. He worked long hours, often repairing broken machinery or obsessing over his craft.

On the road, he frequently stopped to examine the work of other builders, especially bridges. Meanwhile, he struggled to manage cashflow. Several times, NWE nearly missed payroll on projects.[8]

BUILDING THE BADLANDS AND THE BLACK HILLS

Even with these early hurdles, it is hard to fathom better timing for the creation of NWE. When Morris Adelstein first stuffed his papers into his briefcase in 1924, the Black Hills was in the heart of the greatest infrastructure boom in its history. Since the mid-1870s, when whites established the first permanent communities on Lakota land, business-minded settlers had seen that the region's physical beauty and temperate climate could attract tourists from the far reaches of the nation. A sustained forty-year period of development relied on selling the area to ever-growing droves of outsiders. By 1930, the Black Hills contained a state park, a national park, a national monument, miles of national forest, and dozens of private caves, zoos, gift shops, and hotels, and construction had started on the spectacular monument known as Mount Rushmore.[9]

Economic, technological, and social trends powered the explosion of Black Hills tourism. More efficient factories meant affordable automobiles, which rendered locales like the Black Hills and Yellowstone National Park more accessible than ever. By 1931, Americans had registered twenty-six million cars, a fact that both complemented and shaped the American public's sense of itself as a nation of free, independent, and adventurous people. Local politicians lobbied for the creation of parks and amenities even as they marketed the Black Hills. Area leaders also orchestrated the summerlong visit of President Calvin Coolidge in 1927.[10] That same year, Nicholas Black Elk, the venerated Oglala Lakota Holy Man, also harnessed the power of tourism. He partnered with a Black Hills mercantilist, Alex Duhamel, and together they created the first Indian-authored cultural performance business in the region.[11]

One historian has detailed the complicated and contentious milieu in which politicians, policy makers, and entrepreneurs built the physical and political infrastructure that undergirded South Dakota's tourism industry.[12] Another points out how, in addition to being constructed with the state and federal dollars that created public areas and the roads that accessed them, the trade in visitors' adventures depended, in part, on the sale of Native American culture and history, even as Native people were often undercompensated.[13]

CHAPTER 8

All of these issues mattered little to two businessmen from the Badlands whose prosperity was being written on the landscape. Regardless of where the roads led and which gulches would be bridged—let alone who would benefit or suffer as a result—an incredible amount of construction was under way.

The flurry of work that redefined the Black Hills in the late nineteenth and early twentieth centuries also mirrored national developments. Progressive Era conservationists inspired those who could afford it—most of whom were middle-class and wealthy whites—to venture out into nature. This movement surged after World War I, when a generation devastated by war and tantalized by a strong postwar economy sought wilderness and the outdoors.[14]

A few years after the Great Depression hit South Dakota, New Deal relief programs invested heavily in the state.[15] Laborers hired through federal work programs like the Civilian Conservation Corps (CCC) and the Works Progress Administration (WPA) built roads, bridges, parks, and dams, all in the name of putting Americans to work. In the Black Hills, they constructed Iron Mountain Road, the fire lookout on top of South Dakota's tallest mountain, which was at the time called Harney Peak and was later renamed Black Elk Peak, and many other landmarks.[16] The federal government had workers but needed the equipment and expertise that Northwestern was ready and willing to provide.[17]

As they were for heavy constructors across the United States, the years before and during the Depression were good for NWE. The company posted profits in each of its first four years—gains that grew bit by bit as seasons passed and the company gained experience. Morris kept up on industry developments, and after investing $57,000 for the first hot mixed asphalt plant in South Dakota, could staff several projects at once, extending the company's reach into Wyoming and beyond.[18]

NWE carried out several large-scale projects, including—and perhaps most notably—the Beaver Creek Bridge, in the late 1920s. Insufficient advertising, poor roads, and competition diminished attendance at Wind Cave National Park at the end of the decade, and officials sought a remedy.[19] Suspended 115 feet above the ground, the impressive platform at Beaver Creek appeared to grow directly out of the canyon walls, and a dozen columns connected the road above to a graceful arch below. At 225 feet long, it linked Wind Cave and Custer State Park. Using federal funds, Northwestern completed the project—the only one of its kind in South Dakota—in 1929.[20]

"It was always one of Dad's greatest prides, along with the administration building at the School of Mines and his work on the Rapid City High School," Stan recalled, and a photograph of the Beaver Creek Bridge adorned his office for forty years.[21]

Business was good during World War II, but government spending fell by 75 percent between 1944 and 1947. Fortunately, this decrease did not return the nation to economic calamity as many predicted. Instead, consumer spending skyrocketed.[22] Rising investments in defense would compound this confidence within a few short years.[23] The early Cold War created a perfect storm for companies like NWE. Unlike smaller operations, it remained competitive for highway, interstate, airfield, and defense projects. As a result, the company grew steadily. In its first year, NWE had done around $60,000 (almost $875,000 in 2019 dollars) worth of work. By 1947, that number had climbed to $5 million (over $56 million today).[24]

Yet Northwestern was cursed by its own success. As the company grew, it went farther afield, performing jobs outside Colorado and South Dakota. These remote projects raised expenses. Martis Levine, a field manager from Rapid City and Morris's nephew, addressed this problem during an afternoon talk at the NWE superintendents' meeting in 1948. He pointed out that while the company had gradually expanded its volume, "our profits have not increased in the same ratio." "Strangely enough," he continued, "it seems that there is a law of diminishing returns that governs our case." The situation plagued contractors, he said, throughout the industry.[25]

Levine proposed a solution. "If we want to increase our volume and still continue to make money," he pointed out, "it appears we must bid larger jobs." Without a few big projects to bring home the bacon, he predicted, "our ratio of profit could decrease at such a rate that it would disappear entirely."[26]

Levine's idea must have sounded good to Morris Adelstein and John Materi. Over the next two decades, NWE combatted the many challenges of postwar construction—including increasing competition and higher expenses—by bidding major projects that Morris would jubilantly detail in each year's annual message. In 1951, he noted that over its long history, NWE had worked in twelve states for a wide range of local, state, and federal government clients.[27] In 1965, he happily reported, Northwestern had just completed $17.2 million (more than $138 million today) worth of work in the previous year alone.[28]

Other strategies also kept costs low. One revolved around what Morris called "the iron." The company maintained a huge fleet of "several thousand items of heavy equipment and the necessary auxiliary and tools," as well as a staff of technicians and welders who roamed the field repairing machines so they would not need to be replaced.[29]

To lower its tax liability, NWE also undertook an unusual reorganization. In 1948, L.A. Pier had decided to sell his shares of Northwestern. It was an amicable split, with Pier bowing out after it became clear that NWE would be passed on to Morris's children. *"When Pier and Dad discussed L.A.'s retirement, one of them asked the other how much he thought the company was worth. The other, and I'm not even sure which one said it, gave an amount, and both men accepted it immediately,"* with neither attempting to bargain over the value. *"This was typical during the many years that they worked together. Each always took the other's word or decision, and my father said they never had a disagreement."* Pier had also reaped a handsome return on his investment and was almost sixty-five years old. Rather than sell out all at once, however, Pier asked Morris to divide his buyout over the course of ten years. Over the next decade, NWE made annual payments, slowly phasing Pier—who remained an "ex officio" leader—out of the company.[30]

But in 1949, Pier was not yet gone. Quite the opposite—with Morris and Bertha in Colorado, he was the only NWE stockholder in South Dakota. Taking advantage of this situation, late that summer Northwestern announced that it would reincorporate in Belvidere. This was not a physical relocation; Materi would continue to run the show from Rapid City. The company merely intended to change its legal domicile from Pennington County to Jackson County.[31]

A deputy state's attorney in Rapid City, Julius Seiler, cried foul. According to Stan, Seiler's politics were personal: *"by the time I was getting involved in politics, Seiler was a power in the Republican Party, and always opposed anything I tried to do—and it looks like he took a similar approach to L.A. Pier and my father."* Seiler charged that NWE only wanted to amend its articles of incorporation "as a subterfuge in order to avoid [tax] assessment in Pennington County." He asked South Dakota Attorney General Sigurd Anderson to investigate.[32] A short time later, Anderson held a hearing on the issue in the state capital. During the proceedings, the Pennington County Commission did not object to NWE's reincorporation because the commissioners understood that the county could still tax NWE for quarry piles that remained in Pennington County.[33]

When the hearing ended, Anderson explained his office's findings in an expectedly lawyerly fashion: "the motive to avoid, limit, or postpone the tax by a particular transaction," he said, "does not prevent the transaction from affecting, as it otherwise would, the incident of the tax." In other words, NWE had the right to reincorporate in Jackson County—even if its motive was simply to lessen its tax burden. The legal move saved the company $24,000 a year.[34]

Together, these strategies made Northwestern into an expansive, multimillion dollar engine that, by the early 1960s, employed more than 2,400 people across the American West and powered the growth of the Adelstein family's wealth.[35] But bidding huge projects was high-risk, high-reward. By the middle of the decade, intensifying competition would force hairline fractures through the cornerstone of the Adelstein empire.

LOSING MATERI

On a winter morning in 1962, a priest strolled through the third floor of the Pennington County courthouse, his steps echoing through the marble halls. Fresh from administering the Pledge of Allegiance during a naturalization ceremony, he was about to turn into the stairwell when he saw a familiar face in one of the courtrooms.[36]

A devout Catholic, John Materi was a regular attendee at Sunday mass at the Cathedral of Immaculate Conception in downtown Rapid City. The congregation had outgrown its church—one parishioner recalled that they resorted to holding "mass in the Catholic school gymnasium"—and would soon be replaced by the massive sandstone church being built on donated land at the edge of town.[37]

Curious, the priest stepped to the threshold. Materi was about to testify on behalf of NWE, for which he had been a loyal lieutenant for thirty-one years.[38] Two area residents, Louis and Gwyneth Wipf, were suing for $60,000 in damages incurred, they claimed, when an NWE truck struck their home.

Judge Thomas Parker opened the proceedings and ordered Materi, the first witness, to step forth. Materi stood, swore his oath of honesty, and identified himself for the stenographer's records. Then his heart stopped. As the priest watched, Materi struggled for breath, clutched his breast, and slumped forward in the stand. Someone called a doctor, who arrived too late.[39] As the action subsided, the priest came forward from the threshold and administered the last rites that would, according to their shared faith, guide Materi to heaven.⁴⁰

Coronary disease ran in John Materi's blood. His father's clogged arteries caused a fatal heart attack exactly four years and one day earlier in El Paso, Texas, where he and John's mother, Anna, had retired.⁴¹ John's lifetime of stress certainly did not help. When Morris Adelstein addressed the NWE crew to tell them the sad news, he noted that in the preceding weeks he had "suggested . . . that [Materi] should not take part in" testifying in the case because he sensed in his old friend the signs of overwork. Yet Materi "thought it was his obligation to see that certain information was properly presented" in court.⁴²

"No one will ever know," Morris concluded, "whether this last duty hastened his death or not. This is something that is out of our hands, but we do know that John died in the line of duty."⁴³

Indeed, John Materi died as he had lived, in the service of NWE. As he lay staring at the ceiling, his last moments ticking by, the longtime vice president's concentration undoubtedly oscillated between the pain in his chest and thoughts about his wife, Ora; their son, John Steven; and their daughter, Mary Ann. If work crossed his mind in these fatal breaths—and his years of intense devotion to NWE suggest it may have—he might have pondered whether his protégé, Stan, was ready to take his place.

CHAPTER 9
POLITICS *IS* BUSINESS

After returning to Rapid City in 1957, Stan became deeply involved in community affairs. He cared about his community and considered it his obligation to put his privilege and good fortune to work for the disadvantaged. He relished both the fulfillment of doing good works and the recognition that followed. He was a member of the Rotary Club, for example, a national charitable group that had been operating in Rapid City since 1921.[1] So far, however, he had not jumped into the political arena.

That changed when Stan attended a Rotary Club meeting in Denver in 1960. There, he heard a speech by Walter F. Bennett, a World War I veteran, wealthy paint producer, and former president of the National Association of Manufacturers. Bennett had served Utah in the U.S. Senate since 1951 and was part of a growing cadre of probusiness Republicans who helped lay the foundation of modern conservatism.[2] In his speech, Stan remembered, Bennett encouraged businessmen to get involved in politics and help strengthen private enterprise.[3]

The talk piqued Stan's interest. Shortly afterward, he boarded a squat DC-3 airplane for the return trip to Rapid City. *"In those days they gave you magazines and you had time to read. The* Life Magazine *article I read talked about Soviet anti-Semitism."* What Stan read infuriated him, and, as he thought it over, he realized that working through political channels could allow him to effect change related to his business, as well as broader social and policy decisions he cared about. *"By the time I got off the plane,"* Stan recalled, *"I had to get into politics."*

CHAPTER 9

Back in Rapid City, John Materi—who was still two years away from his fatal heart attack—dashed Stan's political hopes, giving him a firm "no" when he asked his boss's thoughts on getting into party politics. *"Here I was, a businessperson, and when I asked John Materi about politics, he said, 'We're contractors and we have got to get along with everyone. You just can't do it.' So I asked if I could get a second opinion from my father. Materi approved but wanted me to make it clear that he didn't want me doing it. Well, anyway, Dad said I could get into politics if that's what I really wanted to do."*

With this, the young Adelstein went looking for Republican connections and quickly found a woman named Kathleen "Tommy" Christensen, who lived about 50 miles northwest of Rapid City in the small town of Spearfish. Born there in 1914, Christensen had moved to a prairie town called Huron, where her husband, Harry, worked for the Federal Crop Insurance Corporation. After Harry died in 1956, Tommy returned home, remarried, and ran a small clothing store before getting into real estate. She was an active Republican and member of several local women's clubs, and according to her obituary "was acquainted with President Dwight D. Eisenhower, President Richard Nixon, and Barry Goldwater."[4]

Tommy Christensen was both queen and kingmaker. She led campaigns, connected people, served as South Dakota's national committeewoman, and was a member of the party's executive committee. *"When someone told me to go see Tommy Christensen, I said, 'Okay, where does he live,' only to have them say, 'It's not a he, it's a her. She lives in Spearfish, and she's the national committeewoman, and she's real powerful,'"* Stan remembered. Already sage by her mid-forties, Christensen recognized that Adelstein came from *"a good family"* and saw value in getting a young, energetic businessman into politics. Christensen also knew how to test newcomers and sought a role significant enough to excite and expose Stan to state and national politics, yet small enough to try his abilities without incurring damage from a potential misstep. With the Republican National Convention set to begin in Chicago in late July, Christensen found the perfect opportunity: she arranged for Adelstein to be named an alternate delegate. He leaped at the opportunity and began preparing himself for the trip to Chicago.

Richard Nixon had all but secured the Republican nomination by the spring of 1960. An adept and cunning California politician, he had distinguished himself during the Red Scare of the early Cold War and served eight years as Dwight Eisenhower's vice president. Nixon suffered an uneasy relationship with Eisenhower. Some party members, like Illinois Governor William Stratton, believed the president might pull his support for Nixon's bid for the White House during the primaries. This did not happen, and Nixon quickly became the party's choice.[5]

Stan spent many hours at the Chicago convention in training sessions. Experienced party operatives taught newcomers how to support Republican candidates and organize voter turnout drives. Stan learned about a strategy employed by several unions that had used telephones to get out the vote for a Democratic candidate in another state. He loved the idea.

"When I got back to South Dakota," Stan said, *"I told Tommy that we should use a phone bank to try and get a Republican back in the governor's mansion."* From 1936 to 1959, the Republican Party had seated six consecutive governors in South Dakota. This "Republican dynasty," as one historian calls it, did not form on its own. Instead, the party drew from a strong pool of charismatic and able candidates. On the other side of the aisle was a Democratic Party that faced a paucity of inspiring and experienced candidates. During this period, many Democrats who might have otherwise been good contenders declined to run rather than face this Republican juggernaut. A series of weaker candidates ran and lost to Republicans in election after election.[6] Then, in 1958 a Democrat named Ralph Herseth, who was himself a former Civilian Conservation Corps superintendent, won on a platform that pushed tax reform and investment in statewide infrastructure.[7]

After a sound first two-year term, Herseth seemed well positioned for reelection—so much so, in fact, that many capable Republican challengers bowed out.[8] Archie Gubbrud, a farmer from Lincoln County who ran a bank and had served on his local school board, spent ten years in the South Dakota legislature, and was the speaker of the state House, was not intimidated.[9]

Gubbrud was not an especially strong orator, and he was not well known outside Lincoln County. But he launched his campaign early in the summer of 1960, casting himself as a solid centrist Republican who dripped integrity and small-town charm. He was, his supporters claimed, the candidate who could reunite a somewhat factionalized Republican Party. It did not hurt that 1960 was a presidential election year, and with the state firmly in Nixon's column, Gubbrud stood to reap a down-ballot boost, even though *"the party was pretty sure that they could not defeat Herseth."*[10]

CHAPTER 9

Stan Adelstein became enmeshed in Gubbrud's campaign under rather unusual circumstances. He had already been a supporter when Gubbrud was injured in an accident in a black 1934 Packard convertible that Stan owned. As a result, the candidate *"spent a significant part of the campaign"* recovering from his injuries in Bennett-Clarkson Memorial Hospital in Rapid City. *"I helped him with speeches that he made by telephone,"* Stan said, *"and even hung a long, twenty-foot banner that said 'Temporary Gubbrud for Governor Headquarters' from his hospital window."*

Stan also set up a series of telephones in the basement board room of a Rapid City office building he had recently purchased. *"This idea,"* he said, *"was seen as sort of foolish, and nobody thought it would work, despite what I had learned in Chicago."* In order to cover the cost, he reached out to Republican friends across the Rapid City business community, asking each to pay one phone bill for a period of two months. Under this system, Stan—who was also the county precinct coordinator—managed nearly two-dozen phones and a team of volunteers. He called this the "Pennington plan of action," and Tommy Christensen organized a similar operation in Lawrence County. Together, Stan said, *"this was the first get out the vote drive in South Dakota."*[11] On election night, the strategy contributed to a strong Republican showing. Although Nixon lost the presidency to John F. Kennedy, he won South Dakota, and state Republicans rode his ticket across the state, capturing firm majorities in both the state House and the state Senate.[12] Gubbrud trailed Herseth in the early returns, but after the ballots were tallied in West River he won by just 4,435 votes.[13]

Stan's role in Gubbrud's underdog victory made him an overnight star in the Republican Party. Before he knew it, he would be the youngest member of Gubbrud's first transition team, involved with the Young Republicans, and secretary-treasurer of the Pennington County Central Committee. The governor also named him to the Industrial Development Expansion Agency (IDEA).[14] Instituted by Governor Joe Foss in the late 1950s, this program encouraged innovation and economic development.[15] IDEA had weathered a scandal during the Herseth administration, when the attorney general prosecuted Noel Tweet, the agency's director, for misusing travel funds.[16] While Stan was on the board, he and his colleagues took steps to ensure bipartisanship by having IDEA commissioners serve overlapping six-year terms.[17]

"In 1960, just after the successful election, Tommy Christensen walked me into a meeting of the Young Republicans and said, 'I'd like you all to meet your new candidate for

Republican national committeeman.' Since I was a newcomer, this wasn't exactly good news for some people in the group. When I took my seat and a question popped up, another Young Republican officer, Jane Boorman, snapped, 'Why don't we ask our new national committeeman since he is not encumbered with any experience or even attendance of a previous meeting?'" Stan served as a Young Republican national committeeman from 1961 to 1963, then as the group's chairman from 1963 to 1964, during which time he helped increase the number of state Young Republicans by 50 percent. "Stan 'The Man' Adelstein," his campaign pamphlet read, raised more money than anyone else for the party's 1960 Eisenhower Dinner, then raked in another $75,000 for an event recognizing Karl Mundt in 1964. Stan was the state's "Outstanding Young Republican" in 1963.[18] And despite their early tension, Adelstein and Boorman—who later spent years as a staffer for Senator James Abdnor—*"became very close friends and teammates later on."*[19]

In Republican circles, the young Adelstein was known for passionately championing the issues he cared about—sometimes to a fault. A news clipping, shared with Stan by his friend Norma Anderson, summed up these perceptions during an intraparty election in 1963. After a sitting member of South Dakota's delegation to the Republican National Committee resigned that year, Stan jumped into the race. As one article put it, Stan was "aggressive and informed, with a will to work hard at the task involved in the committeemanship." The author also pointed out, however, that Stan "steps on toes, to be sure," before reasoning that "who doesn't when the trek is forward?" The author ultimately concluded that, because he was a fighter and because "he has plenty of the green stuff," Adelstein was a good candidate and deserving of his fellow Republicans' support.[20]

Stan lost that race, as well as a bid to become treasurer of the Young Republican National Federation two years later. *"I had been nominated as the moderate candidate for treasurer of the Federation, in the hope that I would be able to give oversight to the $2 million that the Republican National Committee gave to the Young Republicans each year."* This second defeat reflected the emerging bitter struggle between moderates and conservatives within the Republican Party, a tension that would dog Adelstein his entire political career. One of Stan's associates summed up his chances just days before the party elections in 1965: "Stan gained 2 points for every one he lost" during a recent speech to the delegates from California. He was "a little too grim, but they laughed [at] his jokes . . . [and] Stan's qualifications [were] not questioned. However he is absolutely not welcomed with open arms for they know he is not ultra conservative," which imperiled—and ultimately doomed—Stan's candidacy.[21]

Although he had a hard time breaking into the high ranks of the national party, Adelstein was welcomed to the inner circle of state politics by the early 1960s. What he encountered there was unsettling. Early on, he attended a meeting with *"the real powers around West River."* This included a couple of prominent state legislators, a former governor, and *"a big fund-raiser."* As the group chatted, one Republican mentioned his confusion when, while returning home from a recent hunting trip in Mitchell, a state patrolman pulled in front of him and crept back to Rapid City. Another member of the group interjected that, after getting a concerned call from the Republican's wife about whether her husband had been drinking heavily, he had called the highway patrol and asked that his friend be escorted home without incident.

"That was one of the things that kind of shocked me," Stan remembered, *"and it's a little bit of insider stuff."* Political leaders, he naively assumed, held themselves to higher standards, but he soon realized that, regardless of one's party affiliation, *"everything was always decided in the back room."* Stan resisted conflicts of interest when he believed they could do real damage to an institution. He had achieved the rank of captain in the South Dakota National Guard by 1961, for example, but started to notice that during Guard trainings his superiors—several of whom he knew in the civilian world, where Stan's influence outmatched theirs—seemed to afford him favorable treatment. *"When I had generals coming over to make sure this mere captain was comfortable"* following Gubbrud's victory, *"I realized that if I wanted to have any dealings with the Guard, then I should not stay an officer. Remembering my experience with Utah, I resigned."*

Occasionally, Stan's seat in political parlors aroused tension with his father. Only months after Gubbrud's inauguration in 1961, for example, the younger Adelstein dragged NWE into a controversy involving the South Dakota Cement Plant, a state-owned corporation that had been making industrial products in Rapid City since 1925.[22] In 1961, the plant's board purchased 195 lime-rich acres from Pete Lien & Sons for $600,000.[23] This acquisition enraged state Democrats. They called the sale hypocritical because Republicans had opposed a similar deal during the Herseth administration only months earlier. They also charged that the board had overpaid and made the decision over the phone rather than at an official meeting.[24]

Some Republicans, like Speaker of the House Carl Burgess, parried by claiming that in private meetings, Governor Herseth had indicated his willingness to pay $1.5 million for the property. Meanwhile, some Republicans, including Stan, continued to oppose the sale even after Gubbrud was in office, which pushed the price down.[25] This opposition angered local bankers, who thought that Republican meddling had cost them two-thirds of their profit on the hefty deal. Several representatives from First National Bank flew to Pierre in a furor, where they claimed that Adelstein had acted just to spite his family's longtime competitors, the Liens. Gubbrud, a friend, ally, and political beneficiary of Stan's, defended him to the banks, which—in Stan's mind—left them embarrassed and angry at him and, by extension, NWE.[26]

Morris, who had for years expressed his concerns that Stan's outside commitments were crowding his schedule, grew upset that his son had injected NWE into an ugly political fight. The battle threatened to needlessly sour the company's relationship with powerful bankers across the state.[27]

Stan sharply rebutted his father's criticisms. "I think you are being very short-sighted," he wrote in a rare outburst, "when you feel that political power is something that can be completely eliminated from business. There probably was a day when business and this political connection wasn't very significant." But, he continued, "government regulates our business . . . [and] the power and prestige that goes into the political arena has a very significant effect on the friends and contacts that you'll have in business. Ultimately, I think that political power and business success . . . are very closely related."[28]

Stan also engaged in national politics, putting his philosophy about the relationship between politics and business to work in early 1963 when he supported an amendment to the Small Business Act. The change would have exempted the construction industry from "small-business set-asides," or regulations that barred large firms from bidding on certain contracts.[29] As their name suggests, the regulations literally "set aside" certain projects for smaller operators. Proponents sought to prevent big companies from dominating entire industries. They considered set-asides a leg up for smaller operators, many of whom had less experience and fewer resources for navigating the "complex, verbose, and, at times, conflicting regulations" that accompanied federal projects.[30]

NWE opposed construction set-asides by the federal government. As Stan wrote to Senator Peter Dominick, a Colorado Republican who sat on the

CHAPTER 9

Senate Committee on Banking and Currency, although NWE was the largest construction firm incorporated in South Dakota and sat above the threshold that classified a "small business" (a company had to do less than $7.5 million in annual work to be considered "small"), it was still "somewhere below the 250 largest contracting companies in the country."[31] NWE, he insisted, was a middle-tier operator that faced "real hardship" when disallowed from bidding on projects. His family, he pointed out, built its company from the ground up without any help from set-asides, and moreover did not "stifle free competitive bidding on projects." From his perspective, NWE actually supported small businesses by subcontracting around 15 percent of its work to them.[32]

Stan then appealed to Dominick's ideology. Both Democrats and Republicans in Congress had a tendency to support set-asides, which they viewed as an investment in working people.[33] Yet this was still Cold War America, where politicians were steeped in concerns about the creep of socialism. "I do feel," Stan wrote, appealing to Dominick's conservative side, that the program had "all the earmarks of a deliberate attempt to destroy personal incentive instituted by those who abhor our free enterprise system and who seek to remove our individual liberties, by first taking away our economic liberties."[34]

This letter was not Stan's only opportunity to lobby Dominick. Working through his state party connections, he obtained an invitation from Senator Karl Mundt to testify before the Banking Committee in May 1963. The session opened with Mundt telling his colleagues that Stan was an "oldtime friend of mine," and that NWE "typifie[d] sound business in" South Dakota. He then joked about the size of Kadoka, which was so small that he thought he "might have to run for office out there."[35] According to Stan, he had gotten to know Mundt through a family connection that bred a political friendship. *"Karl had been a supporter of my cousin Elliot Cohen and his* Commentary *magazine with regard to several issues dealing with postwar Poland. Mundt did several things for NWE over the years, and from time to time, we even furnished our company plane to him."* As the years wore on, Stan's relationship with Mundt would deteriorate. *"I always wondered about his intentions when he supported Elliot,"* Stan said, *"and it seemed to me that he was trying to make up for his isolationism and for joining up with the anti-Semitic crowd in D.C. before the Second World War."*

A few years later, Adelstein and Mundt would end their relationship after a falling out over Mundt's opposition to some labor legislation that

Stan supported. But they were still close allies during the Senate Banking Committee hearings in 1963. After Mundt finished his friendly introduction, committee chairman Senator Thomas J. McIntyre of New Hampshire gave Stan the floor. The young South Dakotan then laid out several examples that, to his thinking, exemplified the ways in which set-asides had cost taxpayers extra money by awarding government projects to small companies that were less efficient than larger builders like NWE.[36] He then detailed project budgets for some of these set-asides, many of which required more than a million dollars in new equipment to complete. "Is this really small business?" he asked rhetorically. "Is it the desire of the Congress to protect firms that can invest $1,469,000 in new equipment," as was the case in one of his examples, "from firms such as ours" that already "happened to have" millions of dollars of equipment? "It just does not seem logical."[37]

Stan continued in this vein for the duration of his testimony, arguing passionately for the elimination of construction set-asides. He gave example after example from across the country, many of which were drawn from his four-year involvement with the Associated General Contractors of America (AGC), which supported the bill.[38] Stan closed his testimony with a rebuttal to his opposition. Proponents of set-asides, in his estimation, were trying to paint all large companies as monopolistic and in collusion to stifle competition.[39] NWE, he said, did not fit this paradigm.

In the end, President Kennedy's White House Council on Small Businesses rejected the construction set-asides bill, which effectively killed it. This outcome was, as least as far as Stan's willingness and ability to meld business and politics were concerned, less significant than the fact that he had made his way from an office in Rapid City to the hearing room of the Senate Banking Committee in Washington, D.C.—a city he would visit many more times over the years, and where two of his own sons would one day work.[40]

Morris Adelstein was no stranger to these activities and was more politically savvy than he let on. He understood the kinds of connections his son described. In fact, in 1961 Morris Adelstein was more upset with the *visibility* of his son's political activities than his specific actions. This nuance was lost on Stan. In the angry letter to his father, Stan pointed out that the banks were neither as friendly to NWE nor as powerful as Morris thought. "For what reason," he asked rhetorically, "should we seek to acquire more dollars than we can spend in our lifetime" if doing so came at the price of "knuckling down to these bigots and crooks?" Stan, who had never been poor and had rarely worried about securing bank financing, admonished his father for backing off in the face of a challenge. Both Adelsteins were prideful men, Stan wrote, "though lately [your pride has] been battered and you're willing to compromise for the sake of some peace of mind. I am simply not willing to say goodbye, drop politics and admit that they managed to defeat me."[41]

Stan ended the exchange with a short passage summarizing his belief in the relationship between business and politics and his determination to be involved in both. In his view, he had a duty to the Republican Party. He unabashedly expected that "in turn, [he would] receive some of the political benefits therefrom." This, he made clear, was simply how the world worked. He finished with a personal ultimatum. "This struggle," he wrote, "depends on your support of me. If you feel that you cannot go all the way with me if the need arises, then perhaps what I had better do is drop out of this picture and consider some other direction for my future."[42]

STEP OUT OR STEP UP

By late 1961, the tense relationship between father and son brought a foreboding sense of uncertainty about NWE's future. Although the cement plant controversy dissipated almost as quickly as it had formed, the words exchanged between Morris and Stan brought a long-standing concern to the fore.[43] "I think I committed Mortal Sin," Morris had told Stan in a letter. Morris noted that a Catholic friend had just explained the difference between mortal and venial transgressions. He wrote to Stan to say he worried that by not "constantly developing new men so that the loss of one or two" critical figures—in this case, his sons—would seriously hurt NWE, he had increased the risk of a major crisis for the business. "I am putting my faith in you and Robert," he surmised, "and I hope this faith is not misplaced."[44]

This last point lingered in the air. Bob had been struggling for some time. His talents and interests lay outside Northwestern, and he had grown resentful after years of feeling undervalued and overlooked by his family.[45] Stan complained regularly about Bob's performance and business sense.[46] He was not the only one. As Stan wrote to his father, several staff members had approached him during a trip to Denver and said that Bob had grown increasingly difficult at work.[47] It was becoming clear that although Bob was a son, brother, and stockholder to Northwestern, he would not be its leading heir.

Stan's weaknesses came in a different form. Nobody doubted that he took Northwestern seriously and possessed a sharp business acumen, but he was still devoting significant amounts of time volunteering for civic and political causes. In November 1961, he detailed his activities for his father, who, as he wrote, "often wonder[ed] what I do with my days." Although Stan spent more than six hours on NWE business—in meetings, reviewing reports on other jobs, and crafting estimates for new work in Custer State Park and for Boeing missile contracts—the other half of his 11.75-hour day went to Automobile Bankers, Harney Lumber, Hills Tire, and activities related to the AGC. Aware of his own penchant for overwork and injecting himself into other enterprises, Stan mentioned that he thought he would have to "start limiting [him]self to a 70 hour work week."[48]

Then lightning struck. Twice. John Materi died, stripping Northwestern of its seasoned second-in-command in 1962. Just over a year later, with the company still reeling from the loss of Materi, Morris Adelstein had a massive heart attack.[49]

Morris and Bertha had flown to Israel in March 1963, spending time with dignitaries and promoting Israeli interests. Now approaching his sixty-ninth birthday, Morris grew fatigued as their trip dragged on. The couple decided to rest in Florence, Italy. When stabbing chest pain jolted Morris from his bed, Bertha called the concierge. A discordant scene unfolded as Morris clutched his chest. Then a group of local volunteer health care workers burst into the room in medieval-looking black robes—a tradition, Bertha later learned, that reached back to the plague. Despite their frightening appearance, the medics saved Morris's life, and he spent several weeks regaining his strength in an Italian hospital. Although he eventually returned to work and activism, he never fully recovered his stamina.[50]

Five thousand miles from his father's hospital bed, Stan Adelstein scrambled. He had been catapulted into his mentor's chair after Materi's death, becoming the vice president of NWE just a few months before his father went to Italy. Stan had several years' experience managing contracts and bids, checking the progress on projects, and performing other administrative tasks, but he could always turn to his father for advice. With Morris in critical condition and his fears about NWE's line of succession seeming more prophetic than ever, the company's fate now fell to Stan. Morris had granted him temporary control over the company in the event of an emergency, but NWE's lawyers had not crafted a document with long-term incapacitation in mind. Stan's power-of-attorney allowed him to handle a few small-scale decisions, but his authority was tenuous.[51]

Morris slowly recovered over the course of 1963. By early 1964, he was once again penning the annual president's message, reporting on progress, and encouraging the company along. From these writings, NWE looked like a tight-knit, successful family business. The four Adelsteins sat on the board of directors. Morris was president, Stan his vice president. Bertha held the title of secretary/treasurer, while Bob was an assistant secretary, along with four other longtime NWE employees.[52]

Behind the scenes, however, the authority structure was less clear. Morris was in his seventies, in ill-health, and Northwestern was facing serious financial problems for the first time in forty years. In 1966, Morris had to reach out to L.A. Pier, who was still banking in Belvidere, for a loan.[53] The lingering question of NWE's leadership remained unanswered: Bob was disengaged; Bertha, too, had health problems; and perhaps most shockingly, Stan was threatening to leave.[54]

The risks associated with NWE's business plan—the "bid big" strategy that had introduced incredible success since the late 1940s—had grown significantly by the mid-1960s. Increasing competition was a problem, but Morris believed poor management posed a larger threat. "We never bid a job unless we carefully analyze it," he wrote to a friend in late 1966, "and we have a paper profit on every job we bid. But for some reason or other they just don't come out that way."[55]

He gave examples. NWE had bid two recent jobs "with almost a guaranteed profit." Yet somehow, Morris noted with exasperation, "we dropped this profit" on both projects "and developed a loss." "It was not the weather," he wrote, and "it was not the equipment—it was poor management." Too often, supervisors did not catch deficiencies early enough. Rather than running multiple jobs at once to increase the company's margins, Morris would often have to shut one job down, devote extra resources to finishing the first, and then move on. He knew the company needed better management.

"What to do," Morris told his friend, "is clear as crystal. The thing now is how to do it."[56]

Stan agreed with his father, but only in part. Management and competition were certainly problems. A more pressing—and far more sensitive—one concerned Morris himself. His health had steadily deteriorated after his heart attack, but he refused to slow down, relentlessly pursuing his involvement with national Union of American Hebrew Congregations and other activities. On the business front, although Morris's mind was sharp and his intentions good, the industry had shifted, and he could not seem to divorce himself from the "bid big" mantra. *"It seemed to me that my father's ill health had set something off in his mind, almost like a need to do more and larger work to prove something, either to us or to himself,"* Stan said.

The Rifle Gap Dam, a massive three-year Colorado Bureau of Reclamation project, was indicative of NWE's problems.[57] *"Moving hundreds of thousands of cubic yards of earth in an adverse environment was expensive work, and it was not the kind that, in my mind, Northwestern was especially good at,"* Stan said. Instead, the company had taken the project for two reasons: *"because it had a big price tag and because it fascinated Dad,"* neither of which Stan agreed with.

Morris was *"bidding projects he liked"* with little real recognition of their cost. Another project was *"an interesting bridge that he wanted to build,"* even though it was situated at high altitude and vulnerable to prohibitively inclement weather. *"We'd lost money there,"* Stan remembered, *"we lost money all over."* He believed the company was in dire straits. If they could not get control of the problem, especially in Denver, he thought, *"we'd go broke."*

When Stan raised these concerns, Morris gave a prickly response. Stan would never forget the staccato sentence his father used to describe his money and his company: *"'I made it,' Dad said, 'and I can lose it.'"*

Frustrated, Stan decided to look for other work. *"I had a chance to go with a national asphalt company,"* which had made him an attractive offer. Young and ambitious, Stan considered it. Although it would mean that he and Ita and the boys would have to leave Rapid City, he told his father he would be moving on from NWE in the spring.

Stan's decision finally pushed Morris into action. If Stan would stay and run the company, he said, Morris would transition to retirement. Stan agreed to stay, and in the middle of 1966, at the age of thirty-five, he became

CHAPTER 9

president of NWE. Over the next two years, Morris remained chairman, lending consultation when he could and retaining ultimate authority over the corporation, but Stan ran the business on a day-to-day basis.[58]

Throughout this period, Morris's health continued to deteriorate. He was hospitalized several times in the middle of the decade. On December 16, 1968, the long-ailing founder of the Northwestern Engineering Company lay on his deathbed. He turned to Stan, who had spent weeks at his father's side along with his mother and brother, and told his eldest son in a croaking voice: "It's all up to you now." The next day, Morris Adelstein was gone.[59]

CHAPTER 10
FAMILY AND COMMUNITY

Even as he grieved for his father and struggled to pilot a massive company stretched to its breaking point, plenty of other things were going well in Stan Adelstein's life. By careful design, his family was a living metaphor of civic commitment, a respectable image that comported with the expectations of Cold War America and was measured by an adherence to a common way of life romantically embodied in images of white middle-class nuclear families.[1]

Fitting this model underwrote the American way, even as prejudice kept many minority and working-class families from realizing the American Dream. Engaging with their community afforded the Jewish Adelsteins a chance to fold themselves into the social fabric of the very Christian Black Hills. Ita was a stay-at-home mom who kept busy, even as she missed Denver's cosmopolitan culture.[2] She may not have been ecstatic about living in South Dakota, but she was content in her new hometown, even if her family's connection to place was more Stan's than hers. If nothing else, unlike military life, it was stable. She kept up with American Jewish Committee (AJC) activities from afar, stayed active in several local clubs, and taught the synagogue's Sunday school classes at Ellsworth.[3]

When their grandfather passed away late in 1968, Daniel Adelstein had just celebrated his fourteenth birthday; Jim was eight; and Jon was six. Dan—like his father—spent a summer at a 70-acre outdoor camp situated 30 miles southeast of Duluth, Minnesota, on the Wisconsin side of the line. There, the boy, who wore horn-rimmed glasses and a navy blazer adorned with a Camp Nebagamon patch, learned to build a fire and paddle a canoe.

CHAPTER 10

These experiences fit well with his other interests. Although Stan was often away on business, when he was home he spent quality time with Dan, taking him and his friends hiking around Skyline Drive. He bought Dan a .22-caliber rifle and taught him to shoot in the seclusion of the Northwestern Engineering Company's Rapid City quarry.[4] When he got a little older, Dan ran track, and as a junior at Central High School in 1972 he was a delegate to the American Legion's Boy's State event at Northern State College in Aberdeen, where he and others studied government.[5]

Throughout these years, Ita devoted her attention to raising her boys and giving them the playful childhood that had been stolen from her in 1939. Still too young for camp, Jim and Jon climbed on the statues at Dinosaur Hill and scampered up the stone steps of the State Game Lodge in Custer State Park.[6] From Dan's point of view, it was a "traditional family" situation, with Stan at work most of the time and Ita the primary homemaker. She was a "student of parenting" who religiously read Dr. Benjamin Spock's best-selling books on infant and child care.[7] Years later, Ita confirmed that she strived to be "a perfect wife, perfect mother and perfect housekeeper. That was my goal."[8]

The family spent weekends picnicking in the Black Hills, where even in the woods Ita looked like something out of *Vogue*. She and Stan took the kids to Keystone—the small tourist town near Mount Rushmore—where the boys had their photographs taken with a few Lakotas who, harnessing their role in the new tourism economy, spent long summer days in full regalia. The family grabbed ice cream and headed up to the monument, where Stan introduced some out-of-town friends to Ben Black Elk, son of the famous Lakota Holy Man and a longtime fixture at the foot of the mountain.

The Adelstein clan zoomed past the ponderosas in Stan's '34 Packard convertible—the same one Archie Gubbrud had once wrecked. *"I had purchased the car with four of my fraternity brothers in Boulder in 1951,"* Stan recalled. *"As each graduated, I repaid them their $50 investment until I owned it. When I got back from the army, the Packard had been parked in the company's equipment yard in Denver. Somebody offered me $2,500 for it, and I thought that was really special, so I kept the car."* The vehicle fit Stan's sense of style better than newer models on Black Hills highways.

Stan and Ita also traveled widely, visiting California for a meeting of the Beavers (a professional organization for contractors) and relaxing on a trip to the Caribbean in early 1966. Soon after returning to Rapid City, they *"met*

Lincoln Borglum and his wife, Mary Anne, who had been General Ellsworth's wife before his death in 1953," and enjoyed weekends with the Borglums at the same cottage studio where the sculptor Gutzon Borglum had once spent long days refining his artistic vision.

Stan, who by the early 1970s had traded the clean face of a military man for a mustache and then a full goatee, funded this lifestyle by packing in twelve-hour days at the office. He also spent evenings and weekends at the synagogue, at political functions, and in endless meetings with a dizzying array of community groups. He had immersed himself in philanthropy soon after returning to Rapid City, joining the local United Fund, a yearly charitable giving drive, in 1958.[9]

His United Fund experience solidified a firm belief that Rapid City needed a more robust philanthropic sector. *"It became clear,"* he said, *"that there was a real paucity of giving publicly,"* due, in his estimation, to the town's conservative business culture. People clung to a *"concept that the purpose of a business is to make a profit,"* and *"not to be weak-kneed and gift-giving."* Stan agreed with the first half of this sentiment but abhorred the second. He remembered that in Denver the very public nature of giving in the Jewish community had fueled philanthropy, even when it was driven in part by individual aspirations for social standing. So he set out to change things.

Stan joined the founding board of the Rapid City Club for Boys (often called the "Boys Club") in 1963. Led by Executive Director Roger Erickson, the organization had been chartered five years earlier but first began operations in an old train depot in downtown Rapid City in November 1963. The Club provided area youth with a safe and supportive space, but very quickly the depot was bursting at its seams.[10] Stan later expounded to Erickson, telling him that "those early days of the Boys Club gave [us] an opportunity to demonstrate that which makes our American Democracy and capitalist system unique." He noted that many of the board members were extremely successful and represented a variety of sectors of society, and that "with no coercion other than their own [conscience]," they "gave freely of their time and resources" to children "at the bottom of the scale economically, educationally, and socially." By providing the boys a place where they could play, learn, and challenge themselves and one another, Adelstein concluded, the Boys Club created an environment where any child "could dream of being the intellectual equal of anyone," and as a result, "often they became the intellectual superior of many."[11]

Given his enthusiasm, Stan was eager to help the club find a new facility. A joke that circulated through Jewish circles in the United States offered inspiration: *"If you went to Israel and took down all the brass plaques with the names of American Jews on them, all the buildings would just collapse."* Offering donors the chance to see their name emblazoned on the side of a building was by no means a new idea, but it was effective. Around 1965 or 1966—a few years before Morris Adelstein's death—the Boys Club finalized plans for a larger facility. Stan convinced his father of the organization's import, and Morris donated more than $50,000 from the Adelstein Foundation, which he had set up years earlier to manage the family's charitable giving.[12]

The Morris and Bertha Adelstein Club for Boys Building opened in downtown Rapid City in October 1967. The pair were the guests of honor at an open house reception, one of Morris's final public events. His old friend and coworker Boyd Leedom—who had become a successful lawyer, justice of the South Dakota Supreme Court, and chairman of the National Labor Relations Board during the Eisenhower administration—flew to Rapid City and honored Morris and Bertha in a keynote address.[13] Just as important in Stan's eyes, the donation and related publicity aided his larger goal: *"The idea of naming the building occurred to me as a way to change the view that individuals who ran businesses shouldn't give to charities."*

Stan Adelstein spent another fifteen years on the board of the Rapid City Club for Boys, but his involvement with the nonprofit community did not stop there. From the middle of the 1960s on, Stan developed a pattern: if he found an issue interesting, he would seek out supportive organizations and get involved. Occasionally, folks from around the community would reach out to him. And, as Stan put it, *"I had a hard time saying 'no' to a good cause."*

Some of Stan's civic involvement was anchored in hobbies and experiences from his younger days. National defense was a continuing interest and political priority. But increasingly his activities grew out of chance conversations, like the one he had with Major General Duane "Duke" Corning in 1967. Born in Madison, South Dakota, Corning had served in World War II and Korea, where he earned numerous medals as a fighter pilot before spending two decades in charge of the South Dakota National Guard.[14]

"*We ended up sitting next to each other on a plane,*" Stan said, "*and I turned to Duke and said, 'You know, that was the most insulting thing you sent me.'*"

Corning awkwardly searched his memory, trying to remember what Adelstein was talking about.

"'*Duke, I know how old I am. But you are in charge of the selective service.*'

"'*Yes, I am,*' Duke replied."

"So I told him: '*You sent me a card in the mail telling me I had reached the age where I was not considered capable to serve the United States in uniform. Now I know I've gotten too old,*'" Stan said, his stern face slackening, "*but you didn't have to remind me.*"

Realizing Stan's tease, Corning loosened up and chuckled. A few moments later, "*he said, 'Well, you know, if you still want to do something—what do you know about the National Defense Executive Reserve [NDER]?*'"

Stan had never heard of it. Corning explained that the NDER was a classified emergency plan "*that had been established by a secret presidential executive order to provide for continuity of government in the event of a nuclear attack, or some other incident that would render normal governance impossible.*" Under the plan, the United States would set up a series of independent governmental entities organized into several national districts across the nation. There was an opening for an engineer or contractor in Denver, "*which was the headquarters for the Sixth District.*" If Stan was interested, Corning said he would recommend him for the position. This conversation began Adelstein's three-decade stint as one of South Dakota's only members of the NDER.[15]

Per Corning's description, the NDER was an Eisenhower-era agency that trained leaders from industry and other sectors of civilian life who would transition to high-level government positions in the event of a major national defense emergency.[16] "*This group would become virtually the government of Washington in miniature for this area*" following a nuclear attack or something similar, Stan said, "*until the United States could be put back together.*"

Members of the NDER hailed from an array of sectors—construction and engineering, utilities, the financial sector, the food service industry, health care, and others. Their collective job was to "identify what was lost" in an emergency and compensate to the best of their abilities until further resources and order could be restored.[17]

Stan held a rank equivalent to brigadier general in the NDER, and in the case of emergency was ordered to drop everything and report to a 33,000-square-foot facility that sat 11 miles west of Denver. *"We had an extensive office and sleeping quarters underground,"* Stan recalled. Equipped with enough supplies so that a team of 300 people could survive for thirty days, the bunker was buried under 4 feet of earth and 2 feet of bomb-resistant concrete. There, Stan and other NDER service members *"held practice exercises"* to prepare for an emergency.[18]

In 1974, Stan attended an NDER planning meeting in San Francisco along with forty-six individuals from regional branches and the agency's central office.[19] During the meeting, Stan and his colleagues walked through a hypothetical scenario in which the Soviet Union had detonated a nuclear weapon over Sacramento. Agency leaders quizzed attendees on NDER protocols, reaffirming the various principles that would ensure the nation's survival.[20]

"I remember that Ita wasn't happy about NDER," Stan said. *"You know, her position was 'you're going to leave the family if there's a disaster!' but then again, I couldn't really tell her much about it, which was difficult. It operated by fiat under that executive order. That's the reason it was classified. We had all kinds of powers—right of eminent domain, right of acquisition. I could just commandeer construction equipment, and in one training the railroads were down, and we walked through how I would find stockpiles of railroad ties in Kansas and other places, and put them to use to reestablish infrastructure."*

The notes Stan scribbled on Hilton Hotel and Tower letterhead during the San Francisco exercise provide insight into the agency's philosophy. First, he made an important distinction: the NDER existed to help the nation through "catastrophe," not just "crisis or disaster." State and local authorities could deal with floods, earthquakes, and the like. The NDER represented a last resort, created to preserve the Republic under only dire circumstances, *"like when all communication with D.C. and the normal units of government had all been destroyed."* The agency had to avoid confusion and chaos at any cost by establishing a hierarchy of "unquestioned leadership" that could usher a city, region, or the entire nation through the immediate and long-term fallout of a crippling event.[21] According to the government, from their strategically placed bunkers, Stan and his colleagues were to "assembl[e] key regional federal officials and assur[e] their survival," enable "a continuity of government," assess damage to vital resources, prepare for the reestablishment of federal authority, and "assist State and Local Government" in executing "immediate postattack responsibilities."[22]

In 1979, President Jimmy Carter amended Eisenhower's original executive order consolidating five agencies in order to create the Federal Emergency Management Agency (FEMA), which employed nearly 2,500 staff members nationwide and had a broader mission of providing federal assistance in natural disasters, defense scenarios, and other emergencies.[23] Although an ardent political critic of Carter, when Stan's term expired in 1979 he immediately agreed to extend his service another three years.[24] National defense superseded politics, and he re-upped with NDER's successor organization again and again before finally retiring from the agency in 1994.

As a part of his civic activity, Stan also reinvigorated his interest in the fine arts. Drama and music had fascinated him since his days at summer camp and in the high school and college orchestras. In 1971, he became a trustee for the Black Hills Playhouse, a nonprofit organization that maintained a stage and theater troupe for summertime performances at a complex inside Custer State Park. Founded in 1946 by University of South Dakota professor Warren "Doc" Lee, the playhouse offered summer employment and college credits to drama students at the college, as well as "twenty different institutions of higher education and two professional acting studios." Students came from across the United States and, by the late 1970s, at least "one foreign country."[25]

Similarly, Stan spent a two-year term as president of the Rapid City Concert Association in the late 1970s, during which he chaired an eighteen-member board of volunteers who sponsored a performance by the Minneapolis Symphony Orchestra. *"There was a grant that would help pay to have the Minneapolis Symphony play, but the catch was that the union contract for the musicians required them to be back in Minneapolis by midnight, or else we had to pay double the wages for each performer. So I worked with the mayor's wife, Trude LaCroix—who ran a very successful travel agency—and we chartered a North Central Airlines plane to bring them here. We had something like 1,997 seats at the time, as I recall, and we wanted it to be a full house. So we sold over 2,000 tickets, knowing some people might not show up."* That night, the symphony played Rapid City into a new era as the first concert in the newly constructed Rushmore Plaza Civic Center's theater, then made it home on time. Stan served another term on the Concert Association's board in the late 1980s, and over the years the Concert Association hosted performances by groups like the National Folk Ballet of Mexico, the Tommy Dorsey Band, and many others.[26]

Adelstein also got involved with the development and management of parks in and around Rapid City. Sometimes, he simply made a donation, as was the case when he and Ita gave funds and materials to Storybook Island, a nursery rhyme–themed children's park that the local Rotary Club opened in 1959. Stan supervised the construction of a turreted stone "London Bridge" that arched over a pond and welcomed families to the park.[27] On other occasions Stan lent time and expertise. In 1972, he joined the board of trustees for the Mount Rushmore National Memorial Society, which helped manage Mount Rushmore under the terms of a 1952 agreement with the National Parks Service.[28] He and the rest of the board spent several years helping park administrators update the memorial's management plan, which called for an extensive redesign of the traffic flow to and from the monument, new parking structures, viewing platforms, gift shops, and the expansion of the on-site amphitheater.[29]

One of the most unexpected causes with which Adelstein associated himself developed through his close friendship with a group of Benedictine nuns, whose order had been praying and teaching in the Black Hills since 1889.[30] According to one local historian, the sisters had originally provided medical care in the town of Sturgis before anti-Catholic Klan activity pushed them to relocate to Rapid City in the mid-1920s where they reestablished their practice.[31] They built St. Martin's Monastery in the woods of western Rapid City in 1962, and devoted their lives to caring for the sick. Originally called St. John's Hospital, the sisters worked out of "three rented residences on St. Joseph Street." In 1928, St. John's McNamara Hospital, a seventy-five-bed facility, opened in a large brick building on Rapid City's Eleventh Street. It had been named after the late John McNamara, whose *"wife had been a close friend of my mother's,"* Stan pointed out, and whose family was among the hospital's most generous beneficiaries.[32]

In the early 1960s, the nuns invited Stan and other advisers to lend fiscal and administrative advice. *"It was a fantastic organization of giving people,"* Stan recalled. *"I loved their commitment"* and the strength of *"not only the sisters' faith but their values and integrity."* These common virtues overcame the religious schism between the young Jewish man and his new Catholic friends. Years later, Sister Sarto Rogers—one of the top administrators at St. John's—would recall that, although it was sadly "not true of all hospitals," she and her colleagues in Rapid City had "always had a very excellent working relationship" with Stan Adelstein and people from different religious backgrounds.[33]

In fact, their shared commitments bound Stan and the sisters of St. Martin's for decades. He initially advised them on an informal board, later becoming vice president of the St. Martin's Hospital Corporation, which had been organized *"so that I could act as the hospital board chairman, since the Prioress Mother Magdalene didn't feel comfortable managing board meetings or understanding corporate procedures."* This idea had been born, in part, from Stan's own *"interest in having an outside board at my own company—the similarity was with the sisters also having closed, or private, ownership structure for the hospital. It reminds me of the ways different activities and interests were always tied together somehow."* One of the first things he helped the sisters with, however, was political. Around 1962, the prioress had heard that the South Dakota Board of Regents wanted to create a baccalaureate degree nursing program in Rapid City. *"St. John's,* meanwhile, *"had also just completed a new building to house its own nursing school, which would offer an RN Certificate, which I thought was the better program since it offered superior clinical practice."* Concerned that the state would start a separate school that might compete with theirs, Sister Sarto mentioned that she would get together with the sisters and pray for a solution. That's when Stan stepped in, with a dose of humor: *"I said, 'Let me tell you something, Sister, the Board of Regents isn't appointed by God. It's appointed by our Governor Gubbrud. While you pray, let me try something else.'"*[34]

Knowing the strength of his connections in Pierre, Stan *"called each member of the Board of Regents, detailing the need for the existing certificate program and the sisters' good work. I pointed out that the baccalaureate program would continue on at the state university in Brookings, and argued that having two nursing programs in Rapid City would create unnecessary administrative bloat, as well as jeopardize the investment in a brand-new building."* The sisters were nervous about Stan's backroom approach, but it paid off. Over the next several months, the Board of Regents worked with the nuns to accredit the program at St. Johns, which offered thirty-two college credits. Five years later, in 1968, the nursing school started a long affiliation with the South Dakota School of Mines & Technology.[35] Together, these colleges would continue to train nurses in Rapid City for more than thirty years. The nursing program later affiliated with other state universities in South Dakota.

The sisters at St. Martin's quickly came to appreciate Adelstein and his methods, even when they did not fully understand them. He spent a half decade on the board of directors, which he chaired from 1971 to 1973.[36] Stan recalled one incident that tested his commitment to the sisters. A lifelong pro-choice Republican, Stan was not one to advance agendas that limited abortions. The Catholic nuns, on the other hand, were intensely opposed to abortion. Working with them around the time of *Roe v. Wade*, the 1973 U.S. Supreme Court decision legalizing some abortions in the United States, Adelstein and St. Martin's seemed primed for a collision. *"One day, Sister Sarto came to a board meeting very concerned, saying there was a bill in the state legislature that would require any hospital licensed in South Dakota to provide abortions. She said, 'Well, we're not going to do any abortions, law or no law,' and I supported her."*

Then, Harvey Fraser, a West Point grad who had also served in the Army Corps of Engineers and who was now president of the South Dakota School of Mines & Technology, as well as a board member at St. Johns, *said, "'Stan, what are you going to do if this law gets passed?' I told him, 'Well, I'll go to jail.' And he said, 'Why would you go to jail over this? You don't even agree with them!' And I told him: 'Harvey, I knew the rules and the values of the institution when I came here, and I'm going to stick by them. If men and women in positions of influence and power had been willing to stand by their values, regardless of the law, millions of people just like me would not have been taken to Nazi ovens.'"* Fortunately for Stan and the sisters, no such bill made it out of the legislature.[37]

The relationship, of course, had a lighter side. Every October 18 (the feast day for St. Luke, the patron saint of doctors and medical care) the convent hosted a dinner. *"All the nuns always worried that they would serve me something that wasn't kosher. So I was pretty used to them coming up and asking small questions—'Mr. Adelstein, can you eat this?' 'Mr. Adelstein, can you eat that,' you know. But one night, they kept coming up and asking me if they had permission to do this or that, little things and small tasks like sweeping or clearing the table or whatever. I finally brought it up—you know, 'Why is everyone asking me permission for this stuff?'—and two of the younger sisters giggled. They pointed at a bulletin board on a nearby wall, and I walked over and saw a copy of the bylaws for the St. Martin's Corporation,"* which Stan had helped the nuns form. *"And it said that 'the prioress of St. Martin's shall be the president of the corporation, and in her absence the vice president will serve as president.' Because the prioress was gone that night, someone had penciled in 'since Mr. Adelstein is the vice president of the corporation and Mother Magdalene was out of town, tonight he is the prioress of St. Martin's Monastery.'"* As they laughed over rhubarb wine that night, neither party knew that within a few years, the friendship between a Jewish man named Adelstein and some Benedictine nuns would be a key component of a process that would change the fates of St. John's McNamara Hospital and Rapid City forever.

CHAPTER 11
TAKING OVER

Nineteen sixty-eight brought tumult to the United States. At the end of January, the Viet Cong launched the Tet Offensive, a massive, multipronged assault on South Vietnamese and American forces. Assassins cut down Martin Luther King Jr. and Robert F. Kennedy, Lyndon Johnson refused to run for reelection, and a raucous election year featured virulent anti–Vietnam War protests.[1] Riots erupted at the Democratic National Convention in Chicago. Richard Nixon campaigned on a "secret plan" for ending the war in Vietnam and by calling for "law and order" and drafting support from what he would later call a "silent majority" of middle-class, predominately white voters, who were fed up with social unrest and a perceived abandonment of traditional American values. Nixon would ride these messages all the way to the White House.[2]

For Stan, Bob, and Bertha Adelstein, all this unrest paled in comparison to the pain and personal strain they would feel when Morris Adelstein died at the end of 1968. Along with their mother, the Adelstein boys had to work through their grief while settling Morris's estate. Perhaps their most pressing challenge regarded their search for a new mechanism for corporate decision making—a problem made all the more pressing by the need to revitalize the family business.

The Northwestern Engineering Company had begun to falter several years before Morris's death, and conditions only worsened toward the end. As Stan confessed in the 1967 annual report, the year "[had] not been all that we desire, there are some things that are on the positive side and some things that are on the negative side," and several managers were deeply concerned about the future.³

With Morris gone, Stan blamed himself for Northwestern's failures. *"I wasn't doing a good job, and I realized that."* He called himself *"dictatorial in the sense that I decided stuff"* with too little input. The documentary record and the recollections of a few former employees paint a more balanced picture, which describes NWE as a company fighting to stabilize while innovating within the industry. Ed Kroll, for example, was a six-foot, three-inch tall project foreman who ran projects for NWE for several years in the 1950s and 1960s. Described by his stepson, David Super, as the "quintessential strong silent type," Kroll had worked for a couple of regional construction outfits and slowly worked his way up the chain of command. Over the years, David Super and his sister Maryann developed a sense for their stepfather's take on Northwestern. Each also spent a summer working for NWE just after college in the early 1960s.⁴

NWE was a good job to have, David Super said, because the company had a reputation as one that "stabilized opportunities" for its employees. Northwestern had bigger, longer-term projects. Families like the Krolls often lived in trailers on remote job sites. David and Maryann both remembered the hot summers they spent living outside Glendive, Montana, where their stepfather was managing a project while their mother watched the kids and occasionally helped cook for the field crews.⁵ Although far from ideal, this situation kept the family together—a luxury that smaller operations could rarely afford their employees.

Northwestern, moreover, kept more experienced workers on staff through seasonal ebbs and flows. Ed Kroll spent winters working part-time as a mechanic in the maintenance shop in Rapid City. NWE also kept its "protocols and policies more established," meaning that the company was less likely to fire people for small mistakes or treat its workers as dispensable labor. Northwestern—at least as far as David Super could tell—was known as "a relatively humane operator in a very inhumane business."⁶

This reputation also extended to the hiring of women and minorities. Maryann had graduated from nursing school in 1963 when Kroll recruited her for a monthlong job driving the pilot car up and down Boulder Canyon just outside the city of Sturgis in the central Black Hills. She enjoyed her time with NWE, but recalled that, in those days, construction companies simply were not used to making accommodations for women. On her first day, she realized that nobody had built bathroom breaks into her schedule. Expected to work from seven o'clock every morning until about six in the evening, she drove for five straight hours before she got a break on her first day. That night at dinner, she explained the problem to Ed, who, Maryann remembered, had not "thought of it because I was a woman." He fixed the issue the next day.[7]

David Super also worked with women at NWE but recalled how most were given secretarial or administrative jobs in the office, a common practice in the industry during this era. But several women, he recalled, donned a "hard hat and dirty pants" and marched out into the field "in the middle of everybody." Adelstein remembered NWE as one of the region's first companies to hire women drivers. *"People said it was just too heavy of a job for women. I told them 'power brakes, power shifts, and power steering—the only thing they can't do is change one of those huge tires, and the kind of men we have in our company would be more than happy to help them with it!'"* Stan recalled one woman, Jill LaCroix, the niece of a good friend, who was an incredibly skilled truck driver. *"She could whip around any curve while laying two inches of asphalt and going uphill without a machine grader,"* and for that *"was one of Northwestern's highest-paid drivers."* Still, Maryann remembered, most women seemed to work in less physical "clerical positions" or in the scale house where the company weighed quarry trucks.[8]

Stan was given increasing corporate responsibility just as the African American civil rights movement stirred the nation. In the summer of 1963, he sent a memorandum barring hiring discrimination to every field supervisor. The timing of this message correlated closely with a historic moment in the African American civil rights movement: Martin Luther King Jr. delivered his famous "I Have a Dream" speech just twenty-eight days later in Washington, D.C. But in early August, as Stan wrote, there had already been a great deal of "national publicity" on civil rights—African Americans, of course, had been pushing for equality for decades—and he thought "it would be well for Northwestern to put itself firmly on record in this regard." He pointed out federal nondiscrimination regulations and reminded his staff about the fair-hiring posters on display at NWE project sites.[9]

Stan wanted to go further. He sent out a "Constructogram"—the name NWE gave its memos, which were attached to perforated slips so employees could respond directly to management—"to make it firmly understood that company policy is to employ any American who is capable of doing the work required." Northwestern valued diversity and would not deny anyone a job based on "race, creed, or national origin," Adelstein wrote. "Our most successful years at Northwestern," he reminded his staff, "were those in which activities were directed by a President, who was Jewish, an Executive Vice President, who was Catholic, and a Vice President who was Protestant."[10]

Adelstein then instructed each of his field supervisors to give a short report explaining whether they had ever witnessed discrimination in their division. Every single manager wrote back denying any such behavior. E.D. Gaiser, for example, asserted that his team would "never judge a man by his color or religion but on performance only."[11] Another manager said that "we have always followed this policy. We have had Indians, Mexicans, and Negros [sic] working for us" and had never witnessed a problem.[12] Another was even more vocal: "we can be proud of our stance on this 'touchy' problem which today is becoming a national crisis."[13]

Northwestern's supervisors, of course, may not have been entirely candid. Or perhaps the kinds of discrimination Stan banished were invisible. The company certainly had Native American and African American employees, and Northwestern was generally "enlightened for those days," as David Super recalled. But it was far from perfect. Many employees harbored the racial assumptions of their time, including Ed Kroll. "My dad," Super explained, "could be as old-fashioned and racist, or predisposed, as anybody," and these expressions were usually subtle. He remembered that Kroll came home one day talking about an African American man on one of his crews. Midway through his story, Kroll stopped to clarify that the man was a good worker, his interruption intimating that he had expected otherwise. Even at a company as relatively forward thinking as Northwestern, if a position opened for which a handful of minorities applied, Super surmised, "the chance of them getting picked for the job" over a white candidate, especially in tough times, "would be unlikely."[14]

Stan's insistence on a policy of nondiscrimination in 1963 reflected a growing but still somewhat hesitant sense of his own authority as executive vice president. When he first returned to Northwestern in 1957, some employees— and arguably even Stan himself—were uncomfortable with his status as the "boss's son." In the spring of 1958, for example, a fellow employee approached Stan and complained about some warehouse workers who were performing poorly and refusing to take suggestions. The man told Stan "he knew my position" and understood that Stan would be the boss one day. The workers asked Stan to resolve the problem or take it directly to Morris. Stan wrote his father but was not asking for a solution. He wanted to make clear his respect for the chain of command and his discomfort with being perceived as having extra authority. He said he told the man that he would not go over anyone's head, and to take the matter up with John Materi.[15]

A couple of months later, however, Stan broke his own rule. When a colleague told him about a new machine that separated iron oxide particles, which could help Hills Materials get into the North Dakota concrete markets, Adelstein took the idea to Materi. When Materi rebuffed him, Stan wrote his father, "This is the first time I have gone over John's head to talk to you directly." He solicited his father's approval, self-consciously closing the letter by asking if he was being unrealistic and if he was off-base in superseding Materi's authority. Stan even added a revealing postscript, which underscored his own anxieties about his unique position within NWE: it "would be murder to me," he wrote, "if it got out that I had written [you] such a letter."[16]

As time went on, Stan grew more confident, and when Materi's death made him executive vice president, he struggled to fill his mentor's shoes and establish an authoritative presence. When he became president, he ran Northwestern with strong faith in his team and a penchant for quantitative analysis. Stan's correspondence about strategic business decisions, personnel matters, and many other issues offers glimmers of his style.

Safety had long been a priority at Northwestern. As Stan's brother Bob—who oversaw the company's safety program—wrote, "first because it save[d] lives, and, secondly, because it [was] economically practical."[17] Accidents had injured and even killed people, and Morris Adelstein had instituted a safety awards program in the early 1960s offering prizes of up to $300 for supervisors whose divisions had the lowest accident rates.[18] The company was also especially cautious when it came to flying. A charter plane crash had killed Martis Levine—an employee and one of Stan's cousins—in the early 1950s. On his forty-fifth birthday, Levine wanted to get home from a business trip and pushed the company's pilot to fly in bad weather. The plane went down, killing everyone on board.[19] By 1959, air travel had become so routine that the company acquired its own plane and pilot, adding a second aircraft a few years later.[20]

CHAPTER 11

Given the broad geographic expanse of NWE's projects, Adelstein quickly came to see the company airplane as a vital tool for connecting him to projects and the people making decisions on-the-ground, all while getting up to speed with operations in the Rapid City headquarters. *"When John died, I realized that I had the responsibility to make the Rapid City office's projects successful. I also realized that many problems that arose in the field were beyond my expertise, but I had faith in our outstanding field supervisors. If we could find a way for me to get to the job site and work face-to-face with subcontractors, we could make this work. That's where the plane came in. Northwestern bought a Beechcraft Travel Air"*—a small, twin-prop rig with seats for a pilot and four passengers—*"and contracted a pilot and maintenance through Snedigar Flying Services, since Jerry Snedigar was L.A. Pier's son-in-law. Our pilot was a former air force colonel named Bob Higgins, and we used him so much that we just put him on NWE's payroll and made him our company pilot. The plane was so handy that we later bought a Beechcraft Model 18, a larger, twin-tail passenger plane converted from the military C-45s used during World War II. It could seat five passengers comfortably, and even had space where I could sleep."*

Flying proved critical to Stan's ability to *"be two places at once. Often, I would load up a couple of political allies—maybe two or three fellow Young Republicans or something, and in those days you could even give congressmen and their staffs rides"* (a practice restricted by modern ethics rules) *"and I could work on something related to a project, like a project letting, drop it off for submission, hit a job site for meetings, do our political work, and still be back in Rapid City all in one day."* The plane, for example, allowed Stan to fly up and monitor a challenging project building what was known as the "Rim Rock Highway" in Billings, Montana. NWE had to destroy a 60-foot, solid rock wall in order to expand a one-lane road to four lanes. Deeply experienced in removing limestone (the company's quarry near Rapid City was filled with it), NWE crafted what amounted to a massive rubber blanket assembled from old tires, which would catch any loose rock and soften its impact. As a safety precaution, the company housed all of the residents in homes downhill from the job site at a nearby hotel. All except one: *"A local circuit court judge,"* Stan remembered, *"demanded that we purchase his house at some exorbitant price after one piece of rock—the only one that got away—ended up in his yard. I flew up to meet with him at his home, and he was furious. Seeing red, he went into the house and came out with a revolver, shouting as Bob Higgins and I took off for the car, jumped in, and sped away. I swear a few bullets flew over our heads on the way out.*

Later on, I returned to Billings for a court appearance against an injunction the judge brought against us. Before leaving, I called the local sheriff to ask if he could ensure our safety while we were in town. When he told us that could be challenging, since he was an officer of the court and couldn't do much to stop the judge, well, let's just say we ended up paying the judge the price he demanded, then reselling his home after the project was done."

Stan had what he called a *"Mediterranean personality"* in life and business, by which he meant that he could be *"very nice to friends, but very hard on enemies."* This was apparent when Stan coupled his access to a plane with his harder edge in an effort to secure a joint venture on a big paving job in South Dakota. *"I was in Denver, and there was this big job in South Dakota—maybe Chamberlain,"* Stan started. *"And the top guy for another company, named Harold Stillman, was a big, tall guy, a tough son-of-a-bitch. And they had locked into some advantage for this job, and we had one too, and so it was going to be us versus them at the bidding table. I wanted to do a joint venture, but Harold didn't want to. So anyway, the day of the letting comes, and Stillman has to be in Pierre. So I offered to give him a ride on my plane, and he says 'Sure, thanks, Stan.' So we're flying along, and I ask again why he won't do the project as a joint venture with Northwestern. And he told me 'I think you're a little greedy.' The flight starts to feel a little long, so he asks Bob, the pilot, where we are. Bob points out the window and says, 'That's Lincoln, Nebraska, down there.' Stillman says 'Lincoln? I thought we were going to Pierre.' That's when I cut in and told him that we had a full tank of gas and instructed Bob to fly due east until we needed to fill up. That, I pointed out, would be about Cincinnati. Then Harold finally gets it. He says, 'So I won't get there in time for the bid opening, will I?' and I say, 'No.' He says, 'Fine. It's a deal,' and that's how we got the Chamberlain job."*

Business was generally less dramatic. When it came to air travel and efforts to cut costs and get NWE back on track, Stan personally determined the cost effectiveness—both in terms of travel expenses and lost work hours—to drive or fly. He used these calculations to develop a set of detailed guidelines that his supervisors were to follow when they made decisions about the use of the company plane. Seven NWE executives could use the aircraft at their discretion, but nobody could overrule Higgins, who Stan empowered to ground the plane. Higgins would "make his decision without regard to the urgency of the trip and shall not be subject to criticism from anyone," Stan wrote his supervisors in 1969.[21]

No amount of business was worth risking employees' lives. When Stan became president, NWE transitioned to a system that further underscored

Stan's faith in numbers. The new safety program generated a decimal-based "experience modifier"—a rating that could measure the amount of risk the company carried—before offering strategies to continue reducing risk. In July 1969, Robert Adelstein proudly told an official in New Mexico that in the three years since Stan implemented the system, NWE had decreased its modifier from 1.19 to .073. "As you can readily see," he bragged, "our on-going [safety] program has been effective."[22]

The extent of Stan's maturation became clear when Northwestern faced a challenge from organized labor in 1965. Eleven years earlier, employees at Hills Materials had voted to join Local No. 326 of the International Union of Operating Engineers. From that point forward, the company and the union developed contracts, often with some fierce negotiation, but usually with a mutually agreeable result. Occasionally, however, tensions flared. When union leaders asked for things like a forty-hour workweek, paid federal holidays, and eight-hour shifts, Morris Adelstein and his team offered little resistance. But when Local 326 wanted to amend the terms of employees' paid vacation, institute a "last-hired, first-fired" rule for layoffs (and its reciprocal for rehiring), and renegotiate shift start times, Northwestern refused. The company considered this contract "very distasteful," primarily because it meddled in managerial decisions like scheduling and authorizing vacation time, and because the "last-hired, first-fired" clause would privilege employees based on time with the company rather than work ethic or performance.[23]

Stan, like his father, opposed collective bargaining, once calling himself *"a violently anti-union operator"* before clarifying that *"it isn't because I don't want to pay people well."* For him, the decision hinged, as it had for his father, on the question of seniority. *"I'm absolutely opposed to basing pay or benefits off seniority alone, because it doesn't allow for any differential based on skill or work ethic,"* he said. *"I wanted to be able to pay differently and compensate for skill and accomplishment,"* rather than calendar pages.

On July 16, 1965, Northwestern invited three representatives from Rapid City–area unions, including the Operating Engineers, to its office. Up to that point, negotiations had gone relatively smoothly, and Northwestern and the unions had come to a tentative contract agreement early in the summer of 1965. The unions, however, had "two bones of contention"—they wanted to raise the hourly wages for two classes of workers, based only on seniority.[24]

Northwestern refused. Just hours before the meeting, Stan and his team had received reports of vandalism on two project sites. In one case, after hours, someone "turned a D8 Cat loose at Ruby, Nebraska," where the tractor ultimately crashed into a ditch. Adelstein was incensed at the damage to NWE property. More important, he said, he was furious that the tactic could have injured someone. He believed the vandals intended to intimidate Northwestern into raising its wages. "I'd be less than honest," Stan said, if he told the union representatives "that never have either my father or myself taken any position which was anti-union." But, he continued furiously, this went far beyond the company's ideological stance on organized labor. "In 40 years of business we have never experienced sabotage on our equipment," he said, and Northwestern was not about to allow something like this to go unnoticed.[25]

The union representatives apologized and denied any knowledge of the incidents. "We certainly appreciate and know that you're angry and you have justifiable cause, no doubt to be angry," said Bud Muhiville, a representative of the Operating Engineers. But he pointed out that there was no evidence that one of their people was involved, or that the incidents were anything more than coincidence. He appealed to Stan, asking him to remember the many years they had worked together and whether he had ever broken his word.[26]

Stan agreed that "to the best of [his] knowledge," Muhiville had always been honest with him. Yet Stan refused to budge. The sabotage was no accident, but it was a line in the sand. Stan forced the negotiations to impasse—an official stall that would bring the National Labor Relations Board (NLRB) and the Federal Mediation Service into the conversation. Neither the extra hassle nor the cost nor the risk of losing that came with appealing a case before the NLRB bothered Stan. He had decided to stand on principle. Northwestern had come to what it considered a fair agreement, and board members did not intend to change their minds. And whether the incidents in Nebraska were unrelated to the negotiations, the company would not give in to intimidation.

"Gentlemen," Stan said, "I don't know how clear we can make it. We will not move from the contract. If anyone thinks this company can be frightened into changing its position, they are dead wrong." NWE would "pay five times" more "to guard our equipment" from further sabotage "before we'll accept one penny of change from our contract."[27]

CHAPTER 11

The parties eventually resolved their differences, as they would each year until employees at Hills Materials voted to dissolve the union in the early 1970s. *"The union had actually called a strike the year before the final vote to dissolve. When nothing was resolved within twelve months, the law allowed me to call a vote. I did, and our workers decided against the union, but it was contentious. The night before one of the crucial votes, somebody shot out the living room window of my attorney, Ron Banks, at eleven o'clock. Thirty minutes later, the same thing happened at my house. We involved the police, and somehow they figured out who did it—the shooter had left a footprint and they even determined the serial number of the shotgun that was used, but we knew we could never get anyone to testify as a witness, so we dropped it. It was just an effort to scare us and threaten us. But we knew the vote was basically in our pocket because a few weeks earlier, an altercation at a Hills Materials bowling competition ended with someone from the union threatening a woman employee. That really locked it up, and the union went down in something like an 80–20 vote."* Weathering incidents like this one in the summer of 1965 pushed Stan along on his journey from an uneasy, middle manager with family connections to a firm and seasoned executive.

Leadership, however, was about more than becoming a hard negotiator. It was also about repairing frayed relationships and finding creative solutions to challenging problems. An example of the former came when Stan and Chuck Lien—the son of Morris's old rival Pete Lien—found a way to move beyond their fathers' acrimony, and eventually became dear friends.

For years, Stan and Chuck had clung to their fathers' feuds. Stan later admitted in a letter that "as a consequence . . . there were things that I did in business which I see so clearly now were totally inappropriate." Their anger was so deep that Stan had been surprised to see a "substantial donation" from the Liens to one of Morris's favorite charities in the many condolences that poured in after his father's death. When Pete Lien unexpectedly died only a few months later, in April 1969, Stan reciprocated, sending money on his family's behalf to a charity in the Liens' name.[28]

This pair of gestures opened the doors through which Stan and Chuck Lien buried their families' animosity. *"Chuck Lien stopped by my office on a rainy May day to discuss the ending of the feud. We each told each other what we had independently assumed was the cause of the fight back in 1935. We each had a similar ending to the story but a different narrative about its cause. Loving our fathers but also understanding their flaws, we pretty well agreed on what had probably happened, and we agreed not to divulge it. Neither of us has."* Gone were the days when the Lien name carried the tinge of bigotry once associated with the elder Lien's occasional flashes of anti-Semitism. Within a few short years, Stan and Chuck were sharing articles about Israeli issues. In 1980, when Chuck toured the Middle East, Stan arranged for his "non-Jewish friend of intelligence and perception" to stay with some friends in Israel, and, according to Stan, the pair *"were intimate friends for the rest of our lives."*[29]

Stan also had penchant for creative problem solving that occasionally verged upon genius. Late in the 1960s, Northwestern had outbid a competitor on a highway project near Ogden, Utah. *"The largest contractor in the area was Gibbons & Reed,"* Stan recalled, *"and they were a really great, well-established company. In fact, the top guy, Pat Gibbons, was a friend of my dad's. And we beat them pretty badly in the bidding because we found a farm that had some sand and gravel, so we knew we could save big by digging it up and screening it out to make construction materials."* Shortly after the bid was over, Gibbons invited Stan to an event at a country club in Salt Lake City. There, Stan remembered, Pat Gibbons—not knowing about NWE's plans, since they had been secret during the bidding process—*"asked if Gibbons & Reed could sell us the aggregate we'd need for the project. I told him we already had a plan to make our own, and told him that's how we beat them on the bid. But I asked for his offer anyway, and when he told me, it was obvious that we wouldn't make any profit on the job if we bought from them, so I said no, and was feeling pretty smart about the way we had planned this project."*

"Well," Adelstein continued, *"as clever as I was, Pat was clever, too. After I turned him down, he said, 'Well, how are you going to get an excavation permit?' Not understanding his meaning, I told him we'd go to the county office and get a permit, just like everyone else. Well, he had other plans. Gibbons told me, 'No you won't. There are five county commissioners, and I own four of them,' making it clear that he would make sure to block our permit unless we bought aggregate from them. I remember saying, 'Well, that's not a very gracious way to handle this,' and I got up and walked out."*

NWE was stuck. Not knowing about the excavation permit, Stan's estimators, Al Marvin and Don Hutchings, had locked in a low bid on a project that would either cost the company in expensive materials costs or, if it wanted to go toe-to-toe with Gibbons, bribes paid to county commissioners. Adelstein refused the second option on principle, and put his brain to work. The next morning, he had a plan.

"In the morning, I headed down to Zion National Bank where we opened an account for the project, and I asked the banker if they had a Boys Club in Ogden. He said no. So I asked if the Church of Latter Day Saints had any youth programs, and he said nothing really came to mind. Then I asked if they had Boy Scouts, and his face lit up. It turned out that Ogden had one of the largest Boy Scout area councils in the whole country, and that one of their trust officers was the activity director or held some other position with the Boy Scouts. I asked if I could meet him. The guy comes down, and we start chatting. I said to him, 'Where do you teach the boys to swim?' and he says, 'Well, there, we have a problem. It's actually quite a ways up into the mountains, and we have to rent buses and all of this.' By now, the guy realizes I'm a businessman, and I can tell he's got buses in his eyes—he thinks I'm going to donate some buses. I had something else in mind. I said to him, 'So you've got all these kids in Boy Scouts, and each of them has two parents who are voters. What if you had a free, 10-acre lake right here in Ogden, with an acre-and-half of white, sandy beach that the kids could use for swimming and activities?' And he said, 'Of course the county would love that, but how would I build it?' That's when I told him: 'You don't have to. We'll build it for you.'"

In the end, Northwestern never got the excavation permit it needed to pull aggregate from the farm near Ogden. But the Boy Scouts easily won a permit, and there were tons of sand and gravel left over from the digging of that lake. Stan made sure that NWE got it, and the company used the aggregate from the lake to complete its highway project. Everyone was happy: *"we finished our job and made a good profit,"* Stan remembered, and in return, Ogden's Boy Scouts got a new water park—called the Morris E. Adelstein Aquatic Camp—which municipal leaders dedicated at an event on October 3, 1970.[30]

WHO'S MANAGING WHO?

Unfortunately for NWE, success stories like the aquatic center were an outlier in the years surrounding Morris's death. By 1967—a year before his passing—Northwestern suffered from deeply entrenched financial problems. Stan believed that the "continuation of [the government's] arbitrary inflationary controls and increased competition" ensured that the company's challenges were not going away.[31] They were compounded by an increasingly tense dynamic that took shape within NWE's executive strata. Stan possessed a superior intellect and robust sense of initiative, but despite his impressive ability to crunch numbers, evaluate problems, and make snap decisions, he could also be impulsive and impatient, especially when it came to his working relationship with his brother, Bob. Something had to be done to counteract both the financial ills and interpersonal trials that filled the void created by Morris's absence.

NWE underwent an executive shakeup in 1968. Although she had little involvement in the company's day-to-day operations, Bertha Adelstein became executive vice president, Gaiser was named vice president, and Robert became corporate secretary.[32] Stan, Bob, and Bertha each owned shares of NWE stock, so even though Stan was president, he could not make major decisions without their approval. This rarely, if ever, posed a problem with Bertha. Bob, on the other hand, was an entirely different story. He and Stan were in the throes of a long, personal feud, and the company became their battleground.[33]

According to Bob, this conflict had its roots in their genetics and their upbringing. Stan was Stan, and Bob had a form of dyslexia that caused his eyes and his mind to switch numbers and letters around. Although he had a knack for working with his hands and understanding machines—his constant tinkering was a lifelong hobby—he struggled with mathematics and grammar. Morris Adelstein had little patience for Bob. As a result, Stan became the "favored son," in part because he was more articulate than his brother. Bob was very close to his mother but felt that Stan and Morris regarded him as someone who needed to "go play in the corner and don't bother us." This pattern continued when the brothers worked for NWE. Morris regularly forced Bob to rewrite letters and estimates to meet his standards.[34]

After Morris died, Stan sought to fill his shoes. He was the corporate president, which Bob approved, but the two owned equal shares of stock. As a result, they fought constantly, and, in Bob's words, "there were things that Stan wanted to do that I was not in favor of because I thought they would be disastrous." Sometimes, these battles were over strategy. Other times, the feud centered on small things, like the meeting minutes that Bob would write up as corporate secretary, where he detailed what he saw as poor decisions or mistakes by his older brother. Ultimately, Stan made Bob feel as though he was simply "in the way."[35]

Stan gave a similar explanation in a letter to his sons. "For one reason or another," the note began, "your Uncle Bob and I were put in a competition with one another when we were really quite young. The key was the success that we had—or the failure we reflected—in external achievement." Stan suggested that he "had been taught from small boyhood" that the scope of his business achievements "would be the measure of my success or failure" in life. As such, he fought ruthlessly to earn his father's approval, and later derived satisfaction from the notion of controlling Northwestern. It took many years, Stan wrote, before he realized that the illusion of fraternal superiority was as much a ghost as the father he had still been struggling to impress.[36]

Time would bring wisdom and healing, but the friction between the Adelstein brothers was abrasive and painful in the late 1960s. The board managed to cut through the tension and agree on a few short-term steps that would get Northwestern back on track. The board would increase the company's volume and recruit younger workers to keep labor costs low. The company would reaffirm its commitment to the acquisition, maintenance, and repair of corporate iron. In 1969, Northwestern also "institute[d] a profit-sharing program" as an incentive and a "technique for sharing the rewards of good operation" with the staff.[37]

The board even took a step unprecedented in company history, but characteristic of the space age the world had only recently entered: Northwestern bought its first computer, a system that could, as Stan marveled, provide "accurate job costs and comparisons, on a weekly basis." Stan hoped the new technology would help prevent the cost overruns that had for so long plagued the company.[38] These tactics would keep the corporation alive, but they offered only temporary relief. Northwestern needed a long-term strategy, and Stan needed help developing this vision.

Stan found the mentoring and peer support he was looking for in the Young Presidents' Organization (YPO). Founded in New York City in 1950, YPO was a national organization composed of successful young chief executives. *"There were membership requirements,"* Stan recalled, *"like the company had to have an annual volume of at least $1 million and at least sixty employees, and you had to be under forty."* YPO had been created to give young leaders a forum to share their experiences, learn from business leaders, and gain perspective that would help them become better managers.[39] Stan joined the organization's Rocky Mountain Chapter in 1967, and over the next fourteen years participated in conferences and seminars across the world, where he gleaned new ideas on a wide range of topics.[40]

"I joined YPO with some difficulty. A relative of mine was Eppie Lederer, who the world knew as the advice columnist 'Ann Landers,' and she used to babysit us in Sioux City, where she grew up. Eppie gave the annual speech sponsored by the Jaycees in Rapid City one year. After her speech, she came over to our house to visit with Ita and me, then told us about YPO and how her husband was a founding member. I remember she said, 'I've got to get Morris to make you president so you can join!' I was sponsored by an AJC fellow from Chicago, and the way YPO worked was that each chapter could either accept or reject a nominee. The group often discussed very confidential business information, so all these steps were put in place to ensure that the group could trust you. And I had to be interviewed by the chapter president. He showed me photographs of all of the Denver chapter members and asked me if I knew any of them. I said, 'Yes,' and named those with whom Northwestern did business through our Denver office. I had missed his point—when he asked if I 'knew' any of them, he was asking if I socialized with them, not just did business. I later realized my error, but by then had been blackballed. It was clear to me that the chapter didn't have any Jewish members and didn't want any. I told Eppie about this, as well as the president of the Boise Cascade Company, who I knew through the Young Republicans. They made a real stink and I became the first Jewish member of my YPO chapter."

Once Adelstein was a member of YPO, he focused on the organization's national activities rather than those of the Denver chapter. YPO events took Stan to Japan, where he visited the offices and factories of Noritake Company, a global producer of fine porcelain, and the car manufacturer Toyota. He marveled at the difference between Japanese and American work cultures, jotting notes about the absence of women in Japanese production lines or how impressed he was with corporate cultures that emphasized "striving to create good human relationships" rather than "simply offering products and technology" to customers.[41]

On that journey, Stan also visited the memorial at Hiroshima, where he reflected on the destructive power of the atomic bomb and the morality of its use in 1945.[42] He had always understood and agreed that the United States had used the weapon to end the war without carrying out a violent and protracted invasion of Japan, which, Stan believed, *"would have meant a horrendous loss of American lives."* But visiting Japan in person shifted his perspective. *"After visiting the museum at 'Ground Zero,'"* he said, *"and seeing the horrible pictures of permanently scarred Japanese citizens that had been taken immediately after the bomb was dropped, I realized that in the decisions of human beings, there is no 'absolute' truth. What was 'absolutely' correct from my American perspective was equally incorrect for those who had been so terribly injured. From that day forward, I never believed there was an absolute, unfailing truth. Instead, 'truth' depended on the place you were standing and where you were looking."*

In the spring of 1978, he went to Sydney, Australia, for a five-day workshop. Some of the panels he attended focused on politics, foreign policy, and the plight of developing countries, as well as how to maintain focus at middle-age. Stan was so impressed by John D. Stoessinger—a Harvard classmate of Henry Kissinger, Nixon's secretary of state, and Zbigniew Brzezinski, Jimmy Carter's national security adviser—that Stan invited Stoessinger to Rapid City, where he gave a lecture at the School of Mines later that year.[43]

Stan was also deeply interested in the YPO's business sessions. In 1974, he had convened a small seminar in Chicago, where eighteen members met to discuss strategies for "Managing Your Business in the 1970s."[44] This interest carried on, and four years later in Sydney, Stan went to talks entitled the "Dollar's Role in the International Economy," "Who's Managing Who?" and "Preserving Purchasing Power in an Inflationary Economy."[45] Seminars like these deeply influenced his thoughts and the decision-making process he used to reshape Northwestern after his father's death.

Of all the ways that Stan sought advice and training after Morris passed on, none was more important than his decision to expand the board of directors and give the board veto power over his own instincts. In 1968, Stan had attended a Rocky Mountain Chapter meeting in Aspen, Colorado. There, he met a business consultant, Dr. Leon Danko, a professor at John Carroll University in Ohio who had given a strong presentation. Danko agreed to come to Rapid City—for the sizable fee of $1,500 per day—and evaluate Northwestern. After a short meeting in South Dakota, Danko recommended expanding the NWE board to include a group of outsiders who could offset Stan's personality quirks, navigate the personal animosities between Stan and Bob, focus on solving company-wide problems, and help formulate big-picture strategies.[46] *"Danko said that our board members need not have stock interest in the company,"* Stan said, *"but that they needed to be my 'worthy adversaries' so they could give me criticisms and push me to make the best decisions for the company."*

Stan embraced Danko's suggestion and set about finding such a group. In talking to potential board members he offered two arguments: one, solving NWE's problems *"was going to be interesting,"* and two, *"I was willing to pay them a generous board fee."* At Danko's urging, Stan also gave the board an absolute veto power. *"All major ideas had to go to them first, and I agreed not to do anything they strongly disliked, at least not without a chance to revise and reexamine it."* As Bob put it, the board "set limits on" Stan and occasionally prevented him from venturing off into some "wild-haired schemes."[47]

By 1969, the board had been selected and seated. It included the Adelstein brothers and four other men. Allen Kris was a young Jewish banker from Denver who had a sharp mind and an eye for financials. Doug Hawkins was a mobile home manufacturer from Texas, while Henry Moeller was a South Dakotan who had graduated from the U.S. Naval Academy before returning to eastern South Dakota to run an alfalfa drying operation.[48] He and Stan *"had both been appointed by Archie Gubbrud to the South Dakota's Industrial Development Expansion Agency (IDEA)"* in the early 1960s.

Northwestern's final board member was perhaps its most influential. Roland Rautenstraus had grown up in Nebraska and Kansas, then served in the U.S. Navy before moving to Colorado, where he was an engineering professor in Boulder. There, he taught Stan's and Bob's survey courses. "Charismatic and eloquent," with "a most enchanting and captivating presence," Rautenstraus later became president of the University of Colorado Boulder before retiring from that position at age fifty-five.[49] He went on to write six books and lead a successful consulting firm, and, as Stan remembered, *"Roland became very famous in the engineering world."*[50]

Rautenstraus was an invaluable asset. He studied NWE and its history, identified weaknesses, and pushed the Adelstein brothers to come to terms with each other. Rautenstraus took it upon himself to serve as a buffer between them. "He had a way of talking to me one way, and would talk to Bob a different way," Stan told Rautenstraus's biographer, and out of respect and gratitude for these efforts, Stan would later create a scholarship fund in Rautenstraus's name at UC Boulder.[51] With his help, Stan and Bob slowly learned to work amicably and focus on salvaging Northwestern.

Together, the board members came to a stark decision: NWE had overextended itself with its long-running "bid big" strategy and needed to downsize. They agreed with Stan on a phased retreat that would keep the company focused on its strengths, but limit projects to a smaller, more manageable and cost-effective scope.[52]

First, the company had to finish work that, in Stan's view, *"should never have been bid and had been badly managed."* This task would take several years. *"It's hard for me to describe just how terrible the situation was at NWE,"* Stan remembered. *"I looked at the various projects we had running around the country. They were all operating well over the estimated costs—particularly in New Mexico, where we had a large interstate project under way in 1968."* Once again, the question of bribes came up. *"In those days, members of the highway commission and highway department employees often expected to be paid something extra under the table in order to do business with contractors like us. But that wasn't the way we did business, so I hadn't paid any of these bribes. For example, we needed asphalt for the highway's shoulders, but nobody down there would sell me any, even though I drove past three plants on my way between the airport and the jobsite. This was the consequence for failing to pay. So I had to move in a hot mix concrete plant, and the cost of just relocating it and setting it up cost something like $5.00 per ton. This was considerably more expensive for the few times that we needed it on the shoulders than the selling price of around $4.25, which it what it would have cost to just have some mix delivered straight to the job. This ended up pushing that project to a $1 million loss."*

The New Mexico job was indicative of *"the general situation,"* Stan said, referring to losses on various jobs. *"We also had a number of underpriced projects, and the company showed a small loss in 1968, then a slightly bigger loss in 1969. That took us into 1970, and that's where things really got bad."* In order to understand what happened that year, Stan said, one had to know a little about how the construction business worked.

"We determined profitability through a process called 'percentage completion,'" Adelstein continued, *"which basically meant that in the bid, contractors would add up different elements of a project—materials costs, labor, equipment, all of that—and chart out these different payments over various phases of a project. A lot of our work took several years to complete. So, if the estimator only added in profit on parts of the project that came later in the process, and if overhead costs were high for one reason or another, the contract might show a loss in the first year since the extra funds would not have been paid out yet, and these losses would be visible in the company's annual, certified audit. All of this, of course, had implications on everything from how healthy the business looked to creditors to how much tax we had to pay on a given year's revenue. So the standard practice was to understate the uncompleted profit. That way, we could demonstrate the accuracy of our bid over time, but also defer taxes until later on, towards the end of the project, when profits increased our cash flow."*

In good, or even normal, times, all of this made sense. Being short on cash at the start of a construction season was so commonplace, in fact, that each May NWE would negotiate a lending agreement with its bank, which essentially extended a line of credit that could cover work until the following May. As NWE struggled to wrap up the big, problem jobs in New Mexico, Colorado, and elsewhere in 1969, Stan and the board decided that as jobs were completed, NWE would move equipment to Denver, where Stan would organize a massive equipment auction to raise the capital the company would need to recoup its losses, repay its lenders, and position itself for the future.

While the company wound down its projects and prepared its equipment for auction, Stan saw a devastating scenario unfolding before him: if NWE could make it through to 1971, it had a chance to rebuild. If not, the company—his family's company—would fail.

Then, the plan hit a serious snag. *"Because we were so far under on so many projects, I was struggling to get our bank to extend our line of credit for the season stretching from May 1969 to May 1970. If we couldn't get the cash to get through that year, we would lose everything. So, I did something that was very out of line with my previous behavior: I deliberately exaggerated both the percentage of completion and the estimated profit on some of our projects. In other words, I cooked the books to secure enough credit for us to survive. It was a huge, terrible gamble that I never made before or since."*

Everything seemed fine through 1970, and by fall *"most of our highway construction outside South Dakota had been finished,"* Stan recalled. *"But the company was low on cash, and we were in danger of falling behind on some of our payments for the first time ever—we even started rationing payments from state highway departments as they came in."* Then, the unthinkable happened: a brutal winter kicked off 1971, stalling projects and threatening to push NWE beyond its already overstretched limits.

These were the most desperate days of Stan Adelstein's life. *"I vividly remember standing in my living room in Rapid City, facing the west wall of my house. As the disastrous numbers from these bad jobs trickled in week after week, I started to see only one way out: a couple of years earlier I had taken out a $2 million life insurance policy, and it since it had been in effect for the requisite two years, I knew that it would have paid out regardless of the reason for my death. So I stood there, seriously contemplating suicide, knowing that my family could pay off NWE's debts with that policy."*

The company's fate—and, potentially, Stan's—rested on the outcome of NWE's equipment auction. Northwestern had contacted the Forke Brothers auctioneers out of Omaha, Nebraska, to organize the sale. They had an excellent reputation—*"everyone knew their auctions were absolute; they often had great bargains for buyers, and they were very honest. Forke was known to actually end auctions in process if they suspected a seller was back-buying items in an attempt to inflate prices."* Buyers were also attracted to this sale because *"we had a reputation for taking good care of our iron."* Altogether, Stan and the board expected a good turnout. Plus, *"we knew we just needed two serious contenders to show up, so they could bid against one another and make for a strong sale."* Everything looked good, so Northwestern asked the Forke Brothers to set an auction date for the following April, and over the winter made plans to fill a 20-acre lot near Denver with heavy equipment.

Then, *"just two days before the auction date, a huge blizzard blew in,"* Adelstein recalled. *"I was stuck in Rapid City, and by the morning of the day before the auction, the authorities closed Stapleton Airport and issued a no-travel advisory for the highways."* Nervous that bad weather might spell the end for NWE, Stan called the auctioneers and asked if they should reschedule. *"They told me they were booked until June,"* and strongly recommended that the auction move forward despite the weather. *"As I hung up the phone, I really struggled with the decision. A three-month delay would force us into bankruptcy—or worse. And we had mapped out a strong future for NWE. We had plenty of resources, experience, and incredible personnel in Rapid City. I knew I couldn't let this take us out, so I called back and told Forke to go forward as planned."*

When the auction started the next day, Stan sat nervously next to his phone, waiting for updates. *"It turned out that I had forgotten one of the most obvious things about this sale: the resourcefulness of contractors. Everyone knew that the poor weather might limit turnout, which could in turn give them an advantage at the sale. Frankly, if I had been in their position instead of my own, I would have found a way to get there, too. And they did. One contractor flew to Laramie, Wyoming, where the weather was still good enough to land, jumped into a dump truck his company was using for a highway project, and drove to Denver for the auction. Another made it to Fort Collins and took a Caterpillar road grader."*

In the end, hundreds of bidders arrived, and the sale was a huge success. All day long Stan took calls as sale after sale rolled in. At the end of the auction, he tallied up the total: *"We had hoped for a sale of $2.5 million to $3 million, tops, all we needed to get back in the black. But the list in my hand showed that we had exceeded expectations on almost everything, and the total sale was over $4 million!"*

This auction saved NWE. It also allowed Stan and the board to pursue the company's new strategic plan: moving away from its bid-big, multistate strategy. Going forward, NWE would contain its work to South Dakota and the surrounding region. Stan and his leadership team would oversee this transition from NWE's office in Rapid City. By 1972, operations focused on the Hills Materials Company—which eventually operated "three quarries, four ready-mix concrete plants, two hot mix asphaltic concrete plants and an emulsified asphalt production company in South Dakota," as well as the Colorado-Wyoming Improvement Company, the NWE subsidiary that managed projects in its namesake states. The following year Northwestern transitioned away from heavy construction, except in western South Dakota, where the company continued to carry out local projects, including its own ventures into real estate development. The downsizing took time, but Northwestern steadily moved home: by 1978 the company was no longer building in Colorado, and over the 1980s would start to focus on becoming a holding company for Hills Materials, the Colorado-Wyoming Improvement Company, and a portfolio of real estate investment properties.[53]

PHOTOGRAPHY

Morris Adelstein at Bertha Martinsky's homestead in the Badlands near Interior, South Dakota (1920s).

Adelstein family photos (ca. 1938). Top row, from left: Stan and Bob Adelstein. Bottom row, from left: Morris and Bertha Adelstein.

(From left) Morris, Bertha, Stan, and Ita Adelstein at a Denver Town Club event at the lavish Crawford Hill Mansion (1953 or 1954).

Newlyweds Stan and Ita Adelstein pose at Temple Emanuel in Denver with maid of honor Marcia Korn (far left) and best man Bob Adelstein (far right) (December 19, 1952).

PHOTOGRAPHY

A tank crosses the Little Remagen Bridge as Lt. Colonel Joseph Gurfein and Lieutenant Stan Adelstein look on. Stan was part of the U.S. Army Corps of Engineers' "C" Company, which built the bridge outside Tacoma, Washington in 1956.

Stan with three-month-old Daniel Adelstein (February 1955).

Governor Archie Gubbrud (far right) speaks at the dedication of a road near Sturgis, South Dakota (early 1960s). A get-out-the-vote strategy devised by Stan (far left) helped Gubbrud win the 1960 gubernatorial election.

Twenty-two young couples, including Stan and Ita Adelstein, participated in the AJC's first Young Leadership Mission to Israel (March 1965).

PHOTOGRAPHY

Stan traveling with members of the AJC. (Summer 1965). Several participants in the Young Leadership Mission became national leaders of the AJC later in their careers.

Stan originally bought this 1934 Packard with a group of friends while he was a student at UC Boulder. Years later, he piled friends and family into the convertible and toured them around the Black Hills.

Stan would later describe this picture of him working midair from NWE's company plane around 1971 as "a typical day at the office." Over the years, this flying office enabled him to run NWE and stay involved in numerous state and national causes.

Morris Adelstein passed away on December 17, 1968, thrusting Stan into the president's chair at the Northwestern Engineering Company.

The logos for two Adelstein family businesses: the Northwestern Engineering Company and the Hills Materials Company. Flip your book upside down to see Stan's initials—SMA—hidden in the design.

Stan and Ita's three sons (from left) Jon, Dan, and Jim at Dan's West Point graduation (June 1977).

The Rapid City Flood of June 9, 1972 swept vehicles, appliances and debris downstream. The flood killed 238 people. Stan spent the night of the flood helping survivors at St. John's McNamara Hospital. Credit: *Rapid City Journal*.

Stan helped raise funds and support for the construction of a new, 28,000 square foot Rapid City Public Library. The building opened in October 1972—only five months after the flood. Credit: Rapid City Public Library.

With an eagle feather still dangling from his hair, Stan thanks a room of Lakota friends following his naming ceremony in 1984. Pete Catches (seated at right) gave Stan the name *Iyoyanpa u Wakan*, or "Sacred Dawn Arising."

PHOTOGRAPHY

Stan and Ita on a Friday night Shabbat in Israel (1977). The pair traveled to the Middle East many times as part of their service in the AJC and other Jewish advocacy organizations.

Stan and Chuck Lien, shown here at the annual Pete Lien & Sons Christmas Party (1987), became lifelong friends after settling the old rift between their fathers. Stan was one of the first people Chuck called after he received a terminal diagnosis in 2018.

Stan and his friend, long time South Dakota Governor Bill Janklow, tour the new interpretive center and walkway at Mount Rushmore National Memorial in 1998. Stan spent many years with the Mount Rushmore National Memorial Society, which raised funds for the renovation.

Stan with President Ronald Reagan in the Roosevelt Room of the White House (1988). As part of a delegation from the Republican Jewish Coalition, Stan visited the White House to thank the president for his support.

Three generations of service: (From left) Morris, Stan, and Dan Adelstein all served in the U.S. military.

PHOTOGRAPHY

Stan and his longtime business partner, Pat Tlustos, pose at an NWE job site outside Belle Fource, SD in 1986. The 1980s brought big successes and hard lessons.

Stan talks foreign policy with U.S. Senator Larry Pressler as the pair stroll through a Jewish market in Jerusalem (December 1988).

Given its high number of Jewish military families—and Stan's connections to military personnel—the Synagogue of the Hills met for years at Ellsworth Air Force Base. Here, Stan chats with a synagogue member during a Passover celebration in 1987.

PHOTOGRAPHY

Stan observes the Knesset Menorah during a trip to Israel in the early 2000s. Gifted to the State of Israel by the Parliament of the United Kingdom in 1956, the sculpture includes engravings that depict Jewish history.

Stan and his granddaughter, Shirley Adelstein, pose outside a home he built in Keystone in the early 2000s. From the living room and back deck, the house offers a view of Mount Rushmore.

Governor Mike Rounds presents Stan with the 2004 South Dakota Philanthropist of the Year Award. The pair remained close friends for years after Stan helped jumpstart Rounds' first gubernatorial run in 2002.

Scotland holds a special place in Stan and Lynda's hearts. Unseasonably cold, rainy weather (even for Scotland) forced the pair to buy matching hats as they toured Edinburgh in 2011.

Stan and Lynda pose beneath the makeshift *chuppah* they erected for their wedding in Norfolk, Nebraska in 2011. To keep the ceremony out of the South Dakota political spotlight, the pair were married at the home of Lynda's sister and brother-in-law, Beverly and Joe Ferguson.

In between his service as South Dakota governor and U.S. senator, Mike Rounds and his wife, Jean (left), accompanied Stan, Lynda (not pictured), and Dan Adelstein (right) to Israel in 2013. Here, the group poses before the historic Weizmann House in the city of Rehovot.

PHOTOGRAPHY

Taken as part of a photography show that focused on the hobbies of Black Hills residents, this shot of Stan captured his lifelong passion for horned instruments. It was featured at the Dahl Fine Arts Center in Rapid City. Credit: Chris Benson.

Stan carried a small horn as he and Lynda drove through the Scottish Highlands one year. The High Holidays loomed shortly after their trip, and he wanted to practice for the shofar. As Stan stepped out of the car, Lynda teased: "be careful—what if you blow that and a herd of Jews come running over the hill?"

This photograph captured Stan as he appeared many times between 2001 and 2012: standing to give an impassioned speech on the floor of the South Dakota State Legislature.

PHOTOGRAPHY

Stan and Lynda remained active in Rapid City's civic and philanthropic circles. They posed for a quick photograph at a scholarship dinner at the South Dakota School of Mines & Technology in 2017.

Clutching the shofar he picked up during his first trip to Israel in 1965, Stan posed with longtime friend Chaplain Herb Cleveland at the dedication of the statue "Dignity" in 2016. Credit: Katie LeClair.

CHAPTER 12
THE CONTINUAL STRUGGLE

Few people in 1960s and 1970s Rapid City were more tightly thread into community affairs than Stan Adelstein. Yet "survival in South Dakota," he explained in a pitch to the editor of the American Jewish Committee's (AJC) *Present Tense* magazine in 1978, "is not a function of defense as it has been for so many Jewish communities, but rather one of continually struggling to maintain your difference in sufferedness."[1] In other words, the primary challenge facing Jewish people in South Dakota was not an outward, malicious threat as it had been in Russia, Germany, and so many other places. Rather, Jewish South Dakotans constantly fought against the danger of becoming invisible and thus forgotten. If they failed to work for a sense of identity—to maintain a space and commitment to liturgy, rituals, and holidays—they would cease to exist as a separate Jewish community.

Through the 1970s, the Synagogue of the Hills struggled along. During peak attendance, which was heavily contingent on the number of Jewish people who happened to be stationed at Ellsworth at a given moment, more than 200 members met at the base chapel for the High Holidays. When the synagogue waxed, it was an eclectic group. "We probably have the only congregation in the United Sates," Stan marveled in 1978, "that has Sioux Indian children and a [Guatemalan] adopted child."[2] But the organization also waned. Only about thirty people showed up to regular services, which were held on the first and third Fridays of every month.[3]

The synagogue was "too small to have an ordained Rabbi," Stan explained, and relied upon the Union of American Hebrew Congregations

(UAHC) and supporters like Stan to secure people and artifacts for rituals.[4] This included everything from the set of *yads* (small silver bars used to keep one's place while reading from the Torah) and the woven scroll covers that the UAHC provided, to the visiting rabbis that the synagogue had to recruit from out of state for special services.[5]

Rituals like marriage, which had both religious and legal components, posed special problems. Questions about the extent of the lay leaders' ability to marry members of the Jewish congregation first arose in 1964. *"South Dakota law said that weddings could be conducted by anyone 'authorized by a church,'"* Stan remembered, *"but it wasn't exactly clear whether we at the synagogue counted or not."* When he and others inquired, the state attorney general's office released a report suggesting that "designated members of the Synagogue of the Hills [could] solemnize marriages." The congregation operated under that assumption for years, but the issue remained uncomfortably murky, prompting Stan to inquire again in 1977.[6]

Attorney General William "Bill" Janklow was a prominent Republican with a Jewish father and a bright political future who got to know Adelstein through party politics. *"Janklow had a Jewish father and two Jewish brothers, and a lot of people didn't know that,"* Stan said. *"Even though he didn't practice Judaism, Bill identified closely with his family's heritage, and if any stereotyping or anti-Semitism ever came up, Bill would look at them and say"*—with a famously acid tongue—*"'before you go any further, you better understand that I'm Jewiogen,'"* a combination of his father's heritage with that of his Norwegian mother's. Generally supportive when Stan called with issues pertaining to the small Jewish community in South Dakota, Janklow told Adelstein that when it came to lay leaders and marriage, the Synagogue of the Hills should draft bylaws that could distinguish it "from just a group of individuals practicing Judaism which," Janklow said, "probably would not constitute a church as recognized under the marriage statutes."[7]

Stan was the synagogue's on-again-off-again president and full-time supporter. He blew the shofar at important events and during the High Holidays.[8] Sometimes, he recalled, his pride offended the sacred horn. *"You blow the shofar three times, the first time for Rosh Hashanah. One year out at Ellsworth, this first one was awful. I was pretty proud, and I was getting carried away and I could hear the horn failing—the sound just came out terrible. So I said to it, 'I got the message. Don't ruin the service for everyone.'"* He reasoned with the ancient shofar: *"There aren't that many Jews here, you know,"* and closed his eyes, putting his full faith in the horn. On his next try the shofar produced a beautiful sound, *"and now, whenever the shofar is blown I close my eyes."*

Adelstein conducted *"probably sixty or seventy different weddings"* around the Black Hills over the years, *"and one in Sioux Falls,"* following Janklow's recommendations. Stan also spoke or blew the shofar at a handful of funerals. As with almost everything at the Synagogue of the Hills, Adelstein often had to improvise. *"I always relied on the 'rabbi's handbook' that the Union of American Hebrew Congregations put out,"* but sometimes it could only go so far.[9] *"The Jewish wedding ceremony is normally conducted under a 'chuppah,' a cover of cloth often held by four individuals who are friends of the couple. In one case, the wedding couple had met while they were in the National Forest, so the* chuppah *was a covering of pine boughs."* Once, Stan married *"a couple who had met in India while working for two separate Peace Corps—one each from the United States and Israel—which had originally been planned to be conducted by a mayor. They switched to me when they found out there was an eligible Jew in the area. The father of the groom was very religious, and he and I were both interested to see that the Reform ceremony I would conduct, which dated back to nineteenth-century Germany, was nearly identical to that used in his family. Being descendants of a group of Jews that had gone to India during the time of King Solomon, their traditions were ancient. The only real difference was that their ritual had a long preamble acknowledging the dominance of the husband in the relationship, to which the bride had to assent. We left that part out."*

Stan's role as lay leader led him to conduct many unique ceremonies. Sometimes *"the marriage service was conducted jointly with a minister, but even then there are no explicitly Christian references in the ceremony."* He also had no problem conducting interfaith marriages, *"even though most rabbis won't do it. In the Reform movement, they aren't prohibited, but aren't generally supported, either."* Stan, however, took any opportunity to introduce Jewish customs to his home state.

He also conducted many funerals, as was the case when Irene Leedom, Boyd Leedom's wife, passed away in Washington, D.C., in 1982. Her body was returned to South Dakota to be buried next to her husband's. *"She had asked that I conduct the funeral,"* Stan said, *"and since their family was an essential part of our lives from the early days in Kadoka, I really wanted to. But I couldn't do a Methodist funeral because there were things it required to be said that I don't believe in. When I told Al Scovel, who had come to see me about the matter, he said, 'If anyone would have known what you believed in, it would've been Aunt Irene!' I agreed and gave her a Jewish burial."*

When he was not busy with these events, Stan stayed in touch with leaders at national Jewish organizations, and when new Jewish service members arrived at Ellsworth, Stan fired off letters offering to show them around.[10] He and Ita fielded calls from the faithful as well as the curious. Once it was "a distressed widow of three days in Sundance, Wyoming, needing someone to discuss how Jews visualize life after death." Later, a Christian minister in Spearfish "wanted to know exactly what the breakdown was of the ten commandments as the Jews read them." Another time, a young Jewish couple arrived at the Adelstein's door "high on drugs but absolutely broke with no food, a baby, and two dogs."[11]

These encounters were at once exhausting and enriching. One morning, while Stan poured over reports in the NWE office on St. Joseph Street—the same lot as his parents' first home in Rapid City, which Stan had repurchased in 1961—his secretary interrupted him with a pair of very unusual visitors.[12] "Two young Lubavichers," or members of a Hasidic sect, had "arrived at the airport in Rapid City, rented a car and stopped at Jacobs Motor—because the name was Jewish—but were directed promptly to my office," Stan wrote. He invited them to dinner and afterward believed he and Ita had taught their new Orthodox friends a great deal about what it meant to be Jewish on the Northern Plains in the modern world.[13]

As his reputation as a knowledgeable and willing public speaker spread, Stan was regularly asked to speak to audiences of all kinds. He made up a handful of vivid, fictional stories that he thought could convey his version of Jewish values—and were often shaped by elements of his political ideology—that he delivered in church basements, at civic events, and wherever people asked him to share. One story he told often at the height of the Cold War married the plight of Jewish Europeans with his impatience when he heard his upper-crust friends and colleagues complaining about their taxes: *"Imagine I was a Jewish man living in Georgia—the Russian Georgia—and one day, there was a knock on my door. Two men in suits said, 'You know what, we've noticed that you're kind of a go-getter, the kind of person we'd like to have live in the United States. It would be very advantageous to you as a Jew in the Soviet Union. In America, you can go anyplace you'd like. You can read whatever you like, anything by any author. You can say anything you want, and you can't be arrested. As a Jew, you can worship, or not worship, as you wish. You can even own property. And we think you're a productive kind of guy, so you can have your own business, and it will be protected as a corporation. As a matter of fact, you can't* *be arrested for anything unless it's a publicly published law, and those are protected by due process and jury trials.' Well, I couldn't believe it. I asked, 'What's the catch?' And they said, 'The catch is, maybe, that it isn't free. You have to pay about $35,000 a year in income tax.' And I said, 'Well look around my place—I can't come up with that kind of money.' So the men left to talk to his superior. When the men came back, they said, 'Okay, we think you'd be a good enough citizen, and we're gonna make a deal. You can have all those freedoms, and you won't have to pay anything until you make at least $15,000 for yourself. Now, you might have to pay a lot more than $30,000 in taxes, but not until you're making over about $65,000.' And I carefully asked to be sure I could still have all the freedoms—to read, to travel, whatever. The man said those were guaranteed for the small price of income tax. So, looking around Georgia and seeing how limited I really was, I said, 'You've got a deal and I'll be there tomorrow.'"*

By the late 1970s, Myron Rivkin had stepped in as the president of the Synagogue of the Hills, as had other lay leaders like Larry Blass and Barry Schneider. The synagogue, however, still lacked regular attendance and, after a while, even failed to hold regular meetings. In August 1978, the group "had its first meeting in some time," and later that month held its first annual picnic.[14] Joan Levine, an administrator at the Center for Judaic Studies at University of Colorado Denver, reassured Stan in a friendly letter that fall. By her thinking, the picnic's success "indicate[d] the vitality and positive future that exists for the Rapid City Jewish community," even if its members did not get together every week.[15]

As synagogue attendance lagged, Stan expanded his involvement in national and global Jewish affairs. Threats of invasion and war had loomed over Israel since 1948. Many Jewish people saw Israel as their homeland and the state's creation a return thousands of years in the making. To regional Arabs, the Jewish state was an imposition. Sacred and historical sites of three major world religions—Judaism, Christianity, and Islam—dotted the Holy Land. This added fervor and intractability to an already tense geopolitical situation.

Until his death, Morris Adelstein ardently supported the UAHC and the United Jewish Appeal in their efforts to make the State of Israel a place of refuge for Jewish refugees forced to flee persecution in their own countries. So deep was his commitment that, when violence erupted in Israel in 1967, Morris—who was at the time still the majority holder of Northwestern stock—called Stan and told him to calculate how much they could raise for the Israeli war effort if they liquidated all of NWE's assets.[16] The Soviet Union was perennially antagonistic toward Israel, and in the years leading up to 1967 it armed and encouraged aggression by Egypt, Iraq, and the Palestinian Liberation Organization (PLO), which committed itself to expelling the Jewish state through violence. As tensions mounted, Israel braced itself for a long, hard-fought war.[17]

On the other side of the world, Stan Adelstein furiously ran the numbers. *"It was my father's company, and I thought he was right,"* he recalled. *"Jews all over the United States were doing that."* He calculated that if NWE finished out its existing contacts, stopped taking new work, paid its debts, and sold its equipment, the company could give around $6 million to Israel. This, of course, would wipe the company out. The elder Adelstein, however, was not worried. *"He told me: 'I'm an old man, and I'll get Social Security pretty soon. You're young and intelligent and can make it again, but Israel wouldn't have a second chance.'"*

Fortunately for Northwestern—not to mention the thousands of Jewish people and Arabs who would have perished in a protracted conflict—the fight ended as quickly as it began. Israel's preemptive strike was a resounding victory. It destroyed the Egyptian air force and captured strategic territories, including the Sinai, in less than three days. When Jordanian and Syrian forces launched a counterattack, Israel repelled them both, taking artillery damage but, as Stan remembered, *"also capturing the Golan Heights above Syria, all of Jerusalem and the area west of the Jordan River, including Jericho and Bethlehem."* At the conclusion of this "Six-Day War," Israeli forces had, from their perspective, halted Arab aggression.[18]

The Egyptians, Palestinians, Syrians, and Jordanians saw things differently. What Israel considered a preemptive but fundamentally defensive strike, Arab leaders viewed as an invasion. Tensions remained high for years, with periodic outbreaks of violence—like the murder of eleven Israeli Olympians at the 1972 Munich games and the three-week-long Yom Kippur War the following year—marring the slow diplomatic churn that attempted to establish a lasting peace in the Middle East.[19]

Following Morris's death in 1968, Stan carried his family's dedication to Israeli defense into the 1970s and beyond. When it came to Jewish activism, he found, it was useful to be *"the Jew from South Dakota." "If we lived in New York, we would just be lost in a sea of Jewish activists."* Being the most prominent

Jewish couple in hundreds of square miles, however, placed the Adelsteins on a short list of regionally influential Jewish families. As a result, everyone in Jewish circles seemed to have heard of "the Jew from South Dakota."[20] Stan leveraged these connections, and in a trend that mirrored his sprawling membership in Black Hills organizations, secured seats on the founding boards and executive committees of many organizations that rose to prominence during what was a transformative period in Jewish activism. From the 1960s to the 1990s, Adelstein wove Jewish and Israeli advocacy into the many relationships with state and national politicians that grew out of his work with the Republican Party.

Yet of all these activities, harkening back to his telephone call with Morris Abram in the winter of 1964, the AJC remained the primary Jewish organization to which Stan devoted his time. He became a national vice president in 1978, and while serving as a member of the AJC's board of governors two years later, took another trip to the Middle East. This time, Stan and Ita, who were traveling with five of the couples that had also been on that initial 1965 excursion, began their journey in Egypt, rode a ferry through the Suez Canal, then took buses into Israel.

Later on, Stan penned a detailed, sixteen-page account of the 1978 journey. He admitted that "feelings of fear and perhaps trepidation" flared as he "got on an airplane headed for an Arab country." Subtle signs of ethnic tension surrounded him. The in-flight meal came with a large label declaring that "this meal does not contain pork" in four Roman and one Arabic languages. Muslims, like Jewish people, abstained from pork. Yet a Hebrew warning was conspicuously absent from the label; the airline avoided commenting directly on religious tensions, Stan noticed, by offering a universally identifiable message: the package was stamped with a drawing of a pig covered by a large, red "X."[21]

On the ground in Egypt, the Adelsteins went to events intended to educate Jewish Americans to Arab perspectives while building bridges between the AJC and Egyptian leaders. Stan's group spoke with the Egyptian minister of economics, who described the high rates of illiteracy, population growth, imported food, and other challenges his country faced. Later, the Americans attended a service at a local synagogue. Stan enjoyed the session but could not help noticing the two-dozen armed security guards who surrounded that house of worship.[22]

CHAPTER 12

After one dinner with several Egyptian dignitaries, Stan—as the trip's ranking AJC officer—was asked to chant the kiddush, or a blessing of the wine served at Friday night meals preceding the Jewish Sabbath. He relished the opportunity, giddily recounting in his notes how he "trotted up to my room to get my yarmulke" before the prayer. He also recalled how someone in the group mentioned that Stan's was probably the largest kiddush to occur in Egypt since Israeli independence.[23]

The trip was filled with similar moments of reflection and experiences that proved as personal as they were political. Ita, for one, was gripped by emotion upon landing at the Cairo airport, where she encountered several "poorly uniformed young soldiers" who "looked not very different from the sorts of young men" that the Adelsteins had met in Israel years earlier. Stan recounted how Ita "spoke movingly" to their hosts and traveling companions, describing "the feeling of anger at 'statesmen' who had somehow caused these young men to repeatedly kill each other."[24]

Years earlier, Stan had written his senior paper at Boulder examining the design and engineering of several ancient monuments, including the Great Pyramid of Giza. Now, decades later, he stood midway up the monument—the AJC group had taken a day trip to visit historic sites outside Cairo. Stan had been struggling with back pain and, despite the guide's warnings, started up the blocks before realizing his limitations. Now forty-nine, he was firmly in middle-age, and Giza made it abundantly clear that his body was no longer what it had been. While he waited for the rest of his group to descend, Stan pondered the trajectory of his own life. When he hammered out that essay in 1954, he never expected that, twenty-six years later, he would be standing on that historic place.[25]

The gravity of his visit, and of the dire situation faced by Israel and its Arab neighbors, presented itself in other ways on that 1980 trip. To get to Israel, the AJC group boarded a bus and headed northeast. They lingered at an Israeli checkpoint while officials examined the bus and its passengers' passports. With a few minutes to kill, Stan paced the small compound to stretch his legs. A true tourist, his camera dangled from his neck. He raised it and fired, capturing a quiet scene that played out before him: a few yards away, on the desert sand beneath a fluttering Egyptian flag, stood two Israeli lieutenants, visiting politely with the Egyptian border guard.[26]

Stan deemed this moment photo-worthy because it rubbed directly against a very different one he had experienced only minutes earlier. When the AJC buses first approached the Israeli border, an Israeli border guard accidentally directed them to drive through the exit gate. This caused momentary confusion, and the drivers had to wheel their buses around to the appropriate entrance for their security check. Later on, Stan, Ita, and their colleagues discovered the reason for the error. The agent had pointed them the wrong way because, Arab-Israeli turmoil being what it was, "he ha[d] never brought anyone" across the Egyptian border before.[27]

While Stan immersed himself in these broader causes—traveling the United States and the world while harnessing his influence and studying firsthand the issues surrounding Israeli and American security—his local Jewish community struggled for survival. Yet based on his many experiences with Jewish people from across the United States and the world, he maintained that the Synagogue of the Hills would survive. Concluding a letter to the editor of *Present Tense* in 1978, he noted that people frequently asked him how he and his family "managed to stay Jewish for four generations in Rapid City." The answer, Stan typed, was simple. "I remind the questioner that statistically we are a true microcosm of world Jewry. We probably are to Western South Dakota what the world Jewry is to world population. If we cannot survive for four generations in freedom," he asked, "what hope is there for [the] Jewry to survive in a hostile world?"[28]

CHAPTER 13
REMAKING THE GATE CITY

Disaster loomed on the western horizon. In the Black Hills, locals expected storms. Sunny afternoons regularly devolved into a thundering melee of lightning, wind, and hailstones. But on June 9, 1972, the heavens sent down a crushing deluge. Nearly two billion tons of rain poured from the sky, engorging Rapid Creek, which runs through the center of Rapid City. The storm produced enough water to fill Pactola Reservoir, which at the time fed a metro area of some 50,000 people, fourteen times over.[1]

Even with his many years of military and disaster training, the rain still caught Stan Adelstein off-guard. The forty-one-year-old had spent most of the day with Ita and the boys at the Borglum family's ranch near Custer State Park. They left around five o'clock in the evening, and during the one-hour drive home, torrents of water pounded the car and the surrounding landscape. When they reached Rapid City, all the streetlights were out, and, as they would soon discover, so was most of the electricity across town. *"We also heard over the radio that, due to breaks in gas service all over town, the local utility was considering shutting off the city's gas supplies to prevent an explosion."*

Stan dropped off his family at their house high on West Boulevard, where they could stay safely above the flooded streets. He then maneuvered the car carefully, hydroplaning his way for roughly a mile toward St. John's McNamara Hospital, where he had recently been named chairman of the hospital's board of directors. He "arrived early on the scene," according to a report Sister Sarto Rogers wrote after the flood.[2] Years later, Stan recalled that Sister Sarto had been stranded in Keystone, a small town more than 20 miles away. *"In her absence,"* he recalled, *"I was the most senior executive officer at St. John's, so I took charge of the hospital."*

It was a chaotic scene. A stream of volunteers carried the dead and injured through the doors. Some had been swept away from their vehicles or homes by the raging waters in swollen creeks. Others were injured by fallen power lines. Survivors had been banged and scratched by branches, vehicles, trees, and even entire houses unmoored from their foundations and pushed downstream. Victims brought to St. John's were suffering from burns, broken bones, and exposure.[3]

As the downpour entered its seventh straight hour, delivering record amounts of rain, Adelstein worried about whether the power would stay on. Just before the flood, St. John's had installed a brand new $500,000 electrical system, replete with a full backup generator. This investment was supposed to save them from disaster. Around eleven o'clock on the night of the flood, however, shortly after the dam at Canyon Lake had broken, hospital staff heard reports that natural gas lines had ruptured just outside the city limits. Service interruptions continued to spread through the neighborhoods. This posed a serious problem for St. John's, since gas fueled the emergency generator—Sister Sarto reported that the backup lasted until a quarter after midnight.[4]

At 11:15 that night, the lights went out. The nuns gathered candles from their on-site chapel, illuminating the clinic for some forty-five minutes. Yet their wicks could not power the dozens of medical machines that, for many patients, were the difference between life and death.[5]

So the chairman of the board, Stan Adelstein, headed out into the storm, making his way through deadly waters to the Montana Dakota Utilities Company, where representatives informed him that "there was absolutely no way to restore the gas." Disappointed but not deterred, he left for the offices of the Northwestern Bell Telephone Company, where he "managed to get a line through" and convinced the operators to relay power from a substation to St. John's.[6] Adelstein arrived back at the hospital after the lights had flickered back on, and spent the rest of that long and withering night monitoring the radio and carrying casualties up and down the stairs by the light of handheld lanterns.[7]

Daylight revealed an awful scene of devastation. A wall of water had followed the course of Rapid Creek, ripping houses from their foundations, tearing up trees by their roots, and propelling automobiles and other debris through the heart of the city. The flood had killed 238 people and injured 3,000 more. It destroyed 1,300 homes, 5,000 vehicles, and thirty-six businesses. It caused more than $165 million in damage.[8]

In the coming months, organizations across the Black Hills generated flood response reports. In hers, Sister Sarto offered a ten-step prescription for organizations seeking to prepare for natural disasters. The first nine covered expected ground: disaster planning, the need for regular emergency drills, a surplus of supplies, and a backup phone system with a direct line to the local civil defense headquarters.[9]

The tenth and final item on the nun's list was oddly specific. "You want to have as Chairman of your Board of Directors an engineer," she wrote, her gratitude toward Stan Adelstein growing clearer with every stroke on her typewriter. "Not just any engineer—it must be an engineer who [owns a] highway and heavy construction firm," and, as such, has a fleet of "large trucks available to supply water and provide garbage pickup." This engineer must also be someone who would "know exactly who to contact for necessary power and equipment." "It is very basic," Sister Sarto continued, "that this Chairman be able to assist you and function well." With someone like him coupled with some basic preparedness, she finished, any organization should be "perfectly capable of handling a disaster."[10]

The initial recovery lasted for weeks. At dawn the morning after the disaster, Adelstein, like people across Rapid City, helped out where he could. E.D. Gaiser, the longtime manager at Hills Materials, loaded two-dozen company trucks with rocks, which they carried up the highway to fill washed-out sections of the road. This would restore traffic flow and allow emergency crews access to families on Rapid City's west side and farther up the devastated creek bed, which snaked its way west of town. Stan sent other Northwestern Engineering Company iron to clean up at St. John's. He also helped establish an emergency control center and spent long days creating a priority list for the recovery work, much of which relied on company equipment. Meanwhile, everywhere he went Adelstein saw people in shock, many of them homeless and sleeping in shelters, grieving for lost relatives and friends. There were so many deaths, in fact, that local funeral homes were overwhelmed, leading them to hold all services at graveside.[11]

Within days, Adelstein found himself standing over a freshly dug grave intended for Herbert Weisz, a Jewish man from Germany who had died in the flood decades after fleeing Europe at the start of World War II. He had become an engineering professor at the South Dakota School of Mines & Technology, and his weary eyes suggested that he had never fully shaken his midcentury trauma.[12] Weisz knew Stan Adelstein through the university and the synagogue. As Adelstein stood over the grave in the summer of 1972, he *"knew that in addition to everything else that was going on, I would need to conduct Herb's funeral."*

With Weisz's funeral set to begin in only a few hours, Stan stopped by to see where the grave had been dug. The entire community was helping clear debris from destroyed homes, searching for bodies, and doing other gut-wrenching work. *"I had just finished some recovery-related chore. Since there were so many funerals in only a few days, all the burial services were done at graveside. Each gravesite had the name of the person written on a wooden lath."* Then he saw it: Herbert's name had been inscribed on a lath cross, and the Christian symbol was about to adorn his final resting place. Gripped by grief and exhaustion, this small cultural misstep nearly pushed Stan over the edge. Absorbing this casual omission, for what seemed the millionth time, was, in that moment, too much.

Stan's frustration welled inside. Then he felt a nudge at his elbow. *"One of the nuns from St. Martin's had been working at an aid station set up to help grieving friends and family as they entered the cemetery. She saw me, walked up, and said, 'Is something wrong Mr. Adelstein?' Then she looked down and gently said, 'I see. You go home and get ready for the funeral and I'll take care of it.' When I returned, the name was on a lath in the shape of a Star of David. To this day, I have no idea how she did it, and that touching moment still comes back to be."*

Physically and emotionally grueling for Adelstein and the rest of the Rapid City community, the flood also created opportunities for incredible generosity. Given his substantial means, Stan was better positioned to provide relief than most. One example connected Stan's penchant to personal generosity and his devotion to helping fellow Rapid Citians to a rare opportunity to pay back a debt owed, he believed, by Jewish people everywhere.

The story started a few years before the flood, when Stan and Ita regularly attended a discussion group in Rapid City. Once or twice a month, a handful of young couples would get together and talk through current events and other issues. One member of the group, Helge Christiansen, was a professional wood-carver who had been born in Denmark and had lived in Rapid City for several years.[13] Locally, Christiansen was well known for his contributions to the "Chapel in the Hills," a striking Norwegian *"stavekirke"*-style church. In the mid-1960s, a local Lutheran preacher and a wealthy banker had sponsored the church's construction on the west side of Rapid City, hoping that by building an exact replica of a twelfth-century Scandinavian chapel, they could attract tourists and faithful Lutherans to the Black Hills. Christiansen and a Norwegian wood-carver named Erik Friedstom chiseled the intricate patterns on the interior and exterior of the church, which was dedicated in the summer of 1969.[14]

In his conversations with Christiansen, however, Adelstein was more interested in a specific part of Danish history: the refusal of the Danes to participate in the Holocaust. *"When Ita and I took that first trip to Israel in 1965,"* Stan recalled, *"we toured this school. On the walls of one classroom, there was this big chart, and it showed the percentage of Jews who died in each European country during the war. The number was high in many countries, but there was one clear exception: very few Jews died in Denmark."*[15] For years, Adelstein wondered about this, and in conversation with Christiansen found an opportunity to ask. *"I remember saying to Helge: Why were the Danes so different from everyone else? Why didn't your people kill mine? And he said that protecting others—and I'll never forget his answer—'Well, that's what one person does for another.'"* That sentiment astounded Stan and stuck with him for the rest of his life.

In 1972, Adelstein had not forgotten these words. *"A day or two after the flood, I saw Helge walking in downtown Rapid City. I asked him how he was doing, and he was very distraught. The flood had taken his business, his car, and all of his wood carving tools, which had all been located along Omaha Street, one of the heaviest-hit areas of town. I told him to make a list of the tools he lost; we'd replace them for him. And I knew we had some extra space in a warehouse down on Spruce Street, where NWE had a little machine shop. I told him we'd clear out some space for his workbench. I also knew that the company had some extra pickup trucks in its inventory, so I told him we'd have him a vehicle by dark. Helge looked up at me, stunned, and said, 'Why are you doing this for me?' and I told him, 'Helge, you told me the answer to that question years ago.' And he said, 'I did?' and I said, 'Yes, you taught me that this sort of thing is just what one person does for another.'"*

REBUILDING

Rapid City was never the same after the 1972 flood. That catastrophe, however, was not a beginning in and of itself. It was a tipping point in a longer arc of civic activism that had been pushing the town toward a renaissance. Since the early 1960s, Stan had associated with an expansive network of business owners, boosters, politicians, and municipal leaders who sought to improve the quality of life in Rapid City. Some of these individuals were in Stan's immediate social and professional circles; others were not. And the movement to rebuild Rapid City was not shaped by party politics—that was, as Adelstein would later say, *"a whole different issue."* It was driven by influential people with *"a concept of working together with the city council"* to make things better.

For Stan, the movement started in the early 1960s when *"a group of us younger people wanted to get things changed."* They thought that Rapid City was primed for growth. The group included Barbara Bates Gunderson, who had lived in Rapid City since 1947 and was involved in a wide array of civic groups and activities, as well as being active in the Republican Party.[16] Tom Lane became the chairman of the Rapid City Area Chamber of Commerce's board. Jerry Shoener had a long career with the local paper of record, the *Rapid City Journal*, and spent a dozen years on the city council. These were only a few of Stan's associates who seemed to follow a sentiment once expressed by Shoener: "I feel community service is the rent you pay for the space you occupy in that community." He "tried to keep [his] rent paid up," Shoener added, "by staying active in community affairs."[17]

The group's strategy was straightforward, and it mirrored Stan's personal method for attaching himself to local causes. They recruited and supported candidates who shared their interest. They held private meetings, where they *"talked about what we could do to . . . make the town better."* They also organized door-to-door campaigns and sought to fill the mayor's office and city council seats with individuals who shared their plans.[18]

The first person they elected was Phil Schroeder, a young banker who worked under Morris Adelstein's old friend Art Dahl at the American National Bank branch in town. Schroeder, like Stan, volunteered with the Club for Boys. In a pair of close elections that had to be settled with runoffs, he beat longtime mayor Fred Dusek in 1963 and took the mayor's office that year. He held it through a follow-up challenge from Dusek in 1965.[19]

It was a heady time, filled by the desire to get things done and punctuated by a clear record of accomplishment. *"I really loved books,"* Stan recalled, so Schroeder appointed him to the Rapid City Library Board in 1965. There, he joined a group of citizens, led by longtime librarian Faye Crawford, in an effort to replace the city's fifty-year-old library with a new, 28,000-square-foot facility that opened in 1972.[20]

The library project gained momentum between 1965 and 1967, when the board *"convinced the council to issue bonds to pay for a new library. But in order to do that, we first had to establish a trust fund with at least $60,000."* This required diverting funds from the municipal budget to start a building fund.[21] Stan pitched the plan at a council meeting in 1967, where it passed easily—much to the chagrin of Mayor Henry Baker, who had succeeded Schroeder. Baker stormed up to Stan after the meeting, angry because he had other plans for that money. Baker demanded that Stan explain how he talked the council into supporting his plan with only a short presentation. *"I'll tell you how we did it, Henry,"* Stan snapped—revealing that his broader political experience was beginning to shape his approach to local affairs—*"I had six votes going in."*

For all their prowess when it came to whipping council votes, Stan and his friends also faced public opposition to the changes they were trying to make in Rapid City—the library project among them. *"Like so many of the things we thought needed to be done in town, there was a group of what I'll call 'persistent naysayers' who disagreed with the need for a new library, as well as its location. They were absolutely sure that the city didn't need any more books."*

Community members also harbored concerns that certain aspects of the new library's construction and financing were *"going to be a disaster."* For one thing, the building would fill an open lot that provided some of the only public parking downtown at the corner of Seventh and Quincy Streets. The Library Board paid the city $60,000—which was, by no coincidence, the exact amount pulled from the mayor's coffers a few years earlier—to compensate for the construction of off-street parking.[22] Stan and his friends were not the only group of Rapid Citians with a penchant for slick politicking.

Despite his better intentions, Adelstein sometimes let his partisan passions creep into nonpartisan civic affairs. In 1971, as the library project was nearing its end, Don Barnett, a twenty-eight-year-old Vietnam War veteran with Democratic leanings, won the mayor's office by a scarce 168 votes. Barnett defeated John Barnes, an employee of Hills Materials who worked as Stan's assistant.[23] When the newly inaugurated Barnett came to a Library Board meeting to share his views about what kinds of things the board should be focusing on, Stan was not pleased. When the new mayor finished, *"I thanked Barnett for his visit and then told him the board was an independent body, which meant that the mayor's comments carried the same weight as those of any other citizen."* Barnett, on the other hand, recalled Adelstein losing his temper and arguing angrily for fifteen minutes.[24]

Whatever its form, Stan's icy retort cost him his seat on the board, as Barnett refused to reappoint him.[25] Stan remained involved with the library project as a member of the board of a corporation—the Rapid City Civic

Library Building Association, Inc.—that the city council formed in 1970 to manage the financing of the new building. He served alongside his friend Barbara Gunderson and another ally, Dean Nauman, who was a successful local printer.[26] Together with other library supporters, the group helped raise some $250,000 in cash for the building fund and secured pledges, bonds, and a city tax levy that helped cover the $1.08 million cost of construction and furnishings.[27] Stan's point of view was that leaving the Library Board also *"freed me up to work on another project—the development of Rapid City's new hospital, which was under way around that same time."*

The most powerful of Stan's allies, Arthur "Art" LaCroix, succeeded Barnett in 1975. LaCroix had been born in Nebraska to Mdewakanton (Santee Dakota) parents in 1922 and fought at the Battle of the Bulge in World War II. He moved to Rapid City and founded a linoleum business.[28] LaCroix was elected to the city council in 1971. He became the first American Indian to serve on the council and later—after five terms—the longest-serving mayor in Rapid City's history.[29] He and Stan had met in the army reserves, and their wives—Ita and Trude LaCroix (an Austrian woman Art had met in the service)—were also close friends who skied together on the weekends.[30]

Before his long tenure at city hall ended in 1987, Art LaCroix "worked on several big projects" like tarmac extensions and new terminals at the regional airport and the development of a central fire station.[31] To people like Stan and Art, these projects made Rapid City a better place. To others, they were a carefully planned gambit that aimed to line the pockets of Rapid City's rich and powerful. Like his father before him, Stan Adelstein and the Northwestern Engineering Company sat ready and waiting to build the infrastructure Rapid City needed to grow. But Stan's close relationship with LaCroix also opened both men to criticism. Stan remembered how, during one of LaCroix's many reelection campaigns, his opponents *"ran an ad pointing out that Hills Materials had 53 percent of the competitively bid work in town."* Although LaCroix's political opponents took this as a sign of backroom dealing, Stan saw it differently. After seeing the ad against LaCroix, he called the managers at Hills Materials together and asked, *"What's the matter with us? We've got 60 percent of the construction assets in this town, but only 53 percent of the work?!"*

In the end, any criticisms of Stan and Art's relationship did little to break the tide of development. As the postflood cleanup began in 1972, leaders like LaCroix—then a city councilman—championed the creation of green spaces that would serve two purposes: restrict construction along Rapid Creek's flood zone to prevent future disasters and expand the available open space or parkland for recreational uses.[32]

In fact, the reenvisioning of Rapid City had begun several years before the flood. The city first explored its eligibility for federal urban renewal funds in 1965.[33] Two years later, Rapid City Area Chamber of Commerce president James Bell, himself an engineer, arranged a visit at the offices of the American Institute of Architects (AIA), a national organization for professional designers that had been founded in 1857.[34] Bell was in Washington, D.C., for a national Chamber meeting, and believed his hometown needed a more streamlined plan. After a long conversation, the AIA offered a four-person team—a pair of architects and a pair of planners—to visit Rapid City and help lay a framework for urban renewal. For these services, the AIA asked only that Rapid City cover expenses, about $900.[35]

For Rapid City, the AIA's involvement spurred public discussions about the town's future. The AIA team came to Rapid City, which, in turn, started the Community Development Action Committee (CDAC), a group of fifteen powerful local men. They were led by Robert Asheim, a city councilman and executive at the Black Hills Power and Light Company, the regional utilities provider. Together, these groups convinced municipal leaders to hire a full-time city planner and bring in a consulting firm—Hodne Associates, Inc. out of Minneapolis—to evaluate the town.[36] The firm produced what came to be called the "Hodne Report," a fifty-two-page booklet that mapped out a new and improved town center that could be updated, they believed, between 1968 and 1980.[37]

The Hodne Report sought to redesign Rapid City's main business corridor to populate the downtown district. As it stood, a long street bypassed the heart of the city, so Hodne Associates proposed new buildings and a traffic pattern that would follow a "circular or square design" that, the firm believed, would incentivize people to park, walk around, and spend more time and money in Rapid City.[38] The design also sought to open access from major highways and especially from Ellsworth Air Force Base. Meanwhile, the city could consolidate its labor force and tax base "to the twelve block area bounded by Main–Fourth–Kansas City and Ninth streets." In so doing, Hodne Associates argued, Rapid City could revitalize itself, bolster retail and tourism revenues, boost employment, and "create an esthetic and distinct image for Rapid City."[39]

In early 1968, Hodne Associates presented its plan to the CDAC and in public meetings. Support for the downtown renewal proved strong, but according to one community member who wrote to the *Rapid City Journal,* there was little debate as to whether the city should invest in its downtown corridor. Cities everywhere were doing this. But, the author asked, "who will put it into operation, who will be affected, who will pay, [and] who will relocate?" The author's most significant question framed the city's basic obstacle: "how do you proceed?"[40] The community responded by planning projects and seeking federal support, which was available through the recently created Department of Housing and Urban Development (HUD). Funding, however, was hard to get, as cities had to meet eligibility criteria and navigate a long, bureaucratic process to secure HUD funds. As such, Rapid City's revitalization progressed slowly.

Until 1972, that is. A torrent of "emergency disaster assistance and long range community development" money followed the flood into Rapid City. In fact, the situation was so dire that HUD waived several standard application requirements "in order to expedite [Rapid City's] recovery efforts."[41] Over the next decade, state and federal support allowed the community to devote tens of millions of dollars to its disaster-driven renewal and development program.[42]

One capstone project that defined this era of development was the construction of the city's Rushmore Plaza Civic Center—on whose board Stan Adelstein would serve many years—and a nearby conference hotel.[43] Late in the evening on June 22, 1977, the "King of Rock'n'Roll," Elvis Presley himself, headlined the Civic Center auditorium's grand opening. Clad in his signature ivory jumpsuit, with a high, stiff collar and a bare chest covered in gold jewelry, Elvis took the stage. His health had declined significantly in recent months, and members of his Civic Center audience noticed his lackluster performance. Although nobody in the crowd knew it, the underpaced gyration of Presley's famous hips signaled a historic end. The show in Rapid City was one of his last. The King died less than two months later at his home in Tennessee.[44]

Still, Presley had crooned Rapid City into a new era. The downtown had been consolidated and streamlined, and the new Civic Center brought concerts, conventions, rodeos, and other events that would provide local entertainment while boosting revenues across the hospitality industry. Green spaces offered parks and, later, bicycle paths that connected the city from end to end. In only a few years, the local airport would accommodate larger planes, delivering ever-more visitors to the tourism sites that were ready and waiting to accommodate and entertain them. Throughout this process, relationships mattered. Stan Adelstein, Art LaCroix, and their friends were but one group that helped spur these developments. Indeed, speaking broadly of the spirit of civic activism and the networks of influential citizens who revitalized Rapid City during this era, Adelstein would later recall that *"our bunch really kind of did a lot,"* and, in a sense, *"ran this town."*

THE MECHANICS OF MEDICINE

One of the most significant developments in this cascade of new construction—and certainly the one closest to Stan Adelstein's heart—was the creation of Rapid City Regional Hospital. As with the library and so many other things, Stan was simply "fascinated with medicine" and "the mechanics of it." This was not entirely new in the 1970s—what had been a loose, avocational interest in medical technologies and care burgeoned as he became increasingly involved with Sister Sarto and the other nuns at St. Martin's and St. Johns McNamara the decade before. In one of their final conversations, in fact, Morris and Stan had talked about the new blood purification machines in the renal dialysis unit in Denver.[45]

As he grew acquainted with the process and challenges of medical administration at St. Johns, Stan grew deeply critical of Bennett-Clarkson Memorial Hospital—the other hospital in town. *"Their quality of care was so poor,"* he said, *"and there was a duplication of investment in new equipment that was so costly, and one of the first things I learned about medicine is that money isn't everything."* The community, he believed, was wasting money by supporting two hospitals with two administrations, two staffs, and two sets of equipment. Stan also noted the local perception that Bennett-Clarkson had been founded *"out of antipathy towards the Catholic Church and the idea of a major medical facility, St. Johns, being run by nuns,"* a sentiment anchored in religious prejudice that he rejected.[46]

During the 1972 flood, Adelstein recalled how Bennett-Clarkson's basement started filling up with water. Upon hearing the news, Stan offered to transport patients to St. John's, where the situation was chaotic but under better control, *"around 8:30 in the evening, when it still seemed possible to move people from the West Side."* Bennett-Clarkson's director refused to take the offer, Adelstein said, electing instead to move all of the hospital's patients to the upper floors. *"The next morning, two doctors climbed over Skyline Drive, since there was no access by streets early in the day, to check on Bennett-Clarkson. They found patients stranded upstairs, but there were no doctors at the hospital."* Stan was furious when he heard this news. *"We wanted to bring the patients over to St. John's, but the director of Bennett-Clarkson wouldn't let us. Later on, someone told me they heard him say that 'if I move the patients, if I evacuate the hospital, Adelstein will never let me open again.' So he just moved everyone upstairs."*

After the flood, Dr. Thomas T. Coolidge, a physician at St. John's McNamara who lived on Rapid City's west side, explained how the patients at Bennett-Clarkson eventually made it out of the hospital. In a report similar to Sister Sarto's, Coolidge recalled leaving work for the day at around five o'clock in the evening, just as the rain was beginning to pound the Black Hills. He stayed home the rest of the night but woke to an urgent call from the St. John's switchboard at around 4:30 in the morning, imploring him to return to the hospital. Stepping outside, he quickly realized the damage. When a policeman informed him it would be impossible to make it across town to St. John's, he decided to head to Bennett-Clarkson and offer his assistance.[47]

When he arrived, Coolidge was stunned to see "a house roof in the Bennett-Clarkson parking lot," which was also filled with "mud, debris, and motor vehicles." The hospital's main floor "was covered in two inches of mud." After conferring with several on-staff physicians, the group decided that of the ninety patients at Bennett-Clarkson that night, about a third could be sent home, a third required minimal care but should not be discharged, and a third required critical care. Coolidge left for St. John's, where he asked Sister Sarto—who had since made it back to the hospital—if he could transfer patents from Bennett-Clarkson. Ultimately, about twenty patients went to St. John's and about thirty were transferred to Ellsworth Air Force Base. "The evacuation of patients [from Bennett-Clarkson] proceeded in a relatively orderly fashion," Coolidge wrote, and by noon on June 10—the day after the flood—all but four patients "who were in traction due to forehead and cervical injuries" remained. They were located on the third floor of the facility, and Coolidge and his colleagues deemed it too dangerous to move them immediately. They would be transferred by day's end.[48]

According to Adelstein, all of this might have been avoided had the administrator at Bennett-Clarkson heeded his offer of assistance the night before. *"By eleven o'clock, there was no way anyone was getting to Bennett-Clarkson, and their administrator had missed a critical opportunity to save his patients a long and stressful night."* Nevertheless, the officials there had refused to evacuate, setting the stage for the disorderly scene Coolidge encountered when he arrived the next morning.

And, it seems, the alleged exclamation by Bennett-Clarkson's director—that "Adelstein will never let me open again"—was not far off the mark. By the time floodwaters devastated Rapid City, Adelstein had been trying to shut down Bennett-Clarkson for several years. Concerned about the quality of care at Bennett-Clarkson, he said, *"I tried everything to get them closed."* Sometime around 1969 or 1970, for example, he made *"a secret deal with a local heating company so that they wouldn't have to bid on a full air conditioning installation contract at St. Johns, provided that they ordered everything based on my word that they'd be paid and didn't have a contract through the first of May, and that they would have us completely air-conditioned by the first of June. So what do you think happened to the respective occupancies for that summer? Bennett-Clarkson's went down to less than 20 percent, but ours was always full. In business, there would have been no way they would have hung on with occupancy that low, but I learned things were very different in medicine, and they never closed."*

When the misery of a stifling South Dakota summer failed to shutter Bennett-Clarkson for good, Adelstein took another, more collaborative track. *"I reached out to the chairman of the board at Bennett-Clarkson, and suggested that we establish a Joint Liaison Committee, which would include three or four members of the St. John's board and an equal number of members from the board at Bennett-Clarkson. Once he agreed, the Joint Liaison Committee held a series of meetings at the school of nursing that would occur over the course of several months. During that time, we discussed the duplication of equipment and other problems. At one of our last meetings, I suggested that we consider establishing a committee to consider combining the two hospitals. The leader of Bennett-Clarkson, however, didn't think it would be possible to find a committee that everyone could agree on. So I pulled a sheet of paper from my tablet and slid it across the table. We asked that Bennett-Clarkson team go to another room, deliberate, and make a list of six or seven names of people around town they'd want to have as members of what later came to be called the 'Hospital Action Committee.' We would do the same thing, then compare the two papers. Anyone who appeared on both lists would automatically be on the committee, and after that, we'd alternate back-and-forth, with each group getting to select an individual from the other group's list. We gave Bennett-Clarkson the first choice, and eventually developed a list of seven Hospital Action Committee members."*

Once the Joint Liaison Committee had developed its list, the group reached out to the prospective members of the Hospital Action Committee (HAC). After everyone agreed to be involved, the group spent the next couple of years evaluating and negotiating a merger, which promised to do away with the "costly duplication of facilities, equipment, and manpower" at the two competing hospitals and to streamline planning and fund-raising by placing them under one umbrella.[49] As the HAC grew in membership and in prominence, it advocated for a new, consolidated Rapid City Regional Hospital, which would become the hub for local care as well as a clearinghouse for medical referrals to specialists across the region.[50]

By July 1973, the merger was complete, and Rapid City Regional Hospital operated out of two partner facilities. The East Unit filled the old St. John's McNamara facility, while the West Unit was inside the former Bennett-Clarkson. The latter had been patched up—it underwent extensive renovation to repair flood damage and get the building up to code, as well as the installation of a new flood mitigation system. Rapid City Regional Hospital was already planning to consolidate the bulk of its services in a single, massive new building to be erected on a 100-acre lot at the southern edge of town just across from the towering Catholic cathedral that had gone up nearly two decades earlier.[51] When that facility opened, the East Unit would continue to serve as an educational facility; its name simply changed to Rapid City Regional Hospital School of Nursing.[52]

The administrators, boards, and committees that would manage the new hospital filled a sprawling flowchart. It included the names of stakeholders from all across the Black Hills and the medical communities, from experienced physicians and nuns from the old facility at St. John's McNamara to local leaders like Stan Adelstein.[53] *"I served as secretary of the new corporation,"* Stan recalled, *"and asked to be the chairman of the facilities development committee, and helped organize the negotiations to secure the land on the south side of Rapid City, where the new hospital would be built a few years later."*

A member of the new Rapid City Regional Hospital's board of directors, Stan served on three of the nine board subcommittees that helped shepherd the new facility through its first years. Given his profession, it made sense that he was the chairman of the master site development committee, which located, designed, and built the nine-floor facility that began to be constructed in the autumn of 1976. He was also on the community-patient relations group, but perhaps most significant, sat on the professional practice committee, which sought to emphasize quality patient care at the new hospital.[54]

All was not smooth sailing. Adelstein and other nonmedical personnel encountered resistance from Regional's physicians. *"The idea of having a nonphysician dealing with medical practice was anathema to the general thinking about how to administer a hospital,"* he said. *"At St. John's, I'd always insisted upon having a layperson as the chairman of the medical practice committee, so decisions about costs could be evaluated by someone with a more objective, quality and business-oriented perspective."* One example came when Adelstein and the professional practice committee advocated the use of "Medical Care Evaluations" or MCEs, which staff members could fill out for administrators to use as they monitored the quality of patient care. Although the hospital's chief of staff supported the MCEs, many doctors did not. Stan summed up this view in a short note that he scribbled on the cover of a meeting agenda in May 1978: "some physicians see MCE's as a paper exercise."[55]

The doctors' distaste for these evaluations, as well as the clear derision they held for nonspecialists tasked with oversight, nearly pushed Stan to quit the committee that year. "At one time," he wrote to the rest of the board, "I thought that the situation could be enhanced by my resignation." But he later came to see that such drastic action would merely "defer for a short period the . . . acceptance of responsibility" by the doctors, and instead, pushed harder for MCEs and a list of people who would conduct them.[56]

These disagreements reflected the growing pains at Rapid City Regional Hospital in its first five years, but they did not detract from the institution's real progress. Although "continued inefficiencies" and "unending pressures from regulatory bodies" posed serious challenges, the institution increased its patient volume, hired twenty-five new physicians, and raised enough money to add 285 beds to the facility four years earlier than expected. It also added "nuclear medicine, ultrasound, endoscopy/proctoscopy, computerized axial tomography, sophisticated laboratory procedures and equipment, and [a] full-time, in-house, emergency room physician," all of which did not exist in the Black Hills "prior to 1973."[57]

By the mid-1970s, Stan and others in the community could see the fruit of their labors in the development of Rapid City Regional Hospital and other institutions that marked the community's transition from a retail trading center and military boomtown to a small but growing metropolis that was increasingly connected—by interstate highway and air transportation—to the urban centers of the nation. And just as the city expanded its sense of itself through these connections, Stan Adelstein discovered new opportunities to affect issues and politics far from home.

CHAPTER 14
TRUE REPUBLICAN

As his plane taxied in toward the terminal at the Rapid City Municipal Airport, Nelson Rockefeller, the former governor of New York and—though nobody yet knew it—soon-to-be vice president of the United States, prepared himself for another round of handshakes, smiles, and speeches. Rockefeller had spent the day in Mitchell for the first of two stops in South Dakota. Nearly two hours late into Mitchell after a maintenance issue with his plane, Rockefeller had canceled a tour of the Oscar Howe Cultural Center, choosing instead to view a handful of the famed Yanktonai Dakota painter's works with the artist himself. After an hour's visit and a short speech, Rockefeller left for Rapid City.[1]

Years had passed since Stan Adelstein had supported the governor in his failed effort to win the Republican nomination for president in 1964, but Rockefeller remembered Stan, even if at first he could not remember his name. *"I remember a staffer telling me that when Rockefeller got off the plane, he told them to 'find that kid with the mustache!'"* Stan said, *"and that was me."* Fortunately, Rockefeller's staff knew that the governor did not have that political gift, and they were ready to help.[2]

"I heard him shout 'Stan!'" Adelstein recalled, then watched as the burly New Yorker strode straight toward him, the cold wind whipping across his beaming face. *"He walked right up and shook my hand and said, 'The real friends are the old friends.'"*

The year was 1974. Rockefeller had come to Mitchell and Rapid City as the guest of honor for the annual Lincoln Day fundraiser held by local

CHAPTER 14

Republicans in county parties across the nation. As a well-connected member of the executive committee of the Republican State Central Committee, Stan had lobbied to get Rockefeller, his longtime political hero, to give the keynote address to a crowd of about 450 at the Howard Johnson Motor Lodge.[3]

With Stan acting as the evening's emcee and introducing a bevy of speakers and party officials from across South Dakota, Rockefeller stumped for Republican candidates, calling for strong turnout in the upcoming congressional and state elections. During his speech and a press conference that followed, "Rocky," as reporters called him, called for unity within the Republican Party and sought to galvanize its members—many of whom felt torn over the growing severity of the Watergate scandal—ahead of the midterms. He also made it clear that he was not planning a run for the presidency in 1976, then prepared to leave the Black Hills.[4]

For weeks before the governor's arrival, Stan had struggled to think of a gift, a small memento to thank Rockefeller for coming all the way to South Dakota. He asked himself over and over: what do you give to a man who inherited an unworldly fortune and was one of the most well-connected people in America?

Then inspiration struck. *"On the drive back to the airport, I turned to Rockefeller and said, 'Governor, how would you feel if, as you took off from the airport, Mount Rushmore lighted up for you?' And he said, 'You could do that?'"* Little did he know, Stan—who had already been active in the Mount Rushmore Memorial Society for two years—*"had it all set up."* That night, as Rockefeller's jet gained altitude over the Black Hills, *"the pilots turned towards Mount Rushmore"* so the governor could peer out the small, oblong window and see the yellow glow illuminating the monument below.

On Valentine's Day, shortly after the visit, Rockefeller wrote Adelstein to tell him that the Lincoln Day dinner "was all handled beautifully," and that "the job you did as presiding officer was outstanding." He noted that Stan had "been a good friend for a long while," and was "impressed with the new young leadership that is coming up in the party" and the "constructive role you've been playing in all of this." He closed by thanking Stan for a pair of Black Hills gold cufflinks Stan had presented him and said, "we will long cherish the view we got of Mt. Rushmore lighted at night as we flew out. What an extra-ordinary [sic] courtesy you did us in this."[5]

For Adelstein, this gesture connected the Shrine of Democracy with the personification of his politics in Nelson Rockefeller. Like the former governor, Stan viewed himself as a centrist or *"true Republican"*—someone committed to a set of core political principles including limited government, individual liberty, and a strong national defense. As a businessman, Stan understood that government played a necessary role in the economy, and he did not reject the idea of regulation. He characterized his fiscal conservatism as *"enlightened self-interest."* In other words, he thought businesspeople should be expected to work to increase their bottom line. But this was by no means a blanket excuse to do business in an ethical vacuum.

"I wasn't really opposed to government rules," Stan said, as long as they *"were fair in general."* And with rare exception, he had positive experiences working with regulators. He had long believed that, generally, *"the people I dealt with in government were doing their job as best they could."*

For Adelstein, Nelson Rockefeller embodied these ideals, and he modeled much of his own political ideology, as well as his approach to politics, around Rockefeller and his career. Rockefeller, for instance, was a progressive Republican whose positions occasionally rankled members of his own party. In 1960, he had famously negotiated the so-called Treaty of Fifth Avenue with then-presidential hopeful Richard Nixon during a last-minute meeting in Manhattan. As the two figures chatted in Rockefeller's apartment, the governor hung his support for Nixon on a series of changes to the Republican platform. Rockefeller wanted language supporting an increase in nuclear defense spending, a government-led effort to boost the national economy, and an endorsement of civil rights. Nixon wanted Rockefeller's support, and paid a high price for it. Desegregation and federal economic intervention alienated conservatives, who already distrusted Nixon, while his boss, President Eisenhower, advocated lowering the defense budget.[6] In the end, Nixon won Rockefeller's support, but lost the presidency to John F. Kennedy that fall.

Stan had become acquainted with Rockefeller through his involvement with the Republican National Committee, where Tommy Christensen—the Republican Party organizer from Spearfish who helped introduce Stan to the party—served on the executive committee. *"When I was in New York for AJC meetings,"* Adelstein said, *"I'd go to meet with the national committeeman in the Rockefeller Center"* to talk about fund-raising for Republicans in South Dakota, *"and to meet with other Republicans like Senator Hugh Scott"* from Pennsylvania. Stan saw Rockefeller at other political meetings, and the more Stan studied his politics and approach, the more he identified with the governor's brand of Republicanism. Over time, it became clear to Stan that Rockefeller *"was sort of my model."*

By early 1964, Nelson Rockefeller was locked into a fiery presidential campaign. He was also in a fight for the soul of the Republican Party. Rockefeller and Barry Goldwater, a staunchly conservative senator from Arizona, led a field of six Republican candidates. Rockefeller split the party's centrist and liberal coalitions with leaders like Ohio Governor James Rhodes and Pennsylvania Governor William Scranton. Goldwater, on the other hand, had become a conservative hero.[7]

Brutal character attacks filled the primary season. Opponents like Rockefeller dubbed Goldwater an extremist for his intense conservatism and frequent suggestions that increased American military aggression—including the use of atomic weapons—could solve the Cold War conundrum.[8] Among other things, critics questioned Rockefeller's moral fortitude, repeatedly critiquing his divorce and speedy remarriage to a much younger woman with whom the governor had been involved for several years.[9] In the end, Rockefeller fell to Goldwater, who had won most of the party's primaries and went into the 1964 Republican National Convention with a near lock on the party's delegates.[10]

When Rockefeller was called to the convention stage in Daly City, California, in July 1964, Stan was seated with the South Dakota delegation. The convention host had to rap his gavel forty-four times in an attempt to bring the screams under control. This was a Goldwater crowd, and Rockefeller spoke in support of a platform amendment decrying extremism—a thinly veiled jab at Goldwater.[11] When the cheers and jeers finally subsided, Rockefeller launched into a short speech. He had accepted defeat, but used his time on the rostrum to offer an impassioned warning against the fervor—"whether communist, Ku Klux Klan, or Bircher," as he said, lumping them together—that he believed was pulling the party from the basic principles upon which it had been founded. Republicanism, Rockefeller argued, was a blend of "sound and honest conservatism" and "sound and honest liberalism," a delicate balance that had for more than a century made theirs "the party of all the people."[12]

Goldwater's supporters interrupted Rockefeller with bursts of "We Want Barry! We Want Barry!" signifying what everyone in the hall already knew: that Goldwater's conservatism had overwhelmed—at least for this year, and at least within the Republican Party—Rockefeller's centrism.[13] It was a loss that stung Stan Adelstein and would continue to haunt him and other Rockefeller Republicans for decades to come.

Despite Barry Goldwater's Jewish heritage on his father's side (he was raised Episcopalian), Adelstein had little patience for Goldwater and his brand of forceful conservatism.[14] He was crestfallen when the final delegate count came in. As Goldwater's supporters celebrated on the convention floor, Stan remembered, a segment of the Texas delegation launched into a chant. *"Instead of shouting 'We Want Barry,' they started yelling 'Viva Ole! Viva Ole! Viva Ole!'"*—an exclamation akin to "long live Goldwater!"[15] Years later Stan could not forget the chill that recitation sent down his spine. *"I left the convention hall and went back up to join Ita in our hotel room. I told her how 'Viva Ole! Viva Ole! Viva Ole!' reminded me of recordings I'd heard of Nazi rallies from the early 1930s. It was just too much like hearing 'Sieg Heil! Sieg Heil! Sieg Heil!' for me."*

Two nights after Rockefeller's speech, Barry Goldwater accepted his party's nomination. He begrudged red tape and overregulation, charged "corruption in our highest offices," and decried "violence in our streets." A conservative Goldwater presidency, he promised, would return his party and the nation to fundamental principles of individual equality, decentralized government, and self-made prosperity. Toward the end, Goldwater let loose two controversial sentences that would loom over his candidacy for the rest of 1964.[16] "<u>Extremism in the defense of liberty,</u>" he said, reading lines he had underlined in his speech, "<u>is no vice. Moderation in the pursuit of justice is no virtue.</u>"[17] When Goldwater finished, the convention hall thundered in agreement.[18]

The majority of American voters, however, thought otherwise. After denying Rockefeller's claims for months, Goldwater was saddled with the derisive label of "extremist." In November, President Lyndon Johnson won reelection with 64 percent of the popular vote, defeating Goldwater in all but six states.[19]

The conservative movement that propelled Goldwater to the nomination would prove far more enduring than Stan or Rockefeller dreamed in 1964, but its resurgence was slowed for more than a decade.[20] In 1968, the Republican

Party returned to Richard Nixon. In a race defined by civil unrest and virulent anti–Vietnam War protests, Nixon—who shaped his politics with an adroit (if not paranoid) eye toward electoral pragmatism—ran on a platform that promised to restore order and security. He beat several primary challengers, including Rockefeller and California Governor Ronald Reagan, the heir apparent to Goldwater's conservative throne.[21]

While Nixon orchestrated his political comeback, the Democrats were torn by powerful internecine struggles. Lyndon Johnson's popularity flagged with every day that the bloody conflict in Vietnam dragged on. The Democratic field scrambled when the president announced that he would not run for reelection on the last day of March in 1968. Only months later, an assassin cut down New York Senator Robert Kennedy—brother to the slain president and a popular potential nominee—just minutes after he declared victory in the California and South Dakota primaries. The Democratic Party's August convention was beset by wild protests on the convention floor and outside Chicago's International Amphitheatre. Vice President Hubert Humphrey's ultimate nomination was tainted by the protests, and he fell to Nixon in the fall.[22] These twists and turns of history nudged Stan Adelstein on a path that would soon land him at the front door to the White House.

MAYBE THEY DON'T HAVE BOOTS

If anyone in the United States believed that the transition from one decade to the next might bring an end to the tumult that marred the 1960s, time proved them wrong. The war in Vietnam had bled into a blistering bombing campaign over Laos and Cambodia, as well as a brief invasion of Cambodia by U.S. and South Vietnamese soldiers in 1970. Antiwar sentiment raged on as the Nixon administration searched for a way to end the conflict, while inflation and a stagnant economy tore at the United States. Fortunately for Nixon, he successfully stitched together a loose tapestry of economic remedies and stabilized his foreign policy long enough to win a landslide reelection victory over Senator George McGovern, an ardent South Dakota Democrat who ran on a largely antiwar platform, in 1972.[23]

This balancing act kept Nixon in power just long enough for scandal to kick him out.[24] In real time, the events trickled along, each creating more public anxiety than the next. But in retrospect they fall into a neat chronology: In

1973, Nixon's vice president, former Maryland Governor Spiro Agnew, resigned his seat under charges of corruption and graft.[25] Nixon replaced him with longtime Michigan congressman and House Minority Leader Gerald Ford. Meanwhile, investigators explored whether Nixon had orchestrated a cover-up of the break-in at the Democratic National Committee's offices at the Watergate office building in the summer of 1972.

These issues dominated the headlines, and Nelson Rockefeller made them the primary topic of his speeches in Mitchell and Rapid City in February 1974. There, Rockefeller attempted to insulate Republicans from the sins of their leader, claiming that "Watergate is the tragedy of the individual and not the party. We have to follow the Constitution. Everyone gets a fair deal, and that includes the president," and he called on Congress to devise a constitutionally backed response to the problem.[26] Less than six months later, in August 1974, Ford supplanted Nixon in the Oval Office after Nixon chose resignation over impeachment.[27] And, before the year was out, Ford would name Nelson Rockefeller as his vice president.[28]

In this shuffle, Adelstein received a chance to take an active role in the new Ford administration. *"Due to my prominence in the South Dakota Republican Party, my name made its way to Washington,"* where President Ford nominated Stan to the National Advisory Council on Economic Opportunity (NACEO). The NACEO had been created by the Economic Opportunity Act of 1964, which was a pillar of President Johnson's "War on Poverty."[29] The bipartisan council provided annual evaluations of the effectiveness of federal antipoverty efforts to the president, who in turn shared them with Congress. The first report came out in 1967, compiling assessments from reports generated by War on Poverty agencies like the Office of Economic Opportunity (OEO) and the local Community Action Agencies it oversaw. The NACEO coupled these reports with testimony from hearings, meetings, and outreach efforts it hosted in order to gain the perspectives of federal, state, local, and private participants in antipoverty efforts.[30] *"Our role was to give a report to Congress,"* Stan said, *"and to seek additional innovation in the private sector."*

When Richard Nixon assumed office in 1968, he curtailed the War on Poverty. This was a deeply political and ideological decision, informed by critics on both the Right and the Left who critiqued Johnson's approach. Nixon used his executive authority to withhold appropriated funds from the OEO, *"and Nixon destroyed the NACEO by refusing to appoint anyone to the board for years."* The Ford

CHAPTER 14

administration revived it, changing the OEO's name to Community Services Administration (CSA) in 1975, and reactivating the NACEO in March 1976.[31]

President Ford nominated Stan to the NACEO that very month. He attended his first meeting in Washington, D.C., in early May, and credited his ability to keep up with his career and his new appointment—not to mention his Jewish activism and the many civic and charitable causes he served in the Black Hills—to NWE's company airplane. *"All of this kind of work was really enabled by our company plane,"* he said. *"I would leave Rapid City at about four or five o'clock in the evening and be to D.C. or New York by early morning. It was a nine-hour flight, and I could go to meetings for the AJC, the NACEO, whatever. I would work during the day and then fly back at night, sleeping on that little couch in the plane."*

The NACEO met at an office on K Street Northwest, about fifteen blocks from the White House.[32] The room was filled with twenty-one leather chairs, each bearing a brass plaque with a short inscription offering the name and state of each member. *"We had this beautiful conference room,"* Stan said of one of the group's very first actions, *"and we're supposed to be talking about poverty, and there were these gorgeous leather chairs with little plaques. Mine said 'The Honorable Stanford Adelstein, South Dakota.'"* The committee members, however, found it absurd that such opulence would adorn the seats of a committee tasked with ameliorating the poverty that was devastating so many Americans. So, *"we all looked at the staff and we said, 'Get those plaques off those chairs!'"* With the plaques gone, the committee went to work.

The council's efforts to rebuild under the Ford administration were short-lived. That fall, Jimmy Carter defeated Gerald Ford. Shortly after assuming office in January 1977, President Carter appointed Graciela Olivarez to lead the NACEO, and the members of the council understood that they would soon be replaced by individuals chosen by the new administration. But those appointments would take time, and in the interim, Stan and his colleagues were challenged to work with the new administration and the new director.

Olivarez was a Latina lawyer and longtime civil rights activist who had served on the original 1965 council. She sought to reinvigorate the government's antipoverty programs in collaboration with the bipartisan council.[33] But she recognized that her task would not be easy. The CSA "is in shambles right now," she told the council at one of her first meetings. For years, reports of malfeasance by OEO grantees had damaged the agency's reputation. It only survived, she said, thanks to "some friends in Congress" and "some very good lobbying efforts." She confessed that she was directing an empty shell; the CSA had only a few staff members and would operate on shoestrings until the congressional confirmation process seated agency administrators. And times were tough. "There's a move on the Hill to abolish 2,000 and some-odd advisory councils," she said, before noting that it looked like the NACEO would survive.[34]

On the bright side, Olivarez "want[ed] a very strong advisory council." She promised to take the group's recommendations seriously and desired innovative ideas for how the CSA could improve Head Start, Legal Services, and other programs, and, in the process, become a laboratory for testing poverty solutions.[35] Most important, for the first time in a decade, the NACEO had the solid support of the president of the United States. Where the council "had been encouraged to view its role in the narrowest sense" by previous administrations, Olivarez said, President Carter wanted it to "expand its perspective to include much broader policy analysis and to provide advice" for long- and short-term policy making.[36]

The council's task was to advise the director of the CSA on matters of policy, review and make recommendations that could improve programs, eliminate bureaucratic redundancies, and coordinate programs "designed to assist low-income individuals and families."[37]

The chairman, Fernando Penabaz, a Cuban American radio host and longtime Republican from Miami, oversaw a council divided into three subcommittees: Rural Coordination, Urban Coordination, and National Issues. Stan served on the last committee, whose function was to float between the first two groups and offer suggestions about how to identify executive and legislative branch remedies to the local questions they uncovered and to follow up with the CSA to ensure that the agency implemented the council's suggestions.[38]

Where many Republicans long savaged Lyndon Johnson's War on Poverty as a misguided, Keynesian mistake, Adelstein *"really believed in community action."* In a letter just before he left the council in 1977, he encouraged Olivarez not to dismiss the successes of the 1960s. His ideas were not based on conjecture or ideology. Rather, he spoke from experience working with impoverished people in his home state. Volunteers in Service to America, or VISTA—a program that subsidized living expenses for people who did community work in underserved areas—Stan wrote, "has furnished the best support that the poor community has ever had," opening "new 'windows' [into] a world that many poor South Dakotans didn't even realize existed." He had faith in the NACEO, which he believed provided an "excellent vehicle" for "emphasizing interagency cooperation" and, more important, had the oversight capacity to force programs that had been marred by corruption or had their mission changed by politics back on course.[39]

Comprised of fifteen men and six women, the NACEO committee included a Chinese American businessman, three African Americans, a Cuban American member—Penabaz—and one Jewish representative, Stan Adelstein. A looming problem, however, lay in the fact that, as one memo outlining the role and makeup of the council pointed out, "there are currently no true representatives of the poor or of organizations that represent the poor" on the council.[40] Stan recalled one meeting toward the end of his tenure, after the group submitted its report to the president. Diversity had come up in conversation with several members, who were in the middle of reflecting about how their evaluation had included language about the African American poor and the Latino/a poor. *"The Chinese American member said 'What about the Asian poor?' and I said, 'If we specify everyone, let's include the Jewish poor.' When I said that, the group laughed. I was infuriated with their stereotypical response,"* which assumed all Jewish people were wealthy. *"So I pointed out that according to the data, if 15 percent of Americans were below the poverty line, which was unacceptable, then so were 15 percent of the Jews, mostly in big cities like New York, Chicago, and Philadelphia—they were just more invisible. I explained to them that Jewish wealth was simply more concentrated at the top. Even though we only made up about 2 percent of the population, Jews tended to make up about 6 percent of the top 15 percent of income earners overall. But that didn't mean there weren't any Jews who were struggling. In fact, the data in those days showed Jews to be pretty close to other disadvantaged groups in America when it came to poverty."*

"I always saw conversations like this one as an opportunity to show others that, to us, the great thing about being American didn't have much to do with economic prosperity. Given the restrictions on where we could live, what education we could receive, what jobs we could have, and how unequally we were treated in other court systems around the world, the freedoms America offered took a lot of pressure off our backs. Because many Jewish families valued hard work and literacy, a lot of our people were able to excel when we weren't constrained by oppression."

Over the course of eighteen months, Stan and the rest of the NACEO councilors focused on a bevy of problems facing marginalized Americans. They discussed the energy crisis, describing how fuel shortages disproportionately affected inner cities and rural communities. Stan noted that these shortages would almost certainly put extra pressure on civil rights, already a tense issue in many parts of the country. All of these were significant challenges. One sentence that Stan jotted down at a council meeting in 1976, however, crystallized his belief in the CSA and federal efforts to alleviate poverty. Even he, a lifelong Republican and businessman who was committed to personal liberty and responsibility, saw the problem: "Why can't they pull themselves up by their bootstraps?" someone in the room had asked. Adelstein answered the question to himself: "Maybe they don't have boots."[41]

Wrapped in politics and buried under an immense bureaucracy, even Graciela Olivarez admitted that the council's "recommendations" often "ha[d] gone nowhere." Although she promised to reverse that trend, the extent to which the NACEO reports actually affected policy remains obtuse. The hundred-page report that Stan Adelstein and the rest of the council signed and delivered to President Carter in 1977 contained an overview of the challenges that the CSA and its working parts faced. It reviewed statistics about urban and rural poverty and the programs in place to combat these circumstances. It then set forth some fundamental recommendations that the NACEO thought could improve services for impoverished people across the United States.[42]

Eager to serve the nation on issues that were close to his heart, Stan was disappointed to have to step down from the NACEO in 1977. The end of his tenure that year resulted from the outcome of the 1976 presidential election; Democrat Jimmy Carter did not renew Adelstein's nomination. Although the 1980 election cycle would return a Republican to the White House, it would also bring an even more dramatic change to the NACEO. Less than a year into his first term, President Ronald Reagan abolished the committee and the CSA.[43]

For years afterward, historians would debate the efficacy and legacies of many of the Johnson administration's Great Society programs, but for Stan Adelstein, the experience of serving with the other members of the NACEO deepened his concerns for people who had been marginalized in America even as it reinforced his skepticism about the government's ability to address problems related to poverty. As a Jewish man, Stan tended to look to the history of his own people and the importance of solidarity, self-help, and community in the effort to triumph over adversity. This impulse was evident in his continuing effort to play a role in national Jewish organizations, despite his relative religious isolation in western South Dakota.

AMERICAN ISRAELI POLITICAL ACTION COMMITTEE

Adelstein's service on the NACEO reflected his growing prominence in nationally influential political circles by the mid-1970s. By then, he was deeply entwined in local, state, and national Republican politics, as well as national and international Jewish affairs. Positioned this way, Adelstein became a key catalyst when the American Israeli Political Action Committee (AIPAC) transformed itself into a dominant political force in the 1970s.

Founded in the early 1950s, only a few years after the creation of the State of Israel, AIPAC sought to inform members of Congress and presidential administrations about the challenges Israel faced and to secure political support and foreign aid. AIPAC spent about twenty years building a foundation of supporters and knitting expansive connections in the legislative and executive branches.[44] As Adelstein put it, *"AIPAC had been formed to tell the story of Israel and to give truthful responses to negative information being disseminated by the many wealthy Arab countries. It did this by working alongside groups like the Zionist Organization of America and its partnering women's group, Hadassah, and various synagogue associations around the country."* AIPAC's efforts began in coastal states where the largest numbers of Jewish constituents lived. Its efforts paid enormous dividends. Between 1969 and 1977, American foreign aid to Israel averaged around $700 million each year—almost 10 percent higher than the amounts the White House had written into its annual budgets.[45]

In the late 1970s, a few members of AIPAC set their sights on rural "flyover states" with smaller Jewish populations. As Stan said, *"I received a call around 1977 or 1978 from a political friend in Alaska. He wanted to talk about the lack of understanding for Israeli needs among congressional members from rural states like South Dakota, Montana, and Alaska. The idea was to cultivate relationships and regular communication between Jewish constituents and our congressional representatives. After a little organizing, we had developed a very effective group of creative thinkers. Among them was Harlan 'Bud' Hockenberg, a really well-known attorney from Des Moines, Iowa. I was also close to Jerry Weissman, who owned an industrial steel company in Montana and Solomon "Sol" Dutka, who founded Audits & Surveys Worldwide, the company that was a leader in the political polling and marketing world. I also found that several of my fellow YPO members were interested in this work, including Gordon 'Gordy' Zacks,"* who ran his family's footwear company, the R.G. Barry Corporation, for many years and would later become a key adviser on Middle Eastern affairs for President George H.W. Bush. *"Our group devised plans to work with members of Congress from our states."*⁴⁶

In this early era, Stan said, the group focused on raising awareness. He was careful to point out that, despite the name "AIPAC," *"we weren't initially focused on fund-raising, and despite some misconceptions, AIPAC did not operate as a political action committee, or PAC. In fact, there wasn't much discussion about funding or furnishing dollars for political candidates in the early days. Instead, we focused on arranging trips to Israel so members of Congress could see and learn about Israel firsthand. As time went on, however, people started bringing congressional candidates to board meetings, and later on, to the AIPAC annual meeting, to introduce them to our members with an idea to encourage other members to support their campaigns financially. Even though we weren't a PAC, AIPAC grew from an organization established to spread information about public affairs into one that financed political action."*⁴⁷

As this strategy evolved and became successful, Stan said, AIPAC's opponents sought to undermine its legitimacy. *"Unfortunately, the enemies of Israel and AIPAC have come to refer to the organization, and others that support the Jewish State, as 'the Israel lobby,' which is quite an anti-Semitic dog whistle that plays on old stereotypes. The fact is that when American Jews lobby their members of Congress, they are simply exerting their rights as citizens of this free country, just as other citizens lobby for the things they care about."*

Seeking to exercise his rights to affect political decision making, Adelstein became deeply involved with AIPAC shortly after receiving that call from Alaska. Since many Jewish voters were liberal Democrats, Adelstein's work crossed party lines. Among his closest allies was Tom Lantos, a Jewish man who had been born in Hungary and escaped the Holocaust. Stan met Lantos through their Jewish activism in the 1970s when Lantos was working as an economics professor in San Francisco.⁴⁸ Despite their divergent party loyalties, the men were able to find common ground on issues relating to Israel. And, unlike Adelstein, Lantos had no business-related conflicts of interest preventing him from running for office. This realization inspired Stan to encourage Lantos to run for Congress during a visit to the Bay Area in the late 1970s. *"I remember asking Tom, 'Rather than talking from the outside to members of Congress, why don't you run?' and he said, 'How would I do that? Where would the financing come from?'*

So some of us helped arrange for financial support for his campaign, and Tom was probably one of the first major political beneficiaries of AIPAC."

As part of this process, Adelstein connected Lantos with Mathilde Albers, a woman he knew through the Jewish Agency for Israel, a non-profit organization that encouraged Jewish people to connect with their heritage *"and acted as the political leadership organization of the Zionist movement."* Albers was also a Holocaust survivor who had, along with her husband, found success selling medical equipment and then owned a network of nursing homes. Albers, as Stan remembered, remained deeply skeptical of non-Jewish people; throughout her life *"she refused to speak to them after dark"* and committed much of her time to Jewish causes. She helped raise funds for Lantos, who won his first House race in 1980 and would serve thirteen additional terms, earning a reputation as a "tart-tongue[d]" defender of human rights.[49] Lantos allied with AIPAC throughout his long political career, joining what one scholar calls a "formidable group" of members of Congress who supported Israel.[50]

Back home in South Dakota, Adelstein was able to leverage his influence in Republican circles to encourage the state's Republican members of Congress to support Israel. Adelstein had an especially close relationship with Ellis James "Jim" Abdnor, who was the son of Lebanese immigrants who had settled in rural Kennebec, South Dakota. A Republican farmer who had served a term as lieutenant governor, Abdnor won his first House seat in 1972.[51]

Only months into his freshman year in Congress, Abdnor had asked Stan about Israeli and broader Jewish concerns. Exchanging letters, Adbnor and Adelstein discussed major topics, like the extent to which Soviet anti-Semitism differed from the regime's oppression of other groups or commiserating about the many Jewish families struggling to flee the Soviet Union as refugees.[52] This correspondence began a long relationship between the men, and they often mixed personal pleasantries with conversations about electoral politics. Stan even sent Abdnor a plant to decorate his new office in Rapid City after he won a seat in the upper chamber in 1980, and rarely skipped an opportunity to encourage Abdnor to vote against American arms sales to Arab nations or to support legislation advantageous to the Israelis.[53]

Adelstein was on similarly good terms with Larry Pressler, another South Dakota Republican who served alongside Abdnor in the House of Representatives. Pressler had been a Rhodes Scholar and graduated from

Harvard Law before serving in Vietnam, working in the State Department, and running for Congress.[54] In a book he wrote profiling U.S. senators from South Dakota, Pressler characterized himself as "relatively independent" of lobby and political pressures, "particularly in his service on the prestigious Foreign Relations Committee."[55] That did not stop Stan from making the case for Israel.

By the early 1980s, Stan Adelstein had become an influential member of AIPAC. He served on the board of directors for five years beginning in 1982, and for the first two years of that service sat on the executive committee. This service followed on the heels of Stan's term as national vice president of the AJC and overlapped with his work on behalf of the World Assembly of the Jewish Agency, the Jewish Institute for National Security Affairs, and other organizations.

Given this prominence, Adelstein became a gatekeeper between South Dakota congressmen and Jewish and Israeli advocates. Early on, Adelstein tried to put Jewish activists in touch with Pressler and Abdnor whenever possible, thinking "the more Jews they hear from, the more sympathetic they become to our causes." But he found this strategy often backfired, which is why Stan refused Morton Rywick, the executive director of the Jewish Community Relations Council for Minnesota's Anti-Defamation League, who wanted to set up a meeting with the two senators. Jewish people, Stan reasoned, had a tendency to meet with leaders so often that "non-Jews in the political sector have trouble deciding what our real and urgent priorities are." As such, he exercised great care when extending personal connections.[56]

Adelstein reassured Rywick that Pressler was already "well related to the Washington Office of the AJC and to AIPAC," then noted how Abdnor's case was more sensitive. Adelstein was extra careful about setting up meetings between Jews and the senator because, as he put it, "the special nature of Jim Abdnor's background"—his Lebanese ancestry—"and understanding of our issues," Stan wrote, "must be handled very delicately and frankly only by those who know him well, such as Governor Bill Janklow and myself."[57]

THE REAL POWER

In January 1981, Stan flew to Washington, D.C., for the inauguration of President Ronald Reagan. He was a member of Reagan's inaugural committee, and a few months earlier had made a $200,000 loan to help cover the costs associated with the many receptions, balls, and events that would surround the fortieth president's swearing-in. *"After every presidential election, there is a fund-raising effort to help cover costs associated with the new president's inauguration,"* Stan said. *"They only have a couple of months to raise the money, so private donors make loans to give the inaugural committee the cash it needs to start planning, cover deposits from vendors, things like that. I had a friend in the YPO who reached out to me about the Reagan inaugural. He said they were trying to raise $2 million and wanted a $200,000 loan from me. I said, 'Sure,' and wrote the check. Before I turned it in, I said, 'Are you sure they're good for it?' and he just smiled and said, 'Well, we haven't lost any yet!'"*

A member of the executive committee of the South Dakota Republican Central Committee, Adelstein flew to Washington with Bill Duhamel, a friend from Rapid City. Over the next three days, Stan would attend a meeting of the Republican Governors' Association, which the president-elect himself keynoted; network at several luncheons with politicians, their staff members, and party operatives; take in Reagan's inauguration; and celebrate at several balls.[58]

Stan and Carole Hillard—a prominent South Dakota Republican and later the first woman to serve as the state's lieutenant governor—had good seats overlooking the inaugural platform on the west face of the Capitol building.[59] A marine band played patriotic songs as a warm-up to the ceremony. The entire crowd stood, held hands, and joined in a mass rendition of "American the Beautiful." "I still don't permit myself tears," Stan would later write, "but [I] had a wet cheek."[60]

Even if Ronald Reagan was more socially conservative that Stan preferred, Adelstein *"really liked him."* At an AJC meeting about a year before the 1980 election, Stan had scribbled a note-to-self observing that the "Reagan organization, support and philosophical bent is <u>radically</u> different from <u>anything</u> that wing of the party has advocated since I have been in politics."[61] After the multiday political victory lap that was Reagan's inaugural, Adelstein wrote with satisfaction that the new president's supporters did not conduct themselves with the same zealousness that had unnerved him about the Goldwater camp sixteen years earlier.[62] *"I liked Reagan because of our relationship with Israel"*—although a sharp disagreement would soon present itself—and *"I liked him because of states' rights,"* Stan said. Most important, Adelstein *"loathed President Carter for his economics. I loathed him because of the deal on Israel, and because his Evangelical Christian beliefs didn't seem to leave much room for people of other religions."*

For these reasons, Stan believed, Reagan represented a monumental improvement from his predecessor.

Merely hours after the United States dove headlong into what the historian Sean Wilentz has called the "Age of Reagan," Stan's party arrived at The Great Hall of the historic Pension Building for an inauguration-night gala.[63] Stan "foolishly offered" to check everyone's coats and quickly got lost in the crowded building, wondering if he "would never be heard from again." Stan eventually made it back, then reveled with the rest of the victors. At the end of the night, Stan headed out again to reclaim everyone's coats. He "wandered through some back stairways," and on the trail, bumped into someone who "obviously was enjoying himself, although his secret service escort wasn't." In the melee, Adelstein had knocked directly into former Secretary of State Henry Kissinger.[64]

The significance of that moment, and the realization that most people never attended a single black-tie event in Washington, D.C. (let alone three nights of them in a row), much less ran into Henry Kissinger, seemed lost on Stan. When the festivities finally died down, he headed off to chair an AJC panel on the role that Jewish people could play in the electoral process in coming years.[65]

A few days later, Adelstein ruminated on his time in the nation's capital. Rather than reveling in his party's electoral accomplishments, and the years of work that put him at the highest echelons of American politics, he described a peculiar mix of contentment and lamentation, admitting that he had thus far lived "an interesting life."[66] Years later, Stan would tell several family members that, deep down, he understood that he had originally gotten into politics "for reasons of ego and self-gratification."[67] Years of reflection and regret would teach him the folly of his unquenchable thirst for access and recognition. But on that day in 1981, his ego sat unsatiated. Stan Adelstein, the Jewish millionaire from South Dakota who had wined and dined with presidents and prime ministers, wrote of disappointment. Despite it all, he said, he had thus far fallen "just short of the power—the real power," by which he seemed to mean the authority wielded by elected officials.[68]

Stan's reflection hinted at his subtle but growing desire to move himself from the political shadows—the campaign committees, personal lobbies, and strategic war rooms of party politics—and into a race for electoral office. When

Ronald Reagan placed his hand on a Bible that January day in 1981, it would be almost exactly twenty years before Stan Adelstein swore an oath of his own and got his first personal taste of the "the real power."

AWACS

Of all the work Adelstein did on behalf of Jewish and pro-Israel organizations between the late 1970s and early 1980s, an episode in 1981 best captures the complex personal and political channels through which he fought for the issues he cared most about. In March of that year—barely two months after Stan had attended Reagan's inauguration—the White House announced that the United States would sell sidewinder missiles, fuel pods for F-15 fighters, and several state-of-the-art Boeing E-3 Sentry reconnaissance planes—which were known as AWACS—to Saudi Arabia in an $8.5 million deal.[69] One historian argues that Reagan had pushed the sale in order to achieve stability in a chaotic Persian Gulf while preserving American military dominance in the region.[70]

Jewish organizations were upset by the proposed deal. Jewish Republicans, like Stan, believed it threatened Israel's security and reflected a betrayal of their support for Reagan in the election. Reagan, after all, had received 40 percent of the Jewish vote in the 1980 election, which was an historic high for any Republican vying for the Oval Office.[71] The irony, of course, was that the bulk of Jewish disappointment with Carter had stemmed from his administration's willingness to equip Arab nations.[72]

Jewish allies in Congress, AIPAC, and other pro-Israeli organizations mounted their opposition to the proposed arms sale over the spring and summer.[73] Senator Bob Packwood of Oregon—an ally and close personal friend of Stan's—was among those who spoke out against the proposed AWACS sale. Packwood wrote a letter asking Reagan to kill the deal, then convinced fifty-four senators to sign it.[74] That letter grew into a resolution, colloquially called the "Packwood Resolution," which condemned the sale. As it became clear that the Packwood Resolution might be approved by the Senate, President Reagan pushed Republican senators like Larry Pressler to defeat the measure.[75]

In the middle of this legislative battle, Stan Adelstein became personally invested in the issue, and even took Pressler to Israel in August 1981. Months later, he reflected that the senator "seemed to develop a clear understanding of not only the strategic conditions in the area, but the contrasts between the values of the Arabists [sic] and the Israelis." The trip also provided an opportunity, from Stan's perspective, for the two men to develop "a strong—almost intimate—personal relationship."[76]

With this gentle lobbying effort, Adelstein helped secure Pressler's opposition to the arms sale, at least for the time being. But a couple of months later, bad news arrived in Stan's mailbox. His friend Bill Janklow had forwarded a courtesy copy of a letter he had sent to Pressler, asking him to support the president's AWACS plan. The governor opened the letter by telling Pressler that he tended to avoid wading into congressional affairs unless an issue would directly affect South Dakotans. "I do understand the concerns you may have for Israel," Janklow wrote. After all, the governor's own father was Jewish and had served as a prosecutor during the Nuremburg Trials after World War II. After reminding Pressler of this fact, Janklow pushed him to support the Saudi deal, which had the approval of President Reagan and "all living Presidents, Secretaries of State, and National Security advisors."[77]

Next, Janklow went to the heart of his argument. The Saudis had threatened to retaliate against the United States if the deal broke down, promising to tighten access to fuel, the high price of which was already hurting South Dakota farmers and would do further damage to a Caterpillar tractor company in the state. Saudi Arabia, moreover, had hinted that it could pull assets from South Dakota banks.[78] Janklow noted that he had already been forced to "administer a petroleum set-aside program" in 1978 to compensate for the second major oil shortage that decade.[79] Like it or not, he implored Pressler, South Dakota families "directly or indirectly benefit from Saudi Arabia's purchases of food and other agricultural products."[80]

Adelstein was irate. "I had always felt that Bill Janklow would be neither influenced by a preponderance of notables on the one hand or a threat of unreasonable economic retribution on the other," he steamed in his reply to Janklow. He told the governor he did not believe that Saudi threats could pressure South Dakotans to "call a secret meeting with a senator of Larry Pressler's unquestioned courage of conviction."[81] "In the beginning of the Reagan administration," he continued, "the United States began to be seen as a strong and forthright power. The fact that the Saudis could pressure us is damaging to our image not only in others' eyes, but in our own as well." He

CHAPTER 14

admitted that the Saudis could sting South Dakota by driving up gas prices or withholding money for agricultural products, but this was a small price to pay for refusing to be bullied. "Are we so impotent in South Dakota that we would trade the possibility of markets and petroleum products for 1200 side-winder missiles whose only possible application would be the destruction of Israeli aircraft?" He ended the letter on an acerbic, disappointed note. "We have disagreed before, Bill, and perhaps will again," Stan wrote. But "never in the 12 or 13 years that we've dealt with one another have I ever had such a sense of value difference."[82]

The Reagan administration won the day, pushing the Senate to reject the Packwood Resolution by a vote of 52 to 48 on October 28.[83] According to Pressler, he supported the plan only "after the Senate had persuaded the President to strike a harder bargain" with the Saudis. His vote stemmed from his own belief that the sale was in the nation's best interest because, he said, refusing to approve it would damage Reagan's "ability to conduct foreign policy."[84] Even Adelstein eventually softened on the issue. "*I visited Tinker Air Force Base in Oklahoma—I think Janklow might have set up the trip—and actually spent time with the AWACS,*" he said. "*Somebody there told me how the AWACS were going to Saudi Arabia, but as I toured the aircraft, I could see the absence of any hardware or weapons for anything except defense. Since it wasn't being sold as an offensive weapon, I could tell that it wouldn't be able to threaten Israel in the way we'd all been led to believe. That changed my mind, and I decided to back off the issue.*"

It is unclear exactly when Stan took this trip and when his opinion of the AWACS sale started to shift. As of early November 1981, he was still angry. He dejectedly told Alice Ginott, another Holocaust escapee and noted psychologist in Manhattan, that during the August visit to Israel and at a White House dinner later on, he had introduced Pressler to "nearly everyone of any significance in the Jewish-American leadership." The senator "had an opportunity to discuss a number of issues—not least of which was his own ambition—with many of them."[85] These conversations, a mix of impassioned discussion and winking assurances of campaign support, left Adelstein feeling that Pressler would reject the AWACS sale. According to Stan, late in the evening the night before a major Senate Foreign Relations Committee meeting on the deal, Pressler had "assured" Adelstein "that he was unwavering despite pressure from the White House." One of two things seemed to have happened: either

Pressler had fibbed about his decision in his conversations with Adelstein, or something happened between their call and the committee's session. In any case, as Stan wrote, "the next day he changed" his mind and his vote.[86]

Adelstein had another, more biting take on Pressler's oscillation, and it illustrates the rawness of Stan's emotions, as well as the brutal pragmatism that underlay his work as a political operative. In a letter written on the same day he had lauded the senator's "unquestioned courage of conviction" to Bill Janklow, Adelstein noted to a friend that Pressler "is at best a frail instrument. He has few convictions and little strength of character. We didn't mind that so much as long as these were items which could be utilized to our advantage. Now we don't like it so much."[87]

CHAPTER 15
LAKOTAS AND ISRAELIS

Stan's first impressions of Lakota people had come from his mother, who talked about the friendly relationship his paternal grandmother had shared with Native customers in Kadoka. Bertha Martinsky supplied nearby reservation families with staples. *"My mother told me that when the store was filled with Indians, if Grandma wanted to get a quick bite or go to the bathroom, she didn't worry"* because she believed Native patrons *"would never steal from her."* Martinsky, family lore maintained, kept a closer eye on white customers. In fact, Stan remembered once telling his grandmother how her observations about frontier racism shaped his worldview. *"I said to Grandmother, 'the truth as you told it to me was absolutely the opposite of the stereotypical 'thieving Indian' and 'greedy-eyed Jew.'"* These early experiences helped form Stan's approach to the minority rights issues that would continue to plague western South Dakota throughout his life.

By the 1960s, dispossessed of treaty lands, rarely welcomed by the tourism industry, and facing an uphill climb in schools and employment lines, Native people in South Dakota faced all manner of economic and social strife on reservations and in border towns.[1] Influenced by the national civil rights and women's rights movements, as well as organizations like the Black Panthers and the National Council of La Raza, Native people in South Dakota were beginning to organize. The most visible arm of Native activism was the American Indian Movement (AIM), which had been founded in Minneapolis in 1968 and held high-profile demonstrations well into the 1970s. Protesting treaty violations and discrimination, AIM launched a series of occupations, including those of Alcatraz Island and the Bureau of Indian Affairs offices in Washington, D.C.[2]

Adelstein's introduction to Indian rights activists did not begin with AIM. In 1968, members of the Black Hills Council of American Indians were working to improve race relations and economic opportunities for Lakota people in western South Dakota.[3] The council, Stan wrote, "ha[d] recently been reactivated in an attempt to unify a badly divided Indian community." Recognizing Stan's influence, council members reached out to him to express their concerns with "excessive police brutality." In a meeting with Stan, they told him demoralizing tales of instances in which law enforcement officers had used their authority, as Stan said, quoting the council, to "'terrorize' the Indian community."[4]

Listening to these stories, Stan marveled at how little he and most of his friends in Rapid City knew about this issue. As he wrote later to a fellow AJC member, "I was, of course, horrified because . . . I had never realized that such a thing was happening, despite the fact that I supposedly have a position of influence in our area power structure."[5]

The leaders of the Black Hills Council told Adelstein that he was "the first 'powerful' . . . white man with whom they had ever visited" about these issues. Stunned, Stan asked why. They did not believe any white person of consequence would listen, the council members said.[6] Burdened with a sense of injustice, Adelstein resolved to try to help.

Some Native Americans were almost certainly skeptical of this Jewish millionaire who, despite his people's long struggle against prejudice, had never personally felt the burn of discrimination in comparable terms. Nevertheless, over the next several years Stan developed a reputation as an ally to Native people. He pulled strings in local government and among socially active Rapid Citians when he needed to. He organized meetings with the mayor, police chief, area religious leaders, and members of the American Indian community, always seeking to open the lines of communication. In August 1969, he wrote to Charles Undlin, the president of the local First National Bank, and several other members of the business community and invited them to a meeting at the Arrowhead Country Club. Along with Ray Briggs, a Lakota man and employment specialist with the local community action program, Stan moderated a conversation focused on ways to increase employment for American Indians, who, as he said, were "obviously in a substandard economic condition." Throughout these discussions, Stan encouraged candor, telling Undlin that the meeting would be "one of the rare occasions when you're asked to bring your prejudices with you," so they could be laid bare and opened for discussion.[7]

Stan's notes further illuminated these meetings. During one conversation, local Native leaders expressed frustration at the fact that there were "no brown faces" among the police force, probation officers, or judges. They thought that when the police intervened in a conflict between Native and non-Native people, Indians were usually "asked different questions" than whites. Many Native people were hauled to jail while non-Natives received a warning. Once in custody, Native defendants encountered court-appointed attorneys who, many believed, did not care about their cases.[8]

At another meeting, the chief of police said he "[didn't] want anybody abused." Along with a local Methodist minister, he agreed to sit down and have an open, nonargumentative dialogue with Native leaders.[9] The national office of the United Methodist Church even donated $50,000 to a "fund for reconciliation," which was intended to assist Native communities in North and South Dakota. This money was to be paid "directly to the local Indian leadership itself," as one report read, "not a well-intentioned but white-controlled agency or organization with no leverage to effect change." With these resources, local Native people hired a small staff for an organization that would promote race relations by attending cultural awareness trainings and bringing speakers to Rapid City.[10]

As the 1960s drew to a close, all of these efforts seemed to create some meaningful, positive momentum. Yet no amount of discussion between the Black Hills Council and local leaders, or even a robust new reconciliation fund, could stem the tumult that was about to wash through West River. The problems Adelstein discussed with the Black Hills Council in Rapid City were serious, but far less explosive than a brewing dispute between members of the Oglala Sioux Tribe on the Pine Ridge Reservation.

WOUNDED KNEE

By early 1973, Pine Ridge was a powder keg. Over the course of the previous year, tribal members had grown incensed with Tribal Chairman Richard Wilson, whom they accused of nepotism, corruption, and running the reservation like a dictatorship. As his opponents organized against him, Wilson sent a group of his supporters—known as the "GOON squad"—to suppress opposition, often through violence or intimidation.[11] Tribal members tried and failed to impeach Wilson in February.[12] Meanwhile, all of the antagonism stoked anti-Indian sentiment in border towns as well as in Rapid City, where reservation turmoil seemed only to deepen long-entrenched stereotypes about corrupt and chaotic Native American communities.[13]

In mid-February, a local television station aired a special on local race relations. In a telling omission, the special featured Adelstein, not a Native leader. When asked about the single biggest problem facing American Indians, Stan relayed the concerns he had heard in his many meetings with local Natives. Stan told his interviewer that "the fact that [Native Americans] are not really involved in decision making, in the power structure, and in the cultural decisions of our community" tended to separate American Indian people from their non-Indian neighbors. This isolation, he continued, bore wide-ranging consequences, from inequitable treatment in the courts to lower employment and a generally "difficult discriminatory sort of life."[14]

From Stan's perspective, bigotry worked both ways. "I think that the Indian sees the white employer, the white police officer, the white judge, [and] the white elected official," he told viewers, "as someone he can't talk to, who will be unresponsive, who is preconditioned to prejudice." Conversely, he said, "the whites see the Indian as a non-communicative person, as a person not responsible in terms of employment, and [as] someone that can't be counted on."[15]

Adelstein understood the ubiquity of these perceptions but reminded the television audience that his "experience ha[d] shown that both stereotypes [were] inaccurate." He believed improving communication between the Native and non-Native communities was fundamental to solving the problem. He argued passionately against white leaders who "give lip service" to Indian issues, as well as those who anchored their criticism solely in rhetoric about personal responsibility. "We must make some sacrifice," he declared, "and [make] some changes in our attitude in how we integrate [the] minority into the majority culture while still permitting them to keep their culture" and values.[16]

In addition to these public statements, Adelstein organized a private meeting at the Toby Theatre on Sunday night, February 11. In his invitation to participants, Stan promised that "a very small group of the community's actual leaders" would meet with "15 or 20 leaders of the Indian community" and identify some "mutually agreed problem areas." From his point of view, leaders from both communities "need[ed] very badly to delve deeper into what [was] really going on" between the races in Rapid City.[17]

Adelstein's efforts to broker a reasoned dialogue were exploded shortly thereafter when AIM took over the community of Wounded Knee, a tiny town on the Pine Ridge Reservation, in February 1973.[18] As the nation watched on television, hundreds of AIM activists engaged in a seventy-one-day standoff with the FBI, U.S. marshals, and the National Guard. Led by a charismatic Oglala Lakota man named Russell Means and his compatriot Dennis Banks, an Anishinaabe (Ojibwe) man from northern Minnesota, the protesters hunkered down. Shattering the winter silence, sporadic outbursts of rifle fire left a U.S. marshal paralyzed and killed two AIM protesters over the course of the occupation.[19]

Adelstein was enmeshed in two dramatic episodes that took place during the standoff at Wounded Knee. First, sometime early in the impasse, he helped broker a solution to calamity at the Mother Butler Center on the north side of Rapid City. The original Mother Butler Center had been built in 1950 but was badly damaged during the 1972 flood, and the facility was moved later that year. The building consisted of a large, cinder-block gymnasium with an attached kitchen and meeting room. It was owned by an adjacent Catholic church and had served as the town's de facto Native American community center for two decades.[20] A group of AIM activists had been using the center as a meeting space, and according to some rumors were "apparently ready to move in on Pine Ridge at a call from their friends" at Wounded Knee.[21] With the town on edge, the acting mayor, City Council President Larry Lytle, decided to take action.

Mayor Don Barnett was in Pierre for meetings, and in his absence Lytle *"had convinced the bishop to sign an eviction notice,"* Stan said. This would have rendered the AIM folks trespassers as soon as it went into effect, thereby authorizing the police to move in. *"And he brought city police and highway patrolmen and surrounded the building. I had been in there to talk to folks, and I knew they had weapons. The members of the local Community Relations Service"*—a division of the U.S. Department of Justice sent to monitor communities facing racial tension—*"called to warn me that at six o'clock the next morning, the bishop was going to sign the eviction. They were concerned and I was concerned that somebody would get shot. So I called Bill Duhamel, and told him to meet me at the bishop's house at six o'clock the next morning. He said, 'What for?' and I said if I told him the whole story it would keep him up all night—these things always happened in the middle of the night—but just to meet me at the bishop's house at six o'clock. He agreed, and the next morning we went there and convinced the bishop not to sign the order. We didn't know what Lytle was going to do next, and we had to get Barnett back to town. So I called David Volk, who was the state treasurer in Pierre. I didn't know where Barnett was but asked Volk to please find him. I would get the governor to send the state plane to Rapid City, I said, so we could get Barnett back to take charge. Volk shut down the treasurer's office and told his staff to fan out across the capital, find Barnett, and call Stan Adelstein immediately. When they did, Barnett took the governor's plane back to Rapid, and when he got there, he was able to calm things down."* Barnett corroborated this story, noting that Rapid City had been ready to explode when Lytle nearly moved on Mother Butler. "Stan and I didn't agree on a lot of things," he said, "but we sang basically the same song when it came to civil rights issues at that time."[22]

Like many non-Native people living in western South Dakota, Stan's reaction to the takeover was colored by history and the patterns of border-town racism that had been stewing in communities across West River South Dakota for years.[23] For many non-Natives, AIM's tactics were wild and violent disruptions to the local order. To AIM and its supporters, the United States had for too long neglected their complaints about Wilson and his GOONs' tactics. The government evaded responsibility for the turmoil, many Natives believed, by leaning on the fact that Wilson was the duly elected tribal president. Then, when activists took matters into their own hands, they argued, the federal government's response was characteristically heavy-handed. This perception was compounded by the fact that AIM had made its stand at Wounded Knee, the site of a massacre that left hundreds of Lakota men, women, and children dead on the frozen ground at the hands of American soldiers in December 1890.[24]

Meanwhile, several prominent people visited Wounded Knee and attempted to bring the conflict to a peaceful end, including members of South Dakota's congressional delegation.[25] As the standoff dragged on, Stan played an unexpected role in the epic resolution of the conflict. Although a grand jury in Sioux Falls had indicted Russell Means on counts ranging from civil disorder to assault with a deadly weapon, Leonard Garment, a special assistant to President Nixon, had invited Means and others to Washington for negotiations.[26] To enable these conversations, on Thursday afternoon, April 5, the Justice Department and AIM leaders reached a six-point agreement under which, if AIM surrendered, the federal government promised to investigate Indian affairs and charges of corruption at Pine Ridge, consider bringing civil suits to protect the rights of individual Indians from tribal government, and perform a review of the 1868 Fort Laramie Treaty.[27]

After signing the agreement, Means boarded a helicopter and left for Rapid City, intending to continue on to Washington.[28] As Stan recalled, *"Russell's understanding was that he would be free to go to Washington without interruption, but Judge Andy Bogue disagreed with the other judge in Sioux Falls and wanted Means held on the indictments. So he was arrested as soon as he left Wounded Knee."* In his autobiography, Means later mused that he "had always wanted to travel by helicopter, but not until [he] became one of the FBI's ten most wanted did [he] finally get [his] free ride."[29]

Local papers prematurely reported that the standoff had all but ended. Even though Means had left the reservation, AIM occupiers remained at Wounded Knee, and the outcome of the conflict seemed to hinge on his negotiations.[30] Late Thursday evening, Stan received yet another call from the Justice Department's Community Relations Service. The representative asked him to be at the Pennington County Jail at six o'clock the next morning. When he arrived, guards escorted Adelstein to a concrete, second-floor room with no windows, where *"two civil rights attorneys from Minneapolis, two assistant U.S. attorneys and four or five U.S. marshals in blue jumpsuits, who looked like they were six-and-half-feet tall,"* stood next to federal Magistrate Judge Jim Wilson, a friend of Stan's who, that night, was the acting judge for Judge Bogue's court.

Meanwhile, Russell Means was yelling, cursing, and evoking the long history of Native repression. *"He was shouting all kinds of things, like 'Fuck your separation of powers!' and 'Why don't you just run me through like you did Crazy Horse?!'"*

Means clearly believed he had been double-crossed, and the marshals did not want to release him, arguing that even the president's office had no power over the federal court system and could not negotiate around his Sioux Falls indictments. While the marshals wanted to escort Means to Sioux Falls to face trial, his lawyers argued that Nixon's office had granted Means temporary immunity. He, they maintained, should have been freed to help end the standoff at Wounded Knee.

Adelstein knew where he stood. While Means fumed, Stan *"realized that the magic of the constitutional requirement of 'due process,' and even more specifically, the separation of powers, made up the precious difference between the United States and much of the rest of the world."* Stan was intimately aware, for example, of the persecution of Jewish people and others in the Soviet Union, and had been reading reports for years about that government's penchant for imprisoning people without fair trials. *"Immediately when I heard that bit about 'separation of powers,' I could see three Jews in my head. Arrested, locked upstairs, and the prosecutor, the judge, and the Soviet Police were all one person. And it occurred to me, not being an attorney, that if the executive branch could ignore the judicial process in releasing someone,"* he thought, *"they could just as easily jail someone indefinitely. And that was going on daily in the Soviet Union for Jews."* So, Stan believed that Judge Bogue was absolutely correct, and that everyone involved had to follow the law and the process to help get Means to Washington.

Magistrate Wilson clearly understood the severity of the problem. *"Jim was sitting at this little table, and I was across from him."* They both respected the rule of law, but they also wanted Means released so he could go to D.C. and help end the violence in Wounded Knee. As they talked, Means continued to interrupt, *"and I shouted, 'Russell, just shut up and we can see what we can do!' And Wilson said, 'Well, I guess we could bond him out. Would you be willing to furnish bond?' I said, 'Yes, good idea.' So he wrote up a bond that would allow Means to go to Washington, then listed out a set of requirements Russell would have to agree to follow if he was released. When it was done, I walked it over to him and asked if the terms were acceptable—they would allow him to go from Wounded Knee to Washington. He hesitated, but I said, 'This is the only way you're getting out of here,' so he said, 'Okay.' Even though Russell had broken the law and was irate, through everything we had previously worked on together, he had always kept his word. So I agreed to pay the bond."*

Means recalled their interaction differently. While he was waiting for his bond hearing, he wrote, some "lawyers brought in Stan Adelstein, a Jewish liberal Republican and one of the richest men in the state."[31]

According to Means, Stan stared at him, judging him up and down before saying, "You're not going on the run, are you? You're not going to skip to Cuba or anyplace?"[32]

"This is my country," Means said he replied, "no white man is going to run me out of it."[33]

"That's good enough for me," Adelstein answered, according to Means's version of events, and bonded Means out.[34]

Regardless of the details of this exchange, this much is clear: Magistrate

Wilson proposed a deal. If Adelstein would post a $25,000 bond for Means, he would approve conditions that would allow Means to travel between Washington and Wounded Knee until the standoff ended. It took some coaxing and a few minor adjustments to the terms, but Means and his lawyers agreed. The U.S. attorney was harder to convince. Leaning on procedure, he demanded that Stan produce the cash before Wilson released Means. *"He said, 'I don't see any money on the table,' and so Jim Wilson said, 'Alright, I will take judicial notice that Mr. Stanford Adelstein has sufficient means that we know the bond will be covered.' And he let Russell go."*[35]

Immediately after he was freed on bond, Means complained to the press about the terms of this release. His was allowed to return to his family at Porcupine, a small town north of Wounded Knee, and to travel freely as long as he kept his attorney apprised of his whereabouts. He had agreed not to "associate or travel with persons who possess weapons or unlawful incendiaries or explosive devices or ammunition." Per his request, language in the bond also made it clear that he had not surrendered his rights to peaceable assembly and freedom of speech. But as he told reporters, his bond hearing "show[ed] that the white man still refuses to listen and the white people of Western South Dakota will have to deal with me, with my relatives, and with all Indian people." "After . . . listening to the U.S. magistrate," he continued, "I feel I was being judged in a bail bond hearing" rather than at a full and fair trial, "[and] I'm going to be communicating with those at Wounded Knee and giving them instructions and they won't be coming out until there are complete results."[36]

Means went to Washington, but negotiations with White House officials stalled, and the siege continued.[37] *"As time went on, the Justice Department revised Russell's bond several times; each time, I had to approve the extension and ask Russell if he would agree to the new terms. Finally, the Justice Department wanted him to agree to be able to report to any court in South Dakota within twenty-four hours, and he refused. That ended my role."* Shortly thereafter, Means failed to appear for a federal hearing in the Black Hills and stopped informing his lawyer of his travels. He spent time in Los Angeles, where he spoke publicly about Wounded Knee while refusing to report for court dates in South Dakota. FBI agents arrested Means in Los Angeles in late April.[38] Meanwhile, more violence rained down at Wounded Knee after the planned negotiations fell through—it was during this period that federal bullets cut down Native protesters Frank Clearwater and Buddy Lamont.[39]

The standoff at Wounded Knee finally ended nearly two weeks later, after Leonard Garment once again offered to meet with tribal leaders if the occupation came to an end.[40] Federal law enforcement officers arrested hundreds of AIM protesters, hauling them to Rapid City, where their incarceration and trials tied up the local federal court system for months. As the movement's leaders, Means and Banks were tried separately in a federal court in Minnesota, where officials believed they could receive an impartial trial. Both men were cleared of their Wounded Knee charges in September 1974. In the final act of their lengthy trial, one jury member fell ill, and the remaining eleven voted for acquittal. Federal prosecutors sought a mistrial, but Judge Fred Nichol dismissed the case. The next year, a federal court rejected the prosecutors' appeal, and the long ordeal at Wounded Knee was over.[41]

Violence in and around Pine Ridge, however, was not. The reservation murder rate soared in the years after Wounded Knee, as a bloody conflict pitted Wilson, his enforcers, and the Bureau of Indian Affairs (BIA) against the chairman's opponents, dozens of whom died as incidents of violence multiplied across the reservation. Many of these deaths were never investigated, while members of AIM faced intense scrutiny from law enforcement officers.[42] As the battle between activists and federal agents moved from the community of Wounded Knee to the pages of numerous history books and memoirs, the real legacies were apparent to Adelstein and others: the continued divide between Natives and non-Natives in and around the Black Hills.

Stan had continued to look for long-term solutions even in the middle of the conflict at Wounded Knee. On March 4, 1973—just days after the takeover had begun, and a full month before his encounter with Russell Means—Stan hosted another meeting at the Toby Theatre. He called the gathering to order at 7:40 P.M. Twenty-four people attended that night. Nine were leaders from the American Indian community like Jerome Runs After, Basil Brave Heart, Ray Briggs, and Clement Iron Wing. They mingled with a cross section of Stan's network, including Mayor Don Barnett; Rapid City Police Chief Ron Messer; Don White, the president of the Chamber of Commerce; and, of course, Adelstein's friend, the nun Sister Sarto Rogers. Over the next several hours, the group divided into four working groups, each focusing on one of several important issues: housing, employment, law enforcement, and how to provide newcomers to Rapid City, including Lakotas from the reservation, with information about services that were available in town.⁴³ This group may have been unable to quell the bloodshed at Pine Ridge, but it believed it could dull the sharp edge of prejudice in Rapid City.

From Stan's point of view, these conversations were productive: after some prodding, City Council President Lytle talked about how the city might adjust its ordinances to decriminalize public intoxication—a regular excuse for arresting Native Americans—and delineate provisions for treatment rather than incarceration. Others wanted to educate business owners about cultural differences and the stereotypes that prevented them from hiring Native workers. Recognizing that this work would take more than one, or even a dozen, meetings, Stan suggested that they arrange specific working groups and focus on these core issues in coming months.⁴⁴

Two days after the meeting, Barnett—the same mayor who had clashed with Adelstein over the library years earlier—wrote him a grateful note. After stating his appreciation for Stan's "leadership and courage" on racial issues, Barnett assured him that he would come to every meeting and then described how his office would hire more Native Americans for city jobs. Barnett also promised to encourage local businesses to do the same.⁴⁵

Years later, Circuit Court Judge Marshall Young, one of the attendees at the Toby Theatre, said that although the impact of these meetings was difficult to gauge, they "assisted in bringing together the races." He noted that "there ha[d] not been any major demonstrations" matching the bedlam at Wounded Knee.⁴⁶

A STATE APPOINTMENT

In 1975, with Republican Gerald Ford in the White House, the U.S. Commission on Civil Rights asked Stan to serve on South Dakota's State Advisory Committee.⁴⁷ Established by President Eisenhower in 1957, the U.S. Commission on Civil Rights was charged with evaluating and reporting on racial issues and race-related disparities in the United States. As former commissioner and historian Mary Frances Berry writes, however, Eisenhower had "proposed a temporary commission on Civil Rights as a safety valve to relieve discontent and make it possible for him to avoid tough decisions about racial issues."⁴⁸ Subsequent presidents kept the commission alive, and although its recommendations on matters of race, gender, disability, national origin, and other issues were often met with mixed reviews and subject to the vicissitudes of politics and rhetoric, the "commission became known for its integrity" and has been credited with shaping many of the civil rights laws that came about in the middle of the twentieth century.[49]

The commission was supported by state advisory committees made up of local citizens who served without pay and acted as "the eyes and ears of the commission around the country."[50] When Stan accepted his two-year term, he joined eleven other South Dakotans, several of whom he knew from other activities, including his Republican friend Barbara Bates Gunderson and South Dakota state treasurer David Volk. Given that most of the state's civil rights concerns focused on Indian affairs, several of the committee members were either Native Americans or had close ties to Indian Country. Hilario G. Mendoza, a Mexican American from El Paso, Texas, had married a member of the Cheyenne River Sioux Tribe and worked as a program coordinator at the United Sioux Tribes Development Corporation in Pierre and for the Rapid City Community Action Agency. Eric LaPoint, of the Rosebud Sioux Tribe, was a member of the education committee of the National Congress of American Indians. Joining them were Grace Klein, who had been on the committee since 1967 and helped with a study of off-base housing discrimination at Ellsworth; Dorothy Butler, a teacher and member of the National Association for the Advancement of Colored People (NAACP) and the American Civil Liberties Union (ACLU) from Brookings; and others. Meanwhile, the man chosen to serve as chairman was Mario Gonzalez, an attorney from Martin who also served as a tribal judge on the Rosebud Reservation.[51]

Stan served several successive terms on the South Dakota State Advisory Committee, ending in 1985.[52] During that time, he met with hundreds of people across the Dakotas, discussing issues that ranged from fair housing to disparities in Indian and white education, a general lack of local media coverage of Indian issues, and the trouble Native people faced getting access to quality health care.[53] As with his service on Gerald Ford's National Advisory Council on Economic Opportunity, Adelstein often found himself frustrated with political and bureaucratic bulwarks to the committee's work.[54]

Given his experiences working on racial reconciliation issues in Rapid City, Stan had high hopes that the State Advisory Committee could be a catalyst for real changes in race relations and help promote improvements in the quality of life for American Indians in South Dakota. For nearly two years, he and other members of the committee traveled across South Dakota. They interviewed more than 130 people, including citizens, lawyers, law enforcement officers, and court employees. During a fact-finding meeting in Rapid City in December 1976, some fifty people offered testimony that exposed discrimination in housing, employment, and other social sectors.[55] Meanwhile, the advisory committee focused on inequities in the judicial system, taking Pennington County (home to Rapid City) and rural Charles Mix County in southern South Dakota, just east of the Missouri River, as case studies.[56]

The advisory committee issued its report in October 1977. The document revealed the inequities inherent in the legal system. "Despite progress made during the last few years in improving the quality of justice," the committee wrote to the U.S. Commission on Civil Rights, "Indian people continue to face problems in the State's criminal justice system which place them at a severe disadvantage." The committee offered twenty-two recommendations to curb "widespread abuse of police power throughout the State." It also cited "inexperience, difficulties in communication, and inherent conflicts of interest" among court-appointed defense attorneys, as well as "prejudicial attitudes of potential jurors" and "possible abuse of the plea bargaining system," among other problems.[57] The committee recommended hiring more Native law enforcement officers and paralegals, increased training for police officers, the creation of specialized teams to investigate rape cases and work with victims, and a comprehensive investigation of the causes of unemployment and poverty for Native Americans.[58]

Entitled "Liberty and Justice for All," the report offered an unprecedented, in-depth exposé on these issues. Not unexpectedly, the reaction of state officials ranged from tepid acceptance to outright dismissal. Democratic Governor Richard Kneip implemented a few of the recommendations, while noting that some state agencies were already addressing certain problems. He also contacted state law enforcement officials, encouraging them to hire more minorities.[59]

South Dakota's attorney general, Bill Janklow, however, quickly rejected the committee's findings. Janklow was ramping up his first gubernatorial run when the committee released its report. During his campaign for attorney general, Janklow took a hard line against reservation crime and dysfunction, riding intensely anti-AIM rhetoric into office.[60] After the South Dakota State Advisory Committee released its report in 1977, an op-ed writer for the *Argus Leader*, the major daily in Sioux Falls, criticized Janklow for implying that the advisory committee was merely conducting a political witch hunt. Janklow had dismissed "Liberty and Justice for All" as "light weight [sic] reporting." He also questioned the relevancy of the problems contained in the report.[61]

To the frustration of Stan and several other committee members, the media and some federal officials also seemed to disregard the committee's work. Following the release of the report, several members of the U.S. Commission on Civil Rights visited South Dakota for public hearings. During one of the sessions, Art LaCroix stood up and told a personal story that even his close friend Stan Adelstein had never heard. *"I had always known that Art was a veteran of World War II,"* Stan said, *"and that he had fought at the Battle of the Bulge. But I had never heard his story about facing discrimination in Rapid City after the war. Art stood up before the whole hearing and said, 'When I got back from the war, I walked up the steps into the lobby of the Alex Johnson Hotel. I was still in uniform and was feeling proud. Then, an employee told me that they didn't serve Indians there and asked me to leave.' All that changed when he became mayor, of course, and I remember Art finishing up his speech to the advisory committee by saying, 'Now that I'm mayor, I'm welcome everywhere in Rapid City.'"*

Powerful testimony like this, however, seemed to go unheeded. After the hearings, two advisory committee members, William Walsh and David Volk, drafted a letter to Commission Chairman Arthur S. Fleming, complaining that the hearings were cut short. "A number of our Indian witnesses," they wrote, "were let down." Some officials, moreover, "appeared more interested in keeping the hearings toned down to the extent that the Commissioners . . . were shielded from the real impact of racial injustice." Finally, Walsh and Volk added, the South Dakota State Advisory Committee was disappointed with media coverage of the hearings. Only two local television stations showed up, "one local newspaper didn't know anything was going on," and one journalist told the advisory committee that "the people from D.C. were in such a hurry to leave and catch their planes that I couldn't finish my interviews."[62]

For Stan, the experience of serving on the advisory committee had been edifying. In some ways, it even led to real progress. *"After the hearings, during which several Native Americans had told stories about being mistreated by local law enforcement, Art LaCroix called me and said, 'Stan, could my police force really be doing what they're saying?' and I told him, 'Sorry, but I think so, my friend.' So he went ahead and* fired the chief of police and replaced him with Tom Hennies, who established a program to carefully develop a cultural training program to address the issue. The next three police chiefs all went through that training."[63] In other ways, however, the experience was deeply frustrating and fed Stan's deep ambivalence about the government's ability to solve social problems. As he frequently did, Stan searched instead for ways to direct the energy and insights of entrepreneurs toward the needs of society.

AMERICAN INDIAN BUSINESS AND ISRAELI AGRICULTURE

In addition to organizing meetings and working with the advisory committee, Stan had been supporting Native businesses for years. Indian entrepreneurs faced many obstacles. Most lacked adequate capital and could not get loans or employee training, despite federal programs designed to spur economic growth in Indian Country. To confront these issues a group of Native leaders established the South Dakota Indian Businessmen's Association in the autumn of 1971. The following year, they brought 150 Native Americans, including many business owners, together in Rapid City to develop a plan of action. Although membership in the association was limited to citizens of American Indian tribes, a special category—called the "White Brother Membership"—was created for non-Natives hoping to help.[64]

Although it is unclear whether Adelstein became a "White Brother," he served on the advisory board to the Indian Businessmen's Association in 1975 and 1976 and often assisted Indian business start-ups.[65] Sometimes, he offered advice and networking opportunities. In the early 1980s, for example, Adelstein contacted former Rapid City mayor and businessman Earl Brockelsby, who had founded a successful tourist attraction called Reptile Gardens, on behalf of Douglas Fast Horse, the president of a group of Indian entrepreneurs incorporated as the Wambli Group. Fast Horse and his associates had mapped out a Native American theme park called "Indian City U.S.A." and were looking to build on a 170-acre lot near Interstate 90. Their Indian City would include a wax museum, buffet, art gallery, and crafts bazaar, as well as a petting zoo and a "living prairie zoo." All of these attractions would be "intermingled with a vast array of outdoor exhibits and displays from Native Tribes of the North American continent."[66] Adelstein and Fast Horse asked Brockelsby to analyze the business plan and the projected revenues for Indian City, U.S.A. Stan explained that the group had already convinced the city council to agree to a revenue bond, was in talks with lending agencies, and hoped to break ground the following summer.[67]

Brockelsby could not have been happier with the Wambli Group's efforts. "People do come to the Black Hills expecting to see Indians," he replied to Stan, "and if you had a high caliber group operating this park I am sure there would be many pleased visitors." Indeed, he added, three similar ventures had enjoyed relative success in Rapid City's history.[68]

Brockelsby was blunt, however, about "the real side of the tourist business." Noting that competition in the tourism industry had grown dramatically in recent years, he was skeptical of the group's projected revenues. There were, he wrote, "only so many slices you can get from a pie." Indian City would be in direct competition with another successful petting zoo and "four other wax museums." And, Brockelsby added, he "happen[ed] to know that the present wax museums are not getting rich." Closing his letter, Brockelsby reiterated that he thought the venture was a great idea. Given recent market trends, however, he "would give the overall operation one chance in fifty of being financially successful" over the long term.[69] Despite the efforts of the Wambli Group and their assistance from Adelstein, Indian City, U.S.A. never came to fruition.

Over a decade later, a different effort contributed significantly to the largest Native-centric tourist attraction in the Black Hills. In the mid-1990s, Stan got a call from Ruth Ziolkowski. She was the widow of Korczack Ziolkowski, the sculptor who envisioned the massive Crazy Horse Memorial north of Custer along with Lakota activist and Crazy Horse's maternal cousin Henry Standing Bear in the 1940s. Claiming the edifice was the "world's largest mountain carving project," the Ziolkowskis had been working on the still-unfinished monument for decades, famously refusing to accept any government support for the project.[70] Around 1996, Ruth Ziolkowski faced a problem, according to Adelstein. *"A neighboring land owner had a property with a restaurant, gift shop, and theater right next to Crazy Horse, and it was going to be sold to someone who planned on giving free admission with full views of Crazy Horse,"* which would undercut ticket sales at the memorial. *"Ruth said we only had something like seven or ten days before it was sold for over a million dollars, and she asked if I knew of any way to come up with cash to counter the deal. One of the attorneys in the deal was a good friend of mine, and he thought we could get the land if we offered a little more than the going price. I personally guaranteed a loan, and Ruth and I bought the place and operated a business called*

Heritage LLC. It included the restaurant, theater, and a little RV campground, and we ran it for ten years at a cash loss. Every year, Ruth and I each put in $100,000 to pay off the loan, since the operation barely broke even. In the meantime, Crazy Horse grew, received big grants, and was very successful." Indeed, plans to build a museum, cultural center, and theater at the complex were well under way.[71] *"Once the note was paid off, we transferred the property over to Crazy Horse. They repaid my $1 million in ten $100,000 payments, and I'll always be grateful that I was able to help guarantee the continuation of the message and learning that are part of that project. Ruth and I became close friends over the years, and while today Crazy Horse Memorial is a well-funded organization, I remember her once telling me that without my help in those days, she feared that the project would have floundered."*

On other occasions, Stan's involvement in Indian economic development and enterprise stirred controversy. In the 1970s, one individual accused Adelstein of using Indian issues to advance his own business ventures. Shortly after losing reelection to the presidency of the Rosebud Sioux Tribe in 1976, Robert Burnette called for a congressional investigation into "nepotism, politics, and possible corruption in federal Indian housing programs." At the time, Adelstein was a partner in Thunderbolt Enterprises, Inc., a construction company that had been contracted to build ninety-one houses on the Rosebud Reservation. As reported by the *Rapid City Journal*, Burnette said that one of Stan's partners, Lloyd Boyd Jr., had offered him a bribe of $1,000 per house if he could expand the contract to 220 houses. Boyd then threatened that if Burnette refused the offer, Boyd would get his brother-in-law, Ed Driving Hawk, to challenge him for the tribal chairmanship. When Driving Hawk ran and defeated him in the tribal elections, Burnette claimed "nepotism of the rankest sort" was at play.[72]

Burnette further castigated Boyd for his relationship with Adelstein, who had only recently been named to the civil rights and economic opportunity committees. Since those were government agencies and since Thunderbolt served tribal contracts funded by the Department of Housing and Urban Development (HUD), Burnette argued, Stan's involvement was a clear conflict of interest. Indeed, a little investigative journalism showed that Adelstein was still listed as a corporate director on a recently filed financial report. When questioned, Stan stated that while he had once been a partner in Thunderbolt, he had transferred his rights to that company prior to his appointments and until he was approached by reporters, "did not know [he] was still listed as a director." He also denied ever using a political position to get business, then pointed out that he "had lost considerable money trying to aid Indian businesses" over the years.[73]

Burnette's accusations never resulted in any official action, and even if they had, it appears that Stan had disengaged from Thunderbolt before any of the alleged impropriety occurred. The incident, nevertheless, underscored one of the realities of Stan's sprawling approach to business, politics, and community work: his winding march through the world, at least to outsiders, sometimes blurred the lines between his various roles and responsibilities.

Stan's fluid approach to business and community enabled people from very different backgrounds to collide in unusual and productive ways. The stories of Jason Bloomberg and Tom Cook offer cases in point. Clad in a long, thick beard and yarmulke, Bloomberg had come to Pine Ridge in 1986 on what was supposed to be a two-week stay. A charitable organization from San Francisco had donated an ambulance to the Lakota community, only to find that "there were no emergency medical technicians," so he extended his trip and trained a group of volunteers.[74]

Drawn to the life of the reservation, the young Jewish man stayed for the next several years and was involved in various community activities, including raising funds to purchase the first fire truck in the western White Clay District.[75] During his time in Pine Ridge, Bloomberg traveled to Rapid City to celebrate the High Holidays and other services at the synagogue. He usually stayed with Stan and Ita, who had made a habit of "host[ing] anyone who comes our way" because, as Stan wrote to a Jewish friend, "who knows, perhaps it is Eliyahu."[76] Here, Adelstein was referring to the prophet Elijah, who *"comes to Earth from time to time to see if humankind is sufficiently advanced in caring for the coming of the Messiah. No one knows what shape Eliyahu will take; maybe a man or a woman; perhaps a child or an elderly person; perhaps someone well dressed or in rags; maybe hungry or well fed; and maybe wise or ignorant. It could be a person of any skin color."* No matter what, he continued, *"if this person is not well treated, then the coming of the Messiah is postponed—for Jews, this would be the first coming; for Christians, the second."*

Adelstein had a more protracted relationship with an Akwesasne Mohawk man named Tom Cook, who grew up on his people's reservation in New York and moved to Pine Ridge in the early 1970s. In 1983, along with his wife, an Oglala woman named Loretta, Cook founded the Slim Buttes Agricultural Development Project, an organization that helped tribal members plant and maintain gardens on the reservation.[77] Around that time, Cook met Adelstein, who sold him a truck and then offered to help him obtain a loan for a woodcutting venture he tried to launch in 1985. Stan described Cook as a "creative farmer and developer" and "an Indian expert at utilizing emerging agricultural technologies." The pair remained in intermittent contact for years.[78]

Stan had been interested in agricultural development for some time, an outgrowth of the time his son, Jim, spent on a kibbutz. As he learned more about the kibbutz, Stan noticed similarities to *tiospaye*, the Lakota concept of extended kinship. Both social systems emphasized an individual's responsibility to his or her relatives and communities. During his service on the civil rights committee, Stan's personal connections with Israel and Pine Ridge led him to suggest that the committee should raise money to send some Lakotas to Israel. Although the advisory committee could not fund the plan, Stan refused to abandon the idea. In the early 1980s, he tried to get Israel's Ministry of Agriculture interested in the concept.[79] Then he connected with Rabbi Joseph Glaser, the longtime executive vice president of the Central Conference of American Rabbis, and together they raised the necessary funds.[80]

Rinard Yellow Boy, a professor at the Oglala Lakota College, took five students to Israel to observe the kibbutz system, as well as a new technology called "drip irrigation."[81] Based on ancient farming methods, Israel had developed the system in the late 1950s to apply "calibrated amounts of water and fertilizer" in order to "maximize crop yields" in Israel's harsh desert environments.[82] Pine Ridge farmers faced similar challenges given their region's aridity.

Yellow Boy also understood that only a smattering of reservation families grew their own produce, while most consumed high-sugar, high-sodium diets that resulted from government commodity and food stamp programs. Poor diets compounded the soaring levels of cardiovascular disease, diabetes, and obesity among Native Americans. These persistent problems had ignited local interest in gardening, food production, and canning, which Lakotas hoped could introduce a steady, reliable, and healthy food source to their communities.[83]

After the visit to Israel, however, tribal members' first attempt to implement drip irrigation failed. The system was expensive, the requisite hoses were prone to leaks and difficult to replace, and the project was phased out.[84] Cook, however, stayed in touch with Adelstein, and by the end of the 1980s sought to revive the Israeli technology at Pine Ridge. He partnered with several other tribal members to spur economic development on the reservation while providing healthy, fresh food to its residents.[85] The business plan of the Oglala Truck Co-Op, for example, set forth the company's basic argument: "the reservation contains a bountiful land base and excellent agricultural potential," if only local farmers could adapt methods that could better sustain life in the silty Pine Ridge soil.[86]

Cook and one of his colleagues, Charles Decker, tested the drip-irrigation system in the summer of 1987 "with complete success," and the next year Ron Sherzer, an Israeli irrigation expert, met with Adelstein, Cook, and others about a plan to extend drip irrigation to twelve farms belonging to Oglala Truck.[87] The co-op also secured more than $130,000 in grants from a Presbyterian church in Pennsylvania and the Christian Relief Services organization in New York. These funds enabled the purchase of "equipment, supplies, and material for the drip-line irrigation system."[88] Combined with expertise shared by agronomists at nearby Chadron State College in northwestern Nebraska, the co-op launched a plan to grow and market reservation crops. Some of the yield went to tribal elders, while the rest was "sold locally and to area supermarkets." By the summer of 1989, word spread about the progress being made by Cook, Little Finger, and their organizations and even reached Japan's former minister of finance, who came to Pine Ridge in the summer of 1989 to learn about the initiative.[89]

Israeli drip irrigation did not solve the economic or nutritional woes of the Pine Ridge community. The technology added some fresh food and income for a few reservation residents, but even the best of Cook's farms were hampered by hot summer winds and the periodic ravages of high plains hailstones.[90]

Accordingly, Stan and his entrepreneurs were disappointed with their efforts to improve life on South Dakota's Indian reservations. Tensions and inequities persisted between whites and Indians, and the residents of Pine Ridge still faced staggering poverty and poor nutrition. But Stan had not sat idly by. Instead, he held true to "obligation to leadership" with which Rabbi

CHAPTER 15

Joel Messing had tasked him so many years earlier. And in the end his efforts did not go unnoticed. In September 1984—in the middle of his work with Indian start-ups and with the advisory committee on civil rights, and just after he sent Lakota students to Israel—a spiritual leader named Petaga Yuha Mani "Pete" Catches honored Stan with the name Iyoyanpa u Wakan, or "Sacred Dawn Arising."[91]

CHAPTER 16
FAMILY BUSINESS

Stan Adelstein squinted up at the ceiling, his vision blurry. Throbbing pain shot from his wrists, the bursts of agony dulling in increments as the anesthetics slowly took effect, at once relieving his discomfort and clouding his ability to remember where he was or how he had gotten there.

It was June 1986, and the last thing he remembered he was on a bicycle. Riding and globetrotting had become routine in recent years; Stan had biked for exercise and enjoyment nearly every day for most of the previous decade.[1] These rides offered opportunities for relaxation and reflection. *"I remember once riding for miles along the outer perimeter of the Berlin Wall in West Berlin,"* Stan said, *"and watching airplanes fly overhead. All I could think about was how absurd it seemed that here I was, in the end of the twentieth century when people were flying overhead as well as into space, but we were still building walls to keep one another apart."* Years later, after the wall came down, Stan would help bring a large segment of it to Rapid City, where it stood as a reminder of the divisions that pulled at humanity in the 1980s.

Throughout the 1970s and 1980s, Stan's association with the American Jewish Committe, Young Presidents' Organization, and political groups of all kinds had sent him across the United States and to nations like Monaco, Mexico, Brazil, Greece, and Jamaica.[2] In 1986, however, he was back in Germany, visiting the town of Heilbronn where his son Dan was the commander of an infantry company tasked with providing security for a nuclear missile site. On a beautiful Monday morning, he took a ride on a path that followed the Neckar River. He suddenly crashed on the pavement, the impact shattering both wrists. When he skidded to a halt, the rough concrete nearly severed his nose from his face.[3]

CHAPTER 16

As he lay there with blood pooling around him, *"two men approached, looked at me, and moved on. As I laid there, I realized that if I didn't do something, I would likely go into shock. I remember thinking that the idea of being a Jew who died in Germany while on a recreational bicycle ride was horrible to contemplate. So I pulled myself to a nearby bench."* Then, a woman stopped by, told him to sit still and that she would bring help. *"She returned soon with a strong working man, who half carried me to a nearby city swimming pool that had a first aid station. As I laid on a cot, waiting for the ambulance, the woman walked back into the room with tears in her eyes. She told me that when she left home to go into town that morning, she didn't want to take the bike path. But she had a strong feeling—she called it 'a message from Gott'—to take that route, a path that allowed her to find and help me in my moment of need."*[4]

Months passed while Stan's bones healed and his face recovered from reconstructive surgery. During that time, he sent a letter to the editor of the *Heilbronner Stimme*, a local newspaper, thanking the woman and the hospital staff for their generosity and care. He also wrote friends, explaining how the accident, "rather than being a matter of continual distress," had really "been one of enlightenment."[5] He explained that, over the years, stories of Nazi brutality had painted an unflattering picture of Germany in his mind, one that changed dramatically that day in Heilbronn. "I certainly learned a lot about Germans [and] the inaccuracy of my prejudice against them," he wrote.[6]

Since the early 1970s, Stan had sported a full goatee with dark streaks running down either side of his mouth and a single, dark patch on his chin. By 1986, the goatee had become a full beard, and the patches were slowly fading to gray. He had replaced his horn-rimmed glasses with clear aviators, and together with his beard, they obscured much of his face. When he celebrated his birthday that August, several physical signs suggested that Stan's fifty-five years had taken their toll. Among them were the slow silvering of his beard and an almost imperceptible crease—the scar still fresh from his accident—that adorned the side of his nose.[7]

Just as Stan's visage and his predispositions toward Germans changed in the 1980s, so did the Northwestern Engineering Company (NWE). With each passing year, NWE cemented its role as parent to a rambling conglomeration of construction and real estate assets. Northwestern consolidated construction operations in its subsidiary, the Hills Materials Company.

The company's continued development resulted in part from the emergence of a new generation of leaders. Pat Tlustos joined the company in 1979 after Art LaCroix called Stan one day and explained that he had a brilliant young city engineer who had said he planned to resign and look for another job. *"Art told me Pat was extremely talented and that it would be a terrible thing for the city to lose him"* to some other community. After an introductory lunch, Stan realized that Tlustos *"really knew how to listen to people. He knew how to respect individuals."* Soon after hiring this young engineer, Stan realized that he was extremely competent and focused on producing quality work. Even though the pair *"had different ways of seeing the world,"* Stan recognized that he and Tlustos shared the same values.

When he first came on board, Tlustos recalled, Hills Materials "was the rag-tag remnants of a big" 1950s-style "highway construction company that went broke."[8] Recalling the difficult months leading up to the equipment auction that saved his company, Stan pointed out that *"Hills* nearly *went broke"* following its reorganization in the early 1970s. Afterward, Hills remained a trade name of Northwestern and continued to crush rock and build using aged company iron. E.D. Gaiser, a longtime employee, ran the business from a small quarry in Hot Springs at the southern reach of the Black Hills.[9]

Construction fortified Northwestern's bottom line. It had taken more than a decade to get the company's finances in order and refine its new business model. By September 1983, however, Stan could once again write the Hills Materials team, happily telling them that the company had already done "nearly two-thirds more [work] than we completed last year at this time." Hills also cut down on accidents and the cost of repairs, which he believed increased "the productivity of every man and woman in this outfit."[10]

Municipal projects were especially lucrative. Stan had supported Art LaCroix throughout his mayoral career, working as an aggressive fund-raiser for several successive LaCroix reelection campaigns.[11] During this period, Rapid City expanded its airport and continued to build near the Civic Center, and NWE got many of the contracts. These projects entailed "complications and difficult engineering," but nonetheless paid off, and Stan knew it. "That I'm hearing moans and groans from the competition," he gushed, "means that we must really be hitting them where it hurts—in the marketplace."[12] The numbers supported his confidence: Hills Materials regularly secured around $20 million worth of annual contracts throughout the 1980s, providing steady revenues and handsome profits.[13] *"We had a lot of projects,"* Stan recalled. *"I mean, we were still building jobs everywhere"* in South Dakota.

Hills Materials drove Northwestern's resurgence, and in the process strengthened its brand. In and around South Dakota, the name "NWE" rang of longevity. The company's logo, its acronym inside a small diamond, actually came to be *"because that's the way we designated the ownership of automobiles. In fact, I had some little brass plates made to put on the cars, including the one I drove. It was 'NWE' in that little diamond, and it just sort of came to me. And once it started, it kept up,"* eventually moving onto the company's letterhead and into marketing materials.

In 1985, the board launched a new real estate endeavor called the "NWE Management Company."[14] Stan had been interested in property management for years, slowly accumulating assets under NWE subsidiaries and partnerships like the Robford, Harney Lumber, and Lawrence Realty Companies, which owned land and buildings in South Dakota, Colorado, Wyoming, and, for a time, a major office complex in San Diego, California.[15]

Three forces had converged in the 1970s, creating opportunities in the real estate market. First, the Black Hills continued to grow in prominence as a regional and national tourist destination. Recovery from the 1972 flood left Rapid City flush with both the funds and spirit for urban renewal. Within a few years, the town would also invest in a revitalization program that expanded public parking and built retail spaces, office buildings, hotels, and apartment complexes downtown.[16] Finally, the Cold War continued to pump resources into Ellsworth Air Force Base. It became a key center for the military's Strategic Air Command and the control hub for the 150 nuclear Minuteman Missiles and launch centers scattered in West River counties serviced by Rapid City merchants. Federal dollars brought hundreds of more jobs and thousands of personnel and their dependents to the area.[17] Altogether, these developments created both construction opportunities for Hills Materials and a growing demand for more housing in and around Rapid City.

Adelstein moved swiftly, and by the mid-1980s NWE owned a stake in more than 150,000 square feet of commercial space.[18] In the wake of the flood, Stan had also developed Meadowlark Hill Mobile Estates, which was conceived as temporary housing for Rapid Citians displaced by the disaster. Some 150 families moved into the complex on Rapid City's north side within a year of groundbreaking. Ten years later, this community had "blossomed into a permanent neighborhood" of just under 300 homes.[19] Finally, in the late 1970s a Northwestern division called "NWE Development" completed the Woodridge subdivision, which contained approximately seventy high-end townhomes and condominiums in the forest under Skyline Drive, just southwest of Adelstein's home on West Boulevard.[20]

Stan recognized that a centralized management team could oversee and maximize the potential of NWE's growing array of real estate assets while providing similar services to other property owners. On a fateful flight from Sioux Falls to Pierre one night in the late 1970s, Stan sat next to a young, blonde businesswoman named Sandra K. Runde.

"What's a good-looking girl like you doing flying to Pierre on a Friday night?" Stan, a career sweet-talker, asked.[21]

Runde told him that she had studied psychology at the University of Northern Arizona before returning to Sioux Falls, where she managed a series of motels in several midwestern states. Impressed by her work ethic—Runde was also taking night classes to obtain an MBA from the University of South Dakota—Stan told her to get in touch if she ever needed a job. Satisfied with her position, Runde politely thanked him for the offer before they touched down.[22]

A few years later, Runde was ready for a change. She called Stan and was delighted to hear he was looking for an executive assistant. He was also trying to find someone with a master's degree and several years' experience to run a property management company.[23] Runde fit the bill perfectly and began working as Stan's assistant while the pair brainstormed. When Stan finally pitched the management idea to the board in early 1985, a few members questioned the venture. One even wondered if it would be wise to task Runde with a new set of responsibilities that might distract from her current position. It was board member Howard Farkas who recommended setting up NWE Management as a separate operation.[24]

By May, Runde had assembled a strategic plan.[25] She hung a huge chart in her office—a map of Northwestern and its various subsidiaries with each property listed under the entity that owned it.[26] Under her watch, NWE quickly became one of the largest property management companies in Rapid City. She traveled the city, as well as to Denver and Gillette, Wyoming, where NWE had commercial properties, drafting copious reports about general maintenance and other issues. She collected rent and answered inquiries from current and prospective tenants.[27]

"He paid me well," Runde remembered of her time working for Stan. She considered Adelstein a creative businessman capable of leveraging his properties in unique ways. Runde also valued Stan's approach to her as a person and a professional. She recounted how, upon first coming on board, Adelstein set up introductory meetings across the Rapid City business community, which was still dominated by men. In fact, Runde could scarcely remember another woman in a high-level managerial position in the 1980s and appreciated that "Stan was one of the few people who did not like anybody discriminating against me as a woman," largely, she believed, because "he did not like anybody discriminating against him as a Jewish man."[28]

Although NWE Management would remain a relatively small portion of Northwestern's overall business portfolio throughout the 1980s and 1990s—the revenue brought in by Hills far exceeded NWE's management fees—it was a significant development in the history of the company. Runde's efforts to develop a portfolio of real estate assets owned by NWE and managed by a subsidiary presaged the company's full commitment to the property management industry. When she drafted that strategic plan in May 1985, however, that watershed moment was still a decade-and-a-half on the horizon.

More immediately, the relationships between Northwestern and its array of subsidiaries revealed a great deal about Stan's own development as a businessman. As a holding company, NWE offered a corporate and administrative framework capable of overseeing myriad assets and operations. It also provided Stan, as president, a platform from which to observe the big picture and consider new ventures, while also staying divorced enough from daily minutia to fulfill his political and civic obligations. Hills Materials kept the lights on and the coffers full, while NWE Management tested new entrepreneurial waters and kept an eye on long-held properties.

By empowering Tlustos—who replaced Gaiser upon his retirement in 1987—and Runde to manage the core, day-to-day operations at NWE's main real estate entities, Stan helped mitigate his tendencies toward micromanagement and impulsivity.[29] This strategy built on the system of checks and balances that accompanied the creation of the outside board in the early 1970s. On a personal level, his newfound willingness to delegate responsibility to able managers allowed Stan to better strike the ever-elusive balance between his work and other commitments.

Stan was more than willing to incentivize executive performance. Runde earned bonuses based on the success of the real estate management wing.[30] Similarly, as Gaiser approached retirement in the mid-1980s, Adelstein and Tlustos negotiated an agreement under which Tlustos would stay on as president and receive a percentage of the company's growth.[31] Although NWE had changed dramatically since his father's days in Jackson County, Stan carried on at least one tradition from Morris's playbook: when Tlustos became president of Hills, he remembered, there was "no contract, no nothing." Like Morris Adelstein and L.A. Pier before them, Stan and Pat simply agreed on compensation and shook hands. "And he paid me every year," Tlustos recalled. "We'd sit down at the end of the year and we'd argue, just good natured. It was a game more than anything [else] for an hour at the end of every year, and he paid me." Even though "there were a few years [where] that had to be a little painful."[32]

Profit sharing for employees was another piece of this puzzle. In the mid-1980s, Tlustos convinced Stan to distribute a fixed percentage of Hills Materials' profits to employees in an employee stock ownership program (ESOP). These arrangements had become popular in the late 1970s and into the 1980s, largely because they made companies eligible for significant tax breaks while promising to incentivize productivity and a stronger bottom line. Indeed, by the end of the 1980s, ESOP plans covered about a quarter of all American workers.[33] Stan pegged his interest in the idea to YPO: *"I kept learning about more and more management through YPO,"* Stan said, *"and I came to realize . . . that the success of the company wasn't dependent on senior management or even estimating ability"* but on the energy and diligence with which a company's employees did their jobs. During meetings, Stan recalled that one of his *"pet phrases"* to illustrate this point was to look around the conference room and say, *"I don't see any concrete here . . . I don't see any asphalt, I don't see any rock. All of that goes on out there. And the company's future success is going to be related to the people that do the work."*

The ESOP incentivized efficiency, quality, and cost-control at the job site. Adelstein heard one story that demonstrated that fact. *"A new driver at the Hills quarry kept riding the clutch on his dump truck every time he'd back up to the stone pile,"* Stan recalled. *"He did it once, twice, three times in a row. And on the third time, the rotor operator,"* who was in the next machine over, *"jumped out, went over to the truck, and opened the door. Then he told the driver, 'Listen, you son-of-a-bitch, you ride that clutch one more time and you're going to tear up a $1,500 transmission, and I own part of that!'"*

Adelstein allowed Tlustos, Runde, and their teams the freedom to run their respective wings of the company with relative independence. *"I still ran board meetings and reviewed cost and profit statements each week, discussing earnings disparities with our leadership team. I also visited jobs, quarries, and our ready-mix plants, where I observed supervision and met with managers. Pat and I reviewed competitive bids for profit and pricing considerations, and occasionally there were some personnel or capital appropriations I was involved with. But I tried to give my managers room to do their jobs."* Tlustos, who became president of Hills at only thirty-five years old, hired a group of other men in their thirties and forties. Given NWE's deep pockets, Tlustos remembered, he and his team had what amounted to "a blank checkbook" and virtually blanket authority. They "took every penny we could get our hands on every year and we bought equipment," upgrading it to meet modern standards, sometimes purchasing as much as $3 million of new iron in a single year. By the middle of the 1990s, Tlustos surmised, Hills Materials "ended up with . . . a pretty formidable group of people, equipment, and jobs."[34] For his part, Stan *"emphasized buying used equipment and maintaining its appearance"* to keep costs low and promote the visibility of Hills Materials' signature large, yellow trucks.

As it turned out, one of the keys to Hills's—and, by extension, Northwestern's—success in those years was precisely the opposite of what had made and then broke NWE at midcentury. When Tlustos first came on, Hills was mostly doing jobs worth between $100,000 and $250,000. The instinct was to push for bigger jobs, and after a while the company landed a few $5 million projects. But none of them went well. So Tlustos scaled back, looking for the company's "sweet spot." Finding it brought huge success. "Our sweet spot was always that quarter of a million to a million-dollar job," he said. "We could get more markup, run a hundred [projects] a year, and no one . . . else in the business could figure out how we did it."[35]

Altogether, these new strategies brought about an era of long and durable success for Northwestern. Stan was happy to turn over the keys, as he wrote a friend in 1981, because he had been "hit hard by the 'mid-life crisis.'" He described how "numbers and equipment do not mean what they once did." Nevertheless, he found the process of turning over the bulk of his company's operations to "a collection of vibrant, relatively young men . . . very exciting."[36] Adelstein tried to connect with this new generation of leaders. *"Each spring we had a three-day supervisors' meeting,"* he recalled, *"where we shared and discussed the company's performance, financial statements, and future plans. Usually we had an outside speaker—often someone I had met at a YPO conference or one of the 'university' events YPO put on. These meetings were very productive, and there was a very open give-and-take between all of us. For about five years, we also made a deal: if earnings exceeded a million dollars, I would treat three or four of the top performers and their wives to a ski vacation in Colorado. This was a wonderful time and a great opportunity for me to get to know our employees and learn their hopes for our company. Often, these trips changed my thinking dramatically. And I wasn't the only one! One year, two of the women on our trip were successful working wives. One had a child and the other was worried that having kids might hurt her career. Well, the first woman changed her mind, and eleven months after that vacation, her family welcomed a baby of their own!"*

Needless to say, Adelstein continued to take enormous pride in his family's company and viewed Northwestern as an extension of his own identity. The Hills Materials logo, for example, was an intricate, orange print emblematic of 1980s graphic design. Viewed upside down, the angular symbol clearly reads "SMA"—Stanford Mark Adelstein.

HARD LESSONS

The 1980s and 1990s were good for Northwestern. Although Stan had gotten better at delegating authority to his management team, he was still involved with many aspects of NWE's business. This was especially true when he perceived an opportunity to expand the company or diversify its revenue stream. Two of Adelstein's core strengths—his entrepreneurial spirit and his willingness to delegate—usually resulted in success. But they also occasionally brought expensive mistakes, especially when Stan was captivated by a venture. He had to learn the hard way how personal detachment from the finer details of Northwestern's business sometimes came at everyone's peril.

Among the most consequential miscalculations were the Black Forest Inn and the Circle G Construction Company. Stan had acquired the Black Forest Inn—a cozy restaurant and lounge in the woods near Pactola Reservoir, about twenty-five miles west of Rapid City—in 1972, owning it under a company called "Black Forest Development," with a partner, Ted Venners.[37] A young man whose family had been active in Republican politics, Venners had worked as an assistant to Governor Frank Farrar. Stan met Venners in Pierre, and the two went into business when he moved to Rapid City.[38]

The Black Forest property fit Stan's personality and portfolio. His family had ties to the land's previous owners. Morris Adelstein had helped a woman named Bernice Musekamp set up a small restaurant called "Pactola Lodge" or "Moosecamp Park" in 1953. The original restaurant sat at the bottom of the valley that became Pactola Reservoir in 1956. When the Bureau of Land Management reclamation completed a dam at one end of the gully, relocated most of the structures, and flooded the area, Musekamp moved her restaurant to its new location, and it became an Adelstein family favorite. Musekamp ran the eatery for two more decades before selling it to Ted Venners's parents.[39] In the early 1970s, Stan and Ted bought it and took over the restaurant.[40]

Initially, the venture made sense, especially since the pair could use Hills Materials equipment and labor to improve the roads and landscaping around the inn.[41] Adelstein helped with financing, remodeling, and landscaping. Venners ran the restaurant, and for a time it looked like the company might even partner with Marriott.[42] *"At one point, Marriott even designed a hotel that we might build on the property. Part of the problem was that it always seemed like it would only be a short while before the project was finalized."* The venture, however, never materialized. From it, Adelstein learned some hard lessons about trust and business. *"Eventually, when the project was abandoned, Marriott sued Black Forest,"* Stan recalled, *"but lost because the company did not have an architect's license in South Dakota. I was always very troubled by this since one of the Marriott executives had been a friend who I relied on throughout the deal."*

Worse yet, Black Forest was unable to repay NWE's $470,000 investment, forcing the Northwestern board to call a special meeting in 1978. Despite its idyllic location, Black Forest was too far from nearby towns to attract much business, especially outside the peak summer season. The only solution, some board members believed, would be to build an on-site hotel for about $700,000 or offer the inn for sale. The company chose to sell, but even that did not go well. Over the next seven years, NWE tried everything: attracting buyers, making several failed contract-for-deed sales, and even exploring a quarter-million-dollar scheme to build luxury condominiums on the site.[43]

Nothing worked, and after a deal fell through in early in 1985, Sandra Runde vented her frustration to a colleague in Arizona, calling the property "the dreaded Black Forest Inn."[44] Later that year, NWE finally sold the property to an entrepreneur who ran it as a bed-and-breakfast, but it took another four expensive years for the company's attorneys to iron out all the legal details from the failed partnership.[45] The deal took a heavy toll on Stan. *"I had relied on information from weekly reports, which ended up being inaccurate,"* he said. Stan confided to his son Dan that "the facts, sometimes, aren't as bad as the emotions," and knew that even though he was "always troubled by the previous errors in judgment," it would be years before he was "totally free from [the] pain and aggravation arising from the mistake" at Black Forest.[46]

The Circle G Construction Company ended even more disastrously. As 1987 approached and E.D. Gaiser prepared for retirement, a former Hills Materials engineer estimator—someone Adelstein called *"very competent, someone we were sorry to have lost"*—had moved to Phoenix and founded a company called "Circle G." He got in touch with Northwestern and suggested that an excellent construction opportunity had presented itself in Arizona.[47] *"He wanted us to purchase the company he worked for, Circle G, which was undercapitalized. With more resources,"* Stan said, *"we believed it could become a success."*

According to Tlustos, "the idea was hatched that Northwestern would help fund Circle G, establish it, [and] Ed Gaiser would . . . go down there and spot check" throughout his retirement, making sure "everything was kosher, doing okay, and [the former employee] would run it."[48] *"The whole thing seemed like a great idea,"* Adelstein recalled, *"because working in Arizona would allow us to utilize supervisory personnel from Rapid City throughout the winter season."*

For the first couple of years, Circle G was a smash hit. "We had our board meetings down in Phoenix once a year," Tlustos recalled, "and we ate $200-a-plate dinners and drank really good wine because we were making so much money."[49]

Things fell apart shortly thereafter. Northwestern's auditors quickly discovered that someone at Circle G was, as Tlustos termed it, "cooking the books." Nobody at NWE had paid close enough attention, and the company was in dire straits. By February 1987, Northwestern—as parent to Circle G—was receiving notices of nonpayment from paving firms in Arizona alongside warnings of unpaid taxes from the state's department of revenue.[50]

Stan asked Tlustos to manage the situation. He flew to Phoenix every other week trying to save the company. He had "a hundred Circle G stories" that could illustrate the company's mismanagement, but one stood out. Going through the books with Circle G's chief estimator one day, Tlustos quickly noticed that the man had intentionally bid land-clearing projects at about $500 an acre, knowing that it cost between $700 and $800 to do the work. "Well, that's what the market is," the estimator tried to explain, insensitive to the hazards of underbidding expensive work. "That's where we've got to be if we're going to get the job," he said. Stunned, Tlustos struggled to get the bidders back on track.[51]

Circle G filed Chapter 11 bankruptcy shortly thereafter. This was also due, as Stan recalled, to the fact that *"our manager had been spending much of his time gambling in Las Vegas,"* which only added to the challenges the company faced. Together, the Circle G debacle forced NWE to take more than $100,000 in losses in 1987 alone.[52] This, of course, did not include the money NWE lost in start-up capital or the working hours invested in the venture. All told, Tlustos estimated that Northwestern lost more than $1 million on Circle G. It was a serious and sobering hit for Northwestern, which Tlustos chalked up to loose management. In addition to their troubled on-site manager, "Stan never looked at it [and] Ed never looked at it," so both failed to catch the problems early enough, and the company paid dearly for the mistake.[53]

FAMILY BUSINESS IN A BUSINESS FAMILY

Amid these challenges, Stan and his brother, Bob, continued to disagree about the continued growth at Hills Materials, creating endless tension for the family and the board of directors. After struggling for years to appease his father and older brother, and to carve out a space within the family business, Bob Adelstein had left the NWE office just before the corporate reorganization in the early 1970s. Over the years, Bob had worked many jobs, inside Northwestern and out—first as a company laborer, and later as equipment manager and head of safety. He became a licensed insurer and real estate agent in Colorado. Then he enrolled at Metropolitan State College after an administrator recognized his learning disability and offered him a chance to overcome it. By 1975, Bob had graduated from Metropolitan and completed a master's degree at the University of Denver. He became a psychiatric social worker, spending the rest of his career providing individual and family therapy at an office in Denver.[54]

Bob was still a major stockholder and board member, and he stayed abreast of big decisions. He agreed that Stan should run Northwestern, viewing the arrangement as "the only way we could at least work to make things work. And having the board of directors there," Bob "felt comfortable enough [that] they would, and did, set limits" on his brother.[55] The pair also called on Jerry Mizel, a paternal cousin who had agreed to serve on NWE's board of directors. Raised in Mitchell, South Dakota, Mizel *"had been a very successful businessman in Chicago and Israel,"* and agreed to try and help the Adelsteins balance their rivalry with their shared interest in making Northwestern work.

Around 1988, Bob informed Stan that he wanted to sell his stock and leave Northwestern entirely. Stan was irate because *"producing Bob's stock would reduce funds for the company's growth."* As he put it later, *"I was very unreasonable and told Bob, 'You inherited yellow trucks,'"* referring to the equipment at Hills rather than the cash Bob was seeking, *"'and you're going to die with what you inherited. That's what Dad gave us, and that is all you're going to have!'"*

Stan eventually realized that this was unfair, and by 1989 the brothers were negotiating the deal that would eventually end with Stan buying Bob entirely out of NWE. This was not a hostile takeover—both had agreed it was time to part ways. Bob was living in Denver and was ready to leave the board of directors. With no intention of retiring anytime soon, Stan sought to consolidate his ownership and run Northwestern from Rapid City.

The brothers, however, could not agree on the mechanism for dissolving their partnership. With millions of dollars at stake, each had good reason to consider various options. "They were going their separate ways," Mizel recalled, "and they were going back and forth with lawyer after lawyer. They couldn't agree with the lawyers, and it was going to be very costly to them" to continue along this path. Their impasse worsened by the day, until finally Mizel "got a call from both of them individually." Each explained Bob's plans to divest himself of his NWE shares. Mizel could tell it was shaping up to be "a very traumatic," even "painful" experience for the brothers. "They just couldn't agree on a split. They said that the only thing they could agree on [was] that I would mediate [the dissolution] of their partnership and the ownership of the company."[56] Although reluctant to get in the middle of an ostensibly intractable family spat, Mizel agreed. He quickly found that the brothers had a "different philosophy, different focus, different priorities," and "different personalities," all dynamics that shaped their approach to the problem, as well as their inability to deal with one another peaceably.[57]

The three sat down for their first meeting in early 1989, and according to the transcript of that session, Mizel laid the ground rules. "I mean, it's going to be a compromise on both your parts," Jerry responded to Bob, who had recognized that whatever form the buyout took, neither he nor Stan would get everything they wanted out of the deal. "I don't want to see a problem."[58]

"And that is part of your role, too," Bob interjected, "to make sure that we don't get off base because if we do disagree," he said, Mizel would need to step in, halt the conversation, and correct the situation.[59]

"As I have told you both," Mizel reiterated, "I think that you both have good intentions," but he understood why this was going to be so hard. He would intervene if necessary but hoped to marshal the Adelsteins toward a fair and amicable agreement.[60]

The negotiations were "very difficult [and] put a lot of responsibility on me," Mizel remembered years later. In order to ensure an objective and transparent process, he recommended that the Adelsteins hire an external accounting firm from Chicago, where he lived, to go through Northwestern's books. "We met a few times with the accountants," he said, who sorted through an extended patchwork of assets, liabilities, and partnerships that had developed over the course of more than sixty years. As they worked, the accountants explored several options, and the brothers sought to find a buyout that would be mutually advantageous from a tax standpoint but would also provide some long-term security for their heirs. They slogged through all of this while "trying to do it with the least amount of animosity towards each other." After several arduous and delicate meetings, Bob and Stan finally came "to an agreement and dissolved their partnership."[61] Once finalized—and with the exception of some employee stock ownership provisions and a number of shares held for the Adelsteins' dependents and beneficiaries—the deal made Stan the sole owner of the Northwestern Engineering Company.[62]

Stan and Bob's was not the only Adelstein relationship in flux as the 1980s wound to a close. Stan and Ita's three sons had scattered themselves across the planet in pursuit of their educations and careers. After graduating from West Point, Dan served as an army Green Beret. He moved around frequently, spending a total of ten years at Fort Bragg, North Carolina, and four more in West Germany. Later, he was assigned as a special forces specialist in the Pentagon before retiring from the military after twenty-seven years of active duty. He then launched a career as a national security adviser to several members of Congress.[63]

Jim Adelstein, as his father told a correspondent in 1981, "stayed out of school for two years after high school working as a carpenter in Denver, then [worked] on a Kibbutz in Israel." He next attended Brown University, which Stan called "the most perfect place in the world for him," before pursuing screenwriting work in California.[64]

The youngest of the three, Jonathan, attended high school at the Phillips Academy in Andover, Massachusetts, before studying at Lewis and Clark

College in Oregon, where he interned for Stan's political ally Senator Bob Packwood. Jonathan transferred to Stanford University, where he completed bachelor's and master's degrees before going on to the Kennedy School of Government at Harvard. He then began a career in politics and policy that would, a few decades down the road, land him several presidential appointments.[65]

As their boys grew up, Ita and Stan grew apart. As their son Dan put it years later, his parents "were just really different people."[66] Sharp differences separated the ways that Stan and Ita viewed important parts of their lives. When it came to Jewish affairs, Ita felt a deep, personal connection to her people and, according to Dan, "was very aware of her roots as a Jew who had to flee Europe as a kid." She also "felt very strongly about the health and welfare of Israel." Yet Dan qualified this comment, noting that his mother "was not as involved" as Stan "on an emotional level . . . with the religious ritual side of things."[67] Stan, too, found religious truth elusive, but put a great deal of stock in ceremony and tradition.[68]

For decades, Ita had been, as Stan termed it, a *"professional mom"* and *"incredible mother."* Understandably, she struggled to find purpose after the boys left home. As her long-cherished role gave way to an increasingly empty household, Ita tried several occupations, hoping to find something to enrich her days. She became a graphoanalyst—a person trained to evaluate someone's personality based on clues in their handwriting—after meeting a woman in that line of work at a YPO meeting. She quickly moved on after finding that "the lack of personal contact was not for her." Ita was also, as Stan told a friend, "involved in the feminist movement" and became an instructor in Woman's Effectiveness Training after attending an institute in Southern California.[69] In that capacity, she taught women "to be straightforward and direct, rather than passive," and to "take responsibility for their actions, emotions, and desires."[70] She also became quite involved in the teachings of Swami Muktanada, an Indian-born spiritual leader who created a meditation-based belief system called Siddha Yoga. Stan disagreed with Ita's practice—he would have preferred that she focus more closely on Judaism—but recognized that he "must respect her right to learn and grow in her way."[71]

For the boys' sake, neither Stan nor Ita considered divorce. They had much in common, after all, and shared a comfortable life. But Stan was often away on business or in meetings, and—just as he had when they were newlyweds—underappreciated Ita's restlessness. Ita had the time and resources to pursue different interests, and for years, that was enough. Like Morris and Bertha Adelstein before them, the couple traveled and socialized together. Their relationship was imperfect, but it worked.

Over time, the imperfections in their relationship strained their marriage. In 1989, Stan and Ita separated but did not divorce. They preserved their marriage for a variety of reasons. It made financial sense but, more importantly, *"was more a matter that we had agreed to live separately, and the whole concept of divorce troubled us both greatly."* The discomfort and animosity of a dead romance eventually gave way to cordial greetings, and both found new relationships. Over time, Stan and Ita transformed their love from romance to that of deep friendship, and, in a certain sense, this was an improvement. Years after their separation, Stan would tell one of his sons that he and Ita "got along better . . . after [we] were separated than [we] did when [we] were home."[72]

CHAPTER 17
POLITICS AND SERVICE

When Gerald Ford drove past the new Rushmore Plaza Civic Center in Rapid City on October 12, 1978, the marquee blazed a message from local Republicans: "Welcome President Ford."[1] Nearly two years had passed since Ford handed over the White House to Democrat Jimmy Carter, but he had been greeted on the tarmac at the Rapid City Regional Airport by local Republican officials as if he were still the leader of the free world.[2] Ford had visited Rapid City once before, on a brief afternoon campaign stop at Ellsworth Air Force Base that he followed with a photo-op at a local middle school in August 1976.[3] But on this day in 1978, Republicans were glad to enlist his support.

Nationally, the Republican Party was waging a fierce midterm campaign to dislodge the Democratic majorities in both houses of Congress. Democrat James Abourezk, who had served South Dakota in the U.S. Senate since 1973, had decided to leave office. This created a golden opportunity for then-Congressman Larry Pressler to recapture the seat for the Republican Party. To raise money and whip up enthusiasm in the final weeks of the campaign, the party had organized a fund-raiser for several Republican candidates, most notably Leo Thorsness, a former Vietnam prisoner of war and Medal of Honor winner who was running for the House to fill Pressler's seat.[4] Stan Adelstein and Thorsness went back several years. After initially supporting his friend Barbara Bates Gunderson in the 1974 Republican Senate primary, Stan served as national finance chairman for Thorsness's unsuccessful race against George McGovern.[5]

The Ford luncheon presented a veritable who's who of South Dakota Republicans. A press conference was followed by a short meet-and-greet at the Hotel Alex Johnson, where those who bought a special $1,000 ticket shook hands and snapped pictures with Ford. At 12:15, the former president headed to the ornate and high-ceilinged Gold Room, where some 250 donors ate a buffet lunch and listened to the day's speakers. Adelstein and Ford led the two head tables, a podium separating them. To Ford's right (and the audience's left) sat Arlene Ham, South Dakota's Republican Party chairwoman; Thorsness; Nora Hussey (whom Ronald Reagan would later appoint Secretary of the Denver Mint); and Bill Janklow, who was running for governor. On Stan's side sat local party officials and candidates for the state legislature. Of South Dakota's most prominent Republicans, only Pressler, who had remained in Washington for a vote, was absent from the event.[6]

At one o'clock, Stan stood and welcomed the president and the day's guests. Then a local pastor gave an invocation, and Janklow led the audience in the Pledge of Allegiance. Thorsness gave a short campaign speech before Ford addressed the crowd, and before the clock struck three that afternoon, the former commander in chief was back in the air.[7] The program had gone off without a hitch and pulled in almost $50,000. South Dakota Republicans reaped the rewards: a month later, Janklow won his first term in the governor's mansion, Pressler ascended to the U.S. Senate, Representative Jim Abdnor clinched reelection, and the party kept control of both houses of the state legislature.[8] A few days later, Ham thanked Adelstein for his "cooperation in making that day the success that it was."[9]

Still, the excitement surrounding Ford's visit, and even the party's victories that fall, masked an ugly truth for Republicans like Stan Adelstein: the political currents were beginning to flow away from centrists. By pardoning Richard Nixon for his role in Watergate, Ford had saddled himself and his party with the specter of being light on corruption, and Democrats swept the presidency and both houses of Congress in 1976. In South Dakota, Republican power remained fragile. George McGovern held one Senate seat, and despite the Ford fundraiser and success of his colleagues, Leo Thorsness lost South Dakota's First Congressional District to Democrat Tom Daschle by just 139 votes in 1978.[10]

As moderate voters gave Democrats like Daschle a chance, conservatives—who had continued strengthening their political infrastructure and building a coalition of middle-class whites, Christian voters, and business leaders—began to pull the party to the right.[11] California Governor Ronald Reagan had challenged Ford for the 1976 Republican nomination and was already laying the groundwork for a 1980 run. Ford, too, thought seriously about running again, and many moderates hoped he would. When he decided not to, George H.W. Bush jumped into the race and worked to paint Reagan and his supporters as extremists.[12]

Stan could see the tensions in the party reflected locally. Several South Dakota Republicans had skipped the Ford event. "Gerald Ford is really not my man," one invitee wrote, adding that he thought the former president could "perform a great service to the Republican Party by focusing his activities on the role of elder statesman."[13] Another offered a more banal explanation when he wrote Arlene Ham, explaining why he did not think he or anyone else from rural Murdo would make the trek to the Black Hills that October. "I am not sure," he said, "that Ford is a real attraction anymore."[14] To Adelstein, who had once revered Nelson Rockefeller and thought of himself in the long tradition of socially responsive but fiscally conservative Republicans, these divisions were increasingly disconcerting.

TOO LIBERAL

At first, Adelstein barely noticed the signs that voters had tired of the old-guard "true Republicans" who modeled themselves and their party around pragmatists like Rockefeller and Nixon. By the end of 1978, however, the high from so many electoral victories had worn off, and Adelstein perceived a looming challenge. He had recently been named a national vice president of the American Jewish Committee (AJC), a prestigious position he would hold until 1981. Stan was also on the board of the Jewish Institute for National Security Affairs (JINSA), and in these capacities he fought hard to ensure American support for Israel and build a rapport that would create opportunities for Jewish servicemen and women.[15] *"JINSA was different because it was military. It wasn't related to raising money. It was about establishing a relationship that went both ways. Even in the 1970s, when Dan went to West Point, Jews marched to a Protestant chapel. And when people heard you were Jewish and served, they would ask if you had been in the 'Jewish Corps,' which was basically asking if you were quartermaster. At the same time, Jews weren't always very supportive of the American military, so we wanted to build that relationship."* Lobbying was a primary element of this work, and Stan sought to burnish his political connections. But he quickly realized that he had a problem: "as a Ford delegate in the last [presidential] election," he told colleague Mark A. Spiegel, "I had limited contact with the Reagan organization" and wanted to build a better relationship with the new administration.[16]

For decades, Adelstein's links to the Rockefeller political machine had created opportunities for him. After Rockefeller died in 1979 and Ford decided not to run again, Reagan emerged as the party's standard-bearer. Meanwhile, the nation grew more amenable to the conservatism associated with Barry Goldwater's failed 1964 bid for the presidency. During this transition, a new generation of supporters saw their political stock rise.

Adelstein recognized that to effectively serve the AJC in his new role, he would need "an early contact with someone at a policy-making level" inside the Reagan organization.[17] Spiegel quickly put Stan in touch with his father, Albert Spiegel, who had "already been selected," his son wrote, "as the Jewish coordinator of [Reagan's] Presidential campaign for 1980."[18]

Over the next two years, Adelstein made inroads with the Reagan campaign, serving as vice-chairman for a six-state region of a major Reagan-Bush fund-raising committee.[19] In the lead-up to the 1980 election, Adelstein also launched a bid for Republican national committeeman, a position that would make him one of the South Dakota Republican Party's chief representatives at the upcoming party convention in Detroit.

Joining the national committee would allow Stan to fold several personal and political objectives into one. It would, of course, project his authority within the South Dakota Republican Party onto a national stage, where he would have a tangible role in the shaping of the Republican platform.[20] This, in turn, could replenish some of the clout that had slipped away with Rockefeller and Ford. Finally, as a national committeeman, Stan told a pair of friends in April 1980, he would be better positioned to advocate directly on behalf of Jewish people and Israel in foreign policy. Under Carter, he said, the "world political situation continue[d] to deteriorate." If elected, he would at least enjoy the "likelihood of an opportunity" to express "his views to the new Republican president."[21]

Stan's platform would enhance the fund-raising capacity of the state party, focus on dislodging George McGovern, increase communication between the national committee and party members, and, as he said in his nomination speech, "bring forceful, energetic, and effective concentration to the National Committee."[22] Crunching the numbers with some analysts one evening in June

1980—just over a week from the state convention—Stan left for a meeting feeling nervous. He returned to his team and was delighted to see that "the race [was] imminently doabl[e]." With their help, Adelstein told his supporters in a final campaign mailer, "we will do something to change the Republican Party for years to come."[23]

When Stan lost the election to the incumbent William Lenker, an insurance salesman and World War II veteran from Sioux Falls, he was understandably crestfallen, but also furious with the tactics of some of Lenker's supporters.[24] Shortly before the election, someone in Lenker's camp had promulgated a letter warning that, because he was Jewish, Stan would elevate the concerns of Jewish people over those of regular South Dakotans.[25] *"They suggested that I was only running to get Jewish issues on the national platform. That was partially true,"* Stan said, *"but the way they did it was tasteless."* At best, the letter lobbed a veiled jab at Stan's capacity for free thought and action; at worst, he believed, it was blatant anti-Semitism.

Unfortunately, Stan directed his anger at the wrong target. He fired off a note accusing a political friend who had supported Lenker of rubber-stamping bigotry. When the man replied that he, like Stan, had Jewish ancestors who had fled persecution in Europe and that he did not approve of the Lenker campaign's tactic, Stan quickly apologized.[26]

Time settled his temper, and the following year Adelstein gave a more reasoned assessment. Although still shocked that "the issue of my being a Jew was raised," he wrote, that "really did little damage." Opposition to his candidacy, he realized, had calcified around another, equally disheartening issue: his support for Indian Country. "I lost every county near a reservation," he wrote, then claimed to have never heard the term "Indian-lover" until the race. Art LaCroix, Rapid City's first mayor with Native ancestry, had written a flattering blurb on the front of Stan's campaign brochure. In hindsight, Stan realized that the testimonial "was used as only further evidence of my relationship with 'them.'"[27]

Although Stan readied himself for another campaign four years later, support never materialized.[28] Gradually, he focused his energies elsewhere, and worked with the Republican Senate Trust, a committee of elite donors who, according to one *New York Times* report, "gave at least $10,000" to support Republican efforts to maintain the Republican majority in the U.S. Senate.

"*The Trust is actually how I first met Bob Packwood,*" Stan recalled, thinking back to the senator who had been an ally on the AWACS issue in the early 1980s. *"He called me out of the blue one day and said he was the chairman of the Republican Senatorial Campaign Committee. He made the usual fund-raising request. When I asked why he would personally call a contractor from South Dakota, Bob said my name had come up in several conversations and that he thought the two of us shared a lot of moderate positions on the issues. As a consequence, I became a member of the Campaign Committee, and flew to Washington, D.C., quite a number of times for committee meetings, and Bob and I became quite close friends over the years."*

Trust events were lavish affairs, "$1,000-a-person cocktail part[ies]" regularly headlined by President Reagan, Vice President Bush, former president Ford, and Reagan cabinet officials.[29] At least once, Stan had to turn down a personal invitation to a White House luncheon because he would be out of the country.[30]

Adelstein was also involved with the Republican Jewish Coalition (RJC), an organization that sought to increase political participation by Jewish Republicans. *"I had been invited to participate in the RJC,"* he said, *"by some friends from YPO who had been pursuing the idea of creating a specifically-Republican Jewish organization. I sat on the organization's original board"* and started another, four-year term with the organization in 1985.[31] Toward the end of Reagan's second term, Adelstein's service on the RCJ board afforded him a chance to attend an event at the White House. There, Stan met the president, and a photo of the pair shaking hands in the Roosevelt Room adorned the wall of Stan's Rapid City office for years.

Throughout the 1980s, Adelstein demonstrated that he could fit in with the Reagan crowd, even when he found them too conservative or disagreed with the finer points of the administration's foreign policy. Indeed, Stan proved a loyal contributor who consistently devoted his interests and skillset to public service. Alongside his political commitments, he served as a state liaison between the Federal Emergency Management Agency (FEMA) and South Dakota (an extension of his National Defense Executive Reserve days).[32]

Yet one ghoul from his run for the Republican National Committee would quietly haunt him for years to come. In 1980, Stan had sent out mailers to party constituents asking for feedback on political issues and matters of party administration. He wanted to know what the people wanted and to be known as someone who went out of his way to be directly responsive to their needs. Many offered friendly responses, declaring their support and providing insights on the issues. One, however, wrote back with a blunt and revealing response: "I feel I cannot vote for you because you are too liberal. If you would be more conservative, I might consider voting for you."[33]

HIGH PLAINS POLITICS

As he pondered his position in the Republican Party, Stan stayed engaged in South Dakota politics. He had raised funds aggressively for Bill Janklow, and after the 1978 elections busied himself with securing a role in the governor's administration.[34] As he told the governor-elect a few weeks after his victory, "I enjoy government and would enjoy involvement as you begin developing your plans." Acknowledging his own forward nature, he wrote, "I know the demands on your time are enormous, [but] didn't want to sit back and act coy waiting to be asked" to serve. "Any role that you would choose for me would be enjoyable," he pressed, "except possibl[y] no role at all."[35]

Stan and Janklow spoke often, *"usually at eleven o'clock at night,"* and thus shared ideas and talked over issues and political strategy. Although the pair were friendly, they disagreed often, and sometimes intensely. After a late-night conversation about the Middle East—during which, in a rhetorical flourish, Janklow equated Israeli treatment of Palestinians to Nazi oppression—Stan explained that he "felt very badly and was hurting a lot." He agreed with some of Janklow's criticisms of Prime Minister Menachem Begin, but believed the governor had gone too far. "If our relationship is to continue," Stan wrote his friend the next day, "I would hope that out of simple consideration that you would never again . . . compar[e] Israel to Nazi Germany."[36] Their friendship survived the dustup, and, according to Stan, *"Bill eventually became involved with Israel in a very positive manner,"* later visiting Israel as a member of the International Relations Committee in the U.S. House of Representatives.[37]

When the two were not busy debating global affairs, Adelstein helped Janklow by fund-raising to ensure that the state Republican Party was well-oiled.[38] Since 1968, he had served on the Republican State Central Committee. He was elevated to the executive committee in 1973, where he remained for over a decade.[39] A flexible schedule enabled Adelstein to attend party meetings at the King's Inn in Pierre and elsewhere.[40] Once, Stan even hosted the Republican State Central Committee at the Black Forest Inn, where the group discussed politics and strategy.⁴¹ In the lead-up to the meeting, Stan had provided the Republicans with the not-yet-defunct Black Forest Inn's expansive banquet menu, which offered curried apples, Swedish meatballs, a cold sandwich buffet, breaded mushrooms, several entrees, and—whether out of culinary coincidence or a subtle nod to his political hero, after whose grandfather the dish had been named—oysters Rockefeller.⁴²

One meeting memo that outlined the state party's 1983–1984 strategy offers a hint of the incredible work that went into maintaining and expanding the Republican machine. As the Central Committee updated its records during an era when personal computers were just beginning to appear on office desks around the country, it sought to enter every Republican into a computerized database. The committee also had to review and consolidate the state's 1984 presidential primary procedures since South Dakota had moved from two congressional districts to one at-large district in 1982.⁴³

Above all, Republicans were frustrated by their inability to keep control of the state's congressional delegation. Even though there were 11,000 more Republicans than Democrats in South Dakota, Tom Daschle had won the at-large seat. Headed into 1984, the Republican State Central Committee wanted to keep pressure on him.⁴⁴ They also reviewed the party's bylaws and brainstormed an outreach program that might improve Native American perceptions of Republicans. Adelstein and the committee tackled all of this while attempting to add 8,000 new donors and raise a minimum of $250,000 for the 1984 election cycle.⁴⁵

This work helped the party focus its campaign strategies. Looking ahead to 1984, the State Central Committee targeted the 71,000 veterans living in South Dakota, as well as the nearly 32,000 voters attending universities or vocational schools across the state. Another 58,000 South Dakotans were eligible to vote but were unregistered, and the Republicans courted them. Most pressingly, perhaps, were the demographic changes that had been steadily reshaping South Dakota. In the 1950s, of the state's 690,000 people, 53.6 percent lived on farms or in small towns, and in 1954 there were nearly 56,000 farms in the state, averaging just over 700 acres apiece. Yet by the early 1980s, the number of farms had fallen to 37,000, while the average acreage grew to over 1,000. This consolidation of agriculture—the state's largest industry—steadily pushed many South Dakotans to urban centers like Sioux Falls and Rapid City.⁴⁶

The question, then, was whether the party could maintain the loyalty of old voters and attract new ones, all while staying true to its values as new neighborhoods, jobs, and lifestyles reshaped voters' worldviews. Luckily for Adelstein, the committee, and the party, things looked good: since 1960, Republicans had won 78 percent of the statewide races and seventeen of twenty-two congressional elections.[47] Statistics like these made Republican electoral hegemony seem clear-cut and easy, but the intricate tapestry of South Dakota politics meant nothing was ever a given.

Bill Janklow proved enormously capable at bridging the growing urban versus rural tensions in South Dakota. He was arguably the most dominant figure in state politics in the 1980s and 1990s.[48] He talked tough on the American Indian Movement as attorney general, and, as legend has it, once arrived at a hostage situation at the state capitol with a rifle in hand.[49] As governor, he was brash, outspoken, and simultaneously begrudged and celebrated for tongue-lashing anyone who crossed him. He was known for racing to small towns reeling from natural disasters and was famously accessible: Stan once went to pick him up for a meeting, only to find the front door open and Janklow in a bathrobe. *"Where else in the United States,"* Stan reminisced, *"can you walk into a governor's house and walk up and have him coming out of the shower?!"*[50]

Yet when it came to policy, Janklow was a Republican whose "actions," as the journalist Patrick Lalley writes, often "[did] not represent Republican ideals."[51] When term limits forced him from the governor's mansion in 1987, Janklow returned to private practice, but not by choice. Janklow had unsuccessfully challenged Jim Abdnor in the 1986 U.S. Senate primary, and thereafter kept his eyes on another run.[52] His Republican successor, George Mickelson, served a term-and-a-half before perishing in a tragic plane crash in April 1993. Mickelson's lieutenant governor, Walter Dale Miller, finished out his term before Janklow returned; Janklow defeated Miller in the Republican primary campaign, during which Stan was active in his corner. Janklow returned and began an unprecedented third (and later fourth) term in 1995. During his sixteen years at the helm of state government, Janklow "bought a railroad, embarked upon a massive wiring project to connect South Dakota's schools to the internet, and, over the protests of the private sector, started what amounted to a state construction company to build houses at the South Dakota Penitentiary."[53]

RESTRUCTURING THE DEPARTMENT OF TRANSPORTATION

Adelstein had been involved with each of Janklow's gubernatorial campaigns and transitions, and the pair continued to meet and talk on the telephone for years.[54] But it was during the 1994 campaign that Stan sat on Janklow's campaign steering committee and transition team, and, after the election, served in a formal administrative capacity. In late 1995, the governor signed Executive Order 95-20, creating a task force that would review and restructure the South Dakota Department of Transportation (SDDOT).[55] He had done this once before, during his first term, and that review cut $920,000 from the department's budget by reorganizing it into four core divisions and reducing its workforce from 1,750 to 1,375 full-time employees.[56]

More than a decade later, on September 28, 1995, Janklow called Adelstein and asked him to join a task force slated to once again review the SDDOT. Stan recalled the conversation, noting that *"outside Education, [SDDOT] was the largest single spender"* in state government, and that Janklow *"really thought it was badly managed."* Adelstein and the governor agreed that the job *"would be better done by contractors who are used to competition"* than a group of career bureaucrats.[57] This concept was widely shared among members of the committee, who believed that "most bureaucratic agencies foster[ed] cultures that resist change rather than encourage or demand continuous improvement." The memorandum continued with its indictment: "Creativity and decisiveness is [sic] rarely encouraged, rewarded, or recognized" at the agency. This, the committee members believed, left SDDOT employees scrambling to protect their jobs and, over time, led to administrative bloat.[58]

The task force, however, had more than ideological roots: an evaluation had revealed that South Dakota had fallen behind on maintenance and new construction projects, and that it would cost $540 million "to bring highways up to the desired quality." That money had to come from somewhere, and Janklow decided to streamline the SDDOT's budget before turning to the legislature for a larger expenditure.[59]

Even as he agreed with Janklow about the utility of a departmental review, Stan was concerned about the task force's twenty-member makeup. It was politically bipartisan and professionally diverse (there were only three women) and included an academic; a county commissioner; a couple each of farmers, state legislators, and lawyers; an accountant; and two bankers; among others—but only one person from the construction industry: Stan.[60]

Speaking with the governor, Adelstein drew from his old axiom about the difference between executives in offices and laborers in the field. He believed the committee should be better represented by members of the construction industry. *"I said to him, 'Bill, I'm the only contractor on that committee. We don't have enough people that really do the work.' But he looked right at me and said 'No. There's only going to be one contractor, and it's going to be you, and I want it just that way.'"*[61] And so it was done. A few days later, Janklow followed the conversation with a formal letter thanking Stan for his service and putting him in touch with Stephanie Miller-Davis, the staff person who would be coordinating between the task force, the governor's office, and the SDDOT.[62]

Curt Jones, a farmer and longtime Democratic state legislator from rural Britton, cochaired the task force with Ron Wheeler, the secretary of SDDOT and a former CEO of a multimillion dollar manufacturing company based in Watertown.[63] Together, they welcomed the group to its first meeting in a state capitol conference room in late October.[64] Over the next several months, the group would review the structure, budget, and operations of the SDDOT, then propose changes and offer guidance on how to implement them. Jones and Wheeler divided the task force into subcommittees to tackle individual issues. The task force only faced one major restriction: they could not make recommendations pertaining to the SDDOT's annual budget appropriation, as that was the province of the state legislature. Other than about $400,000 that came from South Dakota's General Fund, the SDDOT drew its $274 million budget from state and federal funds dedicated to building, maintaining, and operating the 7,812 miles of highway that crisscrossed the state. This was a massive undertaking, and the department had conducted an average of 314.5 projects every year from the time Janklow left office in 1987 to his return in 1995. The department also handled the administration of South Dakota's "rail, aeronautics, and transit" transportation.[65]

The task force's goal, then, was to cut "duplication, inefficiency, and waste" from the SDDOT's services, largely, as one person scribbled at the bottom of a meeting agenda, by "shift[ing] as much money from non-core or peripheral areas as well as inefficiencies in operation to new construction."[66] These "peripheral" functions were defined as those operations dealing with finance, human resources, data services, right-of-way appraisal, equipment management and maintenance, mapmaking, legal issues, and local government service. Altogether, these operations accounted for $101 million, or about 37 percent of the budget. These stood in contrast to the SDDOT's "core" functions, which included the design, contracting, and maintenance of roads and bridges, as well as planning for future expansions of the state highway system.[67]

Adelstein chaired the Division of Engineering Review Subcommittee, which set out to determine whether it would be feasible to create standardized designs for bridges, culverts, and roads. The group also sought to reduce the SDDOT's central office by outsourcing engineering work or dividing it up among regional offices, and reviewed the legal, fiscal, and other segments of the SDDOT's Engineering and Operations division, searching for redundancies and inefficiencies.[68]

Altogether, Stan's group came up with nine formal recommendations for the final task force report. The Engineering Review Subcommittee's comments ranged from recommending further analysis of specific policies and operations, to developing a list of federal regulations that did not apply directly to South Dakota and, as a result, forced staff to spend time filling out unnecessary compliance forms. The subcommitte also found that the state could generate standard models for certain kinds of construction projects and asked that the SDDOT implement systems for reviewing project contracts and engineering plans online—a new opportunity in this early phase of the internet revolution.[69] These joined twenty-nine other revisions proposed by the other four subcommittees, which examined the SDDOT's organizational structure; its planning office; its operations; and the aeronautics, rail, and transit departments.[70]

At the end of February, the task force submitted its final report to Governor Janklow. It laid out all thirty-eight recommendations and, like the 1980 review, led to a dramatic downsizing within the SDDOT. The Division of Planning and Support Services and the Division of Planning and Engineering were reduced and consolidated, bringing the total number of SDDOT's administrative divisions from four to three.[71] The department also removed 300 positions, 150 of which were supervisory roles, and 106 engineers were "reclassified" to lower pay grades. "None of these actions were popular," Wheeler wrote to task force member Kay Jorgensen in June 1996, "but all of them were valid and necessary." He then explained that he had spent the previous week meeting personally with every division of his department, explaining the changes and why they were needed.[72]

Over the years, the various threads of Stan's political, professional, and community activities had intersected in surprising ways. When Janklow assigned him to the SDDOT task force, however, his long career as an engineer and construction contractor contributed directly to an effort that saved South Dakota taxpayers some $7 million a year.[73] Looking back, Stan characterized the SDDOT task force as an enjoyable experience, during which he and the group *"worked on some pretty interesting stuff"* that made a difference for his state. Although he would have enjoyed more opportunities to contribute directly to state government, Stan lacked the time. After all, he had a business to run and a bevy of community initiatives demanding his time and attention.

CHAPTER 18
NEW LOVE

"My God, he didn't get the dinosaur," the woman said, glancing at the newspaper in her lap. She and a colleague were making the 390-mile trek from the South Dakota Art Museum in Brookings to Rapid City for a fund-raiser. "We thought he would get the dinosaur."[1]

Puzzled, Lynda Clark looked at her coworker, wondering who "he" was and what dinosaur she was talking about. Born in Miami, Clark had attended college in Florida before heading to the West Coast "because," as she said, "it was the thing to do in the late sixties and early seventies." She worked in Los Angeles and San Francisco and then followed her interest in anthropology to a graduate program in northwestern Arkansas. The program was not a good fit, so just before embarking on her thesis, Clark transferred to California State University–Long Beach, where she completed a master's degree in her true passion—studio art. That degree led Clark to work as the director of two museums at the University of Illinois, and ultimately to Brookings, where she worked for the art museum on the campus of South Dakota State University. It was October 1997, and Clark had never even heard of "Sue," an extremely valuable—and exceedingly controversial—dinosaur fossil from South Dakota, let alone Stan Adelstein, the man who was trying to buy it.[2]

Only a few days earlier—and some 1,400 miles away—Stan had looked out over a crowd. He could barely see the top of Sue's 600-pound, sixty-seven-million-year-old head, which was encased in chalky stone at the front of the room in Sotheby's Auction House on Manhattan's Upper East Side. Seated about a dozen rows back from the auctioneer's podium, Stan shifted his weight to the right, his tan jacket pulled taut as he watched the action. Some 300 people filled the chamber, and cameras lined its perimeter. Everyone was there to see who would bring home Sue—the largest, most complete *Tyrannosaurus rex* ever excavated.[3]

The auction capped off a multiyear drama surrounding Sue. In August 1990, a paleontologist working for the Black Hills Institute, a for-profit archaeological research company, found Sue on the Cheyenne River Indian Reservation in northwestern South Dakota. After painstakingly removing the dinosaur's bones from the earth, a vicious six-year battle for ownership of the fossil ensued, as the institute, the federal government, the Cheyenne River Sioux Tribe, and a landowner—an enrolled tribal member named Maurice Williams—asserted their claims. In the end, federal courts determined that the bones belonged to Williams. Peter Larson, the head of the Black Hills Institute, who had carefully excavated and protected the fossil, spent more than a year at a federal prison camp for failing to handle paleontological specimens according to regulations.[4]

In 1997, Williams had decided to sell Sue at auction, and an array of wealthy collectors and museums lined up for a chance to bid. Larson and his family feared that the skeleton would be purchased and taken out of South Dakota. Devastated financially after years of court battles, they had turned to Adelstein, "a successful local businessman, philanthropist, and family friend," hoping that his pockets were deep enough and that his charitable heart might entice him into fronting the more than $1 million they thought it would take to bring Sue back to South Dakota.[5]

Stan's involvement illuminates the ways in which his penchant for personal generosity dovetailed with his sense of justice and appetite for a succulent business venture. *"Peter never should have even been sentenced,"* Stan said of the very controversial trial that landed the paleontologist in deep trouble with the federal government for failing to complete a small stack of paperwork. *"When he got out, he came to see me about his need to try and recover ownership of the dinosaur. He had been to a very successful display in Tokyo and felt that if he could get possession of the dinosaur again he could stage programs in many major cities. He had already been approached about doing one in Dallas. We talked in detail about his plans, including how he would travel with Sue and his track record of making a profit off his dinosaur displays before the whole Sue thing. Later on we had many meetings computing souvenir sales, admissions* *charges, and the like, and after working through the costs, we decided that we could make about $1.5 million if we got the dinosaur for a certain price and pulled off the show."* Stan, who saw the fossil as a state heirloom and major business opportunity, *"successfully negotiated a line of credit"* totaling $1.5 million *"for our plan, using a personal guarantee, of course,"* and headed to New York, where he attended the auction alongside staff members representing both of South Dakota's U.S. senators.[6]

Unfortunately, higher bidders quickly eliminated Stan from the running. Adelstein pushed hard—even offering a bit more than he planned for Sue—but was clearly outbid within the first minute of the auction.[7] In just under eight minutes, the fossil's sale price soared to $7.6 million as Chicago's Field Museum of Natural History purchased the fossil, intending to make it a focal point in its lakeshore facility.[8] *"We came home disappointed,"* Adelstein surmised, *"but glad that we tried."*

Talking about Sue on the drive to Rapid City might have been the first time Lynda Clark had ever heard the name "Stan Adelstein." Within a year, however, he would change her life.

THE JOURNEY CONTINUES

Stan's seat at the Sotheby's auction may have been his highest profile contribution to the museum world in the 1990s, but his major commitment to local history focused on the creation of the Journey Museum in Rapid City. Stan had grown interested in education over the course of the 1980s, perhaps as a result of the time he spent as an adjunct professor at the South Dakota School of Mines & Technology. The school presented Stan with an honorary doctorate in 1980 for his contributions to local engineering and industry, and afterward, the president of the university asked if he would like to coteach some classes. Stan enthusiastically agreed, wrapping his acceptance in a joke: *"if you take any male Jew over the age fifty and say you'll put 'Professor' in front of his name,"* he laughed, *"he'll do whatever you ask!"*[9]

Over the next few years, Stan taught the courses "Business Organization and Management" and "Managerial Economics for Engineers."[10] *"I also team taught the management practices course with my close friend Larry Owen, who was the chairman and CEO of the local energy utility, Black Hills Corporation."* While teaching, Stan reached out to Art LaCroix and Pat Tlustos, asking them to assign a "real-world task" for teams of students to work on as class projects.[11]

Within a few years Stan extended his interest in public education to the realm of history, a subject he had long found fascinating. By 1984, he was a member of the board of the Ellsworth Heritage Foundation, a group that raised funds and built an airplane and missile silo museum inside a series of refurbished hangers next to the base on the outskirts of Rapid City.[12] The Ellsworth experience was the perfect primer for a second major undertaking that brought a multimillion dollar museum—and Lynda Clark—to Rapid City.

For years the local Minnilusa Historical Association had operated a small pioneer museum in a Works Progress Administration-era building in Halley Park near downtown. The museum celebrated the Euro-American founders of the city and its early days. It also offered Native crafts for sale. But it was not a major tourist attraction. Meanwhile, the South Dakota School of Mines & Technology had an extraordinary collection of dinosaur fossils and geology specimens that were also underappreciated by locals and visitors alike. In the 1980s, a handful of community leaders began to talk about bringing these collections together and building a world-class museum that would convince some of the millions of visitors who went to Mount Rushmore each year to spend more time in Rapid City and learn about the deep, 2.5-billion-year history of the Black Hills.[13]

Stan was among an initial group of leaders who convened at the Rushmore Hotel in the late 1980s to begin discussing the new museum. The group included Jeffrey Viken, a Rapid City attorney (and, later, federal judge); Bill Hughes, an administrator and longtime School of Mines professor; Joe Rovere, the retired head of public relations for the local electric utility, Black Hills Power & Light; and Ray Hillenbrand and Gary Brown, two Rapid City businessmen who were active in the tourism and hospitality industries. At one point during the meeting, somebody flipped over a placemat and started scratching out notes about how to make the dream a reality.[14]

One immediate result of this conversation was the creation of the Museum Alliance of Rapid City, a group of volunteers who raised funds and awareness while organizing and planning what was expected to be an $11.6 million museum.[15] The work was time consuming and progress was slow. The Museum Alliance volunteers had to fund, design, and build the museum itself; build local political support for a city funding and zoning plan; secure delicate artifacts from a bevy of private, state, and federal owners; and map

CHAPTER 18

out a collections policy and visitor programming—all while working their day jobs. Viken alone spent over a decade with the Museum Alliance and spoke to more than two dozen public service and community groups in Rapid City. At one point, he realized that he was only spending about ten hours a week at his practice; the rest went to the Journey Museum.[16]

As a proponent of Native American rights and someone deeply concerned with his family's own connection to the Black Hills, Viken remembered, "Stan was one of the most consistent board members we ever had." "Unless he was out of town, he was there" for virtually every meeting. And his contributions went beyond attending meetings and lending advice: Adelstein brought early credibility to the venture among the business community and the Chamber of Commerce crowd. He also had Hills Materials build the Journey's parking lot as an in-kind donation.[17]

In May 1997, after nearly a decade of planning and preparation, the Journey Museum opened its doors to great fanfare. Visitors appreciated the massive, angular building, situated on an expansive acreage landscaped with a variety of regional flora. And that was just the outside. Inside the Journey, visitors could experience interpretive histories from Lakota and non-Native perspectives, engage interactive exhibits that told many stories of the Black Hills' past, and attend community events—all in a city-owned facility managed by a nonprofit corporation whose board coordinated between local, state, and federal entities to manage and display priceless historical collections.[18]

Unfortunately, however, the Journey Museum faced steep challenges from the very beginning. Technological troubles sullied the grand opening when the "sound sticks"—plastic bars with headsets that were supposed to deliver audio narratives directly to individual users as they strolled the museum—failed. This was the first in a series of missteps. The Museum Alliance had brought in a consulting firm to perform a feasibility study in the early 1990s, and that group told Viken, Adelstein, and their colleagues that the Journey could expect to pull in as many as 300,000 visitors a year, a figure *"based,"* as Stan remembered, *"on the huge interest in the local Native American population and its history."* This, of course, would provide a huge boon to Rapid City's economy. Those projections, it turned out, were wildly inflated, and the museum struggled to bring in a tenth of that number, making it difficult to cover operating expenses.[19]

These problems fed a vitriolic chorus of letters to the editor. Some locals challenged the need for a public museum in the first place; others found the name too ambiguous. Still others disagreed with the Journey's emphasis on Native American history and perspectives, while the most biting assaults took aim at the museum's overall cost to taxpayers. Criticisms only grew sharper when admissions rates failed to meet expectations. Within five years of its debut, the staff wondered if their Journey had ended.[20]

Throughout these turbulent years, Stan contributed significant funds to keep the doors open. The museum would later express its gratitude for his patronage by naming a prominent gallery after him.[21] In the meantime, however, the Journey needed an executive director. Fortuitously for them, the South Dakota Art Museum was about to undergo a long renovation, a process that left Lynda Clark open to other opportunities, as Stan said, *"since she had raised the money and approved the design, but didn't want to sit around a largely closed museum during construction."* Several months after the Rapid City road trip when she first learned about Sue the dinosaur, Clark received a phone call from someone wondering if she would be interested in taking the helm at the Journey Museum. She had heard of the challenges the museum faced but agreed to come out to talk about the position.[22]

"Neither of us were blown away," Lynda said of her first meeting with Stan. He was suffering visibly from jetlag as the two shared breakfast. Lynda thought the meal would feel like an interview, but Stan seemed to want to talk about anything *except* the Journey. When they finished eating, Stan escorted her to Mayor Jim Shaw's office, where she finally had a chance to talk through her experience and ideas. Within months, Clark had been hired and moved to Rapid City, where she spent three years "doing basic museum management things like putting together an employee handbook and organizational charts" and developing mission statements for different wings of the museum.[23]

With her new role at the Journey, Clark and Adelstein "were at meetings together all the time." After a while Stan started offering to introduce her to various groups and members of the Rapid City community. "He started taking me to . . . Chamber mixers and things out at Ellsworth, where I could talk about the museum to different people," and before she knew it, "we were dating."[24] If, as Lynda suggested, Stan was not immediately taken with her, he quickly became infatuated. *"She's an amazing and impressive woman,"* he said. *"It's* incredible. When she chose the museum field, she was told that the best job she could expect was to become curator at a minor facility. But she went on to become only the second woman in the United States to become director of a major museum!"

For her fiftieth birthday not long after she and Stan became a couple, Lynda wanted to go camping outside Cody, Wyoming. He was a bit surprised, and she recalled him telling her that "the last time I camped, all the other boys had the same uniform as I did!" Nevertheless, the pair hopped in one of Hills Materials' jobsite campers and headed to Cody, where they spent a long weekend exploring the mountains and visiting the Buffalo Bill Center of the West museums.[25] That trip seemed to cement their relationship.

In the ensuing years, Stan and Lynda cruised the Mediterranean together and traveled frequently—to Italy, Ireland, and Scandinavia. They made several trips to the Edinburgh Arts festival in Scotland, and, of course, to Israel. Photo albums from these journeys show the couple smiling and posing before historic sites. Lynda loved the arts and Stan enjoyed music, so they split their adventures between museums, art shows, and concerts. Like Stan, Lynda was dedicated to community work. Unlike Stan, she had the ability to focus on one primary passion: the arts. After leaving the Journey Museum, she remained in Rapid City and served more than fifteen years on the South Dakota Arts Council and about ten on the Rapid City Arts Council.[26]

Lynda appreciated Stan for his generosity. Once, while the pair were dining at a Korean restaurant, a woman approached Lynda and sheepishly asked if that was Stan Adelstein she was with. When Lynda affirmed, the women told her that some years earlier she had been struggling with a problem: a dear friend of hers had hit hard times just as winter was getting under way. The woman's friend lived on a rural prairie deep in one of the nearby Indian reservations but had run out of wood for her stove and out of money for food. When the woman from the restaurant told an acquaintance about her friend's predicament, the person told her to call Stan Adelstein. Not knowing who he was, the woman tried anyway but never heard back. When she went to visit her friend on Christmas Eve, she found the home warm, with a holiday feast on the table, and even with toys for the children. The mystified woman learned that Adelstein had gotten her message and taken care of her friend.[27]

When it came to Stan and Ita's marriage, Lynda respected their bond and their arrangement. "To me that was Stan's business," she said. She understood that by staying married, Stan was doing what he thought best for his family. After all, he and Ita "had three children in common [and] multiple grandchildren," and Northwestern supported them both. Lynda never worried much about their unconventional situation: she had met Stan years after the separation, and well after he and Ita resolved their problems.[28] Stan remembered that Ita once *"sent a nice letter, kind of extending an olive branch, and thanking Lynda for being in my life."* The feeling was mutual: the two women "were always very friendly," Lynda recalled, and the trio "used to go out to dinner together," she said, smirking because they "kind of raised eyebrows around town."[29]

If she had any early reservations about dating a man with such an unconventional marital status, she dealt with them swiftly. She put it this way: she knew what she was getting into and "remember[ed] deciding that he must be okay" as soon as she saw how her Australian shepherd took to Stan. "As a matter of fact," Lynda said of the dog, "she thought he was taking *her* out."[30]

YELLOW TRUCKS

Alongside Stan's new romance, his work for Janklow, and the dramatic controversy that reached back to the Cretaceous Period, his other activities in the 1990s read routine by the standard of his eclectic interests and energy. He remained deeply engaged in local affairs, serving on the board of the Rapid City Chamber of Commerce for seven years before becoming its chairman in 1993. He worked with the Black Hills Powwow Association and helped Youth and Family Services—an organization that assisted at-risk children and families—locate a facility. He attended national security forums and was named a civilian aide to the secretary of the army in 1999, a largely ceremonial role aimed at smoothing the relationship between military and civilian communities and advising the brass on issues relevant to South Dakota.[31] He also racked up awards: a Distinguished Engineering Alumni Award from his alma mater in Boulder; a Public Service Award from the South Dakota School of Mines & Technology; and the annual George Award, which was given to an individual for self-reliance and persistence in business from the Rapid City Chamber of Commerce.[32]

Amid these achievements, a pressing issue faced the Northwestern Engineering Company. By the late 1990s, Pat Tlustos, the longtime manager of Hills Materials, was ready to leave the construction industry. "My father died when he was fifty-one years old," Tlustos told Stan, and he wanted to be out of that work by the time he turned fifty. Working construction, he reasoned, "was a six-day-a-week, eleven months out of the year" job. "We hauled ass just continually," as he put it. "You were either bidding work or you're building work [or] you're doing personnel stuff." At best, Tlustos would "take a month or a couple of weeks in the middle of the winter, dead of winter, and you'd go to one or the other coasts" to relax. Otherwise, work was a constant, exhausting grind. "I'd always told Stan when I was fifty," Tlustos said, "I was going to do something different."[33]

By the end of the 1990s, as Adelstein was nearing seventy, Tlustos approached his limit. Neither of them wanted to run Hills any longer, nor did any of Stan's boys, who had built careers of their own far from Rapid City and the family business. So Adelstein and Tlustos debated the company's future. "We spent two years . . . arguing about who was going to run the construction company. If Stan liked somebody as a possible replacement, I didn't," Tlustos remembered. Conversely, "if I liked somebody, he wasn't flashy enough for Stan." The two never settled on a candidate and agreed that "it probably made sense to sell the construction company if we could get the right price." The plan was to "transfer as many of those assets or dollars into real estate" as possible. That is exactly what happened.[34]

Three-quarters of a century had passed since Morris Adelstein and L.A. Pier started their construction outfit in rural Kadoka, and nearly fifteen years had come and gone since Sandra Runde helped set up the NWE Management Company. Now, as the twentieth century wound to a close, Northwestern was planning to make the switch and focus its energies on real estate management.

In 1999, Northwestern received an offer that worked. Oldcastle, Inc. was a major supplier of building and construction materials. Owned by an Irish firm called Cement Roadstone Holdings (CRH), Oldcastle was a huge and growing player in the European and American construction industries. "By the time they acquired Hills," according to Tlustos, "they were doing several billion dollars a year in construction across Europe and the U.S." and were a huge manufacturer of glass block and related products. Oldcastle took a long, strategic approach to its business and had been slowly acquiring companies in Colorado and across the Midwest. Hills Materials would soon be one of them.[35]

The transition was anticlimactic. Oldcastle sent some representatives and accountants to South Dakota to appraise Hills and negotiate a price. Stan even took them to Mount Rushmore, and since NWE would still be around and doing business, Pat agreed to help the transition along, keeping an open door for the Oldcastle folks as they learned the ins and outs of Hills.

"Most of the cash from the sale went to the company's employees, whose ESOP owned 30 percent of the company's shares. In the negotiations, I had arranged for a significant part of the price to be paid in exchange for the five quarries that Hills owned." This allowed Northwestern to do "a lot of tax-free exchanges," as Tlustos recalled, which led to the acquisition of property in California, Denver, and Omaha while expanding NWE's holdings in and around Rapid City.[36] Even though Northwestern no longer paved roads, its brand still resonated through the community. "You know," Tlustos mused, "it always amazes me how many people say, 'Oh, Northwestern, Stan's outfit.'"[37]

On a personal level, the Hills Materials sale was much harder for Adelstein. *"It was very uncomfortable for me,"* he admitted, having attached so much of his own identity to his professional success and his ability to connect his achievements to his father's legacy. Northwestern had not gone anywhere, and Stan's day-to-day life hardly changed after the sale. He still kept his office and used it for everything from making calls about community events to looking over NWE spreadsheets. But *"for a long time afterward, whenever we'd pull up to some intersection or light, I'd see some Hills workers doing something on the side of the road,"* and a melancholic pang would wash over him. *"And I'd turn to Lynda and say, 'Those aren't my trucks anymore.'"*

CHAPTER 19
STATE SENATOR ADELSTEIN

As the clock struck midnight on January 1, 2000, the world stood still and with mixed emotions. Revelers across the globe toasted and kissed their sweethearts as each successive time zone rung in the New Year. Others sighed with relief as the noncatastrophe known as "Y2K" failed to end the world or silence people's television sets. Some feared the apocalypse that night, while others grinned at the promise of a new era. Meanwhile, as the world prepared to turn the page toward a new century, Stan Adelstein was still searching for the real power.

Northwestern dove headlong into its strategic decision to systematically acquire property after the Hills Materials sale. Although effectively retired from the construction industry, Stan retained his position as president of NWE, while Tlustos balanced his responsibilities with other real estate ventures, all run out of their central office.[1]

Both men and their staffs moved to a new facility when the company built a commercial and residential complex just behind Founder's Park in 2009. At the center of regional commerce for more than eighty years, Northwestern would thereafter do business near the sandstone outcropping above the "Hay Camp" that later became Rapid City.[2]

During the first decade of the twenty-first century, Stan continued to stoke the entrepreneurial and philanthropic fires that had inspired him for so long. Over the next few years, he would partner in start-ups like Rapidnet, an internet service provider, as well as an (ultimately unsuccessful) effort to build a passenger railroad that, its planners believed, would shuttle tourists between Rapid City and Deadwood.[3] He also funded the creation of the

Soaring Eagle Treatment Center, an addiction counseling facility for area youth, and served for years on the board of the Black Hills Area Community Foundation. He had many memories of the people he met and helped during this time. *"Every year,"* Stan said, *"I'd sponsor an Easter brunch for the local Catholic bishop, and once a woman came up and thanked me for arranging to get computers for her granddaughter and two of her friends. I didn't really remember doing that, but it turned out that there was a new South Dakota program that reduced tuition for nurses who agreed to stay and work in the state. I really supported that and had purchased computers for these three young women because they were required to have a personal computer at the nursing program but couldn't afford it, which was obviously a ridiculous impediment."* His generosity hardly stopped there. Stan donated $50,000 each to commission sculptures of Presidents John Adams and Zachary Taylor for a Rapid City initiative that placed a bronze statue of every one of the nation's commanders in chief on a downtown street corner.[4]

Stan also sought to stay connected with his grandchildren, some of whom were now entering adulthood, and to instill in them an appreciation for the values that had shaped his life. Stan was especially close with his granddaughter Shirley. She had been born in Berlin while her father, Dan Adelstein, was stationed there in the 1980s. According to Shirley, she and Stan had "always been close. I'm his first grandchild, I was born on his birthday, [and] we've always had a special connection." The pair also had a connection to Berlin because of that city's historical significance for Jewish people and because, as Shirley put it, "I guess you could say that's where we first met."

When Shirley spent a college semester studying in Florence, Italy, in the mid-2000s, her grandfather asked if she would meet him in Berlin. Over the course of what Stan called *"an intense, intense weekend,"* he introduced his granddaughter to the American Jewish Committee (AJC), organizing a tour of the committee's Berlin offices, and took her to see many of the powerful historical sites and Holocaust memorials that dotted the city. The trip inspired Shirley to become involved with the AJC, and she would later contribute to the organization's efforts to improve relations between Jewish people and African Americans. It also "allowed me and my grandfather," Shirley said, "to bond over what really has become over the course of my adult life, a deeply shared commitment to the values that we hold as American Jews. Values of freedom and democracy and the importance of standing up for the Jewish people and

CHAPTER 19

ensuring our security and the special role that the American Jewish community plays in ensuring that those values are perpetuated around the world."[5]

Shirley's words captured the ways in which Stan had been trying to serve his people and his country for decades. He, too, enjoyed the trip across Berlin and the chance to reconnect with his granddaughter and to introduce her to the AJC. But one stop was etched in his memory. *"Shirley and I went to Wanssee,"* a mansion in the far southwestern corner of Berlin, *"where the 'Final Solution' was adopted"* by SS leaders in early 1942. *"I had been to Wanssee four or five times before, since after the war it became a museum and an educational institution where police and leaders from all over the world went for trainings to learn about the treatment of people and the consequences of persecution and genocide. Shirley and I got a tour from the director, and as we walked around the exhibits, we saw the actual Nazi plan to eradicate the Jews."*

Several major Nazi leaders had attended the Wannsee Conference, including Adolf Eichmann, and together they planned the extermination of some eleven million Jewish people. As Stan and Shirley took in the exhibits, they came across a quote by SS general Reinhard Heydrich. Museum designers had pulled his words and blown them up for emphasis. After describing how the Nazis would force Jewish people into labor camps, working them to death while building German infrastructure, Heydrich asserted that "any final remnant that survives will doubtless consist of the elements most capable of resistance. They must be dealt with appropriately since, representing the fruit of natural selection, they are to be regarded as the core of a new Jewish revival."[6] *"As Shirley and I approached this part of the exhibit,"* Stan recalled, tears welling in his eyes, *"I remember that our eyes both fell on those words at the same moment. I turned to her and said, 'Honey, you'd better make that true.'"*

The sentiments Stan expressed in that moment—that it was up to Jewish people fortunate enough either to survive the Holocaust, to avoid it altogether (as he did), or to descend from either group (as was Shirley's experience) had a responsibility to live and grow and protect their community and their values—were reflective of the core motivations that had driven him throughout his life.

One manifestation of this mission, of course, had always been politics. Yet for all the political action Adelstein had been involved with, he had never run for public office. He feared that conflicts of interest with his business would constrain his service to constituents. The sale of Hills Materials, then, had opened a new chapter in Stan's life: now beyond the construction business, the possibility for conflicts of interest between his professional and political lives diminished. Without that tug on his conscience, Stan decided to run for the South Dakota House of Representatives, finally pursuing for himself some of the real, voter-endorsed power for which he had pined so many years before.[7]

Stan won his first seat in the state legislature in November 2000. The general election was a three-way race in which the two candidates receiving the most votes would advance to the state House. Fellow Republican and former Rapid City police chief Tom Hennies took first, while Stan edged out the incumbent Democrat, a lawyer named Mike Wilson, by a healthy margin. Adelstein and Hennies both rode a Republican wave that year. Although the presidential race between Vice President Al Gore and Texas Governor George W. Bush was historically narrow nationally, South Dakota went solidly for Bush and Congressman John Thune, a young Republican who first took the state's lone seat in the House of Representatives in 1996. With these two at the top of South Dakota's ticket, Republicans like Stan swept the Black Hills, securing all twenty-one of the region's legislative seats.[8]

Stan's first campaign set the tone for his electoral career. To many South Dakota Republicans, their politics cast in the conservatism of the Reagan Revolution, Adelstein was just too liberal. In a letter to the *Rapid City Journal* just before the June primary earlier that year, one Rapid City voter called Stan "everything from . . . a political chameleon to a socialist."[9] Bill Janklow's brother, Arthur "Art" Janklow, was a close friend and parried with another letter, deploying the kinds of arguments that Stan's supporters would lean on in campaigns to come. He called Stan "a gentleman who is honest beyond question" before noting his many "leadership positions in our community, state, and national organizations [over] many, many years," and ending with gratitude for Stan's philanthropy and generosity.[10]

This dichotomy returned campaign after campaign. Stan's supporters lauded him for his deep commitment to his city and state, as well as his charity.[11] His detractors called him a liberal "RINO" (a duplicitous "Republican in Name Only") and often pointed at Stan's wealth and the way he used it. *"They used 'RINO' in an ad against me, which had a picture of a rhinoceros. A lot of my friends were furious, but I simply loved it, and in public I would ask people whether they'd rather be represented by a big, powerful rhino who was willing to go anywhere with that big horn on his nose, or a 'RABBIT'—a 'Republican Afraid, Bewildered, and Behind In Terror.'"*

Armed with this sharp wit and ample war chest, Adelstein spent nearly $31,000 in his first primary race in the summer of 2000. He hired pollsters who deployed sophisticated campaign strategies and poured money into advertisements.[12] His years hosting presidents and mingling with the erudite Republican Senate Trust had inured him to big money politics. To Adelstein, this was just how the game was played.

The fact remained, however, that Stan had spent more on his campaign than the average South Dakotan earned in a year. His was not only the most expensive South Dakota state legislative campaign: it was more than double the runner-up, a primary in Pierre for which one candidate spent about $15,000.[13] This lavish spending helped Stan's opponents hammer home the narrative that, at best, Adelstein was out of touch with the average voter, and, at worst, that he was trying to buy his way into power.[14] *"People thought I was rich, powerful, and distant, and I didn't mind the first two,"* Stan joked. He fought these perceptions by pounding the pavement and inviting the public to Saturday morning coffee at the McDonald's just down the hill from his house. There, they could ask questions and talk over the issues they cared about. He also started going by "Stan," rather than "Mr. Adelstein." *"By the time I ran for office, Lynda and I had been together for around two years, and when people called me 'Stan,' sometimes I'd say, 'He doesn't know me well enough to call me that!' Maybe it was a generational thing, but Lynda teased me and I got over it. From then on, whenever somebody called me 'Mr. Adelstein,' I would stop them and say, 'Please call me Stan,' and I really got to like that a lot."*

Stan also had a propensity for supporting other candidates through political action committees (PACs), a practice that irked critics who considered his contributions unethical exploitations of a loophole in the state's campaign finance laws, which allowed unlimited donations by PACs.[15] Sometimes, his generosity helped jumpstart the careers of Republican candidates, occasionally helping cement the party's hold on statewide offices for years.

This was exactly the case when Stan met M. Michael "Mike" Rounds, a Republican insurance man from Pierre who spent most of the 1990s in the state Senate, including several terms as Senate majority leader. When Bill Janklow approached the end of his fourth term in 2002, an intense primary battle broke out between two Republicans—Attorney General Mark Barnett and Steve Kirby, who had served two years as lieutenant governor in the early 1990s. Both men were considered frontrunners, but their deeply negative campaigns turned off South Dakota voters. Rounds had been term limited out of the state senate in 2000 and entered the gubernatorial race as an underdog. As Kirby and Barnett slung mud at one another, Rounds cast himself as the dignified, dark-horse alternative. He clinched the primary that summer and won in the fall.[16] And he did so with significant help from Stan Adelstein.

Stan had met Rounds prior to a multiparty debate in 2002 but did not know him well. Unhappy with Kirby and Barnett and impressed by Rounds's performance, Adelstein approached him after the debate. According to Rounds, Adelstein strode up to him and said, "I would like to help with your campaign, and I think you should be the next governor."[17]

Stan had a similar recollection. *"After the debate was over,"* Adelstein said, *"I walked over to him and said, 'Mike, I'd like to visit with you for a minute. Your campaign doesn't have any money, you have the family running it, and you should be governor. I'm going to give you X number of dollars.'"* The number was substantial enough to prepare Rounds's candidacy for a statewide run. Then, Stan continued, *"Rather than put out his hand and say, 'Thank you,' Mike looked me in the eye and said, 'I'll think about it.'"*

That had never happened to Stan in all the years he had been supporting politicians. *"Bill Janklow told me later that Rounds had called him after we met and said, 'Stan Adelstein offered my campaign X dollars, what in the world does he want?' So Bill told him, 'Listen, you've got to know something. Stan is the most generous son-of-a-bitch in this state, and he gives money where his heart is. The only thing you'll ever have to do for him,'"* Stan said, recalling Janklow's words with a smile, *"'is listen to his cockamamie ideas.'"* With that, Rounds accepted Stan's offer and used his contribution to jumpstart his winning bid for governor. Adelstein served on Rounds's transition team after the election, and the pair became allies in state government throughout Stan's time in the legislature.[18]

Even though his giving had helped elevate Rounds to statewide office, Adelstein also frequently earned the ire of his fellow Republicans when he supported candidates across the aisle. Stan, for example, was an ally of Tom Daschle, the Democrat who had climbed from the U.S. House of Representatives into Jim Abdnor's U.S. Senate seat and eventually became the majority leader of the Senate. When Daschle was a young congressman, Stan had fought hard to undo him, something he later described as a simple function of party politics.[19]

As time went on, however, he and Daschle began to relate with one another. Whether this was because of personal chemistry (Stan lauded Daschle's *"sheer intelligence and ability"*), because they shared stances on specific issues (Adelstein also appreciated the senator's *"championship of Israel"*), or because the Republican Party moved to the right during the Reagan years, leaving Stan ideologically closer to a moderate Democrat than a conservative Republican—and likely a combination of all three—Adelstein and Daschle eventually worked together on several issues. Stan voiced his support for Daschle every campaign season, and his youngest son, Jonathan, even worked for Daschle in Washington, D.C. from 1995 to 2002. Then, at Daschle's recommendation, President George W. Bush nominated Jonathan to serve as a commissioner for the Federal Communications Commission, a position he held from 2002 to 2009. Together, this work opened a personal connection that furthered Stan and Daschle's personal relationship.[20]

Stan spent two terms in the state House beginning in 2000, and over the course of a half-dozen terms as a legislator, he would engage many issues. They ranged from supporting a ban on smoking in public indoors to introducing legislation that would expand the state's definition of "church" to allow officials at mosques, synagogues, and other houses of worship to oversee weddings and other ceremonies.[21] *"That bill was strongly opposed by many of the same radical conservatives who opposed gay marriage and my supposedly 'liberal' policies on things like a bill to compensate for the inflation of medical costs for Temporary Assistance for Needy Families (TANF) recipients,"* Stan said. *"The 'church' bill was killed in the state Senate, in part,"* he continued, *"because I steadfastly refused to eliminate references to 'Muslim congregations,' as some members wanted me to."*

Stan's service in the state legislature also overlapped with an erratic and increasingly polarized epoch in South Dakota politics. The state's political winds had always swirled wildly, gusting along a path that had a habit of looking predictable just long enough to twist on a whim. But even by South Dakota standards, the first decade of the twenty-first century was especially tortuous. As they had been for decades, most South Dakota voters were moderate Republicans who could be persuaded to vote for just the right Democrat. Then, for just over seven months beginning in 2004, all three members of the state's congressional delegation were—for the first time since the Great Depression—Democrats.

This came to pass under bizarre circumstances. During 2002, the full last year of his fourth term as governor, Bill Janklow had run for Congress. That year, John Thune had given up his place in Congress to challenge Democratic Senator Tim Johnson, who had first won a seat in the House in 1986 then defeated Larry Pressler in the 1996 Senate race. Thune lost by a razor-thin 524 votes, but Janklow beat Democrat Stephanie Herseth, herself the granddaughter of former South Dakota Governor Ralph Herseth.[22] Shortly after taking office in 2003, Janklow ran a stop sign in eastern South Dakota, killing a motorcyclist. *"It was a tragic thing, Bill's accident,"* Stan said. Janklow's mistake had cost a man his life, for which Janklow was convicted of second-degree manslaughter following a very public trial. According to Stan, Janklow struggled to come to terms with the accident, for which he was sentenced to serve 100 days in jail.[23] *"Bill tried to stay in good spirits throughout all this,"* Stan remembered. *"I remember him telling me that, 'Well, I guess I started politics with you and I guess I will end politics with you.'"* When Janklow resigned from Congress the following January, Stephanie Herseth edged out the Republican candidate in a special election in June 2004, then again in the general election that November.[24]

The reign of the Democrats—Daschle, Johnson, and Herseth—was short-lived, as Thune upended Daschle in an underdog victory in November 2004. *"Despite Tom's loss, which hit me hard, there is something about the kind of political honor that we have in South Dakota,"* Stan said about the race. *"In the years after, Thune never, ever in any way hinted or made any comment about my previous support for Daschle in that race or any other."* Still, Daschle's loss was not the only thing brewing in South Dakota politics that made the Democrats' brief sweep seem counterintuitive, or at least uneven: conservatives in the state legislature were making headway on abortion, a perennially controversial and seemingly intractable social issue.

Of all the campaigns and issues with which Adelstein was involved during his time in Pierre, South Dakota's fiery abortion battle best illustrates this chapter of his life. The South Dakota State Legislature convened in early January each year and normally stayed in session until mid-February, and sometimes longer. Members of the state House and the state Senate serve two-year terms, meaning they are up for reelection in the fall of even-numbered years. Because party primaries occurred in the June that preceded the November general election, both campaigns often focused on an incumbent legislator's position on the issues during that year's legislative session.

CHAPTER 19

In early 2004, while Adelstein was a member of the state House, conservative Republicans introduced abortion bills that sparked an intense debate among South Dakota legislators and voters. The legislation made national news. A lifelong pro-choice Republican, Stan opposed many aspects of the 2004 bill, which barred doctors from performing abortions except when the mother's life was in danger. Under the proposed law, other abortions could be prosecuted as a felony. In short, Stan—like many South Dakotans—considered the bill too extreme and worried that it was a political stunt, as one reporter wrote, "designed to spur a court challenge," with the goal of bringing abortion before the U.S. Supreme Court.[25]

Lynda vividly remembered this tense period. Over the years, she and Stan's romance had matured into a deep bond and partnership. She became the key sounding board for Stan's ideas. She was a close adviser who helped Stan think through his political positions and strategies. Although she was a Democrat, she and Stan often had long conversations that illuminated differing perspectives on the issues of the day.

Lynda was there during a debate over amendments to the controversial abortion bill in February 2004. "I came to watch and support Stan. As I headed up to the gallery, nobody said a word to me on the way in or out," she said, because many people in the room supported the abortion ban and knew Stan did not. "And I happened to sit next to John and Anne Barlow, who might have been the only other people who supported the changes Stan was trying to make to the bill. We sat up there all night, and I just remember watching Stan pop up and down from his seat, saying 'Mister Speaker,' 'Mister Speaker,' and trying to get the floor."[26]

Stan could feel his partner's presence. *"Oh yes, I knew she was up there, and her support helped keep me going,"* he said. As the floor debate proceeded, other legislators introduced amendments to legalize abortion in cases of rape or incest or to allow hospitals to provide counsel and emergency contraception to rape victims. One wanted to refine the definitions and medical timelines that dictated when abortions could be performed. Adelstein, however, introduced two provisions that would loosen the bill's language to accommodate scenarios in which the mother could face permanent physical damage from a dangerous pregnancy, or to permit the abortion "in the case of a severely deformed baby unlikely to survive after birth."[27]

Through these actions and others, Stan became a vocal leader of the opposition to the abortion bill. Although the final bill included exceptions to the abortion ban when medical complications could seriously impair or kill the mother, legislators refused to extend these exceptions to cases of rape or incest.[28] As the session progressed, Adelstein pushed hard to include this latter provision, and even asked his granddaughter Shirley, then a college student, to testify about the issue. When she did, she gave a young woman's perspective on the additional trauma a mother might experience if forced to bear her rapist's child.[29]

Ultimately, the 2004 abortion bill passed both houses of the state legislature following a raucous public debate. Governor Mike Rounds issued a "style and form veto," which required some technical changes clarifying that existing abortion restrictions would continue if litigation suspended the main provisions of the new law. Although the House voted to accept the governor's changes, the state Senate did not. This killed the bill.[30]

Stan Adelstein advanced from the state House to the state Senate following the 2004 elections. Although the abortion bill had died in the state Senate that year, the issue did not. Over the next year or so, anti-abortion conservatives regrouped and revised the bill, then introduced a similar measure in 2006. Again, an impassioned statewide debate ensured. And again, Adelstein opposed the measure—this time from the Senate. Unlike the earlier version of the abortion ban, Rounds signed the 2006 measure without qualification. But it never went into effect because South Dakota voters killed it in a statewide referendum that November.[31]

Throughout the spring and summer of 2006, however, nobody yet knew the bill's fate, and with the referendum looming in the fall, abortion became the dominant campaign issue leading up to the June primaries. On his side of the issue, Stan earned recognition for refusing to budge on what he (and eventually the majority of South Dakota voters) considered an extreme piece of legislation. Stan received the Barry Goldwater Award, an annual national award given to one lawmaker either from a state legislature or from Congress by the reproductive health-care organization Planned Parenthood, for his opposition to the bill.[32]

Stan's primary opponent, an ardently anti-abortion and conservative Republican named Elli Schwiesow, zeroed in on Adelstein's "no" vote on the

CHAPTER 19   295

abortion bill. Schwiesow had been active for years in the Republican women's organization and as a member of the State Central Committee. In 2000, she had served on the platform committee at the Republican National Convention and then served as vice-chair of the South Dakota Republican Party.[33] In 2004, she had run against Adelstein in his first state Senate primary. Their contest for the District 32 Senate seat embodied the growing chasm between the moderate and conservative wings of the Republican Party, with each candidate needling the other on abortion and other issues. That year, Adelstein defeated Schwiesow by only 122 votes.[34]

When Schwiesow challenged Adelstein again in 2006, their race quickly turned ugly. Stan heard stories about members of the opposition campaign leaning hard on his Jewishness when speaking with Republican voters—many of whom were evangelical Christians or Catholics.[35] There was *"some open anti-Semitism that drove support away from me in 2006,"* he said. He also believed that his opponents quietly spun scandal among family values voters by making it well known that Stan lived with Lynda while he was still married to Ita.[36] For her part, Lynda shrugged off political tactics that focused on their personal life. "You know," she remarked years later, her words trailing away with dismissal, "if people are going to get upset with a couple of elderly people that live together . . ."[37]

Yet Stan, too, played hardball. Looking back over Adelstein's career in the state legislature, the *Argus Leader* would describe Stan this way: "He was outspoken. And rich. And not afraid to put his money into the political process, where he punished his enemies and supported his friends."[38] Some of those "political enemies" had even harsher words for Adelstein. "He was not a Republican. He was anything but a Republican," said Bill Napoli, a conservative and often controversial Catholic Republican from West River. "I'm not going to say that he was a very mean, vindictive, spiteful person. I'm not going to say that he didn't belong in government," Napoli said. But the point of these thinly veiled attacks was clear.[39]

Whatever personal, ideological, or religious undertones coursed through the 2006 state Senate primary, abortion remained among the core issues. Stan took heavy flak from Schwiesow for attending Planned Parenthood's annual gala in Washington, D.C., to accept his Goldwater Award that spring. Although Stan framed the event as an opportunity to discuss South Dakota's debate on the abortion issue at a national forum, Schwiesow ran campaign ads that cemented that trip to his "no" vote on the abortion bill. She defeated Adelstein in the primary.[40]

Following his primary loss in June 2006, Adelstein flirted with switching parties and running as a Democrat in the fall. Ultimately, however, having been a Republican for more than fifty years, he could not stomach the idea. Instead, he crossed the aisle in another way, throwing his support behind the Democratic candidate, Tom Katus, who won in November.[41]

Two years later, Adelstein and Schwiesow went at it again in the 2008 Senate primary, fighting for a chance to unseat the incumbent Democrat, Katus.[42] As with 2006, the 2008 campaigns were ruthless. After Stan won the primary, Schwiesow decided to run as an independent. Adelstein's temper flared at an open house at the Republican Party's West River campaign headquarters just after Schwiesow announced her independent bid. The event, not coincidentally, was situated in a Rapid City building that Stan owned and had donated to the party. When Schwiesow arrived with a cake in hand—whether as a coy jab at her opponent or an innocent gesture—Stan ordered her to leave. He argued that the event was for Republican candidates only, and Schwiesow maintained that she had meant no harm. Others claimed that Stan's actions were in poor taste, and the incident grabbed headlines.[43] Within a few months, however, the dust had settled, and the voters in District 32 sent State Senator Adelstein back to Pierre.[44]

SUDDEN TWILIGHT

Coming off the raucous campaigns of 2006 and 2008, Adelstein continued to serve the constituents of District 32. In the fall of 2008, the state Game, Fish, & Parks department purchased 33 acres of the Northwestern Engineering Company's land on the northwestern edge of Rapid City. Adelstein had reduced the price by over 40 percent from the property's assessed value after the state expressed interest in building an outdoor learning campus, which included an interpretive center, a pond, and a series of trails, on the land.[45]

Adelstein would grab headlines several more times in subsequent years. He proposed a temporary one-cent sales tax increase to help South Dakota pay for ballooning educational and health-care-related costs as the state's economy recovered from the Great Recession. That proposal died in South Dakota's staunchly antitax political environment.[46] Adelstein would also prompt the attorney general's office to investigate a Republican employee of the South Dakota secretary of state's office, who had previously run a campaign merchandise business and a conservative blog that was regularly critical of Stan. The individual had failed to separate himself from these activities after accepting state employment, and Adelstein believed this was highly unethical, if not illegal. Although the attorney general found no criminal wrongdoing in the case, the employee resigned.[47]

Outside of Stan's political life, the year 2009 delivered some lows and highs. After she and Stan separated, Ita had settled in California, and, like Stan, found a long-term romantic partner there. With time, she and Stan had resumed a warm friendship and attended family gatherings together. But in the mid-2000s, Ita was diagnosed with Parkinson's disease. Her health slowly declined, and she passed away in February 2009. As Stan mourned the passing of his wife, friend, and the mother to his children, his spirits were lifted when he and Ita's youngest son, Jonathan, received another presidential appointment, this time from Barack Obama, to serve as the administrator of the U.S. Department of Agriculture's Rural Utilities Service.

Another life event helped Stan through these years. Shortly after Ita's passing, he and Lynda decided to get married. According to Lynda, when Stan first proposed, she was not sure it was necessary. "Why do we need to change anything?" she said. "But I think Stan was concerned," she continued, "that it would make things clearer and cleaner if we were married." As the pair discussed wedding plans, they decided against a big, elaborate ceremony. They thought about going to the courthouse for a quick marriage, but realized that, given Stan's elevated public profile, somebody might call a reporter. Since Lynda's sister and brother-in-law lived in Nebraska, Stan and Lynda decided to get married there. "So within like a week," Lynda recalled, "we were in Nebraska, on [my sister's] deck with her grandchildren and her husband and my nieces," getting married.[48]

The pair only grew closer after their rather impromptu nuptials. "We're basically a mixed marriage at every level," Lynda would later say. "We came from different families, we grew up in different places, and we support different political parties," she continued. "But we are always able to make decisions, to work together, and share the same priorities and values about what's really important in life."⁴⁹ Stan agreed, and cherished the fact that Lynda was *"totally devoid of worrying about what other people think, or ever feeling like she needed to be a stereotypical 'politician's wife' who cared too much about the gossip and social aspects of political life."* Instead, Lynda continued to be a support and adviser, helping him think through problems at work, in politics, and in his charitable efforts. *"She has this un-erring ability to understand people when we first meet them,"* he said. *"I haven't been conned that often in my life, but I have been conned. And I don't think it's happened since Lynda has been around to give her impressions of people before we work with them."*

This partnership and sense of mutual support, combined with Stan's unending drive to stay active and involved in his community and politics, kept him running for the state Senate year after year. Stan ran unopposed in 2010 and continued to fight for the things in which he believed. During that time, South Dakota politics shifted again: Mike Rounds left the governor's mansion in early 2011 and returned to private life. He would return to politics in 2014, and would once again receive Stan's full support as he ran successfully to replace Tim Johnson in the U.S. Senate. Once there, Stan's son Dan—who, after retiring from the military, had worked in Bill Janklow's office during his brief stint in Congress—would advise Rounds on national security and other issues. According to Stan, it was important to Dan that his father not use his political influence or friendship with Mike Rounds to help him find work. *"Dan,"* Stan said, *"absolutely forbade me to assist with his effort to get a job on Rounds's staff."* Although his father may not have been directly involved in advancing Dan's career, Dan would later credit Stan for "bringing the Adelstein family into American politics."⁵⁰

As Rounds was preparing to leave the governor's mansion, his lieutenant governor and the former executive director of the Children's Home Society of South Dakota, Dennis Daugaard, won the gubernatorial election in 2010. That same year, Republican Kristi Noem, a farmer from the southeastern corner of the state, rode a conservative Republican wave and unseated Democratic congresswoman Stephanie Herseth Sandlin. The political landscape was showing signs of a seismic shift, and Adelstein wanted to stay in the fight. He ran unopposed again in 2012 and intended to continue his service.

The following October, however, a medical emergency would put a sudden end to Stan Adelstein's career as an elected official. On an October day in 2013, he checked into the Black Hills Surgical Hospital for a routine

CHAPTER 19

procedure. At age eighty-two, he had suffered from persistent hip pain and finally went in to have his hip replaced. The doctors told him that his would be a relatively straightforward, in-patient surgery. He would be hospitalized for a few days, then go through several weeks of physical therapy. Stan would be on his feet, fully recovered fairly quickly. *"It was a reasonable plan, and my friend and former Rapid City Mayor Ed McLaughlin had told me that when he had the same surgery fifteen years earlier, he was up on a ladder only twelve days after the operation. And he was a little bit older than me. So I planned that I'd better be back on my bicycle within twelve days."* Most important, he had timed the procedure so he would be fully healed and ready to serve in the legislature by January.

After all the paperwork was signed, Stan gave Lynda a quick kiss, changed into his hospital gown, climbed into bed, chatted with the nurse who placed an IV in his arm, and then waited for the anesthesiologist and orthopedic surgeon to talk him through the procedure. Within minutes, he had been wheeled to the operating room. Someone strapped a plastic mask over Stan's nose and mouth, and his doctor asked him to count backward from 100. Then everything went black.

EPILOGUE

The front stoop of 1999 West Boulevard faces east, just high enough on the hill to overlook the tree line and see the Black Hills fade into rolling prairie. Ellsworth Air Force Base, for decades home to the Synagogue of the Hills and, for Stan Adelstein, a reminder of his family's years of military service, sits to the northeast. Its massive beige bomber hangers and air control tower are just visible in the distance. It was a long August evening in 1995, and if Stan Adelstein had been looking to reminisce about his family or their days in uniform, he need not have searched beyond his doorstep.

Arriving home from work, Stan found a strange wooden box sitting on his porch. It had metal edges, measured about 3½ by 1½ feet, and had faint, stenciled letters in a font he had not seen in years. His first impulse was a little strained—his years of political and Jewish activism had occasionally earned him anti-Semitic ire, and the box looked vaguely military, a little like an ordnance crate. He would later tell a reporter that he was not sure if he should open it, in case it had been left by someone who meant him harm. He called the National Guard, asking if they had any idea what the letters on the box, "Co.C. 528 ENGRS," might mean. There was no such unit with that designation, his contact at the Guard said, so he called the police. When they arrived, officers inspecting the box found more writing, scrawled in faint orange: "State Room, Lt. M.E. Adelstein."[1]

Stan never discovered who left the box, where they had gotten it, or how they traced it back to him. But one thing was clear: it was his father's footlocker from World War I, and to his knowledge, no Adelstein had seen the artifact

EPILOGUE

since the war ended in 1918. It was a precious bridge to his family's past for which he has always been grateful.[2]

That box was one of the things Adelstein thought about during his many months of recovery in a hospital bed. The hip surgery that was supposed to have caused only a few weeks of discomfort took an unfortunate and unexpected turn. A vicious bacterium known as methicillin-resistant Staphylococcus aureus (MRSA) made its way into Stan's bloodstream, nearly killing him. He underwent a series of surgeries and was transferred to Rapid City Regional Hospital, where he would return several times for repeated hospitalizations until the following March.[3]

Stan's surgery, as it happened, had coincided with Winter Storm Atlas, an aberrant October blizzard of historic proportions. The sky opened up, dumping huge amounts of wet, heavy snow that snapped trees, killed livestock by the thousands, and shut down much of the Black Hills for days. Lynda remembered being there by Stan's side, making sure that the hospital staff—who were short-staffed and exhausted due to the storm—double-checked and revised his medications after Stan showed signs of confusion and delirium. "If there's one message that should get through with this book," she said with a smirk, "it's that every elderly person who has a major procedure has to have someone there to be their advocate. I don't think I was very popular among the doctors and nurses for a few days, but I'm glad I was there—when Stan first woke up, he was so confused from the incorrect opioid dosage that he thought the whole thing was a prank. I told him, 'Listen, you're in the hospital. I don't have the time or the money to pull off a prank this elaborate!'"[4]

Although he and Lynda would later look back on Stan's hospitalization with a sense of humor, Stan's condition was no joke. The MRSA infection nearly killed him, *"and for a while, I just wanted to die,"* he said.

Had the MRSA proven unstoppable, Stan would have left a sprawling legacy. Although it pained him to do so, Stan felt compelled to leave the state Senate when his hospitalizations made it clear that his constituents would be left without representation in Pierre for the second session of his term. *"That was unfair to them,"* he said, *"so I decided to step down."* His illness rendered him unable to speak, so Stan had a letter drafted and sent to the governor, officially relinquishing his hold on "the real power."[5] "It was," he told a reporter later in the week, "the saddest and most difficult decision I've made in a long time."⁶ Governor Daugaard followed the standard application process for legislative succession, eventually appointing Alan Solano, a prominent Rapid City Republican who was the CEO of Behavior Management Systems, Inc., a local mental health facility, and a member of the Rapid City Chamber of Commerce, to fill Stan's seat.⁷

Northwestern was also ready to live on in Stan's absence. Pat Tlustos oversaw the company's full transition toward property management. Stan's son Jim joined the board a few years after the Hills purchase, and eventually succeeded his father as president of NWE in 2018. Jonathan Adelstein, meanwhile, joined the board after reentering the private workforce following his time in political and government service. By then, the company offered a variety of services structured around its management of "1,200 residential units [and] 435,000 square feet of commercial space" at properties in California, Arizona, Colorado, Nebraska, and South Dakota.⁸ Stan and his team had rebuilt the company his father started before the Depression, and it, too, lay primed for its next phase.

The Synagogue of the Hills was also in good shape. In the early 1990s, the congregation left its longtime home at Ellsworth Air Force Base and temporarily moved into a building owned by Hills Materials Company. In 1996, Adelstein donated a house adjacent to some Hills property, and over the next several years the synagogue converted the home into a set of offices and a library and prayer center.⁹ For the first time in its half-century of life, the synagogue had a home of its own.

Stan stayed involved in Jewish affairs there and elsewhere, and in late September 2013—just months before his fateful surgery—Stan helped organize a dinner and presentation to commemorate the seventieth anniversary of the rescue of several hundred Jewish Danes during the Holocaust. *"It all came about because when I was in Pierre for the legislature in early 2013, I was unable to find a Jewish person to light the Hanukkah menorah later that year. So I went and asked the pastors of the Memorial Lutheran Church if they would be willing to light the menorah each night and say the prayers. They were intrigued with the responsibility, and I made an offhand comment about how even though the one in Pierre was electric, it was 'similar to the one hidden in the church in Copenhagen, Denmark.' When they said they hadn't ever heard that story, I told them how on September 28, 1943, the Nazis had tried to force every Jew in Denmark to death camps. But the Danish government interceded and insisted on maintaining contact with its nationals, so most of the Jews were taken to Sweden on fishing boats. Because of this, more than 99 percent of the country's Jews survived. Telling this story reminded me that the seventieth anniversary of that event was coming up, so I sponsored the celebration at Mount Rushmore that year, and former Senator Rudy Boschwitz and Bishop David Zellmer were both there, and we also had an exhibit on the event set up in the visitors' area. Nearly 100,000 visitors saw it."*[10]

The synagogue also found another lay leader, a Jewish physician who had come to the Black Hills in the 1990s. As with so many things in his life, Adelstein called it a coincidence. The connections, however, were plain to see: when Rapid City Regional Hospital added a neonatology unit in 1988, it quickly became the primary care facility for premature and ill newborns in and around West River.[11] In the mid-1990s, a Brooklyn-born neonatologist named Steven Benn—who had served in Rwanda following the genocide and worked on the faculty at Vanderbilt University—moved to Rapid City with his wife and children. *"We had been sad to see an outstanding physician leave Rapid City,"* Stan remembered, *"and we were desperate to find someone to take his place. At the time, Dan was stationed in Nashville, Tennessee, where he met Steve Benn, a fantastic academic specialist in neonatology. Dan told me about him, so I called Steve and invited him to come see what Rapid City had to offer. Luckily, we were able to convince him to give it a try."*

Working in the hospital that Adelstein helped build, Benn became actively involved in the synagogue Adelstein had founded. *"Steve had an extensive Jewish religious education,"* Stan said, *"and it was much better than mine. I learned a lot from him,"* and the two became friends. As Stan busied himself with legislative affairs, Benn became the synagogue's leader. He was a knowledgeable administrator who could help ensure that western South Dakota's small Jewish community would live on for another generation, even as the number of Jewish people in the state dwindled to less than 1 percent—the lowest in the nation—by 2014.[12]

Even as Benn took over the weekly operations at the synagogue, Adelstein was regularly called upon to blow the shofar at religious and community events. *"I continued to learn from the shofar as the years went by."* Two occasions from the year 2012 sprang to mind. First, after Bill Janklow passed away from a brain tumor in January 2012, his family asked Adelstein to blow the shofar during his old friend's funeral. Stan remembered it this way: *"My shofar really only has a few notes, like a bugle. And when I played 'tekiah,' which requires three notes, that's about all I got. But at Bill's funeral, I stood up to blow it in his memory. And for the first time ever, it emitted a third note, somewhere in between the low and high pitches I normally played. I was surprised to hear this, but as I blew it three times, it made sense. In my head, I could hear the sound climbing up, low to high, for each of the syllables I was thinking in my head as I sent my friend to his resting place: 'Good-Bye-Bill.'"*

About six months later, Adelstein had a similarly surprising experience. Once again, he had been asked to blow the shofar to mark a major local milestone: the fortieth anniversary of the 1972 Rapid City flood. *"When we were planning the event, somebody told me to blow the shofar three times. The first one was supposed to be sad, the second one was supposed to be hopeful, and the third sound triumphant,"* to symbolize the tragedy of and recovery from the flood, as well as the optimism Rapid City had about its own future. *"As they told me this, all I could think was, 'Well, it's a ram's horn, and it really does whatever it wants.' But I told them I'd try. And on the day of the ceremony, it pulled through: the first pitch came out like a really long wail; it really was sad, like nothing I'd heard before. The second one was brighter, and I suppose it was pretty close to hopeful. The third time, I did one of the common calls I usually did during Rosh Hashanah, so it was pretty triumphant."*

That, however, was not the end of the story. Months later, while Stan was in the hospital recovering from his hip surgery and MRSA infection, he awoke in the middle of the night. *"I was up there on the tenth floor, and pretty restless from the medication and so many days in bed. And I just happened to turn on the television, just to pass the time. And all of a sudden I hear this familiar wail—like a shofar blowing somewhere in the hospital. Then I realized what had happened: the television was preset to start up on the local channel, and they were playing the tape from the fortieth anniversary! So I was hearing my own shofar, and in some small way, I think that moment helped my recovery along."*

During that long winter in the hospital, Adelstein needed all the help he could get. His infection was severe, and he could have let go when MRSA attacked his body. Yet Stan did not. He battled back to health and was finally released from the hospital months after he first checked in. Nevertheless, the illness slowed Adelstein down. He maintained his office and the title "Chairman Emeritus" at NWE. He still checked in at the office and went back to local affairs and continued to speak publicly, contribute to local charities, and fight for the community and country he loved.

EPILOGUE

Although his battle with MRSA had forced him out of elected office, Adelstein did not slow down following his recovery. Only a few months after he was released from Rapid City Regional Hospital, Stan took his old friend, former South Dakota Governor Mike Rounds, on a tour of Israel. Rounds had just announced his candidacy for U.S. Senate seat—a race he would win in the fall of 2014—and the pair had been discussing the trip for years.[13] Accompanied by Lynda; Rounds and his wife, Jean; and Dan Adelstein (who would go on to serve as a policy adviser in Rounds's senatorial office), Stan took the candidate on a six-day tour, which included meetings with members of the Knesset, Israeli business leaders, and several Israeli generals.[14]

Yet none of these meetings stood out as strongly in Adelstein's memory as an evening mass the group took together. *"I knew that Mike and Jean were Catholic, so ahead of the trip, I had arranged for a private mass at the Church of the Nativity in Bethlehem, which is of course considered the place of Jesus Christ's birth. Lynda, unfortunately, didn't feel well and had stayed back. But Mike, Jean, Dan and I took mass with this priest from Mexico, and even though Dan and I are Jewish, the four of us took this ceremony together. Afterward, as we were leaving, the priest gave Jean this little doll, which was the symbol of the baby Jesus, and as we were leaving, a group of nuns from the Philippines approached Jean. They wanted to kiss the baby and hug Jean, and we all spent a special few moments together. It was one of the most beautiful, touching expressions of unity between a group of people of different faiths and from different parts of the world that I've ever experienced."*

And still Adelstein did not slow down. He remained involved in South Dakota politics, and each campaign season supported candidates whose values matched his own. In the fall of 2016, Adelstein dove back into presidential politics, putting his money and political interest and connections to work, serving as the state chairman for the Libertarian Party's presidential election and bringing the party's ticket—former New Mexico Governor Gary Johnson and former Massachusetts Governor Bill Weld, both of whom had been Republicans when they were in office, but switched their affiliation—to Rapid City for rallies and fund-raisers. His was part of an effort to push the state's three Electoral College votes against Donald Trump and former Secretary of State Hillary Clinton, both candidates who, in Adelstein's words, were "totally unsuitable!" to the Oval Office.[15]

The Johnson/Weld events he sponsored were classically Stan. On October 20, he hosted Weld, escorting him to Black Hills State University, where about

100 faculty members, students, and community members came to hear his ticket's case against the major party candidates.[16] That night, Weld attended a private fund-raiser at the Arrowhead Country Club, a private golf course on Rapid City's west side. The location told a story of its own: the Adelstein family's member number was "1."

"This came about because Art Dahl, who founded the club in 1954, said he would assign membership numbers in the order he received checks from a group of businesspeople that he was soliciting to start the organization. My father, Morris Adelstein, was the first one he received." After Morris passed away and Stan's mother aged, he took special care to preserve and transfer his father's original member number to his own when Bertha retired from the club in 1980.[17]

At the Johnson/Weld event, Stan offered another introduction, his octogenarian voice booming through the small reception room as it delivered a series of anecdotes—many of which a good portion of the crowd had heard a time or two before—seasoned with a practiced blend of humor, passion, and patriotic urgency. Guests sipped wine and enjoyed classy hors d'oeuvres as they talked with Stan, met Weld, and wondered about the two men's vision for the upcoming election.

The following week, Gary Johnson addressed a crowd of around 300 people at the Rushmore Plaza Civic Center. As state campaign chairman, Stan had been asked to introduce Johnson, and when he took the stage, Stan reminded the audience that Johnson had been born in Minot, North Dakota, and raised in Aberdeen, South Dakota. Stan believed the United States needed an honest president and that he could only trust Johnson—who he termed "one of us"—to meet that threshold.[18]

As they mingled backstage just before the speech, a Native American woman and former U.S. Army soldier named Amanda Yellow Robe approached Stan. She worked at NWE and had been asked to introduce Adelstein at the evening's event. As they waited backstage, the two made small talk, and Yellow Robe *"thanked me for what I had done for her while she was stationed in Germany. I asked her, 'What was that?' and she told me."*

According to Yellow Robe, 2006 was her first year in the military, "and [I] was feeling extremely homesick and scared because we were given word we would be deploying to Iraq in 2007." As her unit trained for deployment, "there were a lot of soldiers who couldn't afford to go home or didn't really have a home to go back to." Bonded as a family by their experience, the soldiers decided to spend the holidays together. "So when my parents came to visit me in December," Yellow Robe continued, "I had mentioned to them I had a lot of friends that had nowhere to go for Christmas." Somehow, word had made its way to Stan, and "that didn't sit well with Mr. Adelstein, being a veteran himself, so he donated some money" so the soldiers could celebrate together. "We gathered everyone in the barracks who stayed behind and went down to the beautiful Christmas market in downtown Wiesbaden," she said, and "it was a beautiful time we got to spend together as an extended family . . . and it truly was a blessing what he did for us soldiers that year." So routine were opportunities like this that Stan *"had no recollection"* of making the donation—a gesture that made Yellow Robe "choke up a little thinking about it" eleven years later.[19] These were the kinds of things Stan did because, as he said, *"I could."* Adelstein thanked Yellow Robe for sharing this memory just before she walked off to introduce him to the crowd.

Despite Stan's enthusiasm at these events, the campaign would not pan out as they hoped—Trump defeated Clinton in a historic upset on November 8. While Johnson/Weld's run was through, if you asked Stan, he would tell you that his own story was far from over.

DIGNITY

On September 17, 2016, a dry, late-summer wind whipped across a bluff high on the edge of Chamberlain, South Dakota. Some 200 miles of barren interstate separate Chamberlain from Rapid City in the west and Sioux City, Iowa, in the east, making the town a logical halfway point between the city of Stan Adelstein's birth and that of his life. And more than 200 people had gathered there on a Saturday for the dedication of a shining fifty-foot stainless steel statue of an American Indian woman.[20]

Her name was Dignity and her story a symbol. A wealthy businessman in Rapid City had commissioned a Black Hills sculptor to design and build Dignity. She stood, arms stretched wide as her fingers pinched a sapphire-blue star quilt above her shoulders. She was a representation, the artist said, of "the strength and grace of the human spirit," and the state's Lakota and Dakota heritage.[21] On this day, the crowd had come to dedicate Dignity to the people of South Dakota.

Stan Adelstein listened from his place on the small stage that had been erected at Dignity's feet. He stood beside a Lutheran pastor from Rapid City, a Dakota teacher, and a group of students from the nearby Crow Creek Reservation school—all representatives of South Dakota's ethnic and spiritual mosaic.[22] Stan's dark yarmulke rested on the crown of his head, and a long pearl tallit with Hebrew embroidery hung over his jacket.[23] His hair and beard sparkled white in the afternoon sun, while his face bore the crags of many years. His body stooped slightly forward. Fancy dancers moved to the pulse of hide drums, their full regalia jingling on the prairie grass. A series of speakers—including Governor Dennis Daugaard and Stan's old friend Chaplain Herb Cleveland—addressed the crowd, lauding the artist and his work. They spoke of Dignity's power and called for a new era of respect between cultures. They asked that the people renew the bonds that unite all South Dakotans.[24]

Dignity towered overhead, and the Missouri River, on whose banks Adelstein had been born nearly a century earlier, loomed in the background. When it was his turn, Stan stepped forward and gripped the long, dark horn he had picked up in Israel in 1965. He bent his right elbow ever so slightly, forming an obtuse angle with his outstretched arm. He said a prayer in Hebrew before lifting his left hand to his mouth and squeezing a loose fist near his lips.[25]

Inhaling deeply, Stan knew that everything that had defined him for more than eight decades—the milieu of politics and business, success and failure, coincidence and achievement—was coming together in this moment. Time stopped for a few long seconds, while the crowd waited. Then, just as he had so many times and in so many places before, Stanford M. Adelstein squinted into the Dakota sun and blew his shofar.

Credit: Dick Brown

ACKNOWLEDGMENTS

Many people have helped me assemble this story over the last three years. First and foremost, Eric John Abrahamson presented me with the opportunity to write this book, edited the volume, and managed the entire process. Lois Facer keeps Vantage Point in order and read the manuscript several times and helped organize the photographs and captions. Diana Pavek undertook the enormous task of surveying and organizing the papers of the Northwestern Engineering Company, then helped me sort through them. She also did extensive newspaper research and assembled the index. Steven Benn shared insights about Stan and the project and read the manuscript. Sam Hurst talked me through many ideas and also reviewed the manuscript. Robert Burchfield copyedited the manuscrupt. Matt McInerney at Motel designed the book. A heartfelt thanks to you all.

Katie LeClair, Stan Adelstein's assistant, deserves her own paragraph for keeping this project moving, assembling archival and photographic materials, reading and commenting on the manuscript, and organizing many meetings throughout the process.

The following people tracked down sources and photographs from a variety of libraries, archives, and institutions, for which I am very grateful: Callie Schleusner and Rochelle Zens at the Black Hills Knowledge Network; Wanda Menin at the Jewish Federation of Sioux City, Iowa; Deano Pape and Karen McHale at the National Speech and Debate Association; Laurie Hallstrom at the *West River Catholic*; Lynn Kendall at the Rapid City Chamber of Commerce; Sheri Sponder and Seth Tupper at the *Rapid City Journal*; the staff

ACKNOWLEDGMENTS

at the Rapid City Public Library; Steven Benn and Leonard Running at the Synagogue of the Hills; Marshall Damgaard at the University of South Dakota Archives and Special Collections (who generously gave me advance access to Bill Janklow's papers, which are still being processed); and my younger brother, Christopher Zimmer, who researched in the Janklow Papers on my behalf.

The work of several historians proved critical to my understanding of Jewish history in South Dakota. I am grateful to two couples in particular: Howard and Audrey Shaff and Orlando and Violet Goering. I drew much of the background material on Stan's family from Howard Shaff & Audrey K. Shaff, *Paving the Way: The Life of Morris E. Adelstein* (Keystone, SD: Parmelia Publishing, 1988) and Orlando J. Goering and Violet Miller Goering, "Keeping the Faith: Bertha Martinsky in West River South Dakota," *South Dakota History* 25 (Spring 1995): 37–48. Additionally, portions of this work appeared in Eric Steven Zimmer, Art Marmorstein, and Matthew Remmich, "'Fewer Rabbis than U.S. Senators': Jewish Political Activism in South Dakota," in *The Plains Political Tradition: Essays on South Dakota Political Culture, Volume 3,* ed. Jon K. Lauck, John E. Miller, and Paula M. Nelson (Pierre: South Dakota State Historical Society Press, 2018), 112–39.

I am also indebted to Stan Adelstein and his family members, friends, and colleagues, who sat for long interviews and often responded to follow-up questions. They are Lynda Clark Adelstein, Daniel Adelstein, Robert Adelstein, Jonathan Adelstein, Jerry Mizel, Shirley Adelstein, Pat Tlustos, David Super, Maryann Blackerby, Donald Barnett, Amanda Yellow Robe, and Jeffrey Viken.

Finally, as always, thank you to my wife, Samantha, who has kept me grounded for eleven years and counting.

SOURCES

In addition to extensive interviews with Stan Adelstein and his friends, family, business partners, and acquaintances, this book is based on several archival collections. In the notes that follow, I use the following abbreviations:

AFP: Adelstein Family Photographs

MEA: Morris E. Adelstein

NWE: Papers of the Northwestern Engineering Company (Rapid City, SD)

RAC: Rockefeller Archive Center (Sleepy Hollow, NY)

RCACC: Rapid City Area Chamber of Commerce Archive (Rapid City, SD)

RCPL: Local History Room, Rapid City Public Library

RG: Reptile Gardens Archive (Rapid City, SD)

SMA: Stanford M. Adelstein

SOH: Synagogue of the Hills Library and Archives (Rapid City, SD)

USD: Richardson Collection, William J. Janklow Gubernatorial Papers, University of South Dakota Archives and Special Collections (Vermillion, SD)

SOURCES

INTRODUCTION

1. "24th Amendment, Banning Poll Tax, Has Been Ratified; Vote in South Dakota Senate Completes the Process of Adding to Constitution," *New York Times*, January 24, 1964.

2. See Benjamin E. Griffith, ed. *America Votes! A Guide to Modern Election Law and Voting Rights* (Chicago: American Bar Association, 2008), 202–15. On the broader history of the poll tax, see Joel H. Silbey, Allan G. Bogue, and William H. Flanigan, *The History of American Electoral Behavior* (Princeton, NJ: Princeton University Press, 1978), 199–230; Donald S. Strong, "The Poll Tax: The Case of Texas," *American Political Science Review* 38, no. 4 (August 1944): 693–709. On Jim Crow, see Glenda Elizabeth Gilmore, *Gender and Jim Crow: Women and the Politics of White Supremacy in North Carolina, 1896–1920* (Chapel Hill: University of North Carolina Press, 1996).

3. See Steven F. Lawson, *Black Ballots: Voting Rights in the South, 1944–1969* (New York: Columbia University Press, 1976), 57, 77, 143–44, 290.

4. Ibid., 290.

5. See John Searle, "South Dakotans Leave Convention for Another," *Rapid City Journal*, July 29, 1960; J.V. Yaukey, *The Governor's Scepter: Vignettes of South Dakota Governors from Byrne to Kneip* (Hayes Brothers, 1976), 62–63.

6. Donald Janson, "South Dakota Northern Pocket of Discrimination," *New York Times*, October 22, 1962. See also Donald Janson, "Study Finds Racial Bias in Rapid City, S.D.," *New York Times*, March 3, 1963.

7. "E.C. 'Ping' Murray," *Rapid City Journal*, June 4, 2002.

8. See Irving Bernstein, *Guns or Butter: The Presidency of Lyndon Johnson* (New York: Oxford University Press, 1996), 223–26; Doris Kearns Goodwin, *Lyndon Johnson and the American Dream* (New York: New American Library, 1977), 243–44. On Civil Rights activity during the Kennedy and Johnson Administrations, see Jonathan Rosenberg and Zachary Karabell, *Kennedy, Johnson, and the Quest for Justice: The Civil Rights Tapes* (New York: W.W. Norton, 2003), 11–26.

9. "24th Amendment, Banning Poll Tax, Has Been Ratified."

10. Yaukey, *Governor's Scepter*, 67.

1. Ibid., 46–51, 67.

2. "24th Amendment, Banning Poll Tax, Has Been Ratified."

CHAPTER 1

1. Ora Williams, "Iowa State Capitol," in *State of Iowa Official Register, 1953–1954*, ed. Sherman W. Needham (Des Moines: State of Iowa, 1953), 7–9.

2. See Lowell J. Soike, *Necessary Courage: Iowa's Underground Railroad and the Struggle Against Slavery* (Iowa City: University of Iowa Press, 2013); Andrea Kay Tucker, "Juntos: Viveron, Trabajaron y Aprendieron: The History of Latinos in Valley Junction, Iowa" (MA thesis, Iowa State University, 2008), 11–24.

3. There were some 16,000 Jewish people living in Iowa by 1918. See Michael J. Bell, "'True Israelites of America': The Story of the Jews of Iowa," *Annals of Iowa* 53, no. 2 (Spring 1994): 106.

4. Howard Shaff and Audrey K. Shaff, *Paving the Way: The Life of Morris E. Adelstein* (Keystone, SD: Parmelia Publishing, 2005), 12–14, 82.

5. Edvard Radzinsky, trans. Antonina W. Bouis, *Alexander II: The Last Great Tsar* (New York: Free Press, 2005), xv–xvii, 57–58.

6. Radzinsky, *Alexander II*, xv–xvii, 416–17.

7. For an overview of Jewish struggles in a variety of regions, see Raymond P. Scheindlin, *A Short History of the Jewish People: From Legendary Times to Modern Statehood* (New York: Oxford University Press, 1998). On Jewish Europeans, see 149–98.

8. On the populations of the Pale, see John D. Klier, "Russian Jewry on the Eve of the Pogroms," in *Pogroms: Anti-Jewish Violence in Modern Russian History*, ed. John D. Klier and Shlomo Lambroza (New York: Cambridge University Press, 1992), 5.

9. For a map of the Pale as it existed in 1881, see Klier and Lambroza, eds., *Pogroms*, xiii. See also Klier, "Russian Jewry on the Eve of the Pogroms," 1–7.

10. Klier, "Russian Jewry on the Eve of the Pogroms," 5.

1. Scheindlin, *A Short History of the Jewish People*, 180–81; Grant Wardlaw, *Political Terrorism: Theory,*

Tactics, and Counter-Measures, Second Ed. (New York: Cambridge University Press, 1989), 19–20.

2. Lawrence J. Epstein, *At the Edge of a Dream: The Story of Jewish Immigrants on New York's Lower East Side, 1880–1920* (San Francisco: John Wiley & Sons, 2007), 9.

3. Some scholars argue that the Russian government orchestrated the massacres, absolving itself through claims that the violence simply followed a public desire to avenge their fallen leader. Others have been skeptical of the government's involvement in organizing the violence. See I. Michael Aronson, *Troubled Waters: The Origins of the 1881 Anti-Jewish Pogroms in Russia* (Pittsburgh: University of Pittsburgh Press, 1990), 5–7.

4. Scheindlin, *A Short History of the Jewish People*, 180. On the pogroms of 1881–1884, see the articles by I. Michael Aronson, Moshe Mishkinsky, and Erich Haberer in Klier and Lambroza, eds., *Pogroms*, 39–98.

5. Scheindlin, *A Short History of the Jewish People*, 181. On the execution of Nicholas II, see Wendy Slater, *The Many Deaths of Tsar Nicholas II* (New York: Routledge, 2007), 1–9.

6. Irving Howe, *World of Our Fathers: The Journey of the East European Jews to America and the Life They Found and Made* (New York: Harcourt Brace Jovanovich, 1976), 4–8, 26.

7. Derek Penslar, *Jews in the Military: A History* (Princeton, NJ: Princeton University Press, 2013), 30. See also 28–34; Yohanan Petrovsky-Shtern, *Jews in the Russian Army, 1827–1917* (New York: Cambridge University Press, 2014).

8. Shari Rabin, "'A Nest to the Wandering Bird:' Iowa and the Creation of American Judaism, 1855–1877," *Annals of Iowa* 73, no. 2 (Spring 2014): 103.

9. Gerald Sorin, *A Time for Building: The Third Migration, 1880–1920* (Baltimore, MD: The Johns Hopkins University Press, 1992), 1.

20. Jonathan D. Sarna, "Port Jews in the Atlantic: Further Thoughts," *Jewish History* 20, no. 2, Port Jews of the Atlantic (Spring 2006): 214.

2. Dorothy Schwieder, *Iowa: The Middle Land* (Iowa City: University of Iowa Press, 1996), 117–18.

22. Bell, "True Israelites of America," 87.

23. Rabin, "Nest to the Wandering Bird," 102.

24. Ibid., 102–3.

25. Ibid., 104–5, 108.

26. Orlando J. Goering and Violet Miller Goering, "Keeping the Faith: Bertha Martinsky in West River South Dakota," *South Dakota History* 25, no. 1 (Spring 1995): 38.

27. Shaff and Shaff, *Paving the Way*, 5; Goering and Goering, "Keeping the Faith," 38, n. 2.

28. Goering and Goering, "Keeping the Faith," 38. On the early history of Des Moines, see Johnson Brigham, *Des Moines: The Pioneer of Municipal Progress and Reform of the Middle West, Volume I* (Chicago: The S. J. Clarke Publishing Company, 1911), 47–49, 134–49, 241–48. See also Silvana R. Siddali, "'Principle, Interest, and Patriotism All Combine': The Fight Over Iowa's Capital City," *Annals of Iowa* 64, no. 2 (Spring 2005): 111–38; Schwieder, *Iowa*, 177.

29. Goering and Goering, "Keeping the Faith," 38.

30. Shaff and Shaff, *Paving the Way*, 14–15.

3. Simon Glazer, *The Jews In Iowa* (Des Moines: Koch Brothers Printing Co., 1904), 248–49. See also Schwieder, *Iowa: The Middle Land*, 118, which claims that B'Nai Israel was founded in Keokuk around 1860 and that the Des Moines congregation was known as B'Nai Jeshurun, which opened was founded in 1872.

32. Robert A. Rockaway, *Words of the Uprooted: Jewish Immigrants in Early Twentieth-Century America* (Ithaca, NY: Cornell University Press, 1998), 167–68.

33. Glazer, *Jews in Iowa*, 248.

34. Schwieder, *Iowa*, 117.

35. See Hasia R. Diner, *Roads Taken: The Great Jewish Migrations to the New World and the Peddlers Who Forged the Way* (New Haven: Yale University Press, 2015), esp. 3–7, 51–83, 115–54.

36. Emma Lazarus, "The New Colossus," in *Emma Lazarus: Selected Poems and Other Writings*, ed. Gregory Eiselein (Peterborough, Ontario, Canada: Broadview Literary Texts, 2002), 233.

37. On the Chinese Exclusion Act, see Andrew Gyory, *Closing the Gate: Race, Politics, and the Chinese Exclusion Act* (Chapel Hill: University of North Carolina Press, 1998).

38. John Hingham, *Strangers in the Land: Patterns of*

American Nativism, 1860–1925 (New Brunswick, NJ: Rutgers University Press, 1955), 92, 181–83, 379. See also Naomi W. Cohen, "Antisemitism in the Gilded Age: The Jewish View," *Jewish Social Studies* 41, nos. 3 and 4 (Summer–Autumn 1979): 188.

39. See Eric L. Goldstein, *The Price of Whiteness: Jews, Race, and American Identity* (Princeton, NJ: Princeton University Press, 2006); Karen Brodkin, *How Jews Became White Folks & What That Says About Race in America* (New Brunswick, NJ: Rutgers University Press, 2002).

40. Cohen, "Antisemitism in the Gilded Age," 195.

4. Robert Michael, *A Concise History of American Antisemitism* (Lanham, MD: Rowman and Littlefield, 2005), 92–94. For scholarship that downplays the connections between Populism and anti-Semitism, see Norman Pollack, "The Myth of Populist Anti-Semitism," *American Historical Review* 68, no. 1 (October 1962): 76–80; Robert F. Durden, *The Climax of Populism: The Election of 1896* (Lexington: University of Kentucky Press, 1966); Leonard Dinnerstein, ed. *Antisemitism in the United States* (New York: Holt, Rinehart, and Winston, 1971), 81–83.

42. Cohen, "Antisemitism in the Gilded Age," 198.

43. Shaff and Shaff, *Paving the Way*, 14–15, 17; SMA e-mail to the author, September 21, 2016.

44. Shaff and Shaff, *Paving the Way*, 17–23.

45. Ibid., 24–26; For the quote, see Goering and Goering, "Keeping the Faith," 39.

46. Goering and Goering, "Keeping the Faith," 39–40; SMA interview, November 17, 2015.

47. Kimberly Marlowe Harnett, *Carolina Israelite: How Harry Golden Made Us Care About Jews, the South, and Civil Rights* (Chapel Hill: University of North Carolina Press, 2015), 5.

48. Shaff and Shaff, *Paving the Way*, 81–82; SMA e-mail to the author, September 21, 2016; "Hyman Miller," 1920 U.S. Census, Sioux City Precinct 8, Woodbury, Iowa, roll T625-521, pg. 5a.

49. Shaff and Shaff, *Paving the Way*, 81–82.

50. Ibid., 82–83.

5. "Total Population for Iowa's Incorporated Places: 1850–2010," accessed April 25, 2016, www.iowadatacenter.org.

52. Bell, "'True Israelites of America,'" 99.

53. Ibid., 99–100.

54. Ibid.

55. Shaff and Shaff, *Paving the Way*, 83.

56. Ibid.

57. Ibid.

58. Ibid., 83–84.

59. Ibid.; SMA interview, November 17, 2015; SMA e-mail to the author, September 21, 2016.

60. Shaff and Shaff, *Paving the Way*, 84–85.

6. Ibid., 85–87.

62. Ibid.; SMA e-mail to the author, September 21, 2016.

CHAPTER 2

1. South Dakota Homestead Act advertisement, quoted in Goering and Goering, "Keeping the Faith," 40. Originally published in *Jackson-Washabaugh Counties, 1915–1965* (Kadoka, SD: Jackson-Washabaugh County Historical Society, 1966), 9. For another account of a Jewish woman's homesteading experience, see J. Sanford Rikoon, ed., *Rachel Calof's Story: Jewish Homesteader on the Northern Plains* (Bloomington: Indiana University Press, 1995).

2. See Stuart Banner, *How the Indians Lost Their Land: Law and Power on the Frontier* (Cambridge, MA: Harvard University Press, 2007), 256–92. For a comprehensive history of Indian removal in the Black Hills, see Jeffrey Ostler, *The Lakotas and the Black Hills: The Struggle for Sacred Ground* (New York: Viking, 2010).

3. Goering and Goering, "Keeping the Faith," 39–40.

4. David P. Olson, "A Graphic Summary of South Dakota" (Brookings, Department of Rural Sociology: South Dakota State University, 2006): 6, 10.

5. Goering and Goering, "Keeping the Faith," 41.

6. Bernice Premack, "A History of the Jewish Community of Aberdeen, South Dakota, 1887–1964," p. 2, unpublished manuscript, SOH.

7. See Violet and Orlando J. Goering, "Jewish Farmers in South Dakota—the Am Olam," *South Dakota History* 12, no. 4 (Winter 1982): 232–47.

8. See Premack, "History of the Jewish Community of Aberdeen," 1–3.

9. On the Sioux Falls Jewish community, see "About Our Temple," Mount Zion Congregation, accessed February 22, 2017, http:/mtzionsf.com/about.php; "Congregation Sons of Israel," Jewish American Society for Historic Preservation, accessed February 22, 2017, http://www.jewish-american-society-for-historicpreservation.org/sdakotawyoming/siouxfallssouthdakota.html; Charles A. Smith, *A Comprehensive History of Minnehaha County, South Dakota: Its Background, Her Pioneers, Their Record of Achievement and Development* (Mitchell, SD: Educator Supply Co., 1949), 264; Gary D. Olson and Erik L. Olson, *Sioux Falls, South Dakota: A Pictorial History* (Norfolk, Va.: Donning Co., 1985), 123; Harry F. Thompson, ed., *A New South Dakota History*, 2d ed. (Sioux Falls, SD: Center for Western Studies, Augustana College, 2009), 338.

10. "Treasures of the Black Hills' Past: Honoring Our Origins," text of Jewish history exhibit, p. 1–4, n.d., binder, "Synagogue History 2," SOH.

11. "Treasures of the Black Hills' Past," 2–3.

12. SMA to Norman Mizel, Jerry Mizel, Edmond Mizel, Laura Siegel, and Robert Adelstein, December 30, 1982, folder 71, box 48, NWE (hereafter "folder 71").

13. Goering and Goering, "Keeping the Faith," 41–42.

14. Ibid., 41–42, 45.

15. Ibid.; See also Dorothy Schweider, "Town-Building and Persistence on the Great Plains: The Case of Presho, South Dakota," *South Dakota History* 30, no. 2 (Summer 2000): 201–22.

16. Goering and Goering, "Keeping the Faith," 47. Here, Goering and Goering cite an oral history provided by MEA.

17. Ibid., 43–47; SMA e-mail to the author, September 21, 2016.

18. Shaff and Shaff, *Paving the Way*, 25, 27.

19. Goering and Goering, "Keeping the Faith," 41; SMA e-mail to the author, September 21, 2016.

20. Shaff and Shaff, *Paving the Way*, 39–44.

21. See Holdger Afflerbach and David Stephenson, eds., *An Improbable War? The Outbreak of World War I and European Political Culture Before 1914* (New York: Berghahn Books, 2007).

22. See David M. Kennedy, *Over Here: The First World War and American Society* (New York: Oxford University Press, 2004), 42–49.

23. MEA, quoted in Shaff and Shaff, *Paving the Way*, 47.

24. Shaff and Shaff, *Paving the Way*, 47–48.

25. Ibid., 47–51.

26. Ibid., 54.

27. Ibid., 51.

28. Ibid., 53–54.

29. Ibid., 86.

30. Ibid., 76–77; Iowa Marriage Records, 1880–1922, Vol. 505, Records, Iowa Department of Public Health, State Historical Society of Iowa, Des Moines, Iowa, available through ancestry.com (hereafter "Vol. 505").

31. Shaff and Shaff, *Paving the Way*, 77–78, 85–86; Iowa Marriage Records, 1880–1922, Vol. 505.

32. Shaff and Shaff, *Paving the Way*, 57–58.

33. Al Nystrom, "Recollections of Life in Wall," *Pennington County Biographies, Part III* (Wall, SD: Carrol McDonald Unit, American Legion Auxiliary, n.d.), accessed March 31, 2017, http://files.usgwarchives.net/sd/penning/history/e-penn/biogs3.txt.

34. Thelma Frame, "Time Marches On," in *South Dakota's Ziebach County: History of the Prairie* (Dupree, SD: Ziebach County Historical Society, 1982), 240.

35. Shaff and Shaff, *Paving the Way*, 58.

36. Ibid., 58–59, 64.

37. Ibid., 73.

38. Ibid., 86.

39. Ibid., 93–94.

40. Ibid., 86–88.

41. Ibid., 93–94.

CHAPTER 3

1. Lon Kightlinger, "Infant Mortality Rates, South Dakota, 1912–1910," slide for a presentation of the South Dakota Department of Health entitled "Infant Mortality in South Dakota," June 20, 2011, Sioux Falls, SD. The infant mortality rate has dropped to just above 7.3 in South Dakota, and the number of women who die in childbirth in the United States today is around 18 per every 100,000

SOURCES

births. "Why Are So Many American Women Dying from Childbirth?" *Economist*, August 6, 2015, accessed May 16, 2016, http://www.economist.com/blogs/economist-explains/2015/08/economist-explains-4.

2. Shaff and Shaff, *Paving the Way*, 123–24.

3. Ibid., 124.

4. Ibid.

5. Ibid., 40, 96.

6. Ibid., 96–97; "Financial Statement and Equipment List of the Northwestern Engineering Company," December 31, 1951, pg. 1, folder "Annual Report for the Year 1951," box 74, NWE.

7. Suzanne Barta Julin, *A Marvelous Hundred Square Miles: Black Hills Tourism, 1880–1941* (Pierre: South Dakota State Historical Society Press, 2009), 5; see also 7–69.

8. "Annual Report 1955, Northwestern Engineering Company," p. 1, folder "NWE Annual Report for the Year 1955," Box 74, NWE. See also Shaff and Shaff, *Paving the Way*, 119–21.

9. Ross P. Korsgaard, "A History of Rapid City, South Dakota, During the Territorial Days," *South Dakota Historical Collections Vol. 38* (Pierre: State Publishing Company, 1977), 523; Eric John Abrahamson, *Improving Life with Energy: The First 125 Years of Black Hills Corporation* (Rapid City, SD: Black Hills Corporation, 2008), 14.

10. See the map in Paula M. Nelson, *The Prairie Winnows Out Its Own: The West River Country of South Dakota in the Years of Depression and Dust* (Iowa City: University of Iowa Press, 1996), xvi. The 1930 Decennial Census lists Rapid City at 10,404 people, while Lead/Deadwood had a combined 8,332. See the U.S. Census bureau, accessed May 30, 2016, http://www.census.gov/prod/www/decennial.html.

11. See David F. Strain, *Black Hills Hay Camp: Images and Perspectives of Early Rapid City* (Rapid City, SD: Dakota West Books & Fenske Media Corporation, 2010), 218–27.

12. Shaff and Shaff, *Paving the Way*, 137.

13. Ibid., 128; SMA interview, December 16, 2015.

14. Martha E. Geores, *Common Ground: The Struggle for Ownership of the Black Hills National Forest* (Lanham, MD: Rowman & Littlefield, 1996), 83.

15. Shaff and Shaff, *Paving the Way*, 128.

16. Ibid.

17. Ibid., 129.

18. Samuel Crabb interview, August 16, 2016.

19. *Polk's Rapid City Directory, Volume 6* (R.L. Polk & Co., 1936), 236. "Most Reverend John J. Lawler," Diocese of Rapid City, accessed June 27, 2016, http://www.rapidcitydiocese.org/office-of-bishop/bishop-lawler.

20. Shaff and Shaff, *Paving the Way*, 129.

21. Ibid., 129–30.

22. Mark Hufstetler and Michael Bedeau, "South Dakota's Railroads: An Historic Context," report prepared for the South Dakota State Historic Preservation Office, July 1998, rev. December 2007, 10–11, 18, 72–73.

23. See *Polk's Rapid City Directory*, 49.

24. "Burrington, David," *Rapid City Journal*, February 23, 2014.

25. Federal Writer's Project, *The WPA Guide to South Dakota* (South Dakota Guide Commission, 1938, repr. St. Paul: Minnesota Historical Society Press, 2006), 149–50.

26. Sam Crabb interview, August 16, 2016.

27. Kathy Bunkowske, "Works Progress Administration Projects in Rapid City, South Dakota: Surviving into the 21st Century," 261, *States and Cities: Mt. Rushmore*, accessed June 28, 2016, http://www.livingnewdeal.org.

28. Sam Crabb interview, August 16, 2016.

29. Adrienne Merola Kerst, Jean Oleson-Kessloff, and Patrick D. Roseland, *Rapid City: Historic Downtown Architecture* (Mount Pleasant, SC: Arcadia Publishing, 2007), 43; "To All the World Be Peace," *Pahasapa Quarterly* 8, no. 3 (June 1919): 3.

30. See "History of Kawaga," accessed November 16, 2016, http://kawaga.com/about/history-of-kawaga. On American summer camps' usage of Native American themes and imagery, see Philip J. Deloria, *Playing Indian* (New Haven, CT: Yale University Press, 1998), esp. 95–127.

31. SMA interview, November 17, 2015; Robert Adelstein interview, September 23, 2016.

32. Julia and Aaron Greenberg are buried in the Mount Carmel Cemetery in Sioux City. See also Robert Adelstein interview, September 23, 2016.

33. See Hayyim Schauss, *The Jewish Festivals: A Guide to Their History and Observance* (New York: Schocken Books, 1938).

34. Sam Crabb interview, August 16, 2016; Robert Adelstein interview, September 23, 2016.

35. SMA, quoted in Shaff and Shaff, *Paving the Way*, 136.

36. See Shaff and Shaff, *Paving the Way*, 137–38. The Yosemite Grant of 1864 was the first instance of the federal government setting aside park land. The park was given to the state of California to manage. After the state proved unable to protect the park, it was returned to federal control and became a national park in 1890.

37. Robert Adelstein interview, September 23, 2016.

38. Robert Adelstein, quoted in Shaff and Shaff, *Paving the Way*, 137–38.

39. Robert Adelstein interview, September 23, 2016.

40. SMA interview, November 17, 2015.

41. MEA, quoted in Shaff and Shaff, *Paving the Way*, 154. For a text that embodies the derogatory thinking about American Indians that permeated West River South Dakota in the early- and mid-twentieth century, see Margaret Lemley Warren, *The Badlands Fox* (Black Hills, SD and WY: M.L. Warren, 1991).

42. Charles Rambow, "The Ku Klux Klan in the 1920s: A Concentration on the Black Hills," *South Dakota History* 4, no. 1 (Winter 1973): 69.

43. Ibid., 68–69; John Taliaferro, *Great White Fathers: The Story of the Obsessive Quest to Create Mount Rushmore* (New York: Public Affairs, 2002), 185–218.

44. Rambow, "The Ku Klux Klan in the 1920s," 72–78.

45. Ibid., 72–81.

46. SMA interview, November 17, 2015.

47. SMA e-mail to the author, September 21, 2016.

48. Rambow, "The Ku Klux Klan in the 1920s," 78.

49. Shaff and Shaff, *Paving the Way*, 144–45.

50. Ibid., 79–80; Goering and Goering, "Keeping the Faith," 46.

51. SMA interview, November 17, 2015.

52. Shaff and Shaff, *Paving the Way*, 143–46.

53. Robert Adelstein quoted in Shaff and Shaff, *Paving the Way*, 146.

54. Robert Adelstein interview, September 23, 2016; A.W. Seff in 1940 U.S. Census, available through www.anscestry.com.

55. SMA interview, December 16, 2015.

56. Arthur Hertzberg, *The Jews in America: Four Centuries of Uneasy Encounter, A History* (New York: Columbia University Press, 1997), 270–72. For another interpretation of Roosevelt's relationship with Jewish people, see Richard Breitman and Allan J. Lichtman, *FDR and the Jews* (Cambridge, MA: Harvard University Press, 2013).

57. Hertzberg, *Jews in America*, 274–77. See also Sinclair Lewis, *It Can't Happen Here* (Sinclair Lewis, 1935, repr. New York: Signet Classics, 2014).

58. Walter Laqueur, *A History of Zionism: From the French Revolution to the Establishment of the State of Israel* (New York: Schocken Books, 2003), 595.

59. Hertzberg, *Jews in America*, 277.

60. Kurt F. Stone, *The Jews of Capitol Hill: A Compendium of Jewish Congressional Members* (Lanham, MD: Scarecrow Press, 2011), 184.

61. For a classic essay on the histories of integration and diversification, see Alfred D. Chandler, Jr., "Integration and Diversification as Business Strategies—An Historical Analysis," *Business and Economic History* Second Series 19 (1990): 65–73.

62. Shaff and Shaff, *Paving the Way*, 132.

63. Ibid., 149–53. For the quote, see 150.

64. Shaff and Shaff, *Paving the Way*, 154.

65. Goering and Goering, "Keeping the Faith," 47.

CHAPTER 4

1. This estimate is based on Denver populations given by the U.S. Census Bureau in 1930 (about 316,000) and 1960 (about 493,000). See U.S. Census Bureau, 20th Century Statistics, Figure 1415: "Population of the Largest 75 Cities, 1900 to 1996," in *Statistical Abstract of the United States, 1999*, 871, accessed November 30, 2016, https://www.census.gov/prod/99pubs/99statab/sec31.pdf.

2. SMA e-mail to the author, September 21, 2016.

3. Shaff and Shaff, *Paving the Way*, 165–67; "Annual Report 1955," 1.

4. Ira C. Selkowitz, "National Register of Historic

SOURCES

Places Registration Form, East High School, Denver, Colorado," sec. 7, p. 1, copy in the author's possession.

5. David Rusk, "Denver Divided: Sprawl, Race, and Poverty in Greater Denver," September 4, 2003, 7–8, accessed May 29, 2016, http://www.law.du.edu/images/uploads/library/evert/DenverDivided.pdf; SMA interview, December 16, 2015.

6. "Original Oratory National Champions," accessed May 29, 2016, http://www.speechanddebate.org/originaloratorychampions.

7. SMA interview, December 16, 2015.

8. Karen McHale, National Speech & Debate Association, e-mail to the author, July 13, 2016. On the NSDA point categories, see "Points and Degrees," National Speech and Debate Association, accessed July 15, 2016, http://www.speechanddebate.org/pointsanddegrees.

9. Shaff and Shaff, *Paving the Way*, 166. See also Allen duPont Breck, *The Centennial History of the Jews of Colorado: 1859–1959* (Denver, CO: Hirschfield Press, 1960).

10. SMA interview, December 16, 2015.

11. Denver East High School 1949 yearbook, 134, from *U.S., School Yearbooks, 1880–2012*, available through ancestry.com.

12. Chaim I. Waxman, "American Jewish Identity and New Patterns of Philanthropy," in *The Call of the Homeland: Diaspora Nationalisms, Past and Present*, ed. Allon Gal, Athena S. Leoussi, and Anthony David Smith (Leiden, The Netherlands: Brill, 2010), 81, 87.

13. SMA interview, December 16, 2015.

14. Dennis Hevesi, "Rabbi Herbert A. Friedman, Israel Backer, Dies at 89," *New York Times*, April 4, 2008, accessed June 2, 2016, http://www.nytimes.com/2008/04/04.

15. Kerry M. Olitzky and Marc Lee Raphael, *The American Synagogue: A Historical Dictionary and Source Book* (Westport, CT: Greenwood Press, 1996), 73.

16. Shaff and Shaff, *Paving the Way*, 171–78.

17. Waxman, "American Jewish Identity," 88; SMA interview, December 16, 2015; Olitzky and Raphael, *American Synagogue*, 73.

18. Hevesi, "Rabbi Herbert A. Friedman."

19. Shaff and Shaff, *Paving the Way*, 181.

20. On the ACJ, see Thomas A. Kolsky, *Jews Against Zionism: The American Council for Judaism, 1942–1948* (Philadelphia: Temple University Press, 1990).

21. Richard Weingardt, *Raut: Teacher, Leader, Engineer* (College of Engineering and Applied Science, University of Colorado at Boulder, 1999), 34, 51, 54.

22. Ibid., 34.

23. SMA interview, November 17, 2015.

24. SMA interview, December 16, 2015.

25. "Klauder Years, 1918–1939," Campus Master Plan, History, University of Colorado Boulder, accessed June 23, 2016, http://www.colorado.edu/masterplan/history; Post card, women's dormitory, University of Colorado Boulder, 1950, accessed June 23, 2016, http://www.terapeak.com/worth/boulder-colorado-university-campus-womens-dormitory-1950s-postcard/291639463162.

26. SMA interview, December 16, 2015.

27. On the Brandeis Camp Institute, see "Founding of BCI," Marilyn and Sigi Ziering Brandeis Collegiate Institute, accessed June 24, 2016, http://bci.aju.edu/Default.aspx?id=1738.

28. SMA interview, December 16, 2015.

29. Ibid.

30. Shaff and Shaff, *Paving the Way*, 196.

31. SMA interview, December 16, 2015.

32. "Captivating Crystal," *Denver Post*, March 23, 1953.

33. "Actors in Drama to Fight Polio," *Rocky Mountain News*, February 28, 1954.

34. SMA interview, December 16, 2015; Shaff and Shaff, *Paving the Way*, 196–98.

35. William B. Breuer, *Vendetta! Fidel Castro and the Kennedy Brothers* (Hoboken, NJ: Wiley, 1997), 103.

36. Shaff and Shaff, *Paving the Way*, 198–99.

37. AFP #33.

CHAPTER 5

1. SMA interview, December 16, 2015.

2. "Engineering Firm Holds 3-Day Meet," *Rapid City Journal*, February 6, 1957; Shaff and Shaff, *Paving the Way*, 196–97.

3. See "Report on First Annual Superintendents'

Meeting, February 3, 4, and 5, 1948 at Denver," folder "Superintendents' Meeting, Feb. 3, 4, & 5, 1948;" "Northwestern Engineering Co. 1950, 3rd Annual Superintendents Meeting, Feb. 7-8-9, Cosmopolitan Hotel, Denver, CO," folder "1950 Superintendents' Meeting;" "Northwestern Engineering Company, 1957 Annual Staff Meeting, Feb. 4, 5, & 6, Sheraton-Johnson Hotel, Rapid City, South Dakota," folder "1957 Staff Meeting," all box 68, NWE.

4. Shaff and Shaff, *Paving the Way*, 197.

5. Ibid.

6. SMA interview, December 16, 2015.

7. See John Lewis Gaddis, *The Cold War: A New History* (London, UK: Penguin, 2005); Odd Arne Westad, *The Global Cold War: Third World Interventions and the Making of Our Times* (New York: Cambridge University Press, 2007), 1–7.

8. On the McCarthy hearings generally, see Edwin R. Bayley, *Joe McCarthy and the Press* (Madison: University of Wisconsin Press, 1981); Robert Griffith, *The Politics of Fear: Joseph R. McCarthy and the Senate* (Amherst: University of Massachusetts Press, 1987); Ted Morgan, *Reds: McCarthyism in Twentieth-Century America* (New York: Random House, 2004). On Mundt's role in the hearings, see John R. Milton, *South Dakota: A History* (New York: W.W. Norton, 1977), 124.

9. SMA interview, December 16, 2015; Daniel Adelstein interview, September 11, 2016.

10. Karen Psiaki, "Stanford Adelstein: Jewel of the Hills," *Black Hills Faces* 12, no. 1 (Winter 2016): 12.

11. See Bruce Cumings, *The Korean War: A History* (New York: Modern Library, 2011), v. See also Mark Atwood Lawrence, *The Vietnam War: A Concise International History* (New York: Oxford University Press, 2010).

12. Joe N. Ballard, *The History of the U.S. Army Corps of Engineers* (Alexandria, VA: U.S. Army Corps of Engineers, 1998), 103, 115. On the nuclear missile program in South Dakota, see Gretchen Heefner, *The Missile Next Door: The Minuteman in the American Heartland* (Cambridge, MA: Harvard University Press, 2012).

13. SMA to MEA and Bertha Adelstein, January 2, 1956, folder "Adelstein Foundation & Trust," box 21, NWE.

14. See Andrew Rawson, *Crossing the Rhine: Remagen Bridge* (South Yorkshire, UK: Pen & Sword Books, 2004).

15. SMA e-mail to the author, September 21, 2016.

16. SMA interview, December 16, 2015.

17. *The Caine Mutiny (Collector's Edition)*, directed by Edward Dmytryk, (1954: Columbia Pictures, 2007), DVD.

18. SMA to MEA and Bertha Adelstein, January 2, 1956.

19. "Joseph I. Gurfein Dies at 79," *Washington Post*, June 7, 1997.

20. Betty Sowers Alt and Bonnie Domrose Stone, *Campfollowing: A History of the Military Wife* (Westport, CT: Praeger, 1991), 111.

21. See Howard P. Willens, *History Will Prove Us Right: Inside the Warren Commission Report on the Assassination of John F. Kennedy* (New York: Overlook Press, 2013).

22. SMA interview, December 16, 2015.

23. Psiaki, "Stanford Adelstein," 13.

CHAPTER 6

1. "Transcription of Tapes of Barbara Korn, October 24–28, 1992, in Coconut Creek, Florida," 39, copy in the author's possession (hereafter "Barbara Korn tapes").

2. J.D. Ames, "Ita Adelstein: Refugee, Survivor, and She's Still Growing," *Rapid City Journal*, January 19, 1982.

3. Ibid.; Barbara Korn tapes, 34. See also Robert M. Kennedy, *The German Campaign in Poland, 1939* (Hoosick Falls, NY: Merriam Press, 2015), 51–52.

4. Ames, "Ita Adelstein;" Barbara Korn tapes, 41. On the Free City of Danzig, see Ralphe Wilde, *International Territorial Administration: How Trusteeship and the Civilizing Mission Never Went Away* (New York: Oxford University Press, 2008), 111–116; Gunter Grass, Gershon C. Bacon, Joseph Gutmann, and Elizabeth Cats, *Danzig 1939: Treasures of a Destroyed Community* (New York: Jewish Museum of New York, 1980).

5. Barbara Korn tapes, 28, 30.

6. Ibid., 32.

SOURCES

7. Ibid., 39.

8. Ames, "Ita Adelstein."

9. Joshua D. Zimmerman, "The Polish Underground Press and the Jews: The Holocaust in the Pages of the Home Army's *Biuletyn Informacyjny*, 1940–1943," in *Warsaw: The Jewish Metropolis: Essays in Honor of the 75th Birthday of Professor Antony Polonsky*, ed. Glenn Dynner and Francois Guesnet (Leiden, The Netherlands: Brill, 2015), 448.

10. Barbara Korn tapes, 38.

11. Virginia Culver, "Nazi-Compelled Odyssey Led to Home in Denver," *Denver Post*, February 19, 2009; Ames, "Ita Adelstein."

12. Culver, "Nazi-Compelled Odyssey Led to Home in Denver," Ames, "Ita Adelstein;" SMA interview, December 16, 2015. Masza went by "Marcia" in the United States and Mavrycy went by "Michael." For their names as they appeared on the manifest, see "List or Manifest of Alien Passengers for the S.S. President Harrison, Sailing from Bombay, January 14, 1941," available through the Statue of Liberty—Ellis Island Foundation, accessed June 1, 2016, http://www.libertyellisfoundation.org.

13. Michael, *Concise History of American Antisemitism*, 184; "List or Manifest of Alien Passengers for the S.S. President Harrison;" Barbara Korn tapes, 68–69.

14. Ibid.; Breitman and Lichtman, *FDR and the Jews*, 2, 135–38.

15. There are several accounts of how Barbara Korn met the *New York Times* reporter. The journalists may also have been there to report on a fight that had broken out amongst several sailors on the *President Harrison*, or to interview several noted Polish academics who were on their way to teach at American universities. See SMA interview, December 16, 2015; Ames, "Ita Adelstein"; Barbara Korn tapes, 67; "Cruise Enlivened by Sailor's Fight; President Harrison Returns from Long Voyage with 3 in Brig," *New York Times*, February 23, 1941.

16. "List or Manifest of Alien Passengers for the S.S. President Harrison;" SMA e-mail to the author, September 21, 2016.

17. Barbara Korn tapes, 67–68; "History" Hebrew Immigrant Aid Society, accessed July 7, 2017, https://www.hias.org/history.

18. Barbara Korn tapes, 70.

19. See Joseph Persico, "The Kremlin Connection," *New York Times*, January 3, 1999; Peter Duffy, "The Congressman Who Spied for Russia: The Strange Case of Samuel Dickstein," *Politico*, October 6, 2014, accessed July 7, 2017, http://www.politico.com/magazine/story/2014/10/samuel-dickstein-congressman-russian-spy-111641.

20. Barbara Korn tapes, 70–71.

21. Ames, "Ita Adelstein."

22. Ibid.

23. "Korn, Barbara, 6867330" and "Korn, Leopold, 6867331," both dated July 23, 1948, in *Soundex Index to Petitions for Naturalization filed in Federal, State, and Local Courts located in New York City, 1792–1989*. New York, New York, USA: The National Archive at New York City, *New York, Index to Petitions for Naturalization filed in New York City, 1792–1989*, available through ancestry.com; Ames, "Ita Adelstein."

24. Ames, "Ita Adelstein."

25. Alex Grobman, *Rekindling the Flame: American Jewish Chaplains and the Survivors of European Jewry, 1944–1948* (Detroit, MI: Wayne State University Press, 1993), 200.

26. Milton J. Rosen, *An American Rabbi in Korea: A Chaplain's Journey in the Forgotten War* (Tuscaloosa: University of Alabama Press, 2004), 99; "Rabbi Major Joseph Messing, Seattle, Washington, Ca. 1956–1957," Digital Collections of the University of Washington Special Collections, accessed July 2, 2016, http://digitalcollections.lib.washington.edu/cdm/ref/collection/jhp/id/1085. SMA e-mail to the author, September 21, 2016.

27. Molly Cone, "The Founding of Temple Beth Am," Temple Beth Am, accessed July 2, 2016, http://www.templebetham.org/about-us/history. See also "Temple Beth Am's First Board, Seattle, Washington, ca. 1956–1958," Digital Collections of the University of Washington Special Collections, accessed July 2, 2016, http://digitalcollections.lib.washington.edu/cdm/singleitem/collection/jhp/id/1095/rec/1.

28. Herb Scott, "USAREUR Pays Final Tribute to Kennedy," *Stars and Stripes*, November 27, 1963, reprinted by Stripes.com, accessed July 6, 2016, http://www.stripes.com/news/usareur-pays-final-tribute-to-kennedy-1.57014.

29. "Legacy of Achievement: Hall of Fame Inductee

Herb Cleveland," South Dakota Hall of Fame, accessed September 29, 2016, http://sdexcellence.org/Herbert_Cleveland; Nancy Giguere, "Herb Cleveland: Serving the Nation's Vets," *Story Magazine*, 2003, accessed September 29, 2016, http://www.luthersem.edu/ story/default.aspx?article_id=54.

30. See Dan Kurzman, *No Greater Glory: The Four Immortal Chaplains and the Sinking of the Dorchester in World War II* (New York: Random House, 2004).

31. SMA offered a similar quote in Psiaki, "Stanford Adelstein," 13.

32. Ibid.

CHAPTER 7

1. George A. Larson, *Thunder Over Dakota: The Complete History of Ellsworth Air Force Base, South Dakota* (Atglen, PA: Schiffer Publishing, 2013), 6–8.

2. Abrahamson, *Improving Life with Energy*, 53.

3. Larson, *Thunder Over Dakota*, 93, 113–14, 117–18.

4. Abrahamson, *Improving Life with Energy*, 53.

5. Alison R. Bernstein, *American Indians and World War II: Toward a New Era in Indian Affairs* (Norman: University of Oklahoma Press, 1991), 149.

6. Shaff and Shaff, *Paving the Way*, 155.

7. See the annual reports from 1961 to 1965, box 18, NWE.

8. "1961 Annual Report: Northwestern Engineering Company," 1, bound volume in box 18, NWE. On the B-36 and B-52's, see Heefner, *Missile Next Door*, 9–11, 20–26.

9. "1961 Annual Report," 8.

10. See folder "Photographs," box 19, NWE.

11. "1961 Annual Report," 9; "Harney Lumber Company," folder "1972 Family Book-Original," box 12, NWE.

"Automobile Bankers of South Dakota," folder "1972 Family Book-Original," box 12, NWE.

12. Campaign pamphlet describing Stanford Adelstein, folder 124A, box 52, NWE Archive (hereafter "folder 124A"); "The Robford Company," folder "1972 Family Book-Original," box 12, both NWE; Robert Adelstein interview, September 23, 2016.

13. John Rapp, "An Economic Analysis of South Dakota," report to Governor Nils Boe, South Dakota Industrial Development Expansion Agency, 1965, p. 43, bound volume in box 65, NWE.

14. "Epsoe Printing Co," n.d., folder "Wage and Salary Schedules," box 2, NWE.

15. "1999 West Boulevard Floorplan 2010 Appraisal," description of the house at 1999 West Boulevard, copy in the author's possession; SMA e-mail to the author, September 21, 2016.

16. SMA e-mail to the author, September 21, 2016.

17. Shaff and Shaff, *Paving the Way*, 199.

18. See the photograph of Materi in Shaff and Shaff, *Paving the Way*, 207.

19. See the letters in folder "J.L. Materi to/from ME Adelstein," box 21, NWE.

20. "John L. Materi Dies in Court, Mass Saturday," *Rapid City Journal* February 8, 196; "History: 1940s," South Dakota School of Mines & Technology, accessed November 26, 2018, https://www.sdsmt.edu/About/History/1940s.

21. Shaff and Shaff, *Paving the Way*, 122–23.

22. "John L. Materi Dies in Court."

23. MEA to SMA, August 6, 1959, folder "Adelstein, Morris E. Correspondence w/ SMA 1959," box 65, NEW (hereafter "folder MEA/SMA 1959").

24. SMA to MEA, October 29, 1958, folder "MEA Reading Copies, to December 31, 1958," box 65, NWE.

25. MEA to SMA, August 6, 1959.

26. Ibid.

27. Ibid.

28. MEA to SMA, July 21, 1959, folder MEA/SMA 1959.

29. MEA to SMA, August 6, 1959.

30. MEA to Materi, August 29, 1960, folder "Morris E. Adelstein Correspondence w/ SMA 1960," box 65, NWE.

31. The once significant number of Jewish people in Deadwood seems to have dwindled by about 1940, likely after a generation of Jewish parents encouraged their children to pursue education and employment outside the small mining town. See "History of the Synagogue of the Hills, Rapid City, South Dakota."

32. "History of the Synagogue of the Hills."

33. Ibid.

34. SMA, e-mail message to Synagogue of the Hills (Ann Stanton), December 31, 2003, binder "Synagogue History 2," SOH.

35. "History of the Synagogue of the Hills."

36. Ibid.

37. See folder "David Lesser Kaplan, Organizing the New Congregation: A Kit for the UAHC Representative, May 1968" box 75, NWE.

38. SMA interview, January 25, 2016. SMA claimed that this incident occurred when he and his friends were "teenagers . . . high school kids." The Israeli Philharmonic Orchestra's website, however, states that the symphony did not tour the United States until December 1950. See "History of the Philharmonic," Israeli Philharmonic Orchestra, accessed June 2, 2016, http://www.ipo.co.il/eng/about/history/.aspx.

39. SMA interview, January 25, 2016.

40. SMA to "The Family," March 20, 1965, folder "Europe SMA 1965," Box 65, NWE.

41. "Milestones of the AJC," pamphlet in folder "American Jewish Committee 2 of 2," box 21, NWE.

42. SMA, "Impressions on Egyptian Trip," folder 20, box 51, NWE (hereafter "folder 20").

43. SMA to "The Family," March 20, 1965.

44. Anita Shapira, *Ben-Gurion: Father of Modern Israel*, trans. Anthony Berris (New Haven, CT: Yale University Press, 2014), 2.

45. On the founding of Israel, see Scheindlin, *A Short History of the Jewish People*, 217–33.

46. Shlomo Aronson, *David Ben-Gurion and the Jewish Renaissance* (New York: Cambridge University Press, 2011), 352.

47. SMA to "The Family," March 20, 1965.

48. "Meeting with Mr. Ben-Gurion, at Kibbutz Institute of City Beh Boker," meeting minutes, folder "Europe SMA 1965," box 65, NWE.

49. SMA to "The Family," March 20, 1965.

50. Ibid.

51. "Meeting with Mr. Ben-Gurion, at Kibbutz Institute of City Beh Boker."

CHAPTER 8

1. Shaff and Shaff, *Paving the Way*, 104–7.

2. Ibid., 96–98. For quote, see 98.

3. Ibid., 97.

4. "Agreement," January 1, 1928, signed by L. A. Pier and Morris Adelstein, copy in the author's possession.

5. MEA, quoted in Shaff and Shaff, *Paving the Way*, 98.

6. Shaff and Shaff, *Paving the Way*, 102.

7. Ibid., 104–5.

8. Ibid., 106–8.

9. Julin, *Marvelous Hundred Square Miles*, 5. See also 7–69.

10. Ibid., 13–14, 7–101. See also Sam Hurst, *Rattlesnake Under His Hat: The Life and Times of Earl Brockelsby* (Rapid City, SD: Vantage Point Press, 2016), 16–21.

11. David O. Born, "Black Elk and the Duhamel Sioux Indian Pageant," *North Dakota History* 61, no. 1 (Winter 1994): 22–29; Linea Sundstrom, "The 'Pageant of Paha Sapa': An Origin Myth of White Settlement in the American West," *Great Plains Quarterly* 28, no. 1 (Winter 2008): 18.

12. Julin, *Marvelous Hundred Square Miles*, 4–6.

13. Elaine Marie Nelson, "Dreams and Dust in the Black Hills: Race, Place, and National Identity in America's 'Land of Promise,'" (Ph.D. diss., University of New Mexico, 2011), esp. 1–20, 91–127.

14. See for example Douglas Brinkley, *The Wilderness Warrior: Theodore Roosevelt and the Crusade for America* (New York: Harper Perennial, 2009); Donald Worster, *A Passion for Nature: The Life of John Muir* (New York: Oxford University Press, 2008).

15. Julin, *Marvelous Hundred Square Miles*, 102–4. On the Great Depression in South Dakota, see also Nelson, *Prairie Winnows*, 116–63.

16. Linea Sundstrom, "The Sacred Black Hills: An Ethnohistorical Review," *Great Plains Quarterly* 17, no. 3/4 (Summer/Fall 1997): 190.

17. Julin, *Marvelous Hundred Square Miles*, 110–13.

18. Shaff and Shaff, *Paving the Way*, 117–18.

19. Julin, *Marvelous Hundred Square Miles*, 102–6.

20. "Historic District-Beaver Creek Bridge," Wind Cave National Park, accessed May 20, 2016, https://www.nps.gov/wica/learn/historyculture/national-historic-district.htm.

21. Shaff and Shaff, *Paving the Way,* 119.

22. Cecil Bohanon, "Economic Recovery: Lessons from the Post-World War II Period," *Mercatus on Policy* 112 (August 2012): 2–3.

23. Robert Higgs, "U.S. Military Spending in the Cold War Era: Opportunity Costs, Foreign Crises, and Domestic Constraints," *Cato Policy Analysis* 114 (November 1988), accessed July 13, 2016, http://www.cato.org/pubs/pas/pa114.html. See also Dana Walker, "Trends in U.S. Military Spending," *Council on Foreign Relations,* July 15, 2014, accessed July 13, 2016, http://www.cfr.org/defense-budget/trends-us-military-spending/p28855.

24. M. Levin, "Discussion of Company Policy Regarding Volume and Type of Work to be Undertaken," in Report of the First Annual Superintendents' Meeting, February 3, 4, and 5, 1948, at Denver," p. 16, folder "Superintendents' Meeting Feb. 3, 4, & 5, 1948," box 68, NWE.

25. Ibid.

26. Ibid.

27. "Financial Statement and Equipment List of the Northwestern Engineering Company, December 31, 1951," folder "Annual Report for Year 1951," box 74, NWE.

28. "1965 Annual Report, Northwestern Engineering Co.," sec. 3, p. 3, bound volume in box 18, NWE.

29. "Annual Report 1955: Northwestern Engineering Company," folder "Annual Report for the Year 1955," box 74, NWE. See also David Super interview, July 5, 2016.

30. Shaff and Shaff, *Paving the Way,* 184–85.

31. "County Loses Fight to Tax Northwestern Engineering," *Rapid City Journal,* September 19, 1949.

32. "Northwestern Engineering to Leave County," *Rapid City Journal,* n.d., clipping in folder "1950 Superintendent's Meeting," box 68, NWE.

33. "County Loses Fight to Tax Northwestern Engineering."

34. "Northwestern Engineering to Leave County."

35. SMA interview, January 5, 2016.

36. Ibid.; Weather" and "Today's Weather: 24-hour Reads to 7 AM Today," *Rapid City Journal,* February 7, 1962. A slightly different version of this story appears in Shaff and Shaff, *Paving the Way,* 206–7.

37. Laurie Hallstrom, "Remember When the New Cathedral Was Built," *West River Catholic* (April 2013): 1. Laurie Hallstrom, "50 Years Ago the Mother Church of the Diocese Was Dedicated," *West River Catholic* (April 2013): 1, 12.

38. MEA to NWE Staff, March 6, 1962, folder "Constructograms 1961," box 65, NWE (hereafter "Constructograms 1961").

39. "John L. Materi Dies in Court."

40. SMA interview, January 5, 2016.

41. Peter Materi death certificate, February 6, 1958, El Paso, TX, available through ancestry.com.

42. MEA to NWE Staff, March 6, 1962.

43. Ibid.

CHAPTER 9

1. "Rapid City Rotary Club," Black Hills Knowledge Network, accessed July 13, 2016, https://www.blackhillsknowledgenetwork.org/news/rapid-city-rotary-club.html.

2. See Kim Phillips-Fein, *Invisible Hands: The Making of the Conservative Movement from the New Deal to Reagan* (New York: W. W. Norton, 2009), xii; "Bennett, Walter Foster," in *Biographical Directory of the United States Congress, 1774–2005* (Washington, D.C.: U.S. Government Printing office, 2005), 644.

3. SMA interview, February 29, 2016.

4. "Kathleen Howe," Fidler-Isburg Funeral Chapels & Crematory Services, November 24, 2010, accessed July 20, 2016, http://www.fidler-isburgfuneralchapels.com.

5. Edmund F. Kallina, Jr. *Courthouse Over White House: Chicago and the Presidential Election of 1960* (Orlando: University of Central Florida Press, 1988), 59. For competing views of Eisenhower and Nixon's political relationship, see Jeffrey Frank, *Ike and Dick: Portrait of a Strange Political Marriage* (New York: Simon & Schuster, 2013; Irwin F. Gellman, *The President and the Apprentice: Eisenhower and Nixon, 1952–1961* (New Haven, CT: Yale University Press, 2015).

SOURCES

6. J.V. Yaukey, *The Governor's Scepter: Vignettes of South Dakota Governors from Byrne to Kneip* (Hayes Brothers, 1976), 23.

7. Ibid., 61; Robert Thompson, "Ralph E. Herseth: 1959–1961," in *Over a Century of Leadership: South Dakota Territorial and State Governors*, ed. Lynwood E. Oyos (Sioux Falls, SD: Center for Western Studies, 1987), 169.

8. Yaukey, *Governor's Scepter*, 62.

9. Ibid., 63; William O. Farber, "Archie Gubbrud: 1961–1965," in Oyos, ed., *Over a Century of Leadership*, 175–176. "Archie Gubbrud," National Governor's Association, accessed July 20, 2016, https://www.nga.org/governor/archie-gubbrud.

10. Yaukey, *Governor's Scepter*, 63; Farber, "Archie Gubbrud," 176.

11. John Searle, "South Dakotans Leave Convention for Another," *Rapid City Journal*, July 29, 1960; SMA interview, February 29, 2016.

12. Thompson, "Ralph E. Herseth," 177; Farber, "Archie Gubbrud," 177.

13. *Gubernatorial Elections, 1787–1997* (Washington, D.C.: Congressional Quarterly Incorporated, 1998), 142.

14. "Please Vote for Stanford M. Adelstein, An Experienced Republican Who Wants to Serve YOU," pamphlet ca. 1960, unlabeled folder, box 65, NWE.

15. Bob Lee, "Joseph Jacob Foss: 1955–1959," in Oyos, ed., *Over a Century of Leadership*, 167.

16. Thompson, "Ralph E. Herseth," 171.

17. Farber, "Archie Gubbrud," 177; *Lead Daily Caller*, January 13, 1967.

18. Larry Bartle, draft text for speech on behalf of SMA's run for Young Republic National Treasurer, n.d.; "South Dakota Presents Stan Adelstein: Platform," campaign pamphlet, n.d., both folder "SMA YGOP-Nat'l Trsr.," box 21, NWE (hereafter "SMA YGOP").

19. Elizabeth Kaston, "The Farewell at Hart 306," *Washington Post*, December 22, 1986.

20. News clipping by Theodore "Dates" Werner, n.t., n.p., n.d., shared by Norma M. Anderson in a letter to SMA, March 4, 1963, unlabeled folder, box 65, NWE.

21. "California," notes on SMA speech to California delegates, June 1965, folder "YGOP SMA."

22. Federal Writer's Project, *WPA Guide to South Dakota*, 44.

23. Denise Ross, "S.D. Cement Plant has Operated 76 Years," *Rapid City Journal*, December 23, 2000; Yaukey, *Governor's Scepter*, 64–65.

24. Yaukey, *Governor's Scepter*, 64.

25. Ross, "S.D. Cement Plant has Operated 76 Years;" Yaukey, *Governor's Scepter*, 64–65.

26. SMA to MEA, August 2, 1961, folder "Adelstein, ME (Corr. With SMA) 1961," box 65, NWE.

27. Ibid.

28. Ibid.

29. See Fredric T. Suss, "Set-Asides and Certificates of Competency—Positive Programs for Small Business in Government Procurement," *Law and Contemporary Problems* 29 (Spring 1964): 418, n. 2.

30. Ibid., 419.

31. SMA to Peter H. Dominick, April 27, 1963, folder "Correspondence SM Adelstein 1963," box 72, NWE; "Construction Set-Asides, 1963. Hearings Before a Subcommittee of the Committee of Banking and Currency, United States Senate, Eighty-Eighth Congress, First Session on S. 757, May 7, 8, and 9, 1963" (Washington, D.C.:U.S. Government Printing Office, 1963), 178.

32. SMA to Dominick, April 27, 1963.

33. Jonathan Bean, *Big Government and Affirmative Action: The Scandalous History of the Small Business Administration* (Lexington: University Press of Kentucky, 2015), 31.

34. SMA to Dominick, April 27, 1963. On Dominick's conservatism, see Joseph B. Treaster, "Peter H. Dominick is Dead at 65," *New York Times*, March 20, 1981.

35. Karl Mundt, quoted in "Construction Set-Asides, 1963," 178.

36. "Construction Set-Asides, 1963," 179.

37. Stan Adelstein, quoted in "Construction Set-Asides, 1963," 180.

38. SMA's personal resume/CV (hereafter, "SMA CV"). On the AGCA's support for this bill, see Bean, *Big Government and Affirmative Action*, 29–31.

39. See "Construction Set-Asides, 1963," 181–85.

40. Ibid., 232–33.

41. SMA to MEA, August 2, 1961.
42. Ibid.
43. Yaukey, *Governor's Scepter*, 64.
44. MEA to SMA, May 12, 1959, folder "MEA Reading Copies to December 31, 1958," box 65, NWE (hereafter "MEA RCC to December 1958").
45. Shaff and Shaff, *Paving the Way*, 186–88.
46. See SMA to MEA, July 9, 1958, folder "MEA Reading Copies to December 31, 1958;" SMA to MEA, November 23, 1959, folder "Adelstein, Morris E. Correspondence w/SMA 1959," both box 65, NWE.
47. SMA to MEA, November 23, 1959.
48. SMA to MEA, November 9, 1961, folder "MEA Correspondence with SMA, 1961," box 65, NWE. See also SMA CV.
49. Shaff and Shaff, *Paving the Way*, 227.
50. Ibid., 226–29.
51. Ibid., 228–29.
52. "1964 Annual Report: Northwestern Engineering Company," p.3, bound volume in box 18, NWE.
53. L.A. Pier to MEA, December 21, 1966, folder "Adelstein, ME Reading Copies 1964–1965, 1966, " box 65, NWE (hereafter "MEA RC 64–66").
54. MEA to L. A. Pier, December 28, 1966, folder "MEA RC 64–66."
55. MEA to Thomas C. Ledgerwood, December 19, 1966, folder "MEA RC 64–66."
56. Ibid.
57. "1964 Annual Report," 1.
58. SMA interview, January 5, 2016.
59. MEA quoted in Shaff and Shaff, *Paving the Way*, 235.

CHAPTER 10

1. See Elaine Tyler May, *Homeward Bound: American Families in the Cold War Era* (New York: Basic Books, 2008), 8.
2. Shaff and Shaff, *Paving the Way*, 203.
3. Ames, "Ita Adelstein."
4. Daniel Adelstein interview, September 11, 2016.
5. AFP #358; "Rapid City Central High Names Boys State Delegates," *Rapid City Journal*, April 19, 1972.
6. AFP #353.
7. Daniel Adelstein interview, September 11, 2016.
8. Ames, "Ita Adelstein."
9. Stan Adelstein CV; SMA interview, January 25, 2016.
10. Molly Barari, "Club for Boys Looks Back at 50 years of Service," *Rapid City Journal*, November 23, 2013; Jim Stasiowski, "Founder of Rapid City Club for Boys, Roger Erickson, Dies," *Rapid City Journal*, February 10, 2015.
11. Stan Adelstein to Roger Erickson, July 16, 1987, folder 31, box 30, NWE (hereafter "folder 31").
12. Shaff and Shaff, *Paving the Way*, 214–15; 229–31.
13. Ibid., 229–31; Barari, "Club for Boys Looks Back at 50 years of Service."
14. "Dakota Images: Duke Corning," *South Dakota History* 47, no. 2 (Summer 2017): 196.
15. Daniel Adelstein interview, September 11, 2016; Harvey F. McPhail to Members of the Office of Defense Resources, May 22, 1974, folder 13A, box 17, NWE (hereafter "folder 13A").
16. See Henry B. Hogue and Keith Bea, "Federal Emergency Management and Homeland Security Organization: Historical Developments and Legislative Options," in *FEMA: An Organization in the Crosshairs*, ed. Linda A. Burns (Hauppauge, NY: Novinka Books, 2007), 9.
17. SMA, hand-written notes on Hilton Hotel and Tower Letterhead, n.d., probably May 1974, folder 13A.
18. "Federal Regional Center, Denver, Colorado," folder 22A, box 6, NWE (hereafter "folder 22A").
19. McPhail to NDER, May 22, 1974.
20. "Nuclear Detonation Problem, For Discussion Purposes Only," folder 13A.
21. SMA notes, May 1974.
22. "Federal Regional Center, Denver, Colorado," folder 22A.
23. Hogue and Bea, "Federal Emergency Management and Homeland Security Agency," 14; "Discussion Materials for the National Defense Executive Reserve Meeting," February 14, 1979, folder 22A.

24. John W. Macy to SMA, October 9, 1979; SMA to Macy, October 16, 1979, both folder 22A.

25. Leland D. Case, *Lee's Official Guide Book to the Black Hills and the Badlands* (Sturgis, SD: Black Hills and Badlands Association, 1949), 32; "Black Hills Playhouse Board of Directors, July 31 1977," folder 9, box 2, NWE.

26. Deanna Darr, "Storybook Island Had a Fairy-Tale Beginning," *Rapid City Journal*, August 18, 2009; "Rapid City Concert Association;" "Attractions 1978–79 Season, Rapid City Concert Association," both folder 140, box 4, NWE (hereafter "folder 140"); SMA CV.

27. "London Bridge," photograph of the plaque inscribed "A Gift From Mr. and Mrs. Stanford M. Adelstein, Hills Materials Company," folder 17, box 2, NWE (hereafter "folder 17").

28. Harvey D. Wickware to Hoadley Dean, April 18, 1978, folder 113, box 3, NWE (hereafter "folder 113").

29. "Review of Alternatives, Draft General Management Plan, Mount Rushmore National Memorial, South Dakota," folder 113.

30. On the early history of the Benedictine order in the Black Hills, see M. Magdalene Callahan, O.S.B., "The Beginnings of the Benedictine Convent of St. Martin, SD, 1889–1915" (M.A. thesis, St. John's University, 1963).

31. Rozella Bracewell, "Society Hears About Ku Klux Klan," *Belle Fourche Post*, February 16, 1979. Bracewell, a journalist, paraphrases a presentation by local historian Charles Rambow, whose independent research detailed how "Catholics were afraid to go to a Protestant hospital, so [the nuns] built their own hospital in Rapid City."

32. "St. John's McNamara/Rapid City Regional Hospital School of Nursing: History, 1927–1991," (Rapid City: St. John's McNamara, 1992), 1, RCPL.

33. Sister Sarto Rogers, "St. John's McNamara Hospital," in *The Black Hills Flood of June 9, 1972: A Historical Document* (Midwest Research Publishers, 1972), 72; Mary Voboril, "Rapid City Flood Victims Fed and Clothed, but Many Emotional Scars Still Remain," *Columbus Telegram* (Columbus, Nebraska), January 24, 1973.

34. SMA, "Some Not-So-Recent Rapid City Health Care History," January 17, 2013, accessed March 13, 2018, *https://way2gosd.com/2013/01/17/some-not-so-recent-rapid-city-health-care-history*.

35. "St. John's McNamara/Rapid City Regional Hospital School of Nursing," 16.

36. SMA interview, January 25, 2016; SMA CV.

37. "Harvey R. Fraser 1939," West Point Association of Graduates, accessed July 31, 2017, http://apps.westpointaog.org/Memorials/Article/11344/.

CHAPTER 11

1. See Don Oberdorfer, *Tet!: The Turning Point in the Vietnam War* (Baltimore, MD: The Johns Hopkins University Press, 1971); Michael Eric Dyson, *April 4, 1968: Martin Luther King Jr.'s Death and How it Changed America* (New York: Basic Books, 2008); Larry Tye, *Bobby Kennedy: The Making of a Liberal Icon* (New York: Random House, 2016), 436.

2. Matthew Lassiter, *The Silent Majority: Suburban Politics in the Sunbelt South* (Princeton, NJ: Princeton University Press, 2006), 232. See also Lisa McGirr, *Suburban Warriors: The Origins of the New American Right* (Princeton, NJ: Princeton University Press, 2001), 204, 213–15.

3. SMA, "The President's Report," in "1967 Annual Report, Northwestern Engineering Co.," ii, bound volume in box 18, NWE.

4. David Super interview, July 5, 2016; Maryann Blackerby interview, July 21, 2016.

5. Super interview, July 5, 2016.

6. Ibid.

7. Maryann Blackerby interview, July 21, 2016.

8. David Super interview, July 5, 2016.

9. SMA to All Supervision, Constructogram, August 1, 1963, "Constructograms 1961." See also Jacqueline Dowd Hall, "The Long Civil Rights Movement and the Political Uses of the Past," *Journal of American History* 91, no. 4 (March 2005): 1233–63.

10. SMA to All Supervision, August 1, 1963.

11. E.D. Gaiser to SMA, Constructogram response, October 1963, "Constructograms 1961."

12. G.L. Unser to SMA, Constructogram response, October 1963, "Constructograms 1961."

13. Barlow to Stan Adelstein, Constructogram

response, October 1963, "Constructograms 1961." On discrimination in the construction industry, see Gerald Finkel, *The Economics of the Construction Industry* (New York and London: Routledge, 2015), 144–45.

14. David Super interview, July 5, 2016.

15. SMA to MEA, April 9, 1958, "MEA RCC to December 1958."

16. SMA to MEA, August 28, 1958, "MEA RCC to December 1958."

17. Robert Adelstein to Dan Clark, July 17, 1969, folder "Constructograms Northwestern Engineering Company," box 70, NWE; Robert Adelstein interview, September 23, 2016.

18. "Safety Awards Program," June 24, 1963, folder "Consutructograms 1961," box 65, NWE.

19. SMA interview, January 5, 2016.

20. MEA to John Materi, October 9, 1959, "MEA RCC to December 1958."

21. SMA, memorandum to field supervision and office personnel, "Transportation and Use of Company Aircraft," June 16, 1969, folder "Constructogram Northwestern Engineering Company," box 70, NWE.

22. Robert Adelstein to Clark, July 17, 1969.

23. For the quotes, see "Hearing Before the National Labor Relations Board at the Pennington County Courthouse, 9:30 AM, June 11, 1954, Northwestern Engineering and Local Union 326 of the International Union of Federated Engineers;" "Agreement" (blank copy of the agreement sent to NWE by Local Union 326 of the International Union of Operating Engineers)." See also Drew W. Jackson to NWE, September 23, 1954; Morris Adelstein to W.A. McCullen, October 28, 1955; Morris Adelstein to McCullen February 28, 1955; Jackson to McCullen, February 21, 1955; Jackson to McCullen November 1, 1955; Jackson to McCullen, September 24, 1955, all folder "National Labor Relations Board—Union Organizing," box 77, NWE.

24. "Meeting Held on July 16, 1965, at Northwestern Engineering Company Office, Rapid City, South Dakota, Between Northwestern Engineering Representatives and Representatives from the Teamsters, Operating Engineers and Laborers," meeting minutes in folder "Original of Minutes of July 15, 1965 Meeting, NW Eng. Co. & Unions," box 19, NWE.

25. Ibid.

26. Ibid.

27. Ibid.

28. SMA, "Feuds are Evil—and This One Wasn't Romeo and Juliette," August 28, 2014, accessed March 13, 2018, https://way2gosd.com/2014/08/28/feuds-are-evil-and-this-one-wasnt-romeo-and-juliette-3.

29. SMA to Chuck Lien, October 22, 1985, folder 31; SMA to Djuki and Hava Hagoel, April 16, 1980, folder 20.

30. "Boy Scouts, Civic Leaders Join for Aquatic Park Rites," *Ogden Standard-Examiner* (Ogden, UT), October 4, 1970, 19.

31. "Message from the President," vii, in "1968 Annual Report, Northwestern Engineering Co.," bound volume in box 18, NWE.

32. "Board of Directors," ii, in "1968 Annual Report, Northwestern Engineering Co."

33. Richard Weingardt, *Raut: Teacher, Leader, Engineer* (Boulder, CO: College of Engineering and Applied Science, University of Colorado Boulder, 1999), 65.

34. Robert Adelstein interview, September 23, 2016.

35. Ibid.

36. SMA to Dan, Jim, and Jon Adelstein, January 23, 1981, folder 22, box 54, NWE (hereafter "folder 22").

37. "Message from the President," vii.

38. "The President's Report," ii.

39. Keith R. McFarland, "Not So Lonely at the Top," Bloomberg, July 9, 2006, accessed July 2, 2017, https://www.bloomberg.com/news/articles/2006-07-09/not-so-lonely-at-the-top.

40. SMA CV.

41. SMA, "Observations, Thursday, March 5, 1981," folder 22.

42. Ibid.

43. SMA notes on John D. Stoessinger's lecture in Sydney, folder 168; William F. Duhamel to SMA, September 26, 1978; Richard A. Schleusener to John D. Stoessinger, September 13, 1978, both folder 169, all box 5, NWE.

44. SMA to Robert M. Holder, November 18, 1974, folder 167A, box 15, NWE.

SOURCES

45. "Young Presidents' Organization, Inc. Statement of Foreign Convention Attendance," folder 168, box 5, NWE.

46. Weingardt, *Raut*, 65.

47. Robert Adelstein interview, September 23, 2016.

48. SMA interview, January 5, 2016.

49. Weingardt, *Raut*, 1–2.

50. Ibid., 190–99.

51. SMA quoted in Weingardt, *Raut*, 66.

52. "Copy for Approval, Northwestern Engineering Company," folder 124A.

53. Ibid.; "Pamphlet: Adelstein for Republican National Committee."

CHAPTER 12

1. SMA to Murray Polner, December 15, 1978, folder 40, box 2, NWE (hereafter "folder 40").

2. Ibid.

3. Gilbert Kollin to Barbara Blass, October 17, 1977, folder 150, box 2, NWE (hereafter "folder 150").

4. SMA to William Janklow, September 16, 1977, folder 150.

5. See folder "Photographs 1962," box 65, NWE; "Services Marking Rosh Hashanah set in Synagogue of Hills," *Rapid City Journal*, September 8, 1977.

6. See Janklow to SMA, September 29, 1977, folder 150; SMA to Janklow, September 16, 1977.

7. Janklow to SMA, September 29, 1977.

8. AFP #347.

9. See Hyman E. Goldin, *Hamadrikh: The Rabbi's Guide; A Manual of Jewish Religious Rituals, Ceremonials, and Customs* (New York: Hebrew Publishing Company, 1956).

10. SMA to Lt. I.B. Maltz, May 24, 1978, folder 17.

11. SMA to Polner, December 15, 1978.

12. Shaff and Shaff, *Paving the Way*, 121.

13. SMA to Polner, December 15, 1978, folder 40.

14. SMA to Larry Blass, August 20, 1978, folder.

15. Joan Levine to SMA, September 20, 1978, folder 17.

16. SMA interview, January 25, 2016.

17. Scheindlin, *A Short History of the Jewish People*, 238–39.

18. Ibid., 239–40.

19. See Roman Czula, "The Munich Olympic Assassinations: A Second Look," *Journal of Sport and Social Issues* 2, no. 1 (March 1978): 19; Asaf Siniver, ed., *The Yom Kippur War: Politics, Legacy, Diplomacy* (New York: Oxford University Press, 2013). See also Scheindlin, *A Short History of the Jewish People*, 236.

20. SMA Interview, January 25, 2016.

21. SMA, "Impressions on Egyptian Trip," folder 20.

22. Ibid.

23. Ibid.

24. Ibid.

25. Ibid.

26. Ibid.

27. Ibid.

28. SMA to Polner, December 15, 1978.

CHAPTER 13

1. "Intriguing Facts Part of Flood Data," *Rapid City Journal*, June 5, 1997.

2. Sister Sarto Rogers, "St. John's McNamara Hospital," in *The Black Hills Flood of June 9, 1972: A Historical Document* (Midwest Research Publishers, 1972), 72–73.

3. "The South Dakota Noon News Roundup," clipping, June 1972, accessed October 17, 2016, https://library.biblioboard.com/viewer/ec290f1d-9c57-489e-9be5-7f788b2c0689/1.

4. Rogers, "St. John's McNamara Hospital," 72.

5. Ibid., 73.

6. Ibid.

7. SMA Interview, January 25, 2016.

8. "The Black Hills Flood of 1972," National Weather Service, accessed August 29, 2016, https://www.weather.gov/unr/1972-06-09.

9. Rogers, "St. John's McNamara Hospital," 69–71.

10. Ibid., 71–72.

11. SMA interview, January 25, 2016.

12. "#218, Herbert Weisz, 69," in "1972 Flood Remembrance Wall," exhibit pamphlet published by the Rapid City Public Library, 2015, in binder "Rapid City Flood Remembrance," RCPL.

13. "Dedication Slated July 6 for Norwegian Stavkirke in Hills," *Mitchell Daily Republic* (Mitchell, SD), June 28, 1969.

14. "History of the Chapel in the Hills," Chapel in the Hills, accessed April 16, 2018, http://www.chapel-in-the-hills.org/history.html. See also Chris Nelson, "Chapel in the Hills," National Register of Historic Places Registration Form, United States Department of the Interior, National Parks Service, June 22, 2012, 9.

15. See "The 'Final Solution': Estimated Number of Jews Killed," Jewish Virtual Library, accessed April 16, 2018, http://www.jewishvirtuallibrary.org/estimated-number-of-jews-killed-in-the-final-solution.

16. "Former Senate Candidate Barbara Gunderson Dies," *Rapid City Journal*, July 29, 2007.

17. "Inductees: Jerry Schoener," South Dakota Hall of Fame, accessed July 29, 2016, http://www.sdhalloffame.com.

18. SMA interview, January 25, 2016.

19. "Phil G. Schroeder," Rapid City Public Library/Black Hills Knowledge Network, accessed July 29, 2016, http://bhkn.rapidcitylibrary.org/bhkn.

20. "Your New Rapid City Public Library: 1972–1982," (Nauman Printing, 1982), RCPL, 1, 7; Donald Barnett e-mail to the author, March 7, 2018.

21. "Your New Rapid City Public Library: 1972–1982," 9–10.

22. South Dakota Library Bulletin, Volumes 56-58 (Pierre: South Dakota State Library Commission, 1970), 103.

23. "Donald V. Barnett," Rapid City Public Library/Black Hills Knowledge Network, accessed July 29, 2016, http://bhkn.rapidcitylibrary.org/bhkn.

24. Donald Barnett interview, June 10, 2017.

25. SMA interview, January 25, 2016.

26. "Your New Rapid City Public Library: 1972–1982,"12; "Ida may Nauman," *Denver Post*, September 4, 2000.

27. "Your New Rapid City Public Library: 1972–1982," 2–4, 11.

28. "Arthur P. LaCroix," Rapid City Public Library/Black Hills Knowledge Network, accessed July 28, 2016, http://bhkn.rapidcitylibrary.org/bhkn/KnowledgeNetwork/includes/bios/lacroix-bio.asp. See also Betty Paukert Derrick, "Interview with Mary Myrick Hinman Lacroix, February 8–14, 1980," Minnesota Historical Society, copy in the author's possession.

29. "Arthur P. LaCroix;" "Arthur Paul LaCroix," *Rapid City Journal*, May 28, 2005.

30. SMA interview, February 29, 2016; SMA interview, December 16, 2016.

31. "Arthur P. LaCroix." See also Thomas & Associates, "Rapid City Regional Airport Proposed Runway Improvement Project Needs and Alternatives: An Historical and Data Report," December 23, 1981, RCPL.

32. Charles Michael Ray, "40 Years After Killer Flood, A Reshaped City Reflects," June 8, 2012, National Public Radio/South Dakota Public Broadcasting, accessed August 29, 2016, http://www.npr.org. See also, "Rapid City Flood Disaster Program, Urban Renewal Project, Project # SD-R3, Rapid City South Dakota," 10–11, March 27, 1975, RCPL.

33. Paul Cross, "Rapid City Moves Cautiously on Urban Renewal," *Rapid City Journal*, n.d., clipping in folder "Rapid City Renewal," box 9, RCACC.

34. For the AIA, Bell's meeting led to the creation of the first Regional and Urban Design Assistance Team. Over the next twenty years, nearly a hundred of these AIA "R/UDATs," as they were known, helped plan communities across the United States. Peter Batchelor and David Lewis, eds., *Urban Design in Action: The History, Theory, and Development of the American Institute of Architects' Regional/Urban Design Assistance Teams Program (R/UDAT)*, volume 29, Student Publication of the School of Design, North Carolina State University, 1985, 4; Benjamin Forgey, "The Transformation Team: A Program to Help Cities Plan the Future," *Washington Post*, March 12, 1988. On the AIA, see Tracy Ostroff, "Richard Upjohn: The Foundation of the Institute, *AIArchitect* (October 2005), accessed August 30, 2016, http://info.aia.org.

35. Batchelor and Lewis, *Urban Design in Action*, 4;

SOURCES   331

Forgey, "Transformation Team."

36. Batchelor and Lewis, *Urban Design in Action*, 4.

37. "Central Area Revitalization Guide for Rapid City Center, Rapid City, South Dakota, Concept Team, Hodne Associates, Inc., January 30, 1968," in binder "James G. Bell, Chamber of Commerce," box 9, RCACC; "Asheim Predicts Redevelopment Enthusiasm Will Bring Buildings," *Rapid City Journal*, February 15, 1968. On Asheim, see Eric John Abrahamson, *Improving Life with Energy*, 74–75. See also "Minutes, Redevelopment Executive Committee," June 30, 1967, folder "Rapid City Renewal," box 9, RCACC.

38. Sally Farrar, "Decision on City Redevelopment Now Approaching Critical Stage," *Rapid City Journal*, February 7, 1968.

39. "Central Area Revitalization Guide for Rapid City Center," v.

40. "We've Got the Ball Now," *Rapid City Journal*, February 8, 1968.

41. "Rapid City Flood Disaster Program, Urban Renewal Project, Project # SD-R3," 5.

42. Since the flood recovery and urban renewal programs were expansive and spread over many years, it is difficult to pinpoint the program's total costs. The initial funding applications that followed the flood, however, totaled $48.3 million. See "Rapid City Flood Disaster Program, Urban Renewal Project, Project # SD-R3," 5.

43. "Arthur P. LaCroix."

44. Samuel Roy, *Elvis: Prophet of Power* (Brookline, MA: Branden, 1985), 71; Peter Guralnick, *Careless Love: The Unmaking of Elvis Presley* (Boston: Little, Brown & Company, 1999), 634.

45. Shaff and Shaff, *Paving the Way*, 234.

46. SMA, "Some Not-So-Recent Rapid City Healthcare History," January 17, 2013, accessed August 30, 2016, https://way2gosd.com/2013/01/17/some-not-so-recent-rapid-city-health-care-history.

47. "Dr. Coolidge Flood Report," in *The Black Hills Flood of June 9, 1972*, 88–89.

48. Ibid., 89–90.

49. SMA, "Some Not-So-Recent Rapid City Healthcare History."

50. "Rapid City Regional Hospital: The First Five Years," May 1978, folder 143, box 4, NWE (hereafter "folder 143").

51. Service Unit Director, Rapid City Service Unit to Area Director, Aberdeen Area Indian Health Service, May 18, 1976; "Rapid City Regional Hospital: The First Five Years," May 1978, both folder 143.

52. "St. John's McNamara/Rapid City Regional Hospital School of Nursing," 17.

53. Operational Flow Chart, July 1980, in binder "Rapid City Regional Hospital," box 5, NWE.

54. "RCRH Board Committees," July 1980, in binder "Rapid City Regional Hospital," box 5, NWE; Service Unit Director, Rapid City Service Unit to Area Director, May 18, 1976.

55. Stan Adelstein to RCRH Board Members, October 24, 1978, folder 143.

56. "Professional Practice Committee, Thursday, September 21, 1978, 8 AM, Agenda," folder 143.

57. SMA to RCRH Board Members, October 24, 1978.

58. "Rapid City Regional Hospital: The First Five Years."

CHAPTER 14

1. Bill Hanna, "Rockefeller Calls for Party Unity," *Mitchell Daily Republic*, February 14, 1974.

2. Richard Norton Smith, *On His Own Terms: A Life of Nelson Rockefeller* (New York: Random House, 2014), xvi.

3. Paul Cross, "Watergate Issue Must Not Leave Unresolved Doubt," *Lead Daily Caller* (Lead, SD), February 13, 1974; "Not a Candidate," *Lead Daily Caller*, February 13, 1974.

4. Lyn Gladstone, "Rockefeller Speaks at GOP Dinner Here," *Rapid City Journal*, February 13, 1974; Associated Press, "Rocky Urges Decision on Watergate," *Huron Daily Plainsman* (Huron, SD), February 13, 1974.

5. Nelson A. Rockefeller to SMA, February 14, 1974, folder 14, box 1, Nelson A. Rockefeller Gubernatorial Records, 55th Street, Series 16 (FA362), RAC.

6. Smith, *On His Own Terms*, 345–47.

7. Timothy J. Sullivan, *New York State and the Rise of Modern Conservatism: Redrawing Party Lines* (Albany, NY: SUNY Press, 2008), 36–37.

8. Gary Donaldson, *Liberalism's Last Hurrah: The Presidential Campaign of 1964* (Armonk, NY: M.E. Sharpe, 2003), 80.

9. Ibid., 63–65; Sullivan, *New York State and the Rise of Modern Conservatism*, 37.

10. Donaldson, *Liberalism's Last Hurrah*, 190.

11. John Dickerson, "Never Goldwater: The Attempt to Wrest the 1964 GOP Nomination from the Arizona Senator and the Birth of the Modern GOP," *Slate*, May 12, 2016, accessed September 16, 2016, http://www.slate.com/articles/news_and_politics/politics/2016/05/never_goldwater_the_failed_attempt_to_wrest_the_1964_gop_nomination_from.html.

12. Nelson Rockefeller, speech to the Republican National Convention, 1964, accessed September 16, 2016, https://www.c-span.org/video/?c3807346/governor-nelson-rockefeller-addresses-64-convention.

13. Ibid.

14. Bart Barnes, "Barry Goldwater, GOP Hero, Dies." *Washington Post*, May 30, 1998.

15. See Ed Kilgore, "Viva Ole!," *Washington Monthly*, October 2, 2013, accessed September 16, 2016, https://washingtonmonthly.com/2013/10/02/viva-ole.

16. Donaldson, *Liberalism's Last Hurrah*, 180.

17. "Acceptance Speech By Senator Barry Goldwater, Republican National Convention, San Francisco, California, July 16, 1964," folder "Republican Party," box 72, NWE (emphasis original).

18. Barry Goldwater, 1964 speech to the Republican National Convention, CSpan2, accessed September 16, 2016, https://www.youtube.com/watch?v=RFSiyueal7Q.

19. Barnes, "Barry Goldwater, GOP Hero, Dies."

20. See John A. Andrew III, *The Other Side of the Sixties: Young Americans for Freedom and the Rise of Conservative Politics* (New Brunswick, NJ: Rutgers University Press, 1997), 6–8.

21. Lewis L. Gould, *1968: The Election That Changed America* (Chicago: Ivan R. Dee, 2010), 97. On Nixon's personality and brand of pragmatic politics, see Allen J. Matusow, *Nixon's Economy: Booms, Busts, Dollars, and Votes* (Lawrence: University Press of Kansas, 1998), 6.

22. Matusow, *Nixon's Economy*, 4–6, 68–69; Rick Perlstein, *Nixonland: The Rise of a President and the Fracturing of America* (New York: Scribner, 2008), 477–80; Theodore H. White, *The Making of the President 1972* (New York: Harperperennial Political Classics, 2010), 122.

23. Matusow, *Nixon's Economy*, 5–6.

24. On Agnew's resignation, see Richard M. Cohen and Jules Witcover, *A Heartbeat Away: The Investigation and Resignation of Vice President Spiro Agnew* (New York: Bantam Books, 1974), 342–55.

25. "Rocky Urges Decision on Watergate."

26. Rick Perlstein, *The Invisible Bridge: The Fall of Nixon and the Rise of Reagan* (New York: Simon & Schuster, 2014), 180, 269–70.

27. Ibid., 308.

28. Arthur I. Blaustein, ed., *The American Promise: Equal Justice and Economic Opportunity*, Fourth Edition (New Brunswick, NJ: Transaction Publishers, 2009), xi; "National Advisory Council on Economic Opportunity," memorandum, n.d., folder "Council on Economic Opportunity 1 of 2," box 15, NWE. On the War on Poverty, see Annelise Orleck and Lisa Gayle Hazirjian, *The War on Poverty: A New Grassroots History, 1964–1980* (Athens: University of Georgia Press, 2011).

29. Greta de Jong, *You Can't Eat Freedom: Southerners and Society Justice after the Civil Rights Movement* (Chapel Hill: University of North Carolina Press, 2016), 80; "National Advisory Council on Economic Opportunity."

30. See "Ninth Report: National Advisory Council on Economic Opportunity," discussion draft, February 8–9, 1977, folder 26 (1 of 2), box 15, NWE (hereafter "folder 26 (1 of 2)"). See also "Management Deficiencies in the Community Services Administration: Ninth Report by the Committee on Government Operations, January 26, 1976" (Washington, D.C.: U.S. Government Printing Office, 1976), 3–4.

31. "National Advisory Council on Economic Opportunity;" Nancy Pettis to Walter B. Quetsch, April 26, 1977, folder 26 (1 of 2).

SOURCES

32. SMA to Graciela Olivarez, June 29, 1977, folder 26 (1 of 2).
33. "Presentation by Dr. Olivarez, Director, Community Services Administration, June 2, 1977," folder 26 (1 of 2).
34. Ibid.
35. Ibid.
36. "Role of the National Advisory Council on Economic Opportunity," folder 26 (1 of 2).
37. "National Advisory Council on Economic Opportunity," memorandum, n.d., folder 26 (1 of 2).
38. Monica Rhor, "Cuban Americans Move Toward Democratic Party," *Sun Sentinel* (Palm Beach, Florida), August 7, 1988; Memo re: proposed committee assignments, June 1, 1977; Committee Mission Statements, memorandum to NACEO members, May 25, 1977, folder 26 (1 of 2).
39. SMA to Olivarez, June 29, 1977.
40. "National Advisory Council on Economic Opportunity," memorandum outlining the statutory basis for the NACEO, n.d., folder 26 (1 of 2).
41. NACEO meeting minutes, May 26, 1977, folder 26 (1 of 2). See also "Role of the National Advisory Council on Economic Opportunity;" "National Advisory Council on Economic Opportunity," memorandum, n.d., folder 26 (1 of 2).
42. "Presentation by Dr. Olivarez;" "Ninth Report" discussion draft.
43. Blaustein, *American Promise*, xi.
44. John P. Miglietta, *American Alliance Policy in the Middle East, 1945–1992* (Lanham, MD: Lexington Books, 2002), 151.
45. Howard Morley Sachar, *A History of Jews in America* (New York: Vintage Books, 1993), 871.
46. Collin Binkley, "Gordon Zacks, 1933–2014: Compassionate Businessman was Friend to Israel," *Columbus Dispatch*, February 3, 2014, accessed July 11, 2018, http://www.dispatch.com/content/stories/local/2014/02/ 03/gordon-zacks-obit-compassionate-businessman-friend-to-israel.html.
47. PACs are a legal vehicle for political fundraising. Although they have existed since the 1940s, PACs were less common in American politics until campaign finance reforms in the 1970s made them attractive to fundraisers. The number of PACs has grown dramatically in subsequent decades.

48. David M. Herszenhorn, "Tom Lantos, 80, Is Dead; Longtime Congressman," *New York Times*, February 12, 2008.
49. Ibid.
50. Miglietta, *American Alliance Policy*, 151.
51. Larry Pressler, *U.S. Senators from the Prairie* (Vermillion, SD: Dakota Press, 1982), 181–82.
52. "Questions to be Answered for Congressman Jim Abdnor, December 7, 1973," folder 3, box 11, NWE.
53. Stan Adelstein to James Abdnor, October 8, 1985, folder 30, box 30, NWE (hereafter "folder 30"); Abdnor to Stan Adelstein, February 20, 1981, folder 22.
54. Pressler, *U.S. Senators from the Prairie*, 171.
55. Ibid., 173–74.
56. SMA to Morton Rywick, February 17, 1981, folder 22.
57. Ibid.
58. Stan Adelstein, "Impressions from the Inaugural of President Ronald Reagan, January 17–20," folder 22.
59. Steve Miller, "Carole Hillard Dies at 71," *Rapid City Journal*, October 24, 2007; SMA, "Impressions from the Inaugural."
60. SMA, "Impressions from the Inaugural."
61. SMA, hand-written notes on an AJC Board of Governor's Meeting agenda, September 18, 1979, folder 40 (emphasis original).
62. SMA, "Impressions from the Inaugural."
63. Ibid. See also Sean Wilentz, *The Age of Reagan: A History, 1974–2008* (New York: HarperCollins, 2008).
64. SMA, "Impressions from the Inaugural."
65. Ibid.
66. Ibid.
67. SMA to Robert Adelstein, May 4, 2006, copy in the author's possession.
68. SMA, "Impressions from the Inaugural."
69. Nicholas Laham, *Selling AWACS to Saudi Arabia: The Reagan Administration and the Balancing of America's Competing Interests in the Middle East* (Westport, CT: Praeger, 2002), 10, 39, 151.
70. Ibid., xi.

71. "AWACS Sale Costing Reagan Support Among Jews," *New York Times*, October 22, 1981.

72. David M. Shribman, "Hosts, Not Visitors: The Future of Jews in American Politics," in *Jews in American Politics: Essays*, ed. Sandy L. Maisel and Ira N. Forman (New York: Rowman & Littlefield, 2004), 277.

73. See Laham, *Selling AWACS to Saudi Arabia*, 1–34.

74. Ibid. See also SMA to Jonathan Adelstein, June 22, 1981, folder 22. Stan's son Jon interned in Packwood's office as a young man. See SMA to Martha Kaufman, November 3, 1981, folder 22.

75. Laham, *Selling AWACS to Saudi Arabia*, 188–92.

76. Stan Adelstein to Alize Ginott, November 4, 1981, folder 22.

77. Janklow to Pressler, October 14, 1981, folder 22.

78. Ibid.

79. Ibid.

80. Ibid.

81. SMA to Janklow, November 3, 1981.

82. Ibid.

83. Laham, *Selling AWACS to Saudi Arabia*, 216.

84. Pressler, *U.S. Senators from the Prairie*, 173.

85. "Cohn—Dr. Alice Ginott," *New York Times*, March 2, 2015; SMA to Ginott, November 4, 1981.

86. SMA to Ginott, November 4, 1981.

87. SMA to Kaufman, November 3, 1981.

CHAPTER 15

1. See Janet A. McDonnell, *The Dispossession of the American Indian, 1887–1934* (Bloomington: Indiana University Press, 1989); The Harvard Project on American Indian Economic Development, *The State of the Native Nations: Conditions Under U.S. Policies of Self-Determination* (New York: Oxford University Press, 2007); Ostler, *Lakotas and the Black Hills*; Nelson, "Dreams and Dust in the Black Hills."

2. See Paul Chaat Smith and Robert Allen Warrior, *Like A Hurricane: The Indian Movement from Alcatraz to Wounded Knee* (New York: The New Press, 1996); Joane Nagel, *American Indian Ethnic Renewal: Red Power and the Resurgence of Identity and Culture* (New York: Oxford University Press, 1996).

3. These Native leaders took their name from an earlier group that had been advocating for the return of the Black Hills since the early twentieth century. Edward Lazarus, *Black Hills/White Justice: The Sioux Nation versus the United States, 1775 to the Present* (New York: Harper Collins, 1991), 130.

4. SMA to Harry Fleischmann, December 14, 1968, folder 52, box 17, NWE (hereafter "folder 52").

5. Ibid.

6. Ibid.

7. SMA to Charles T. Undlin, August 15, 1969, folder 52.

8. "Police, Indians, from Conference in Apartment, 7 Dec. '68," hand-written notes in folder 52.

9. "Blk Hill Council Amer Ind.," hand-written notes, probably 1968–1969, folder 52.

10. "General Observations Regarding Police-Minority Relations and Possible Avenues of Approach in Improving Such Relations in Rapid City, SD;" "A Statement on the History and Background of this Proposal," both n.d., probably 1968-1969, both folder 52.

11. Akim D. Reinhardt, *Ruling Pine Ridge: Oglala Lakota Politics from the IRA to Wounded Knee* (Lubbock: Texas Tech University Press, 2007), 159.

12. Ibid., 3–6. See also 158, 168, 175–77.

13. Ibid., 126.

14. "Stanford M. Adelstein's Answers on KOTA Television Special, 'WHY?', February 13, 1973," folder 52.

15. Ibid.

16. Ibid.

17. SMA to Dave True, February 5, 1973, folder 52.

18. Andrew H. Malcolm, "Occupation of Wounded Knee is Ended," *New York Times*, May 8, 1973.

19. Reinhardt, *Ruling Pine Ridge*, 12, 127.

20. Richie Richards, "Mother Butler Center Staff Was Only Following Rules," *Native Sun News*, February 24, 2014, accessed August 24, 2017, https://www.nativesunnews.today/articles/mother-butler-center-staff-was-only-following-the-rules.

21. Stanley David Lyman, *1973: A Personal Account* (Lincoln: University of Nebraska Press, 1991), 5. "The History of the Diocese and Catholic Education in Western South Dakota," Rapid City

SOURCES

Catholic School System, accessed March 1, 2019, https://rccss.org/development/alumni/history.

22. Donald Barnett in conversation with the author, June 10, 2017.

23. Reinhardt, *Ruling Pine Ridge,* 126, 168, 192.

24. Ibid., 14–18. On tribal politics in Pine Ridge, see Thomas Biolsi, *Organizing the Lakota: The Political Economy of the New Deal on the Pine Ridge and Rosebud Reservations* (Tucson: University of Arizona Press, 1992).

25. James G. Abourezk, *Advise and Dissent: Memoirs of an Ex-Senator* (Chicago: Lawrence Hill Books, 1989), 209–12.

26. Lyn Gladstone and Jack Weaver, "Means Unhappy with Bail Terms, But Sees Victory," *Rapid City Journal,* Saturday, April 7, 1973.

27. Gladstone and Weaver, "Means Unhappy with Bail Terms."

28. Ibid.

29. Russell Means with Marvin J. Wolf, *Where White Men Fear to Tread: The Autobiography of Russell Means* (New York: St. Martin's Griffin, 1995), 287.

30. Gladstone and Weaver, "Means Unhappy with Bail Terms."

31. Means with Wolf, *Where White Men Fear to Tread,* 287.

32. Ibid.

33. Ibid.

34. Ibid.

35. Gladstone and Weaver, "Means Unhappy with Bail Terms."

36. Ibid.; "Means Absent at Bond Hearing; 68 Kyle Arrests," *Rapid City Journal,* April 26, 1973; "Means Says He'll Ignore Bogue Order," *Rapid City Journal,* April 27, 1973.

37. "Indians in Capital for U.S. Talks," *Chicago Tribune,* April 7, 1973, p. 5.

38. Means with Wolf, *Where White Men Fear to Tread,* 290.

39. Malcolm, "Occupation of Wounded Knee is Ended."

40. Ibid.

41. Harvey Jewett in conversation with the author, September 22, 2016; "Dennis Banks and Russell Means Cleared of Charges," *NBC Nightly News,* New York, NBC Universal, September 16, 1074, accessed January 23, 2017, https://archives.nbclearn.com/portal/site/k-12/flatview?cuecard=37580. On the aftermath of the Wounded Knee standoff, see John William Sayer, *Ghost Dancing the Law: The Wounded Knee Trials* (Cambridge, MA: Harvard University Press, 1997).

42. Reinhardt, *Ruling Pine Ridge,* 205.

43. "Minutes of a Special Meeting to Discuss Rapid City Indian-White Relations Toby Theatre, March 4, 1973," folder 52.

44. Ibid.

45. Donald Barnett to SMA, March 6, 1973, folder 52.

46. Marshall Young, e-mail to the author, August 23, 2016.

47. Isaiah T. Creswell to SMA, September 24, 1975, folder 151, box 1, NWE (hereafter "folder 151").

48. Mary Frances Barry, *And Justice for All: The United States Commission on Civil Rights and the Continuing Struggle for Freedom in America* (New York: Alfred A. Knopf, 2009), 3.

49. Ibid., 4.

50. Ibid., 5.

51. "SD Advisory Committee, Biographical Data," folder 151; United States Commission on Civil Rights, South Dakota Advisory Committee, "Liberty and Justice for All: A Report" (Washington, D.C.: The Commission, 1977), v.

52. Bill Muldrow to SMA, May 15, 1985, folder 173, box 32, NWE (hereafter "folder 173").

53. "United Sioux Tribes: Indian Civil Rights Consultation, October 23 and 25, 1984, South Dakota," folder 173.

54. SMA to Rudy Boschwitz, September 2, 1983, folder 152, box 22, NWE.

55. "Remarks to be Delivered by Stanford M. Adelstein, July 27, 1978," folder 161, box 4, NWE (hereafter "folder 161").

56. See U.S. Commission on Civil Rights, South Dakota Advisory Committee, "Liberty and Justice for All," ii–iii.

57. Ibid., ii.

58. Ibid., 38–41.

59. Richard Kneip to Ed DeAntoni, February 16,

1978, folder 161; "Remarks to be Delivered by Stanford M. Adelstein, July 27, 1978."

60. Abourezk, *Advise and Dissent*, 59–60.

61. Percival Quinn, "Report on Indian Civil Rights Upheld," *Argus-Leader* (Sioux Falls, SD), January 29, 1978.

62. William Walsh and David Volk to Arthur S. Fleming, draft, n.d., folder 161.

63. Jomay Steen, "Former Rapid City Police Chief, Lawmaker Tom Hennies Dies," *Rapid City Journal*, August 10, 2009.

64. "South Dakota Indian Businessmen's Association Prospectus and Program Proposal for Funding," n.d. folder 52.

65. Douglas Fast Horse, business plan for "Indian City, U.S.A.," December 19, 1983, folder "General Correspondence 1983," RG.

66. SMA to Earl Brockelsby, December 19, 1983, folder "General Correspondence 1983," RG. See also Fast Horse, business plan for "Indian City, U.S.A." On Brockelsby, see Hurst, *Rattlesnake Under His Hat*.

67. Brockelsby to SMA, December 27, 1983, folder "General Correspondence 1983," Reptile Gardens Archive.

68. Ibid.

69. Ibid.

70. See Kiara M. Vigil, "Who Was Henry Standing Bear? Remembering Lakota Activism from the Early Twentieth Century," *Great Plains Quarterly*, 37, no. (Summer 2017): 158–59.

71. Ibid., 157.

72. Lyn Gladstone, "Corruption Charged in Housing Program," *Rapid City Journal*, June 8, 1976.

73. Ibid.

74. SMA to Richard Schifter, June 16, 1988, folder 82, box 44, NWE (hereafter "folder 82").

75. Ibid. To illustrate the need for this vehicle, Bloomberg described to a reporter in March 1988 how volunteers would "load the back of the ambulance with five-gallon buckets of water, blankets, and shovels and off we'd go" to a fire. With the money they raised, the group acquired a refurbished fire truck through a South Dakota Division of Forestry program. See Joan Morrison,

"Community Gets Its First Fire Truck," *Rapid City Journal*, March 28, 1988.

76. SMA to Schifter, June 16, 1988.

77. "Learn About Tom Cook," Running Strong for American Indian Young, August 2, 2016, accessed January 26, 2017, http://indianyouth.org/news/detail/learn-about-tom-cook.

78. Thomas Cook to SMA, June 2, 1985; SMA to Cook, October 22, 1985, both folder 30.

79. "Meeting Minutes, March 24, 1976," folder 151; SMA to Gordon Bronitsky, n.d., folder 82.

80. SMA to Bronitsky, n.d; Eric Pace, "Rabbi Joseph B. Glaser, 69; Led Reform Group," *New York Times*, September 24, 1994.

81. Ivan Star Comes Out, "New Ground Forged in Oglala Community Hopes for Self-Reliance," *Lakota Times*, May 16, 1989.

82. This, of course, was crucial to Israel, a place covered by desert and, given the Jewish State's precarious relationship with its Arab neighbors, one in which access to imported food was never a given. See "Oglala Truck Gardening Cooperative Association, 1988 Agricultural Project," folder 82. Megh R. Goyal, *Management of Drip/Trickle or Micro Irrigation* (Point Pleasant, NJ: Apple Academic Press, 2013), 104. On Israel and imported food, see Victor Perlo, *Israel and Dollar Diplomacy* (New York: New Century Publishers, 1953), 42.

83. Star Comes Out, "New Ground Forged in Oglala."

84. "Executive Committee, the Lakota Produce Growers Association, August 31, 1989," folder 71; Star Comes Out, "New Ground Forged in Oglala."

85. Star Comes Out, "New Ground Forged in Oglala."

86. "The Oglala Truck Gardening Cooperative Association, 1988 Agricultural Project," folder 82.

87. "The Oglala Truck Gardening Cooperative Association, 1988 Agricultural Project," folder 82. Cook to SMA, April 15, 1988, folder 82.

88. Star Comes Out, "New Ground Forged in Oglala."

89. Ibid.

90. "Oglala Truck Gardening Cooperative Association."

SOURCES

91. Robert D. Fast Horse to SMA, September 30, 1984, in AFP #738.

CHAPTER 16

1. SMA to Jan and Marjorie de Hartog, August 18, 1986, folder 187, box 33, NWE (hereafter "folder 187").
2. "Stanford M. Adelstein, YPO Activities," folder "Young Presidents' Organization, Rocky Mountain Chapter," box 24, NWE.
3. SMA to the editor of the *Heilbronner Stimme*, February 10, 1987, folder 196, box 39, NWE.
4. Ibid.
5. SMA to Vickie Moyle, September 2, 1986, folder 187.
6. Stan Adelstein to De Hartogs, August 18, 1986.
7. AFP #873.
8. Pat Tlustos interview, November 9, 2016.
9. Ibid.
10. SMA to Hills Materials employees, September 2, 1983, folder "SMA Correspondence July to September 1983," box 24, NWE.
11. See ledger, n.d., folder 138A, box 22, NEW (hereafter "folder 138a").
12. SMA to Hills Materials employees, September 2, 1983.
13. See for example "Hills Materials Company Income Statement, Years Ended December 31, 1988 and 1987," folder 202, box 49, NWE.
14. "News Release," July 22, 1985, folder 31.
15. "1973 Annual Report, Northwestern Engineering Company," A-12, bound report in box 18, NWE.
16. K. Bordner Consultants, "Retail Revitalization and Expansion Program, Rapid City, SD, Central Business District," December 17, 1979, 2, bound report in box 24, NWE.
17. Heefner, *Missile Next Door*, 130. See the image inset following pg. 110.
18. "News Release," July 22, 1985, folder 31; Sandra Runde interview, November 23, 2016.
19. "1973 Annual Report," A-8. See map of the Meadowlark Mobile Home Park, folder 129, box 31, NWE (hereafter "folder 129").
20. "News Release," July 22, 1985.
21. SMA quoted in Runde interview, November 23, 2016.
22. Runde interview, November 23, 2016; "About Sandra Runde," personal biography provided by Keller Williams Realty Black Hills, copy in the author's possession
23. Runde interview, November 23, 2016; SMA interview, December 12, 2016.
24. "Northwestern Engineering Company Annual Meeting of the Board of Directors, Sunday and Monday, February 24 and 25, 1985," folder 129.
25. Ibid.
26. Runde interview, November 23, 2016.
27. Sandra K. Runde, "Strategic Plan for a Property Management Company," May 8, 1985, folder 129; Runde interview, November 23, 2016.
28. Runde interview, November 23, 2016.
29. "Hills Materials Company: Action of Board of Directors Without Formal Meeting," October 29, 1987, folder 533, box 41, NWE.
30. "Northwestern Engineering Company Annual Meeting, 1985."
31. Tlustos interview, November 9, 2016.
32. Ibid.
33. Howard J. Wiarda, *Conservative Brain Trust: The Rise, Fall, and Rise Again of the American Enterprise Institute* (Plymouth, UK: Lexington Books, 2009), 146.
34. Tlustos interview, November 9, 2016.
35. Ibid.
36. SMA to De Hartogs, April 2, 1981, folder 22.
37. "Stanford M. Adelstein, 1999 West Boulevard, Rapid City, South Dakota, 57701," folder 2, box 32, NWE.
38. SMA interview, December 12, 2016.
39. Ibid.; "Black Forest Inn History," Black Forest Inn Bed & Breakfast, accessed December 20, 2016, http://www.blackforestinn.net/inn-history.htm; Janet M. Carter, Joyce E. Williamson, and Ralph W. Teller, "The 1972 Black Hills-Rapid City Flood Revisited," U.S. Geological Survey Fact Sheet FS-037-02, accessed December 20, 2016, https://pubs.usgs.gov/fs/fs-037-02.

40. SMA interview, December 12, 2016. "Stanford M. Adelstein, 1999 West Boulevard."

41. "Stanford M. Adelstein, 1999 West Boulevard."

42. Richard W. Stafford to Ted Venners, April 21, 1975; "Management Agreement, April 25, 1975," both folder 48, box 14, NWE (hereafter "folder 48").

43. SMA to Ted Venners, June 18, 1975, folder 48, box 14; "Special Meetings of the Board of Directors of the Northwestern Engineering Company, July 24, 1978," folder 16; SMA to Dan Adelstein, June 26, 1978, folder 5, both box 2; Runde to Jerry Schriver, December 27, 1983, folder "Oct. 1, 1983–Dec. 31, 1983," box 24; Runde to Lawrence Feiler, October 23, 1985, unlabeled folder, box 32; SMA to NWE board of directors, October 21, 1985, folder "NWE Stockholders Meeting—Rapid City, SD August 19, 1985," box 31, all NWE; Runde interview, November 23, 2016.

44. Runde to Rol Johnson, n.d., folder 132, box 31, NWE (hereafter "folder 132").

45. See *Norwest Bank South Dakota v. Venners*, 440 N.W. 2nd 774 (1989), accessed December 20, 2016, http://law.justia.com/cases/south-dakota/supreme-court/1989/16330-1.html; SMA to Venners, October 3, 1985, unlabeled folder, box 32, NWE.

46. SMA to Dan Adelstein, August 4, 1978, folder 5, box 2, NWE (hereafter "folder 5"); SMA to Dan Adelstein, February 6, 1978, folder 17.

47. Tlustos interview, November 9, 2016.

48. Ibid.

49. Ibid.

50. Susan Cleveland to SMA, March 26, 1987; David Crabb to Arizona Department of Revenue, December 15, 1987, both folder 688, box 41, NWE (hereafter "folder 688").

51. Tlustos interview, November 9, 2016.

52. Crabb to Arizona Department of Revenue, December 15, 1987; David Crabb to SMA, Pat Tlustos, and Sandra Runde, September 14, 1987, folder 688.

53. Tlustos interview, November 9, 2016.

54. Robert Adelstein interview, September 23, 2016; SMA interview, December 16, 2015.

55. Robert Adelstein interview, September 23, 2016.

56. Jerry Mizel interview, January 18, 2017.

57. Ibid.

58. Transcript of a meeting between SMA, Robert Adelstein, and Jerry Mizel, n.d., probably March 1989, folder 70, box 48, NWE.

59. Ibid.

60. Ibid.

61. Mizel interview, January 18, 2017; "Transcript of a meeting."

62. SMA to Dana Schwartz, Debbie Morrison, David Adelstein, November 17, 1989, folder 71.

63. Daniel Adelstein interview, September 11, 2016; SMA to Marjorie de Hartog, April 2, 1981.

64. SMA to De Hartogs, April 2, 1981.

65. "Biography of Former Commissioner Jonathan S. Adelstein," Federal Communications Commission, accessed December 1, 2016, https://www.fcc.gov/general/biography-former-commissioner-jonathan-s-adelstein.

66. Daniel Adelstein interview, September 11, 2016.

67. Ibid.

68. Ibid.

69. SMA to De Hartogs, April 2, 1981.

70. J.D. Ames, "Ita Adelstein: Refugee, Survivor, and She's Still Growing," *Rapid City Journal*, January 19, 1982.

71. SMA to De Hartogs, April 2, 1981. See Swami Prajnananda, *A Search for the Self: The Story of Swami Muktananda* (Ganeshpuri: Gurudev Siddha Peeth, 1979).

72. SMA, quoted by Daniel Adelstein in Daniel Adelstein interview, September 11, 2016.

CHAPTER 17

1. SMA to Jack Beckman, October 5, 1978, folder 145A, box 4, NWE (hereafter "folder 145A").

2. Dignitaries included Sturgis resident Nora Hussey, South Dakota's Republican National Committeewoman; the party's Pennington County Chairwoman Ellie Plummer; and Congressman Jim Abdnor. "President Gerald R. Ford's Schedule for October 12, 1978," September 22, 1978, folder 145A.

3. "The Daily Diary of President Gerald R. Ford, August 29, 1976," President's Daily Diary

SOURCES

Collection, box 83, Gerald R. Ford Presidential Library, accessed January 31, 2017, https://www.fordlibrarymuseum.gov/.

4. "Leo Thorsness," pamphlet, n.d., folder 132A, box 14, NWE.

5. "Stanford M. Adelstein for National Committee," pamphlet, n.d., folder 124A.

6. "Head Table Guests, President Ford Luncheon," October 12, 1978, folder 145A; "Hussey to Celebrate 102nd Birthday," *Rapid City Journal*, March 20, 2017.

7. "Ford's Schedule for October 12, 1978."

8. "Republican Ford Dinner, October 12, 1978," folder 145A; SMA to Richard Nixon, October 18, 1978, folder 17; "GOP Continues to Register Gains in Legislature," *Rapid City Journal*, November 8, 1978; "Republicans Get 24 Senate Seats, 43 House Seats to Retain Majority," *Rapid City Journal*, November 8, 1978; "Election Victory Comes Into Sight," *Rapid City Journal*, November 8, 1978.

9. Arlene Ham to SMA, October 17, 1976, folder 145A.

10. Alan Abramowitz and Jeffrey Allan Segal, *Senate Elections* (Ann Arbor: University of Michigan Press, 1992), 209.

11. On the rise of the conservative wing of the Republican Party, see Lisa McGirr, *Suburban Warriors: The Origins of the New American Right* (Princeton, NJ: Princeton University Press, 2001); Kim Phillips-Fein, *Invisible Hands: The Making of the Conservative Movement from the New Deal to Reagan* (New York: W.W. Norton, 2009); Wilentz, *Age of Reagan: A History, 1974–2008* (New York: HarperCollins, 2008); John A. Andrew III, *The Other Side of the Sixties: Young Americans for Freedom and the Rise of Conservative Politics* (New Brunswick, NJ: Rutgers University Press, 1997).

12. See Arthur Paulson, *Realignment and Party Revival: Understanding American Electoral Politics at the Turn of the Twenty-First Century* (Westport, CT: Praeger, 2000), 151.

13. Carl A. Tiffany to SMA, August 28, 1978, folder 145A.

14. Dan Parish to Ham, September 28, 1978, folder 145A.

15. SMA CV.

16. SMA to Mark A. Spiegel, December 7, 1978,

folder 145, box 4, NWE (hereafter "folder 145"); "About RJC," Republican Jewish Coalition, accessed August 22, 2017, http://www.rjchq.org/about.

17. SMA to Spiegel, December 7, 1978.

18. Spiegel to SMA, December 11, 1978, folder 145.

19. "Stanford M. Adelstein, 1999 West Boulevard."

20. Ibid.

21. SMA to Hagoels, April 16, 1980.

22. "Nomination Acceptance, June 28, 1980," folder 124A.

23. SMA to "Key Campaign Leaders," June 19, 1980, folder 124A.

24. The relatively close race had been lost, according to Stan, because of a mistake by his campaign team in one county. SMA to Philip D. Winn, July 1, 1980, folder 124A; *Daily Republic* (Mitchell, SD), June 23, 1959, pg. 1

25. SMA to Winn, July 1, 1980.

26. Rollyn H. Samp to SMA, June 30, 1980; SMA to Samp, July 1, 1980, both folder 124A.

27. SMA to De Hartogs, April 2, 1981.

28. SMA to Jim Nelson, March 11, 1981, folder 22.

29. Alison Muscatine and Saundra Saperstein, "A Long Shot," *New York Times*, September 27, 1982; "Stanford M. Adelstein, 1999 West Boulevard."

30. SMA to Frank J. Fahrenkopf, June 13, 1983, folder 140.

31. The Republican Jewish Coalition was initially called the National Jewish Coalition. See "Statement of Purpose," National Jewish Coalition, folder 30.

32. SMA to Joseph Glaser, February 24, 1983, folder "January 1, 1983–March 31, 1983," box 24; "Federal Emergency Management Agency, Region VIII, National Defense Executive Reserve, Position Description, State Liaison Officer, ODR," folder 2, box 32, both NWE.

33. Anonymous to SMA, June 10, 1980, folder 124A.

34. SMA to Leonard Bell, August 21, 1978, folder 146, box 4, NWE (hereafter "folder 146").

35. SMA to Janklow, November 27, 1978, folder 146.

36. SMA to Janklow, June 10, 1982, folder 23, box 23, NWE.

37. "Janklow Leaves on Israeli Junket," *Rapid City*

Journal, February 14, 2003.

38. SMA interview, February 29, 2016.

39. "Stanford M. Adelstein, 1999 West Boulevard."

40. "Executive Committee Agenda, King's Inn, Pierre, January 7, 1983," folder 141, box 22, NWE.

41. "Agenda: Republican State Central Committee District Meeting, Black Forest Inn, Saturday, June 4, 1983–12:30 PM," folder 141.

42. "Black Forest Inn, Keystone Route 3123, Highways 385, Rapid City," folder 141.

43. Jeff Stingley, "1983–84 Political Plan of the South Dakota Republican Party, March, 1983, Overview," folder 141.

44. "Specific and Broad Tasks Needing Consideration by South Dakota Republican Party in 1983–1984," folder 141.

45. Stingley, "1983–84 Political Plan."

46. Ibid.

47. Ibid.

48. On South Dakota political culture more generally, see Jon K. Lauck, John E. Miller, and Edward Hogan, "Historical Musings: The Contours of South Dakota Political Culture," *South Dakota History* 34, no. 2 (Summer 2004): 157–78; Patrick Lalley, "Historical Musings: Comments on 'The Contours of South Dakota Political Culture, The Politics of Pragmatism," *South Dakota History* 36, no. 3 (Fall 2006): 318–22.

49. Richard Goldstein, "Bill Janklow, a Four-Term Governor of South Dakota, Dies at 72," *New York Times*, January 12, 2012.

50. "South Dakota: Janklow Boosts Reelection Bid in Disaster Scene," *Washington Post*, June 12, 1998, accessed February 2, 2017.

51. Lalley, "Politics of Pragmatism," 319.

52. Jon K. Lauck, *Daschle v. Thune: The Anatomy of a High Plains Senate Race* (Norman: University of Oklahoma Press, 2007), 15.

53. Lalley, "Politics of Pragmatism," 319.

54. SMA interview, December 12, 2016.

55. Janklow to SMA, October 4, 1995, folder "Dept. of Transportation General 1995 (folder 5 of 6)," box 76, USD.

56. Eugene Rowen to Janklow, September 11, 1980, folder "DOT Reorganization," box 16;

"Department of Transportation Review Task Force Meeting, October 24 and October 25, 1995," folder "DOT Task Force 1995," box 77, USD.

57. SMA interview, December 12, 2016.

58. "Department of Transportation Task Force," folder "DOT Task Force 1995," box 77, USD.

59. "Governor Janklow's South Dakota Department of Transportation Review Task Force, February 27, 1996," folder "DOT Task Force 1996 # 1," box 106, USD.

60. Curt Jones and Ron Wheeler to Janklow, February 24, 1996, folder "DOT Task Force 1996 # 1," box 106, USD.

61. SMA interview, December 12, 2016.

62. Janklow to SMA, October 5, 1995, folder "Dept of Transportation General 1995 (folder 5 of 6)," box 76, USD.

63. Curt Jones and Ron Wheeler to Janklow, February 24, 1996; Bob Mercer, "Fort Sisseton Plaques to Honor a Great Pair from Our State's Past," *Black Hills Pioneer* (Spearfish, SD), September 24, 2012; Janklow to JoAnne Heikes, February 21, 1997, folder "2001-016m 1997 GOED/Vitals/C.T. Bank/Economic Development Finance," box 156, USD.

64. "Department of Transportation Review Task Force Meeting, October 24 and October 25, 1995."

65. "Department of Transportation Task Force;" "Governor Janklow's South Dakota Department of Transportation Review Task Force, February 27, 1996;" "Highway Construction–Accomplishments 1987–1994," folder "2003-010 5072 Transition Briefing Documents Book 1-2, 2 of 2," box 368, all USD.

66. "Department of Transportation Task Force."

67. "The 'Core' Functions of the SDDOT," folder "DOT Task Force 1995," box 77; "Governor Janklow's South Dakota Department of Transportation Review Task Force, February 27, 1996," both USD.

68. "Governor Janklow's South Dakota Department of Transportation Review Task Force, February 27, 1996," 6–7.

69. Ibid., 8–40.

70. Ibid.

71. South Dakota Legislative Research Council,

"Reorganization of the Department of Transportation," Issue Memorandum 96-25, August 7, 2000, 4, copy in the author's possession.

72. Wheeler to Kay Jorgensen, June 18, 1996, folder "DOT Task Force 1996 # 1," box 106, USD.

73. South Dakota Legislative Research Council, "Reorganization of the Department of Transportation."

CHAPTER 18

1. Lynda Clark Adelstein interview, September 13, 2016.

2. Ibid.

3. Steve Fiffer, *Tyrannosaurus Sue: The Extraordinary Saga of the Largest, Most Fought Over T. Rex Ever Found* (New York: W.H. Freeman and Company, 2000), 2–3; "USA: Chicago Museum Pays $8.4 Million for Tyrannosaurus Rex," AP News Archive, published July 21, 2015, accessed February 6, 2017, https://www.youtube.com/watch?v=SJa6y7zpO3c.

4. Peter Larson and Kristin Donnan, *Rex Appeal: The Amazing Story of Sue, the Dinosaur that Changed Science, the Law, and My Life* (Montpilier, VT: Invisible Cities Press), 324.

5. Larson and Donnan, *Rex Appeal*, 323. SMA says the figure was actually $1.5 million.

6. Ibid., 324.

7. Fiffer, *Tyrannosaurus Sue*, 209.

8. Larson and Donnan, *Rex Appeal*, 324. See also 356.

9. SMA interview, January 5, 2016.

10. "Business Organization and Management: Spring of 1984," syllabus for course instructed by SMA and Tony Rusek, unlabeled folder; "Homework Assignment, February 26, 1982," folder "SDSMT 'Managerial Economics for Engineers, 1980," both box 24, NWE.

11. SMA to Tlustos, September 21, 1982, folder "SDSMT 'Managerial Economics for Engineers, 1980;" SMA to Art LaCroix, October 21, 1983, folder "Oct. 1, 1983–Dec. 31, 1983," both box 24, NWE.

12. SMA CV. See also folder 529, box 40, NWE.

13. Jeffrey Viken interview, November 28, 2016.

14. Ibid.; Heidi Bell Gease, "After 10 Years, The Journey is Alive and Growing," *Rapid City Journal*, May 13, 2007.

15. Gease, "After 10 Years, Journey Alive and Growing."

16. Viken interview, November 28, 2016.

17. Ibid.; Gease, "Journey Alive and Growing."

18. "Alliance Vision Becomes the Journey Museum Reality," *Turtle Times: The Journey Museum Newsletter* (Winter 2007), 7; Gease, "Journey Alive and Growing."

19. Gease, "Journey Alive and Growing;" "Bumps on the Journey," *Turtle Times: The Journey Museum Newsletter* (Winter 2007), 7.

20. Gease, "Journey Alive and Growing;" Viken interview, November 28, 2016.

21. Viken interview, November 28, 2016; Gease, "Journey Alive and Growing."

22. Lynda Clark Adelstein interview, September 13, 2016.

23. Ibid.

24. Ibid.

25. Ibid.

26. Ibid.

27. SMA e-mail to the author, August 1, 2017; story confirmed by Lynda Clark Adelstein.

28. Lynda Clark Adelstein interview, September 13, 2016.

29. Ibid.

30. Ibid. (emphasis added).

31. SMA CV; Steve Miller, "Rapid City Native Survives Pentagon Attack," September 28, 2001; Army Public Affairs, "New Civilian Aide to the Secretary of the Army Invested," U.S. Army, August 26, 2016, accessed February 7, 2017, https://www.army.mil/article/174106/new_civilian_aide_to_the_secretary_of_the_army_invested.

32. SMA CV.

33. Tlustos interview, November 9, 2016.

34. Ibid.

35. Ibid.

36. Ibid.

37. Ibid.

CHAPTER 19

1. Tlustos interview, November 9, 2016.

2. Mary Garrigan, "Nine in '09: Stan Adelstein, Incoming Senator," *Rapid City Journal*, January 5, 2009.

3. Dan Daly, "Golden West Buys RapidNet," *Rapid City Journal*, April 30, 2001; "Black Hills Transportation Announces New Board Members," *Black Hills Pioneer*, May 25, 2006.

4. Heidi Bell Gease, "Fighting Addictions at Home," *Rapid City Journal*, September 28, 2001; "2008 Annual Report: Black Hills Area Community Foundation," copy in the author's possession; Bill Cissel, "Presidential Statues Preside Over Downtown," *Rapid City Journal*, November 10, 2000.

5. Shirley Adelstein interview, April 20, 2018.

6. Reinhard Heydrich, "The Wannsee Protocol," January 20, 1943, reprinted in Mark Roseman, *The Wannsee Conference and the Final Solution: A Reconsideration* (New York: Picador, 2002), 164–65. See also "Wannsee Conference and the 'Final Solution,'" United States Holocaust Memorial Museum, accessed April 24, 2018, https://www.ushmm.org/wlc/en/article.php?ModuleId=10005477.

7. SMA interview, December 12, 2016.

8. Bill Harlan, "Election Defeat Sparks Dem Defection," *Rapid City Journal*, November 7, 2000.

9. This phrasing comes from a defensive letter by Arthur Janklow, a supporter of Stan's, who was paraphrasing the original letter by Larry Baker, *Rapid City Journal*, May 27, 2000. See Arthur W. Janklow, "True Contributor," *Rapid City Journal*, June 4, 2000.

10. Arthur Janklow, "True Contributor."

11. Joyce Hazeltine, "Hazeltine Says District 32 Lucky to Have Adelstein," *Black Hills Pioneer*, October 29, 2008.

12. Denise Ross, "Adelstein Spends Record on Campaign," *Rapid City Journal*, January 3, 2001; Ray M. Graff, "Adelstein Using Push Poll to Persuade Voters," *Black Hills Pioneer*, October 29, 2008.

13. Ross, "Adelstein Spends Record on Campaign."

14. Ibid.

15. David Montgomery, "Finance Laws Offer Loopholes for Campaign Donors," *Rapid City Journal*, May 1, 2011.

16. Jonathan Ellis, "Health Problem Forces Stan Adelstein to Resign from State Senate," *Argus Leader*, January 1, 2014.

17. Mike Rounds, quoted in Ellis, "Health Problem Forces Stan Adelstein to Resign from State Senate."

18. Ellis, "Health Problem Forces Stan Adelstein to Resign from State Senate."

19. On SMA's early opposition to Daschle, see folder 138a.

20. "Jonathan S. Adelstein, President and CEO," Wireless Infrastructure Association, accessed May 21, 2019, https://wia.org/staff/jonathanadelstein.

21. Emilie Rusch, "Smoking Ban Supporters Hope for Senate Victory," *Rapid City Journal*, February 28, 2009; Denise Ross, "Bill to Include Jews, Muslims in Marriage Law," *Rapid City Journal*, January 30, 2002.

22. Lauck, *Daschle v. Thune*, 31.

23. "Janklow Sentenced to 100 Days in Jail," CNN, January 22, 2004, accessed July 18, 2018, http://www.cnn.com/2004/LAW/01/22/janklow.sentencing/.

24. Lauck, *Daschle v. Thune*, 14. 93–95.

25. Denise Ross, "House Oks Anti-Abortion Bill," *Rapid City Journal*, February 10, 2004.

26. Lynda Clark Adelstein in conversation with the author, July 3, 2018.

27. Ross, "House Oks Anti-Abortion Bill."

28. "Governor Supports Bill to Ban Most Abortions in S. Dakota," *Los Angeles Times*, March 4, 2004, accessed July 12, 2018, http://articles.latimes.com/2004/mar/10/nation/na-abort10.

29. "SD: Committee Rejects Requiring Emergency Contraception for Rape Victims," *Ms. Magazine*, February 6, 2004, accessed April 23, 2018, http://msmagazine.com/news/uswirestory.asp?id=8270.

30. "Governor Supports Bill;" Monica Davey, "South Dakota's Governor Says He Favors Abortion Ban Bill," *New York Times*, February 25, 2006; Nieves, "S.D. Abortion Bill Takes Aim at 'Roe.'"

31. Davey, "South Dakota's Governor;" Stephanie Simon, "Abortion Foes Energized By Their Losses," *Los Angeles Times*, November 9, 2006.

SOURCES

32. Kevin Woster, "Adelstein Draws Fire on Award," *Rapid City Journal*, April 20, 2006.

33. Tom Lawrence, "Adelstein-Schwiesow Feud Flares At Campaign Office Opening," *Black Hills Pioneer*, June 25, 2008; Kevin Woster, "Adelstein Defeats Schwiesow," *Rapid City Journal*, June 1, 2004.

34. Woster, "Adelstein Defeats Schwiesow," *Rapid City Journal*, June 1, 2004.

35. SMA interview, December 12, 2016.

36. Ibid.

37. Lynda Clark Adelstein interview, September 13, 2016.

38. Ellis, "Health Problem Forces Stan Adelstein to Resign from State Senate."

39. William Napoli, quoted in Ellis, "Health Problem Forces Stan Adelstein to Resign from State Senate."

40. Kevin Woster, "Adelstein Draws Fire on Award," *Rapid City Journal*, April 20, 2006;

41. Kevin Woster, "Conservative Victories Mark Trend," *Rapid City Journal*, June 7, 2006; Kevin Woster, "Adelstein Declines Party Switch, Backs Katus' Candidacy," *Rapid City Journal*, July 13, 2006.

42. "Tom Katus," West River Blue Dog, June 16, 2006, accessed February 8, 2017, http://penndemocrats.blogspot.com/2006/06/district-32.html.

43. Lawrence, "Adelstein-Schwiesow Feud Flares At Campaign Office Opening,"

44. Jeremy Fugleberg, "Adelstein Narrowly Wins in District 32 Three-Way Race," *Rapid City Journal*, November 4, 2008.

45. Kevin Woster, "GF&P Buys Land for RC Development Project," *Rapid City Journal*, October 22, 2008.

46. David Montgomery, "Adelstein's Temporary Tax Bill Killed," *Rapid City Journal*, January 7, 2012.

47. "Jackley: No Violations By SOS Gant, Powers," *Associated Press State Wire, South Dakota*, July 17, 2012.

48. Lynda Clark Adelstein in conversation with the author, July 3, 2018.

49. Ibid.

50. Daniel Adelstein interview, September 11, 2016.

EPILOGUE

1. Heidi Bell, "Long Lost Army Locker Mysteriously Appears," *Rapid City Journal*, September 14, 1995.

2. Bell, "Long Lost Army Locker;" SMA, "A Mysterious Box in the Driveway," January 12, 2015, accessed November 30, 2016, https://way2gosd.com/2015/01/12/999.

3. Lynda Clark Adelstein interview, September 13, 2016.

4. Lynda Clark Adelstein in conversation with the author, July 3, 2018.

5. SMA interview, December 12, 2016.

6. Ellis, "Health Problem Forces Stan Adelstein to Resign from State Senate," *Argus Leader*, January 1, 2014.

7. "Gov. Appoints Rapid City Businessman to South Dakota Senate," *Rapid City Journal*, January 13, 2014; Lynda Clark Adelstein interview, September 13, 2016.

8. "About Us," Northwestern Management Company, accessed January 11, 2017, https://www.nwemanagement.com/about-us/.

9. Ann Haber Stanton, "A Destination in the Wilderness," Synagogue of the Hills, accessed January 30, 2017, http://www.synagogueofthehills.org/index.php?option=com_content&view=article&id=339:a-destination-in-the-wilderness&catid=2&Itemid=1112.

10. See Leo Goldberger, *The Rescue of the Danish Jews: Moral Courage Under Stress* (New York: NYU Press, 1987).

11. "A Condensed Case Statement for Rapid City Regional Hospital's Proposed $5,000,000 financial development program," May 2008, folder 82.

12. Regina Garcia Cano, "South Dakota's Jewish Community Small, Tight-Knit," *Associated Press*, December 28, 2014.

13. "Mike Rounds Spends Time in Israel," Rounds for Senate, March 30, 2013, accessed April 16, 2018, https://roundsforsenate.com/news-and-events/news/mike-rounds-spends-time-in-israel.

14. SMA, "Rounds Traveling to Israel for Six-Day Briefing," May 15, 2013, accessed April 4, 2016,

https://way2gosd.com/2013/05/15/rounds-traveling-to-israel-for-six-day-briefing/.

15. Mike Anderson, "Gary Johnson Plants His Flag in South Dakota," *Rapid City Journal*, October 27, 2016.

16. Jim Holland, "Libertarian VP Candidate Bill Weld at BHSU," *Rapid City Journal*, October 21, 2016.

17. SMA to Arrowhead Country Club, March 19, 1980, folder 20.

18. SMA quoted in Mike Anderson, "Gary Johnson Plants His Flag in South Dakota," *Rapid City Journal*, October 27, 2016.

19. Amanda Yellow Robe, e-mail to the author, August 23, 2017.

20. "'Dignity Statue Honors Native Americans," KOTA, September 19, 2016, accessed October 3, 2016, http://www.kotatv.com/content/news/Dignity-statue-honors-Native-Americans-394005521.html; Chris Huber, "Behemoth 'Dignity' Sculpture Heading East for Dedication," *Rapid City Journal*, September 13, 2016.

21. Dale Claude Lamphere, quoted in "Dignity," accessed October 3, 2016, www.lampherestudio.com/dignity.

22. "Dignity of Earth and Sky Celebration," South Dakota Public Broadcasting, September 17, 2016, accessed October 3, 2016, http://watch.sdpb.org/video/2365844810/.

23. "Dignity Unveiled," *South Dakota Magazine*, September 19, 2016, accessed October 3, 2016, https://southdakotamagazine.com/dignity-unveiled.

24. Deb Holland, "Dignity: Of Earth and Sky," *Meade County Times-Tribune*, September 21, 2016; Evan Hendershot, "50-Foot-Tall Statue of Woman Lends 'Dignity' to South Dakota's Skyline," Inforum.com, September 19, 2016, accessed October 3, 2016, http://www.inforum.com/4117594-dignity-celebrated-south-dakotas-skyline.

25. "Dignity Unveiled."

INDEX

Abdnor, James "Jim," 122, 217-18, 263, 270, 290
Abram, Morris, 11-13, 16, 17, 186
Adel Jewelers, 99
Adelstein, Bertha, 36-39, 46-54, 56-57, 59, 62-63, 65-66, 71, 110-11, 128-29, 135, 142, 154, *164*
Adelstein, Daniel "Dan," 78, 86, 97, 132-33, *165*, *169*, *172*, *176*, 246, 255, 259-60, 264, 286, 298, 303, 305
Adelstein, Ita, 12-13, 74-78, 81, 85-93, 99-100, 102-3, 105-6, 132-34, 137, *164*, *166*, *171*, 183, 186-88, 192, 193, 196, 208, 260-61, 281-82, 297
Adelstein, James "Jim," 100, 132-33, *169*, 243, 259, 302
Adelstein, Jonathan "Jon," 100, 132-33, *169*, 259-60, 291, 297, 302
Adelstein, Lynda Clark, *175*, *176*, *178*, *179*, 275, 277, 278, 280-82, 284, 289, 293, 295, 297-98, 299, 301, 305
Adelstein, Morris, 34-35, 44-54, 56-63, 65-67, 69, 71, 72, 73, 80, 82, 97-104, 110-17, 126-31, 135, 142-43, 146, 151, 153-54, *164*, *168*, *172*, 184-85, 252
Adelstein, Robert "Bob," 53, 56, 57-59, 63, 66, 71, 77, 80, 99, 127-29, 142, 146, 154-55, 157-58, *164*, 257-59
Adelstein, Shirley, *175*, 286-87, 294
Adelstein Foundation, 135
Albers, Mathilde, 217
Aliber, Sam, 44
Aliber, Sarah, 44

American Indian Movement (AIM), 225-34, 237, 270
American Institute of Architects (AIA), 197
American Israeli Political Action Committee (AIPAC), 215-18, 221
American Jewish Committee (AJC), 11-12, 16, 19, 105-8, 132, 156, *167*, *171*, 180, 186-88, 206, 211, 218-20, 226, 264-65, 286-87
Anderson, Norma, 122
Anderson, Sigurd, 18, 115-16
Associated General Contractors of America (AGC), 126, 128
AWACS, 221-23, 267

Baker, Henry, 195
Banks, Dennis, 229
Barnett, Donald "Don," 195-96, 229-30, 234, 235
Bell, James, 197
Ben-Gurion, David, 7-8, 10, 71, 108-9
Benn, Steven, 303
Bennett, Walter F., 118
Bennett-Clarkson Memorial Hospital, 121, 199-202
Black Forest Development, Inc., 254
Black Forest Inn, 254-56, 268-69
Black Hills Council of American Indians, 226-27
Black Hills Institute, 276
Black Hills Playhouse, 138
Black Hills Powwow Association, 282

Blackerby, Maryann, 143-44
Bloomberg, Jason, 242
Boe, Nils A., 17-18
Borglum, Gutzon, 61, 134
Borglum, Lincoln, 134, 189
Boyd, Lloyd Jr., 241
Briggs, Ray, 226, 234
Brockelsby, Earl, 239-40
Butler, Dorothy, 236
Bureau of Indian Affairs (BIA), 225, 234
Burnette, Robert, 241-42
Bush, George H.W., 216, 264, 265, 267
Bush, George W., 288, 291

Carter, Jimmy, 138, 211, 212, 214, 219, 221, 262, 265
Christiansen, Helge, 192-93
Christensen, Kathleen "Tommy," 119-22, 206
Circle G Construction Company, 254, 256-57
Clark, Lynda. *See* Lynda Clark Adelstein
Cleveland, Herb, 94-95, *179*, 308
Clinton, Hillary, 305, 307
Cohen, Beila. *See* Beila "Bertha" Martinsky
Cohen, Elliot, 106, 125
Cohen, Tillie, 32, 34, 36
Cohen, Joseph, 31, 32, 36
Cold War, 80-81, 97, 105, 108, 125, 183, 207, 249
Colorado-Wyoming Improvement Company, 162
Cook, Tom, 242-44
Coolidge, Calvin, 47, 112
Coolidge, Thomas T., 200-201
Community Services Administration (CSA), 211-14
Community Development Action Committee (CDAC), 197-98
Corning, Duane "Duke," 135-36
Crabb, Sam, 55, 60, 75
Crawford, Faye, 194
Crazy Horse Memorial, 240-41

Danko, Leon, 157-58
Daschle, Tom, 263, 269, 290-92

Daugaard, Dennis, 298, 302, 308
Department of Housing and Urban Development (HUD), 198, 241
Dignity (Dale Lamphere), *179*, 307-8, *309*
Dominick, Peter, 124-25
Duhamel, Bill, 219, 229-30
Dunmire, Joe R., 15-17
Dusek, Fred, 194
Dutka, Solomon "Sol," 215-16

Eckel, Clarence L., 73-74
Edelstein, Anne, 34
Edelstein, Beila. *See* Beila "Bertha" Martinsky
Edelstein, Meyer, 26, 31-34, 36, 43
Edelstein, Sarah, 34
Eisenhower, Dwight D., 98, 119-20, 122, 136, 138, 206, 235
Ellsworth Air Force Base, 14, 60, 98, 102-103, 132, *174*, 180, 181, 183, 197, 200, 236, 249, 262, 300, 302. *See also* Rapid City Air Base
Ellsworth Heritage Foundation, 278

557th Aircraft Control and Warning Squadron, 105
528th Engineers, 45
Fast Horse, Douglas, 239-40
Federal Emergency Management Agency (FEMA), 138, 167
Ford, Gerald, 210-11, 235-36, 262-67
Friedman, Herbert, 71-72, 104

Gaiser, E.D., 145, 154, 191, 248, 251, 256
Garment, Leonard, 230, 234
Gibson, Mark, 68, 72
Great Depression, 62, 64, 65, 110, 113, 291, 302
Greenberg, Aaron, 27, 36-38, 56-57, 63
Greenberg, Anna, 38
Greenberg, Bertha. *See* Bertha Adelstein
Greenberg, Ida, 38
Greenberg, Israel "Jack," 38
Greenberg, Julia, 27, 36-38, 56-57
Goldwater Award, 294-95
Goldwater, Barry, 119, 207-8, 219, 265

INDEX   347

Gonzalez, Mario, 236
Gubbrud, Archie, 13-15, 120-21, 123-24, 133, 140, 158, *165*
Gunderson, Barbara Bates, 194, 196, 236, 262

Ham, Arlene, 263-64
Harney Lumber Company, 99, 128, 249
Hawkins, Doug, 158
Herseth, Ralph, 14, 120-21, 123-24, 292
Herseth, Stephanie, 292, 298
Higgins, Bob, 13, 17, 147-48
Hills Materials Company, 65, 98-99, 146, 149, 151, 162, *168*, 191, 196, 247-49, 251-57, 279, 282-85, 302
Hockenberg, Harlan "Bud," 215-16
Hodne Associates, Inc., 197-98
Hodne Report, 197-98
Holocaust, 13, 19, 64, 66, 88-93, 107, 108, 193, 216-17, 286-87, 302-3
Hospital Action Committee (HAC), 201-2
Hotel Alex Johnson, 53, 79, 263

Industrial Development Expansion Agency (IDEA), 121, 158
International Union of Operating Engineers, Local No. 326, 149-50

Janklow, Arthur "Art," 288
Janklow, William "Bill," *171*, 181, 218, 222-24, 237-38, 263, 268, 270-74, 288-90, 292, 298, 303-4
Jewish Institute for National Security Affairs (JINSA), 218, 264
Johnson, Lyndon B., 15-16, 142, 208-10, 212, 214
Johnson, Tim, 292, 298
Johnson, Gary, 305-7
Jones, Curt, 272
Journey Museum, 277-81

Kennedy, John F., 12-13, 15, 81, 86, 121, 126, 206
Kennedy, Robert, 13, 86, 142, 209
Kissinger, Henry, 157, 220

Klein, Grace, 236
Korean War, 94, 105
Korn, Bela "Barbara," 90-92
Korn, Ita. *See* Ita Adelstein
Korn, Leibel "Leo," 78, 90-92
Korn, Masza "Marcia," 74-75, 77, 90-92, *164*
Korn, Mavrycy "Michael," 90-92
Kris, Allen, 158
Kroll, Ed, 143-45
Ku Klux Klan (KKK), 60-61, 63, 139, 207

LaCroix, Arthur "Art," 196-97, 199, 238-39, 248, 266, 277
LaCroix, Jill, 144
LaCroix, Trude, 138, 196
LaPoint, Eric, 236
Landers, Ann, 156. *See also* Eppie Lederer
Lane, Tom, 194
Lantos, Tom, 216-17
Larson, Peter, 276
Lawrence Realty Companies, 249
Lederer, Eppie, 156. *See also* Ann Landers
Leedom, Boyd, 48, 97, 135
Leedom, Chet, 47, 110
Leedom, Irene, 182
Levine, Martis, 114, 146
Lien, Chuck, 151-52, *171*
Lien, Pete, 65, 151-52
Lytle, Larry, 229-30, 235

Martinsky, Beila "Bertha," 26, 31-32, 34-35, 40-44, 48-49, 56-57, 66, *164*
Marvin, Al, 100, 152
Materi, John, 100-102, 114-17
McGovern, George, 209, 262, 263, 265
Means, Russell, 229-34
Mendoza, Hilario G., 236
Messing, Joseph "Joel" B., 93-96, 101, 245
Miller, Burmond "Grandfather Miller," 36, 38
Miller, Hyman, 36, 38
Minnilusa Historical Association, 278

Mizel, Jerry, 257-59
Mizel, Philip, 46-47, 63
Moeller, Henry, 158
Morris E. Adelstein Aquatic Camp, 153
Mount Rushmore National Memorial Society, 139, 171
Muhiville, Bud, 150
Mundt, Karl, 81, 97, 122, 125-26
Murray, E.C. "Ping," 15-17
Museum Alliance of Rapid City, 278-79

National Advisory Council on Economic Opportunity (NACEO), 210-15, 236
National Defense Executive Reserve (NDER), 136-38
National Labor Relations Board (NLRB), 150
Napoli, Bill, 295
Nauman, Dean, 196
Nixon, Richard, 119-20, 121, 142, 157, 206, 209-10, 230-31, 263, 264
Northwestern Engineering Company (NWE), 11, 19, 20, 51-52, 54, 58-59, 62, 65-67, 78-80, 86, 98-102, 111-17, 123-31, 133, 142-62, *167*, *168*, *173*, 183, 184-85, 191, 193, 196, 211, 247-59, 282-85, 296, 302, 304, 306
NWE Management Company, 249-51 283

Office of Economic Opportunity (OEO), 210-11
Olivarez, Graciela, 211-14

Packwood, Bob, 221, 223, 260, 267
Pete Lien & Sons, 65, 123-24, *171*
Piatigorsky, Gregor, 66
Pier, Louis "L.A.," 51, 56, 61-62, 65, 98, 100, 110-11, 115, 129, 147, 252, 283
Pressler, Larry, 91, *173*, 217-18, 221-24, 262-63, 292
Present Tense, 180, 188

Rapid City Air Base, 97. *See also* Ellsworth Air Force Base
Rapid City Area Chamber of Commerce, 194, 197, 234, 279, 282, 302
Rapid City Club for Boys, 134-35, 194

Rapid City Concert Association, 66, 138
Rapid City Flood of 1972, *169*, *170*, 189-203, 229, 249, 304
Rapid City Journal, 194, 198, 241, 288
Rapid City Library Board, 194-96
Rapid City Regional Hospital, 199-203, 301, 303, 305
Rapid City Rotary Club, 69, 118, 139
Rautenstraus, Roland, 74, 158
Reagan, Ronald, 95, *172*, 209, 214, 218-23, 263-65, 267, 288, 291
Republican Jewish Coalition (RJC), *172*, 267
Republican National Committee, 121-22, 206-7, 265-67
Republican Senate Trust, 266-67 , 289
Republican State Central Committee, 121, 205, 219, 268-69, 295
Reserve Officer Training Corps (ROTC), 11, 68, 76, 78, 84, 105
Rivkin, Myron, 102-3, 184
Rivkin, Sarah, 102
Robford Company, 99, 249
Rockefeller, Nelson, 204-10, 264-65, 269
Rogers, Sister Sarto, 139-41, 189-91, 199, 200, 234
Rounds, M. Michael "Mike," *176*, 289-90, 294, 298, 305
Runde, Sandra K., 250-52, 255, 283
Rushmore Plaza Civic Center, 138, 198, 262, 306

Schroeder, Phil, 194-95
Schwiesow, Elli, 294-96
Shandler, Neal, 102
Shoener, Jerry, 194
Sioux City Bottling Works, 37-38
South Dakota Department of Transportation (SDDOT), 271-74
South Dakota Indian Businessmen's Association, 239
South Dakota National Guard, 102-3, 123
South Dakota School of Mines & Technology, 100, 114, 140, 141, 157, *179*, 191, 277-78, 282
South Dakota State Advisory Commission (U.S. Commission on Civil Rights), 235-39

INDEX

Spiegel, Mark A., 265
St. John's McNamara Hospital, 139-41, *169*, 189-91, 199-203
St. Martin's Hospital Corporation, 140-41
St. Martin's Monastery, 140-41, 192, 199
Stillman, Harold, 148
Super, David, 143-45
Synagogue of the Hills, 102-5, *174*, 180-82, 184, 188, 300, 302-3

Temple Emanuel, 69-71, 75, 76, *164*
Thorsness, Leo, 262-63
Thunderbolt Enterprises, Inc., 24-42
Thune, John, 288, 292
Tlustos, Pat, *173*, 247-48, 251-53, 256-57, 277, 282-85, 302
Trump, Donald, 305, 307
Twenty-Fourth Amendment, 12-19

Undlin, Charles, 226-27
Union of American Hebrew Congregations (UAHC), 69, 104, 130, 181, 184
United Jewish Appeal (UJA), 71, 184
University of Colorado Boulder (UC Boulder), 68, 70, 72-77, 158, *167*
U.S. Army Corps of Engineers, 11, 79, 82, 86-87, 141, *165*
U.S. Commission on Civil Rights, 235-39

Vandervort, Edwin, 79-80
Venners, Ted, 254-55
Vietnam War, 142, 209
Viken, Jeffrey, 278-79
Volk, David, 230, 236, 238

Walsh, William, 238
War on Poverty, 210, 212
Weissman, Jerry, 215-16
Weisz, Herbert, 191-92
Weld, Bill, 305-7
Wheeler, Ron, 272
Willens, Howard, 85-86

Willens, Susan, 85-86
Wilson, Jim, 231-33
Wilson, Richard, 227-28, 230, 234
World War I, 33, 44, 58, 64, 73, 113, 118, 300
World War II, 33, 59, 60, 63, 65, 70, 71, 80, 82, 85, 97, 99, 114, 125, 135, 147, 191, 196, 222, 238, 266

Yellow Boy, Rinard, 243
Yellow Robe, Amanda, 306-7
Young, Marshall, 235
Young Presidents' Organization (YPO), 19, 155-57, 215-16, 219, 246, 252, 253-54, 260, 267
Young Republicans, 18, 19, 121-22, 147, 156

Zacks, Gordon "Gordy," 215-16
Ziolkowski, Ruth, 240-41